Our Ultin

Life, the Universe and Destiny of Mankind

Adrian P. Cooper

Ultimate Reality Publishing
An imprint of Mind Power Corporation

What readers are saying about Our Ultimate Reality

It is rare indeed, when a book of this monumental importance comes along. For contained within its covers, are answers to all manner of questions spiritual seekers will certainly ask along the path. It appears that every possible topic has been covered in this book. Just a few examples include: healing, meditation, dreams, quantum physics, universal laws, descriptions of the non-physical realms and much more. Reading Our Ultimate Reality has left a profoundly deep impression on me, as I have been a seeker for most of my 56 years. The brilliance of this book is both that the author details all the subjects so clearly, and that these details all ring true for this reader. My advice to anyone interested learning what their ultimate destiny is, and the true nature of this multi-dimensional universe, would be to read this book.

Nick Falcone, Santa Fe, New Mexico, USA.
Retired criminal law attorney.

I scanned through the various chapters and couldn't believe just how much detailed information there is, which is written in an intelligent, articulate and very easy to understand manner just as though you are speaking directly to the person who is reading this. You have covered everything. I am truly blown away with the sheer magnitude of this and I fully resonate with everything you have written about because much of what you talk about I have experienced myself. The subject matter is awesome and exhilarating.

Margaret Hill, Paisley, Scotland.

I could not stop reading your book. It is truly a masterpiece! Over the past 4 and one half years I have read many metaphysical books and experimented with various techniques. I am amazed at what you have done. I have come across aspects of some of your material, but it took a lot of reading to locate it and as I have said, several years. I can't wait to get into some of the exercises that I know are forthcoming. At this point I believe that I will be able to accomplish things that up until this time seemed like a fairy tale.

Charles Humphrey, St. Louis, Missouri .

Our Ultimate Reality
Life, the Universe and Destiny of Mankind

Second edition, November 2007, Ultimate Reality Publishing
An imprint of Mind Power Corporation.

ISBN 978-0-9799106-0-9

Contact: sales@ourultimatereality.com

Website: http://www.ourultimatereality.com

Gifts: http://www.ourultimatereality.com/gifts.html

Narrated Audio Book

Our Ultimate Reality, Life, the Universe and Destiny of Mankind is also available as a fully narrated Audio Book for listening in high quality MP3 format:

http://www.ourultimatereality.com/audio.html

Dedication

For My Sons

Tristan, Darryl, Declan

With Love

Table of Contents

Prologue

From the earliest days of thinking man, people the world over have pondered the nature of the Universe, our planet, and of ourselves. What does it all mean? Why am I here? What is the real purpose of my life? What will happen to me after I die? Will I return once again for another life on Earth?

The solutions to these ancient mysteries are at once both Universal and timeless, having always been available to mankind throughout the ages. More recently, modern quantum physics is only recently beginning to realize the true nature of the infinite Universe of intelligent, vibrating Energy and Consciousness in which we have our live and move and have our Being, emphasizing that there is, always has been, and always will be only one ultimate reality, a Universal reality that can never be the sole claim of any individual, race, culture, science or religion.

Over the millennia, the insidious agents of creed, dogma, doctrine, and national and self-interest have frequently sought, often with considerable prejudice, hatred and violence, to suppress or destroy those who would reveal and teach the truth to mankind, resulting in most of mankind being deprived of their true reality, purpose and destiny.

During the last two millennia in particular, much of humanity has steadily succumbed to the increasingly detrimental effects of materialism, egocentricity, avarice, greed, prejudice, intolerance, discrimination and inequality, as well as the frenetic pace of "modern life" in general. The result has been widespread misery, fear, instability, uncertainty and suffering—a progressive moving away from The Sources of true knowledge and the ultimate destiny of all humankind. People find themselves erroneously believing that they are completely separate individuals housed in a body of matter, physically separated from the Universe and from everything and everyone else in existence, struggling to survive in a lonely or even hostile environment where nothing ever seems to make sense.

Many people today are suffering the debilitation of stress and the overwhelming feeling that their lives, reality, peace, harmony, happiness and even fundamental daily needs are at the mercy of "fortune", "chance" or other people, as well as numerous other situations and factors beyond their control.

Throughout the world we witness increasing extremes between wealth and poverty, with the wealthy becoming progressively wealthier and the poor becoming progressively poorer. This inevitably results in more stress and psychological problems, sometimes leading to feelings of simply being unable to handle "life" at all anymore.

However, during the last few decades remarkable changes have been steadily taking place, coinciding with the transition of a great age in which we are now living on Earth and the rise in popularity of the Internet and other large scale global communications media reaching hundreds of millions or even billions of people throughout the world. This convergence of factors is most assuredly no coincidence. Mankind is now moving into a new and pivotally important era, where Universal knowledge of who we are, why we are here and where we are going, must and will become much more available to everyone, particularly if humanity is to profoundly benefit in ways most people have yet to fully comprehend, both at an individual level, the level entire human race and indeed all life and Earth Herself.

Today, we increasingly see and hear of "miraculous phenomena", with people from all walks of life experiencing spontaneous and sometimes even dramatic Spiritual experiences. Following such an experience, these people often seek their true purpose with the overwhelming realization that there must be more to "life" than the physical, material world that most people erroneously identify as "reality".

Such life-changing experiences continue to arrive in many and varied forms and degrees, including spontaneous Astral Projection or "Out of Body Experiences", Lucid Dreams, near-death experiences, or just sudden inspiration or intuition received from "inner" sources. Countless people are intuitively sensing that there are changes occurring in many different ways, and in particular in the form of increased awareness.

As these profound experiences become more widespread, the Internet is being used as the ideal medium to communicate them to larger numbers of people, many of whom are awakened to the greater levels of reality beyond the temporal, physical world of matter. The conclusion of this progression of events will in all probability be realized by a long prophesied transition of Consciousness, coinciding with the transition of a great age. The dogma, indoctrination, materialism, power and control of the past will eventually give way to a new and glorious direction leading to the true destiny of mankind and the "Kingdom of Heaven on Earth".

Traditional sciences have perceived the physical three-dimensional Universe of matter as their only reality, but the field of quantum physics is rapidly concluding that the three-dimensional Universe of physical matter is but a very small component of what has been hitherto recognised as "reality" and actually the lowest extension of an infinitely larger, interconnected and integrated Universal reality comprised of multiple dimensions and inner states of life and "Being".

Quantum physics is also recognizing that these inner dimensions are, in fact, true reality, and the entire three-dimensional physical Universe of matter that remains the basis of most of the sciences is but a pale reflection of the inner levels of true reality. Earth is a large scale illusion perceived only in accordance with the restrictions of the five physical senses. Quantum physics has metaphorically perceived the Universe as a magnificent fluid hologram known as the "holomovement", a Universal projection of Consciousness and Energy in the form of vibration, in and of which everyone and everything in all dimensions are inseparable aspects.

Science, particularly from the days of Newton, has generally sought to explain everything in terms of the three dimensions of physical matter when these are in fact an extremely small subset of an infinitely greater multi-dimensional Universe. Science has also historically taken the view that everything, including all life, must have originated from this matter. It is only when science and mankind begins to fully understand and accept the true nature of the infinite Universe and of the ultimate destiny of mankind (as has been consistently taught by the many cultures of the world throughout the ages) that there will be progress toward a world of peace, plenty, harmony, health and happiness, "the Kingdom of Heaven on Earth".

In the first section of this book, we will compare and contrast wisdom and knowledge from both ancient and modern sources. We will discuss the profound importance of this knowledge in the context of the entire Universe, the Macrocosm, and each and every human being—the Microcosm. We will discuss how to apply the maximum ongoing benefit of this knowledge to living successfully, happily and securely with all needs fulfilled. We will explore how to progress in the inner spheres of life and, most importantly, how to focus on the most sacred task and destiny of all mankind—the path of ascent as immortal Spiritual Beings back to our Divine creator, the First Cause, God from whence we originally came.

We will also discuss in this book the many dimensions of existence and reality beyond the three-dimensional material world often known as "planes", "realms" or "spheres", both from the perspective of the ancient wisdoms and of modern quantum physics. We will consider the nature of the many

Beings and intelligences inhabiting these realms including human Beings, and the great Universal principles or "laws" prevailing. We will also discuss the significance of each of our own individual lives, and the process occurring after each physical "death". We will discover why people return to Earth time and again within inner planes of reality, including deceased friends and relatives.

Finally, we will explore how you can achieve and maintain absolute control over your own life, how to manifest into your life anything and everything that you truly need and desire, how to create for yourself the life you have only dreamed of, how to maintain perfect health and to heal yourself and others, and how to protect yourself and loved ones from dark psychic influences. Most importantly, we will discover the true nature of the most fundamental Principle in the Universe—Mind, and the most powerful force, vibration and manifestation of Energy in the entire Universe—Unconditional Love.

Part 1

Our Infinite Universe

Chapter 1
The Nature of the Universe

Under normal circumstances, most people perceive, understand and interact with their surroundings and the material world in terms of the five physical senses—sight, hearing, smell, taste and touch. Understandably, these are accepted as the only source of feedback for what is commonly believed to be "reality". In fact, unless something conforms to one or more of the five physical senses, it is usually deemed not to exist at all, or it might be considered an "illusion" or a "figment of the imagination". To most people, the only exception to any extrasensory existence is the perception of a "God" or the gods of various world religions, which is a complete act of faith.

Religions teach their congregations how to live their lives and worship their particular God or Gods in accordance with a "belief system", often based upon the teachings of their various "books" or bibles, and doctrines. At the same time, a wholly materialistic outlook of the world causes people to feel separate from the Universe and each other. People then place their primary emphasis on temporal, material objects as if they are all that is meaningful in life. The mission of the many is to gather as much material and monetary wealth as possible during the course of what is perceived to be an only "life" in order to increase comfort and "keep up appearances".

This situation has contributed in no small degree to the state of the world today with a gross imbalance between those who have more than they could ever need and those who have little or nothing. Therefore, we often see a world where greed, dishonesty, avarice, hate and sometimes violence exists side by side with fear, poverty and suffering.

For a very long time, the world has been in the grip of a major imbalance that has not only escalated for decades, but now threatens the entire immediate future of humanity and the planet. Mankind is directly responsible for this imbalance due for the most part to the gross misuse of the freewill granted by our Creator. Accordingly, only mankind can now reverse this situation and bring about a state of harmony, peace, happiness and balance for everyone, the "Kingdom of Heaven on Earth".

The true nature of the Universe has been known about and taught throughout the ages by many and varied sources, all of which are highly consistent and in broad agreement. Yet, it is now also substantiated by the work of modern quantum physics and increasingly by other branches of the sciences as well. All areas of the sciences will soon have to accept the fact that true Universal reality is not, and never can be based entirely in the familiar three-dimensional world of physical matter as has been assumed since the days of Isaac Newton. Instead, it will be recognised as an infinite, multi-dimensional reality—a Universe of vibrating, living Energy and Consciousness in which everyone and everything without exception is an integral and equal aspect. Throughout the ages, there has been a prevalent misperception of a "God" Who is completely separate from everyone and everything else in existence, and Who "rules" over "his" three-dimensional world of matter from high places. Therefore, the true nature of the Universe will certainly challenge the perceptions of most people.

Mankind has always perceived the three-dimensional Universe and the physical world of matter as "reality". It will be evident to most people, however, that beyond the perceptions of the five physical senses, there is a much more substantial reality. Throughout time, mankind has contemplated and attempted, with varying degrees of success to define the nature of this more substantial, greater reality.

Over the course of many thousands of years, from the dawn of intelligent man, the reality of the Universe has been taught throughout the world by a variety of Beings whose mission it is to teach these matters to mankind. These Beings range from highly advanced Spiritual intelligences of the inner spheres of life, to the greatest Masters ever to walk the Earth. They are often ascended human Beings who incarnated on Earth to teach mankind the Universal truths and offer direction for people to fulfil their ultimate destinies as immortal Spiritual Beings.

These ageless teachings have been taught to many other teachers over the ages, who have often remained in relative obscurity in order to avoid persecution, as they progressively taught the students who were able to understand and go on to teach others. And so it has been, down through the ages.

Some of the greatest of these teachers became very well-known, and performed an invaluable service to humanity. Over the millennia, however, these teachings have been drastically distorted, misused and misunderstood and even became the basis for orthodox, dogmatic religions and doctrines. The truth is both one and eternal, however, and is now ready to finally reach a much wider proportion of the human race, ultimately resulting in a global expansion of Consciousness where true reality, purpose and destiny will eventually become an integral aspect of the lives of everyone.

The following chapters are a comparison of some of the better known and more widely available sources of wisdom and knowledge originating from a diverse range of Eastern and Western cultures. These comparisons will highlight the profound consistency of their respective teachings, which are now being substantiated by modern quantum physics.

4-19-13

Chapter 2
Definition of God

Before reviewing the wisdoms of the various world cultures, the word "God" must first be defined. The word "God" will be used frequently in this book, but I must stress from the outset that I am not in any way referring to God in a religious, theological or dogmatic sense, or as the deity personified and worshipped by many orthodox world religions.

The Universal God has numerous names in accordance with individual cultures and the way Universal truths are taught to followers. Over the centuries God has been referred to as: The Universe, The Source, The First Cause, The Ether, The Akasha, The One, The All, Spirit, The Great Spirit, The Prime Creator, and by many other names. Again, this is the Universal aspect of God Who exists, has always existed and always will exist beyond the temporal confines of space and time—the same God of which we are all integral aspects, each having our own existence in the Universal Mind of God, existing as individuated, immortal, Spiritual Beings, made in the Spiritual image of God. This is the very same God who is in every single one of us, just as we are in God. The true God to which this book refers is Universal Mind.

Throughout this book, I will principally refer to "God" by three different names depending on the context of the discussion:

The Source: Everything in the Universe, all Energy, vibration and life flows from The Source of All that Is, within the Universal Mind. Everything in the Universe is an integral aspect, expression of and channel of experience of The Source. Nothing can exist outside of, or separate to The Universal Mind of The Source. The Source is at once omnipotent, omniscient, and omnipresent.

The First Cause: Source Energy is the First Cause of everything within the Universal Mind. We, as human Beings, and expressions of The First Cause, made in the true Spiritual Image of The First Cause, are co-creators within the Universal Mind of The First Cause. We are, therefore, secondary creators within Universal Mind, the Macrocosm, and primary creators of our own Universe—the Microcosm.

God: The Universal Mind of The Source, The First Cause is All that Is. God is a name, although subject over the ages to much creed and dogma and often even personified as a deity in a human form, is recognized by almost everyone in the world as meaning the Supreme Being and Creator in and of the Universe. Therefore, "God" is a name that is entirely appropriate in the context of a Universal, non-dogmatic form. God is both Universal Mind in Whom we live and move and have our Being, and the infinite Mind of God is The First Cause and The Source of all creation within Universal Mind.

Chapter 3
Hinduism

For many thousands of years the Far East has been a very rich source of Universal practice, wisdom and knowledge, especially within the countries and cultures of India, China and Tibet, which have given rise to many philosophies and pseudo-religions including Buddhism, Hinduism, and Taoism.

Hinduism is one of the world's oldest religions if it should even be called a "religion". Hinduism cannot even be referred to as a single philosophy because in fact it encompasses numerous different social and pseudo-religious philosophies, cults and sects, although all ultimately originating from a common origin. These include many colourful rituals, ceremonies and Spiritual practices. Hinduism has three main names: "Sanatana Dharma", meaning "eternal religion", "Vaidika Dharma" meaning "religion of the Vedas", and "Hindu", the absolute origin of which is not precisely known.

One theory as to the origin of the name "Hindu" is a derivation from an ancient inscription that has been translated as meaning: the country lying between the Himalayan Mountains and Bindu Sarovara, known as Hindustan by combination of the first letter "Hi" of "Himalaya" and the last compound letter "ndu" of the word "Bindu". Bindu Sarovara is called the Cape Comorin Sea in modern times. The origins of Hinduism trace back to the Indus Valley civilization dated at between 4000 and 2200 BCE. (Note that "BCE" is an acronym for "Before Common Era", previously known as "BC" or "Before Christ").

Among the most sacred of all Hindu texts are the "Vedas"—the Rig Veda, Sama Veda, Yajur Veda and Atharva Veda, which contain hymns, incantations and rituals from ancient India. Rig Veda (also known as Rigveda) is the oldest work, having been originally composed around 1500 BCE and written around 600 BCE.

Another group of important primary Hindu texts are known as the Upanishads. These are a continuation of the Vedic philosophy written between 800 and 400 BCE. The Upanishads expand upon how the Soul—Atman—can be united with the ultimate truth—Brahman—through contemplation and meditation as well as through the law of karma.

The Mahabharata were written around 540 to 300 BCE and have been attributed to the sage, Vyasa. They record "the legends of the Bharatas", one of the Aryan tribal groups. A very well-known work is the Bhagavad Gita, which is the sixth book of the Mahabharata. The "Gita" is a long and highly colourful poem describing a conversation between the warrior Arjuna and the God Krishna. It is an ancient text that has become central to Hinduism and other belief systems.

The Ramayana, another important text, is a love story with moral and spiritual themes. The Ramayana is dated to the first century CE and has been attributed to the poet, Valmiki. Other important texts in the Hindu culture include the Brahmanas, the Sutras, and the Aranyakas.

Although Hinduism contains many different variations and practices according to its component traditions and regions, there are spiritual Principles central to its various levels of teachings. These Principles are encompassed by a collection of works known as the "Vedas" which were written by a number of ancient sages known as "Vedic seers".

There are four separate Vedas, the oldest of which is the "Rig Veda". The Vedas are written in ancient Sanskrit, the sacred language of India, and are considered to be the very highest source of religious authority for most branches of Hinduism. The Vedas comprise several sections composed between 1500 BCE and 500 BCE. The most ancient components of the Vedas consist of sacred hymns and prayers. Later additions to the Vedas include rituals associated with Vedic hymns, and the final part is the Upanishads, which form the basic spiritual aspect of Hinduism and the Hindu concepts of Universal reality.

Most Hindus learned their traditions through a variety of stories and plays which teach them about the Universe and of their own nature, purpose and destiny in an entertaining, enjoyable and easily understandable way. Some of these stories and plays are massive epics that still form the basis of teachings for the majority of today's Hindus. The Bhagavad Gita is one of these, which as mentioned previously, is an elaborate and colourful story describing the quest of human nature for enlightenment—the truth of our true Spiritual nature and destiny.

The basis of the teachings of Krishna is completely in accordance with Universal knowledge and the wisdom of the ages as taught by almost all world traditions. It is also in accordance with the Principles of quantum physics. Krishna teaches that all things around us are actually manifestations of the same one and only ultimate reality. In Hinduism, this ultimate reality is called "Brahman" and is exactly the same as The Universal Mind, "The One", "The All", Spirit, "The Source", "The Prime Creator" or "All that Is". In the West, it might be regarded as the true definition of "God". Brahman or Universal Consciousness is considered to be the ultimate reality. Brahman is infinite, exists beyond the restricted perception of the five physical senses, and is incomprehensible.

Most ancient wisdoms of the world teach that human Beings are "God" in the Microcosm—immortal Spirits "made" in the "true Spiritual image of God". Hinduism teaches the same Principle in the form of "Atman", which is equivalent to the human Soul. The Hindu culture teaches Atman and Brahman—the individual reality and ultimate reality are one. This completely affirms ultimate reality as recognized by many other sources of the wisdom and knowledge of the ages, which teaches that the Microcosm, human Beings, and the

Macrocosm or "God" are one, and that everything in the entire Universe is an intimate, integral, inseparable aspect of everything else. *There is no separateness.*

The Upanishads affirm this most succinctly thus:

"That which is the finest essence—this whole world has that as its Soul. That is reality. That is Atman. That art though".

These truths are taught to the masses of followers of the Hindu traditions in the form of elaborate stories and plays in which Brahman is a great magician who uses his magical powers to transform himself into the World. In the Rig Veda, this is the original meaning of "maya", which does not simply imply "illusion" as is commonly believed, but rather means "power" and "might". Hinduism views the world, therefore, as an ever-changing and fluid manifestation of the powerful magic of Brahman, Universal Mind, where nothing ever stands still and everything is in a constant state of motion. This is the real meaning of "maya" and is exactly the same as the Universal Principle of "rhythm" a fundamental Universal Principle as taught within the ancient wisdom of the West and which will be discussed in more depth later in this book.

Another aspect of Brahman is "karma", which literally means "action". This is also an aspect of the important Principle taught by the wisdom of the West—that of "Cause and Effect". These principles teach that the entire Universe is always in a constant state of movement and action, and everything in the Universe is dynamically and eternally connected with everything else. Karma, in accordance with Hindu teachings, represents the ultimate force of creation, The Source of all life. Karma has also been associated with a more fundamental meaning which is widely applied at a personal level—the accumulation and equilibration of good and bad, or positive and negative actions in life. These actions can then carry over into multiple lives.

This is a reduction of meaning, which also applies to "maya", which has been reduced from its original Universal meaning as applies to the Macrocosm, to the more personal level of the Microcosm. When taken together, maya and karma teach that while people usually perceive everything in the Universe as being separate from themselves, they are still bound by the causes and effects of karma and reincarnation. Only when people finally realize their complete unity with the Universe in all of its aspects and live in total harmony with all that Is, never causing a "bad" effect, can they be freed from the bonds of karma and, ultimately, the cycle of reincarnation.

The Bhagavad Gita states the incorrect view of most people today in the following statement:

"All actions take place in time by the interweaving of the forces of nature, but the man lost in self-delusion thinks that he himself is the actor. But the man who knows the relation between the forces of Nature and actions, sees how some forces of Nature work upon other forces of nature and becomes not their slave".

This very profound and wise statement means that all mankind is an integral part of nature, of the Universal Mind, of The All, of God, and accordingly, everyone must always strive to work in perfect harmony with the Universe, the Universal Mind, as an integral and inseparable aspect. Instead, most people work against the Universe by perceiving a state of separateness, which places the Universe and everyone and everything within the Universe in an adversarial position, only to be conquered for selfish, material, and egocentric purposes and personal gain.

Only those who realize beyond all doubt that the Universe, The All, God, or the Brahman within exists beyond the five physical senses and lives in total selfless harmony with the Universe can understand true personal peace and harmony while journeying the sacred path back to our Divine creator.

The Principle of Cause and Effect is especially apparent in true individual progress—each effect achieved in the direction of true progress is directly related to a preceding cause. Ultimately, all requirements for progress are the same, only the methodology and individual approach differing in accordance with the teachings of the particular tradition or individual Spiritual path being followed.

There are many paths leading back to The Source, God, The First Cause from whence we came in the beginning. The Universal Mind does not formally recognize any particular religion, creed, dogma method or concept, but rather operates in complete, immutable, perfect harmony as taught by Hinduism and other Eastern cultures, as well as with those taught by the ancient wisdoms, teachings and knowledge of the West.

Many Hindus still approach Brahman through a large number of separate individual deities all serving to provide followers with a point of focus, inspiration and understanding provided by each one. The most popular of these deities are Shiva, Vishnu and the Divine Mother. This approach to the Divine is very similar to the pagan traditions of the western world, where numerous deities in Roman, Greek and Celtic pantheons are all equal aspects of "The One". Also, particularly in pagan traditions, "The One" is approached through the mediation of both male and female deities, all of which are ultimately considered to be both the male and female aspects of The One.

This is in stark contrast to the doctrines of the popular dogmatic orthodox religions of the West that erroneously consider a single deity, usually known as "God", to be totally separate, above and beyond everything and everyone else.

Both The Hindu and pagan approaches to God or Brahman fully agree with the Principle of gender in accordance with the teachings of the ancient wisdom of the West. Hindu deities are not considered to be separate from The All as is the case with the Christian God, but are all considered to be equal and integral aspects of the one Universal Divinity known as Brahman.

Shiva, one of the oldest of the Hindu Gods, is seen by his followers in many different and diverse forms, each of which ultimately represents a different aspect of the ultimate Divinity of Brahman. When Shiva appears as the fullest aspect of the Divinity of Brahman, he is known as "Mahesvara" or the "Great Lord". One of the most celebrated aspects of Shiva is his appearance in the form of the "Cosmic Dancer" known as "Nataraja", who is the God of creation and destruction through his dance as the eternal rhythm of the Universe. Once again, this can be likened to the teachings of the Universal Principle of rhythm in ancient Western Universal knowledge. It is apparent, therefore, that the deities of the Hindu tradition are simply another means of teaching the immutable Principles of the Universe through artistic rather than intellectual or philosophical means. The absolute meanings and importance of both methods of teaching are identical however, only varying in accordance with the unique approach of each tradition.

Hinduism has a strong philosophical and intellectual approach to Universal truths and realities, most notably through a Spiritual tradition known as "Vedanta", which is based upon the "Upanishads". Vedanta is one of the world's oldest religious philosophies and also one of the broadest. Vedanta is based upon the "Vedas"—the sacred scriptures of India, which affirm the oneness of all existence, the Divinity of the Soul, and the harmony of everything in the Universe. Although Vedanta is the philosophical school of Hinduism, it is Universal in its application and is equally relevant to all countries, cultures and backgrounds. The word "Vedanta" is a combination of two words—"Veda", which means knowledge and "anta", which means "the objective of". In this context, Vedanta is not a search for knowledge in absolute terms, but the search for self-realization and, ultimately, Brahman.

According to Vedanta, Brahman is the infinite existence, the infinite Consciousness and the infinite bliss, which is exactly the same Principle as the Mental Universe of the teachings of the ancient wisdom of the Western world.

The term given to this impersonal transcendent reality in Vedanta is Brahman—the very same Brahman approached by most Hindus through the mediation and form of deities such as Shiva, Vishnu and the Divine Mother. An extremely important aspect of Vedanta is the truth that Brahman dwells in the hearts of people as the Divine self, or "Atman", the ultimate reality, Atman and Brahman being One. Atman the human Spirit, was never born, will never die, and is immortal.

In western terms, Spirit or Atman was created in the true image of God (Brahman). Atman in His/Her purest form is not subject to any human failings, the fluctuations of the body or Mind, or the human emotions and traits including grief, despair or ignorance. Atman at the purest is free from all limitations. The ultimate objective, therefore, for all paths in accordance with Vedanta, and Universally, is to fully realize the Atman within as Brahman.

Vedanta also teaches that the only objective of all human life as manifested in the physical world is to realize that the true nature of all human Beings is Divine, and that the realization of the Brahman within is our birthright. This is totally in accordance with the age-old traditions of both the East and the West, which teach that every single person, after many incarnations of the Higher Self, or physical "lives" and subsequent progress through the inner spheres of reality, will ultimately manifest Divinity, for the greatest truth in the Universe is the Divine nature of man.

Vedanta also teaches there is only one truth, and that all religions, philosophies and traditions are related to each other, all teaching the true nature of the ultimate reality. Many thousands of years ago, long before the days of the beginnings of Christianity, the Rig Veda made an extremely profound statement:

"Truth is one, sages call it by various names".

The unity of all Universal existence is one of the central themes of Vedanta, and, like most world Spiritual traditions, has for many thousands of years taught exactly the same realities in different ways. Vedanta says that the Divinity at the very core of our Being is the very same Divinity that illumines the sun, the moon and the stars.

There is no place in the Universe where we as human Beings, infinite in nature, do not exist. In accordance with Vedanta and all true spiritual traditions, Oneness means with Everything and Everyone, from the very smallest atom, molecule and subatomic particle, to the Quanta at the quantum level, through micro-organisms, through all animal life and through all human Beings, no matter what the Ego might think of "another" person, life form or "thing".

This is the epitome of Unconditional Love, which is quite literally "unconditional". The Self within you, Atman, is exactly the same Self within everyone and everything else, no matter whether the "you" happens to be a Saint, a dog, a fly, a tree or a co-worker, and no matter how irritating the Ego might find any of these other Beings. As affirmed by Isha Upanishad:

"The Self is everywhere. Whoever sees all Beings in the Self, and the Self in all Beings hates none. For one who sees Oneness everywhere, how can there be delusion or grief?"

These truly are most profound and wise words, and ones which equally apply to every human being as immortal, Divine inseparable aspects of God, "made" in the "true image of God".

These same truths have always been taught down through the ages in both the East and the West. Vedanta goes on to teach the profound truth that all fear and misery arise from this sense of separation from the Universe. *"There is fear from the second"* stated the Brihadaranyaka Upanishad. The second refers to "duality", which is the sense of separation from the rest of creation but which is always a misperception since it implies that something exists other than Brahman.

There can be and is no other. The Self is the essence of the Universe, the One Universal Mind—the essence of all Souls as is aptly affirmed by the Upanishads:

"You are at one with the Universe. He who says he is different from others, even by a hairs breadth, immediately becomes miserable. Happiness belongs to him who knows this oneness, who knows he is one with the Universe".

Hinduism is an ancient, wise and diverse culture approached by honouring many different deities by means of song, dance and ritual, and by the philosophy of the Vedanta—ultimate Universal reality in the form of Brahman and the reality of the personal Soul in the form of Atman. All Hindu traditions teach the same ultimate reality—Atman and Brahman, God, the Universal Mind, and the human Soul and Spirit are one.

Chapter 4
Taoism

Tao is another great culture of the Orient, based on the nature and destiny of mankind and the Universe. Taoism teaches its followers how to progress in life and to evolve as immortal aspects of the Divine. As with other ancient wisdoms the world, Taoism teaches that there is an ultimate reality which is the basis for everything and everyone in the Universe. The Tao can be approximately translated as meaning “the path” or “the way” and refers specifically to a “power” or “force” enveloping, surrounding and flowing through all things, both living and non-living. The Tao regulates natural processes, promotes balance in the Universe, and embodies the harmony of opposites.

The founder of Taoism is believed to have been Lao-Tse, 604-531 BCE, a contemporary of Confucius, who was searching for a way to end the constant tribal warfare and disharmony prevalent at the time.

Along with Confucianism and Buddhism, Taoism became one of the three main traditions of China. With the end of the Ch’ing dynasty in 1911, official state support for Taoism came to an end, and much of the Tao heritage was destroyed. When the communists came to power in China in 1949, religious freedom of all types was severely curtailed. The communist government was particularly hard on Taoism, forcing Taoist monks to endure manual labour, and they also confiscated ancient Tao temples and plundered the Tao heritage.

Several million Taoist monks were reduced to a number of around fifty thousand by 1960. Then, during the cultural revolution of 1966 to 1976, much of what remained of Taoist heritage was destroyed by the communist government. This is a typical example of a government which denied the truth of life and the Universe to its people for no other reason than self-interests, power and control. Later, the Chinese government restored some leniency towards Taoism and other ancient traditions.

Throughout the world, Taoism currently has about twenty million followers and continues to have a significant impact on the culture of North America, particularly in the areas of acupuncture, herbalism, holistic medicine, meditation and the martial arts.

After the decimation of the ancient Tao culture by the communist government of China, Taoism is now making a very significant comeback in China and other countries throughout the world. Like other ancient traditions of the East and West, Taoism is an extremely important source of wisdom, knowledge and teachings which no tyranny or suppression can ultimately destroy. The truth must and will always prevail.

Taoism teaches that the Tao is the First Cause of the Universe. The ultimate and most sacred objective of the followers of Taoism is to become one with the Tao. A very well-known Taoist symbol is “Yin-Yang” which represents the balance of the opposites in the Universe. When Yin and Yang are equal and balanced, all is calm and harmonious. When either Yin or Yang becomes dominant, the inevitable result is confusion and disarray. Yin-Yang can be considered as the same Principle of gender that is taught by the wisdom of the West. Yin represents the aspects of the feminine—soft, cool, calm, introspective and healing, while Yang represents the aspects of the masculine—hard, hot, energetic, moving and sometimes aggressive. As nothing in nature is completely positive or negative, however, the Yin-Yang symbol recognizes this reality by including a small black spot in the white swirl and a corresponding white spot in the black swirl of the symbol. Yin and Yang are considered to be opposing forces within nature.

Huai Nan Tzu, a philosopher of around the second century BCE said:

"He who conforms to the course of the Tao, following the natural processes of Heaven and Earth, finds it easy to manage the whole world".

This literally means "going with the flow" of life rather than striving to oppose it, recognising that ultimately everything is a manifestation of the same Energy within Universal mind. Most people today tend to force their lives in the direction the Ego, reacting to conscious interpretation of the perceptions of the five physical senses. This creates ongoing imbalances that can escalate until such people are severely and negatively impacted.

Going with the flow of life is often known as "going with the Tao" - being in complete harmony with the Universe means enjoying a harmonious life. It becomes easier to manifest your needs in your life when you live within the present moment and the natural and immutable flow of the Universe, the Tao.

Chapter 5
Buddhism

Buddhism has become widespread throughout many Asian countries including India, China, Tibet, Nepal, Korea, Japan and Sri Lanka, as well as many countries in the western world where there is an increasing Buddhist following. There are currently approximately three hundred million people following the Buddhist tradition in its various forms.

The title "Buddha" derives from the word "budhi" which means "to awaken". The "awakening" to which this refers is a Spiritual awakening through the seeking of enlightenment, the finding of "Buddha within". This is analogous to discovering the truth that the Universe or God is within everyone. The person who became known as Buddha—Siddhartha Gautama—achieved full awakening, or enlightenment, at the age of thirty-five years.

As with many enlightened traditions, Buddhism transcends the title of a mere religion due to the fact that it is not dogmatic or orthodox in its teachings, and contains no rigid doctrines. Like Hinduism, Buddhism is more of a philosophy and a way of life than a religion. Philosophy means "love of wisdom", and the Buddhist philosophy broadly embraces the need to live a moral life, to be Mindful and aware of all thoughts and actions at all times, and to develop Universal wisdom and understanding.

Notwithstanding being born into a royal family with all the wealth he could possibly need, Siddhartha Gautama realized at the age of twenty-nine that wealth and luxury did not equate to ultimate happiness. After several years of dedicated searching and meditation, Siddhartha finally discovered the middle path and was enlightened, after which he devoted the remainder of his life to teaching the Principles of Buddhism, known as the "Dhamma" or "truth", until his death at the age of eighty years.

Although there are many variations and traditions of Buddhism, the central focus is always to teach the truth. Buddhism is based upon four noble truths and the eightfold path. The four noble truths may be summarized as follows:

The first noble truth teaches that to most people, life is suffering, which includes pain, disease and untimely death. Suffering also includes loneliness, fear, frustration, disappointment and anger. Buddhism teaches how to avoid these pitfalls, all of which due to the way people live and think.

The second noble truth states that suffering is due to craving and aversion. It teaches that people will suffer if they expect others to conform to their own expectations. This noble truth also teaches that "wanting" deprives people of contentment and happiness because it causes a constant striving for more and more material gain, wealth and possessions. A lifetime of craving and wanting, especially the craving to continue to exist in the current physical body, creates a powerful Energy in which people become trapped. This causes the cycle of reincarnation to continue, as the Higher Self must send further incarnations in order to learn the lessons that were not learned in the previous life.

The third noble truth states that suffering can be overcome and happiness attained. This noble truth teaches that if all useless craving and desires are set aside, living each day one at a time, without dwelling on the past or an imagined future, people will be set free and attain happiness and contentment, as well as have more time to help others to achieve the same. This is a state known as "Nirvana".

The fourth noble truth states that the "Eightfold Path" is the path that leads to the end of suffering.

The Noble Eightfold Path consists of eight Principles that may be summarized as follows:

First: “Samma-Ditthi”—complete or perfect vision. The vision of the true nature of reality and the path of transformation.

Second: “Samma-Sankappa”—perfected emotion or aspiration. This is to maintain rightful thinking and attitude, liberating emotionality and acting from love or compassion.

Third: “Samma-Vaca”—perfected or whole speech. Clear, truthful, uplifting and non-harmful communication.

Fourth: “Samma-Kammanta”—integral action. An ethical foundation for life based upon the Principle of non-exploitation of self or others.

Fifth: “Samma-Ajiva”—proper livelihood based upon correct action and ethical Principles of non-exploitation. This is the basis for the ideal society.

Sixth: “Samma-Vayama”—complete or full effort, Energy or vitality. Consciously directing life Energy to the transformative path of creative and healing action, thus fostering wholeness. This is conscious evolution.

Seventh: “Samma-Sati”—complete or thorough awareness, also called “right Mindfulness”. Levels of awareness and Mindfulness of everything, oneself, feelings, thought, people and reality.

Eighth: “Samma-Samhadi”—full, integral holistic “Oneness” with The Source or The All. This includes concentration, meditation, and single pointedness of Mind, and the progressive establishment of the whole Being into the many levels of conscious awareness. Note, the word “Samma” means whole, perfect, integral complete, thorough.

The importance of the four noble truths and the eightfold path simply cannot be underestimated, not only for those practicing

Buddhism but for anyone who genuinely desires to make true progress. In other cultures and traditions, these principles might have different names and be taught in different ways, but all ultimately lead in the same direction toward ennoblement, realization of true Spiritual nature and ongoing progress in the Light on the path back to The Source, The First Cause, God, from Whence we came in the beginning.

Although Buddhism is more of a philosophy than a religion, its ultimate objective is to teach the way to enlightenment, a full realization of self and of the whole Universe, "All that Is". The four noble truths and eightfold path are the ways the Buddha put forward to achieve this based upon his own years of strenuous and arduous efforts, finally achieving his ultimate objective which now forms the basis of Buddhism throughout the world.

In addition to the teaching and realization of enlightenment through the four noble truths and eightfold path, Buddhism also fully recognizes the "holistic" nature of the Universe as identical to the wisdom and traditions of the West, as well as modern quantum physics. Buddhism teaches the "wholeness" of everything in the Universe and the methods for becoming One with wholeness. This is the ultimate objective of enlightenment, and once enlightenment has been achieved, there are no longer any doubts as to the true nature of the Universe, of reality or of true purpose. This is the same ultimate reality and the ultimate destiny of all mankind that everyone will, sooner or later realise.

The Buddhist is acutely aware of the existence and nature of karma and of the continuous cycle of birth and rebirth known as "reincarnation", all of which are discussed in more depth later in this book. It will become the life's work of a Buddhist to transcend both karma and the cycle of reincarnation.

By comparison with the wisdoms of the West and of Hinduism and quantum physics, Buddhism does not teach the very nature of the Universe in depth or at a philosophical level. These are instead taken for granted as truths to be discovered by those who achieve "Buddhahood". Therefore, these precepts are left to the dedicated follower of Buddhism to discover through the process of enlightenment or "Nirvana". Buddhism does, however, teach three important Universal characteristics: impermanence (Anitya), suffering (Dhukha), and "not-self" (Anatama).

Like the wisdom of the ages of the traditions of both the West and the East, Buddhists fully recognize Unconditional Love as the most powerful force in the entire Universe, and unconditional compassion for everything and everyone, known as "Metta or "loving kindness", are fundamental tenets of Buddhist culture, teachings and aspirations.

Chapter 6
The Wisdom of the West

Over the millennia, there have been many very great teachers of the wisdom and knowledge of the Universe, some of whom have remained in relative obscurity while others became legendary names. Some even became the basis of major, orthodox world religions. It was most assuredly never the intention of these great teachers to become the focal point of such dogmatic religions, or to be responsible for the indoctrination of millions of people in their names, or for an instrument of violence, misery and death that ensued as those purporting to represent these teachers exerted their control, usually for their own purposes. These great masters and teachers rather simply sought to offer selfless service as messengers of pure Universal truth and knowledge for Spiritual growth for the benefit of humanity, and how to live a life of perfect joy, abundance and health. It is a most unfortunate fact that the creation of some orthodox religions with their associated creeds, doctrines and dogmas have resulted in exactly the opposite of the intentions of these great teachers of the past.

Universal knowledge was available long before the beginnings of the great world civilizations of the Middle East and elsewhere. The knowledge was known to most ancient civilizations of the world, which are mostly no longer visible due to environmental cataclysms or the actions of humanity. These early civilizations provided future civilizations with the sacred knowledge that mankind should continue to fulfil its true destiny.

It is generally recognized that the seat of the ancient knowledge and wisdom in the western world, the Occident, was set in ancient Egypt long before the first pyramids were constructed. The greatest of all teachers of the time, and in the opinion of many ever since, was a man known as Hermes Trismegistus, who dwelt in ancient Egypt thousands of years before Christianity and the other modern world religions ever came into being. Hermes Trismegistus was widely known and respected as the "Master of Masters" and the teacher of teachers. People came from both the West and the East to learn Universal truths, knowledge and wisdom directly from Hermes himself, and much of the ancient wisdom of both the East and the West originated directly from this great master.

Hermes was dedicated to sowing the seeds of truth regarding the true nature of the Universe and of mankind, that this knowledge and wisdom would be handed down from generation to generation. As decades, centuries and millennia passed, the words, wisdom and teachings of Hermes and other great Masters were kept alive throughout the western world by word of mouth and writings which were kept safe from those who would seek to destroy this truth for their own purposes.

Hermes was later deified and became known as "Thoth", the messenger of the Gods, carrying his vital messages and teachings to humanity. When depicted as a God, Hermes is pictured with wings attached to the sides of his helmet.

At around the same time, there were other great and ancient civilizations possessing the true knowledge, which were almost certainly in direct and frequent communication with the civilizations of ancient Egypt. These ancient but advanced civilizations were lost to the visible world many thousands of years ago due to cataclysmic events, although some evidence of their existence still remains, often resting under what is now thousands of feet of water on the ocean bed. Further evidence will most certainly be discovered in the future.

During the years of Hermes, the wisdom and knowledge of the Universe and of the spiritual nature and destiny of mankind was taught far and wide, having a most profound influence on many diverse cultures. It remained this way until thousands of years later when the advent of orthodox religions brought about an attempt to destroy those who were in possession of the true knowledge. While they did not succeed, dark ages followed where the creed, dogma and oppression of orthodox religions became prevalent, and the ancient wisdom was closely guarded by the few until it became safe for it to be made available to mankind again.

Of course, Hermes Trismegistus was by no means the only teacher of Universal knowledge over the millennia. Other great civilizations of the western world before, during and after the time of Hermes were also in possession of these ancient truths. Such great civilizations existed in Central and South America, including the Inca, Toltec and Maya, as well as the Assyrian, Sumerian, Anatolian and Babylonian civilizations of Mesopotamia in the Middle East. All of these civilizations knew or were taught the ancient wisdom and knowledge that still exists today.

These great ancient civilizations include the lost legendary continent of Atlantis and Lemuria, also known as Mu, which was widely thought to have existed in the area of the Pacific Ocean around Easter Island, the home of the famous giant statues.

Many firmly believe the Atlanteans were in direct contact with the ancient civilizations of both the Americas and the Middle East. Indeed, artefacts such as ancient writings in the form of glyphs have been found which link all of these great ancient civilizations together. Both Atlantis and Lemuria were thought to have been destroyed by global cataclysms which caused them to suddenly sink beneath the ocean, and many believe such global cataclysms are also the basis for the Old Testament account of the great flood.

It is highly probable that evidence of these ancient and long lost civilizations will soon be discovered in abundance, at which time considerably more will be known of their cultures and links to ancient Egypt and other civilizations. Many ancient teachings from a diverse range of western sources have thankfully survived to this day, having been closely guarded, maintained and taught over the millennia, and are now being taught more widely as the influence and power of the orthodox churches diminishes.

All knowledge and wisdom of the West is totally consistent with the legacy and teachings originating in ancient Egypt at the time of Hermes Trismegistus. All of the knowledge and wisdom handed down throughout the ages fully explains that which most modern people regard as miracles, supernatural, paranormal, occult or mystical.

According to the ancient teachings of the West, the Occident, the true nature of the Universe is described by seven fundamental Principles by which everything in the Universe functions and can be explained. These are the Principles of Mentalism, Correspondence, Vibration, Polarity, Rhythm, Cause and Effect and Gender. All of these Principles at their most complex are highly involved and would require an entire book to discuss and analyze each of them in detail. However, the fundamental characteristics of each of these Principles can be summarized in the following seven chapters on these important Universal Principles.

Chapter 7
The Principle of Mentalism

This Principle embodies the truth that the entire Universe is an infinite living Mind, the Universal Mind, and Consciousness, of which everything and everyone is an integral aspect. Everything in the Universe in all of its dimensions or spheres exists within the infinite living Universal Mind, and this living Mind, in which we live and move and have our Being might truly be called "God", The First Cause, or Source Energy.

This Principle fully explains and accounts for all of the "phenomena" which people regard as "miracles", "supernatural" or "paranormal", abilities such as psychic powers, telepathy, telekinesis and many others. This Principle of Mentalism also explains the true nature of Energy, power and matter, and why these are ultimately under the control of, and subordinate to the power of, the Mind. Mentalism or infinite living Mind explains why we, as humans, made in the "image of God", can create mentally in the Microcosm just as God, The Source, The First Cause, The All, Universal Mind created the entire Universe, the Macrocosm.

Chapter 8
The Principle of Correspondence

This is another extremely important Universal Principle, teaching there is direct correspondence between all planes of reality. As we will discuss later in this book, the material universe of matter is but the very lowest plane, realm or dimension of an infinite Universe of ever more subtle planes of Energy of increasing vibration and decreasing relative density.

Everything in the entire Universe—without exception—is subject to Divine order, otherwise, there would be chaos, and the Universe would collapse in an instant. This Divine order is prevalent between all of the great planes of life because anything which occurs on one plane will be reflected on all other planes in exactly the same degree. This has to be the case in order to maintain a perpetual state of balance, harmony and Universal equilibrium.

The Principle of Correspondence is most aptly represented by the famous axiom "as above, so below".

4-20-13

Chapter 9
The Principle of Vibration

The basis of the Principle of Vibration is that everything in the Universe is constantly in motion. Nothing ever rests for a single moment. Vibration is, in fact, a characteristic of Energy, a fact which quantum physics is now rapidly coming to accept as the fundamental basis of the laws of the greater Universe.

The Principle of vibration also explains the differences between all manifestations of matter, Energy, and Spirit, all of which are ultimately pure vibration, or Energy. Everything from the highest aspect of God, pure Spirit, the very highest manifestation of vibration of all, all the way out to the physical world of matter are degrees and manifestations of vibration or Energy—all within the infinite Universal Mind.

Chapter 10
The Principle of Polarity

The Principle of Polarity affirms the fact that everything in the Universe is dual, i.e. having two poles. This Principle also provides for the fact that there are no absolutes in nature. For example, when people refer to "hot" or "cold", these are not absolutes. They are rather degrees of hotness and degrees of coldness relative to, or in comparison with each other.

There are therefore no extremes, but rather only degrees of the same thing. North and South, East and West are merely degrees of direction. Similarly, light and dark are only degrees of illumination, the question being where would light begin and darkness end? The same Principle applies to large and small, black and white, hard and soft, noise and quiet, high and low, positive and negative, and so on.

Another example are the concepts of "love" and "hate", which again, are only degrees of the same emotion, with "like" and dislike" being within these two parameters. There can be no absolute love or absolute hate, and the experience of these two polarities, as with all experience, will vary according to the perceptions of each individual. Something one person might perceive as being associated with "hate" might well be "loved" by the next person. This particular example of the Principle of polarity highlights the possibility for mental transmutation, also known as "Alchemy". In alchemy, the "hate" of something can be transmuted to "love" of the same thing with transmutation taking place along the same polar axis. Similarly, bad or "negative" attributes of the Soul or Spirit can be transmuted along the same axis to their corresponding "good" or positive attributes. The Principle of polarity is, therefore, extremely important in the process of the ennoblement and perfection of every human being on the sacred path back to our Divine Creator.

Chapter 11
The Principle of Rhythm

The Principle of Rhythm encompasses the truth that there is always action and reaction along the same axis of polarity. A pendulum swings from side to side, the tides of the seas ebb and flow, and on a much wider scale, we witness the rise and fall of people claiming power over others such as dictators, the rise and fall of businesses and other entire organizations and most will be aware of the rise and fall of empires of which there have been many examples throughout history. All of these are examples of the Universal Principle of rhythm. The entire Universe and everything and everyone within are all subject to the Principle of rhythm from the very highest to the very lowest aspects and in an infinite degree of magnitude.

The entire Universe operates in these cycles of rhythm, also known as "cycles". Ancient civilisations such as the Maya were expert at observing, measuring and recording these great cycles which they recorded in their advanced calendrical systems, the Maya long count calendar, the current cycle of which ends on December 21, 2012 being a famous example, and one which will be discussed later in this book.

Chapter 12
The Principle of Cause and Effect

The Principle of Cause and Effect, also known as "Causation", is another extremely important Universal law. Some would say this is the most important and exalted Principle, and one which affects everyone in a profound way. The Principle of Causation will be discussed in much more detail later in this book.

The Principle of Cause and Effect is based upon the truth that nothing in the entire Universe ever happens by chance. Everything, including every thought and every action, results in an "effect", always being associated with a preceding and directly corresponding "cause". There can never be any exceptions to this Principle. The vast majority of people progress through life completely oblivious to this exalted Universal law, ascribing everything that happens to them to such notions as "chance", "coincidence", "luck", "fortune", all of which are nothing more or less than superstition. One of the most important aspects of Causation is karma. Karma is important to everyone, and will accordingly be discussed in much more detail later in this book.

Chapter 13
The Principle of Gender

The Principle of Gender embodies the truth that everything in the Universe has both masculine and feminine Principles. This Principle not only applies to humans, animals or other life where it manifests in the physical world, but to everything in creation, animate or inanimate.

The Principle of gender constantly works in the direction of generation, regeneration and creation. Every male element includes a degree of the female element, and conversely every female element contains a degree of the male element. The Principle of Gender also operated in full accordance with the Principle of Polarity, where there can be no absolute male or absolute female, but only relative degrees of "maleness" and "femaleness".

As we will discuss later in this book, all of these Universal Principles are vitally important and integral to the harmony of the Universe in all dimensions and are integral aspects of the truth that everyone and everything in the Universe is an equal and integral aspect of God, The All, The Source, and of each other. There is no separateness in the Universe whatsoever.

This brings us to the most important truth of all, a truth which has been taught by all civilizations throughout the ages—that every single person, without exception, is an immortal Spiritual being, a true son or daughter of God.

Chapter 14
The Emerald Tablet of Hermes

The Emerald Tablet of Hermes is an extremely important and very ancient text that was originally found written on a green stone tablet, documenting the nature of the Universe and how it came into being. Although the tablet is “emerald”, it is thought to actually be a green stone such as jade, and the writing was raised as opposed to carved. The Emerald Tablet was originally thought to have been discovered by a person by the name of “Balinas”, who subsequently wrote down the entire text in the ancient Syriac language, from which it has since been translated into many different languages.

The Emerald Tablet is not only very important from the point of view of describing the process of creation and the nature of the Universe, a process that is fully supported by many other independent sources including modern quantum physics, but is also the basis of alchemy. Contrary to popular belief, alchemy is not necessarily the transmutation of base metals into gold, but rather refers to the ennoblement of the Soul and Spirit on the path to perfection, the ultimate mission of everyone and everything in creation.

Following is a 12th century Latin literal translation of the Emerald Tablet of Hermes:

“True without falsehood, certain most certain
What is above is like what is below, and what is below is like that which is above. To make the miracle of the one thing.
And as all things were made from the contemplation of The One, so all things were born again from one adaptation.
Its Father is the Sun, its Mother is the Moon.
The Wind carried it in its womb, the Earth breastfed it.
It is the Father of all works of wonder in the World.
Its power is complete.

If cast to Earth, it will separate Earth from Fire, the subtle from the gross.
With great capacity it ascends from Earth to Heaven. Again it descends to Earth, and takes back the power of the above and below.
Thus you will receive the glory of the distinctiveness of the World. All obscurity will flee from you.
This is the whole most strong strength of all strength, for it overcomes all subtle things, and penetrates all solid things.
Thus the World was created.
From this comes marvellous adaptations of which this is the procedure.
Therefore I am called Hermes Thrice Crowned, because I have three parts of the wisdom of the whole World.
And complete is what I had to say about the work of the Sun".

These are most profound and important words, which, although written with highly symbolic meaning can be explained as follows:

"True without falsehood, certain most certain":

The text of the Emerald Tablet starts by affirming that everything that follows is Universally true and accurate and applies to "everything that is" without exception.

"What is above is like what is below, and what is below is like that which is above. To make the miracle of the one thing":

This statement affirms that the entire Universe in all spheres of life and reality is not separate in any way whatsoever, but is a continuum from the very highest aspect of "The One", "The Source", the "First Cause", out to the physical world of matter. This phrase also affirms that the continuum of the Universe is equally effective and integral in all directions, above and below, below and above, all working in complete harmony as an inseparable aspect of the whole. This is in accordance with the Universal Principle of Correspondence. The word "miracle" does not mean a miracle in absolute terms, but simply working in complete harmony with the Universe, the results of which might well seem like miracles to some.

"And as all things were made from the contemplation of The One, so all things were born again from one adaptation".

This is an important statement affirming that the entire Universe is a "Mind world" from which everything originated and is held entirely within the infinite Mind of "The One", of God. It also affirms that the entire Universe was created by the contemplation or meditation of "The One" and is a projection of, a Thought Form, contained entirely within the Mind of "The One" —the Universal Mind.

This statement confirms that everything in the Universe is an integral aspect of everything else in the Universe and of "The One", all mirroring and following the power of "The One" by adaptation of the process of following "The One".

"It's Father is the Sun, its Mother is the Moon".

This is analogous to the creative process where the sperm of the father seeks the egg of the mother. The constant cycles of the Sun and the Moon represent the rhythm of the Universe and infinite creation.

"The Wind carried it in its womb, the Earth breastfed it".

In this statement, "wind" is analogous to the Universal element of air which is the mediator of the Universal elements of Fire and Water, as opposed to the physical element of Air. Wind or Air is a mediation of Fire and Water and represents the forces involved behind the process of creation, which ultimately resulted in the final Universal element of Earth, representing solidification. Earth nourishes the creation, providing for independent form and existence as can be clearly witnessed by the presence of the physical world of matter.

"It is the Father of all works of wonder in the World".

Father represents the Prime Creator, The One, The All, the First Cause, The Source, the Quintessence of the four elements of Fire, Air, Water and Earth, the Ether, often known as "God" from Whom the aforementioned processes originated.

It is particularly important to note this statement also confirms that the creative process was carried out by "The One" as an act of full, ultimate, infinite conscious awareness within the Universal Mind of The One, within which all the Universe exists as infinite living Mind and Consciousness.

"Its power is complete. If cast to Earth, it will separate Earth from Fire, the subtle from the gross".

This affirms that the power of the Consciousness of The One is absolutely complete in every aspect. It goes on to say that the forces involved—Fire, Air, Water and Earth—which originally acted in an "outwards" manner and created the Universe from the highest aspect of The One, eventually reach the physical world of matter where there is a reversal of the forces back toward The One. This results in a separation of force from form, thus leaving in place the physical aspect of the Universe in the form of solidification. The Fire of creation is separated from the solidification of the Earth, thereby separating the "subtle" inner worlds and the Astral and Mental planes from the "gross", which is the physical Universe of matter.

It should also be noted that while the Emerald Tablet and sources generally talk in terms of "higher" and "lower", The Source, The First Cause, God is at the very centre of all creation—the innermost level of Energy—while the physical space-time bound material Universe is the outermost Energy level forming the "epidermis" of the Universe. So in reality "lower" is "outer" and "higher" is "inner relative to the Source.

"With great capacity, it ascends from Earth to Heaven. Again it descends to Earth, and takes back the power of the above and below".

This tells us that the conscious awareness of The One releases itself from the solid aspect of Earth, the physical Universe, and returns upwards once again through the continuum of vibration (Energy) back toward the highest aspect of The One.

As this process occurs, Consciousness brings with it the experience of "capacity" or "wisdom".

It is important to note that Spirit exists, has always existed and always will exist in the "Eternal Now" but does not become an "individual" or "individuated" with physical, Astral and Mental bodies until the time of a physical incarnation of the Higher Self. The destiny of every single person, as with the very process of creation itself, is to first descend to the Earth and then rise back, first to the Higher Self, the total of all physical lives, to the highest aspect of The One, our Divine creator, during the process of ennoblement and perfection. This is the ultimate meaning of life, whereby after all physical incarnations are complete, the Higher Self having gained sufficient knowledge and state of perfection to continue on the path, will assume the character of the final incarnation, and continue the journey inwards as a unique Spirit with God-given powers.

This statement then goes on to tell us that the Consciousness of The One descends a second time to Earth, integrating all aspects "above and below", and finally resulting in a fully aware force infinitely uniting the "above" with the "below" as integral aspects of the continuum of the entire Universe from the very highest to the physical world.

"Thus you will receive the glory of the distinctiveness of the World. All obscurity will flee from you".

This confirms that as a result of the processes involved, force descends into form during the original act of creation, and form then acts upon itself with Consciousness once again ascending into a formless state.

Finally, the force thus self-realized descends back into form in which to consciously express its Self, thereby receiving the "glory of the distinctiveness of the World", and receiving the Light (distinctiveness) as the dark (obscurity) is expelled ("flee from you").

"This is the whole most strong strength of all strength, for it overcomes all subtle things, and penetrates all solid things".

This confirms that through the act of creation as previously described, the Consciousness of The One is "whole", complete and of infinite strength, and has the ability to work without restriction in all directions of the continuum of the Universe from above to the below and below to the above at any level of density and vibration. In particular, the power of The One can surpass any "upwards" travelling entity. This statement also affirms that this infinite power is similarly unrestricted in the downward motion toward the physical Universe because it can inhabit the lowest vibration and the highest density of matter. This also confirms the truth that The One exists in everything and everyone and that everything and everyone in the Universe ultimately exists as Energy in the form of conscious awareness or Spirit, each individual being an individuated Energy field, or "spark" of Energy within the great Energy field of the Universal Mind.

"Thus the World was created".

This affirms that this process of force descending into form and realizing self-awareness, followed by another cycle of creation, followed by a further descent into form, eventually results in the physical "world" or the entire physical Universe of matter in space-time reality. Science only recognizes the physical aspect of the creation of the Universe, often known as the "big bang". Scientists remain largely unaware of the Divine forces of infinite and ultimate Consciousness that started this entire creative process or of its true origin which is not within the physical Universe—the true origin being very highest and most incomprehensible aspect of all—The One, God.

"From this comes marvellous adaptations of which this is the procedure".

The "marvellous adaptations" referred to mean the physical Universe of matter as a marvellous adaptation of The One. Beyond the physical Universe, everything consists of subtle Energy with vibration being a principle characteristic. Therefore, by comparison, the physical Universe consists of "marvellous adaptations". Eminent physicist David Bohm very aptly describes the outer physical Universe as "frozen light".

Everything and everyone in the Universe, including the physical Universe, contains the Light of The One.

Human Beings and all other life within the physical Universe are mirrored powers of the "one thing", causing "marvellous adaptations" as opposed to the "miracles of the 'one thing.'" Working within the physical world of matter, humans therefore "adapt" to the physical world, and these adaptations are mirrored as an aspect of the "one thing".

Physical Consciousness (or awareness or the Spirit of the human being) is an example of "force" within the "form" of the human body, with which we develop the future self by the process of perfection and ennoblement as it ascends the Divine path back to the Prime Creator from whence Spirit first came.

"Therefore I am called Hermes Thrice Crowned, because I have three parts of the wisdom of the whole World".

This statement is not in any way intended to be a self-proclamation of greatness on the part of Hermes, but it rather represents the trinity of the levels or aspects of the continuum of the Universe—physical, Astral and Mental. This specifically refers to the physical, Astral and Mental levels of Energy, or of vibration within the continuum of the Universe and the corresponding bodies within each human being. Specifically, this refers to the physical body, the Astral body also known as the Soul, and the Mental Body also known as the immortal Spirit. The final part of the statement affirms that this is a Universal level of knowledge or experience.

"And complete is what I had to say about the work of the Sun".

This final statement affirms the testimony of Hermes as to the creation and true nature of the Universe of Energy. Hermes Trismegistus, Hermes the Thrice Crowned was a true symbolic "messenger of the Gods" and one of the advanced Spiritual Beings of the inner spheres of reality to bring this most sacred knowledge to mankind. "The work of the Sun" affirms that this is an ongoing and active process within the glorious continuum of the Universe, the Universal Mind, Source Energy, the "Sun", representing the Divine creative process. Here we see another example of the perfect harmony of the Universe where everything is made in the "image of God", in that just as the "Central Sun" is the Source Energy that sustains the entire Universe and all in Creation, the Sun of our solar system likewise is the source of Energy that sustains life on Earth.

Chapter 15
The Kabbalah

Kabbalah is a philosophy originating in ancient Judaism, long before the beginnings of Christianity and the orthodox church. It is an important western source of Universal wisdom and principles based upon age-old knowledge originating from intelligences of the inner spheres of life and reality.

Kabbalah can be complex, multi-level and multi-faceted but at its most basic level it represents the wisdom to realize the Divine within. When viewed from a Universal perspective, the physical world of matter with its lowest vibrations and highest density is the outermost aspect of the Universe, analogous to an "epidermis" or "shell", akin to the skin of an apple, where The Source, God is the innermost, at the core of all creation existing at the very highest vibration, Unconditional Love and lowest density of all. Divine Energy radiates outward from The Source, pervading the whole Universe, finally reaching out to the lowest manifestation of vibration where differentiation of Energy into matter occurs.

Kabbalah teaches that in order to move inward closer toward God, it is necessary to understand the stages and nature of the creation of Universal reality. This commences with an understanding of how all creation originally occurred and continues to take place within the "Eternal Now".

In the beginning there was only "The Source", God, the "Eternal Now" existing beyond all space and time. The book of "Genesis I" symbolically and mystically chronicles the creation and formation of the Universe in the beginning, a process which is also documented in a related holy text known as the "Sephir Yetzirah", the "Book of Formation". This whole process of creation was symbolically put into motion by those well-known words "let there be light" or "fiat lux".

It should be mentioned that when ancient texts refer to "The Word", such as "in the beginning was The Word, and the word was with God", this does not mean a spoken word. "The Word" is actually a conscious act of creation on the part of God, involving the issuing forth of a Thought Form, vibrations in the form of colour, sound and other Divine manifestations of vibration, most of which are beyond the comprehension of humans still focussed in the physical world. These creative acts result in highly complex Energy patterns or Thought Forms, the basis of all creation within the Universal Mind.

As we know, the entire continuum of the Universe is Mind, fundamental characteristics of which are Energy and vibration. Nothing exists or can exist outside of Universal Mind or Energy.

Judaism originated with Abraham who devoted his entire life to realizing God within himself—one of the most sacred objectives of all humans focussed in a physical body. During the course of his life, many secrets of creation were made known to him by the intelligences of the inner spheres of reality and by the inspiration of God. The very first and most important work of the Kabbalah, the Sephir Yetzirah (the Book of Formation) is attributed to Adam himself.

The basis of the philosophy of Kabbalah and the method in which it teaches its Divine wisdom is to symbolically explain the 32 paths of wisdom, all of which are aspects of the ultimate act of creation. These 32 paths are based upon an important symbolic structure known as "The Tree of Life", which directly represents all of the inner spheres of reality from the Astral worlds to The Source.

The Tree of Life consists of ten "Sefirot" which are considered to be "Divine lights" acting as conscious channels of creation, and the twenty-two letters of the Hebrew alphabet. Together, these represent the "building blocks" of creation, permutations of which are said to be used by God to create the entire continuum of the Universe of Energy within the Universal Mind.

Around 100 CE, Rabbi Shimon Bar Yochai was granted permission from intelligences of the inner spheres to reveal, discuss and teach the complexities of the Kabbalah. This resulted in a work known as the "Sefer Hazohar", also called the "Zohar" or the "Book of Brilliance".

Over one thousand years later, another famous Rabbi, Yitzach Luria, studied the Zohar and discovered that there were even more inner levels to the Kabbalah that were not immediately apparent. This resulted in the great works of the Arizal, which explain the complexities of the interplay between all of the factors involved in the act of creation and with the secrets and purpose of the Soul.

Two hundred years later, a person by the name of Ba'al Shem Tov also known as "Besht", revealed yet another deeper aspect of the Kabbalah. This resulted in the "Kabbalah of the Besht", also known as "Chassidut". The great importance and significance of Besht is to not only focus on the various stages of creation, but to also bring into focus the individual Soul and Spirit, the ultimate Divine Light of God, the same eternal primordial Divine light as has always been present before, during and after all creation, and which Divine light will always be omnipresent in the Universe.

Again, the ultimate meaning of Kabbalah is exactly the same as that of the other great cultures of the world—each and every human being is an immortal Spirit made in the image of God, and is an equal partner in the creative process of the Microcosm of Universe, with God, the Macrocosm.

The ultimate destiny of every human being is to achieve the potential to reunite with God through the process of ennoblement, perfection and the full realization of God within.

The “true image of God” does not, as widely believed, imply that God has a human form after which everyone is physically fashioned. It means that all human Beings are immortal Spirit, “made” in the same Spiritual image, Thought Form, as God.

In Judaism and therefore Kabbalah, the true name of God is said to be only known by a very few and must never be spoken. The true, ineffable name of God is, therefore, often represented by four ancient Hebrew letters, together known as the “Tetragrammaton”. The letters of the Tetragrammaton, originating from ancient Hebrew, are “YHVH”, sometimes written “IHVH”, pronounced “Yod, Heh, Vahv, Heh” or “Yud, Heh, Vavh, Heh”.

Judaism generally avoids writing down any name of God lest it be later treated with disrespect in any way. In Judaism and Kabbalah God has therefore been associated with alternative names such as “Adonai”, which literally means “Lord”. When writing down the word “God”, Judaism usually represents this word in written form as “G-d” so that the written word cannot later be defiled, altered or treated with disrespect in any way.

The “Tree of Life” of the Kabbalah consists of a total of eleven “Sefirot” or “kingdoms”, often known as “vessels”, each of which represents a connected channel of Divine Energy. From a symbolic perspective, each Sefirot is also analogous to a particular attribute. There is usually considered to be ten Sefirot, as “Keter” and “Da’at” are considered to be the same, each representing a different dimension of the same God force. The Sefirot, together with their respective analogous attributes, are as follows, descending from the highest to the lowest:

“Keter”: Crown is the first and the highest of the ten Sefirot, and corresponds to the super-conscious realm of experience. Keter is represented by a crown representing an aura around the Consciousness.

Chochmah: Wisdom is the first power of conscious intellect within Creation.

Binah: Understanding is the second power of conscious intellect within Creation.

Da'at: Knowledge is the third and final power of conscious intellect within Creation.

Chesed: Loving Kindness is the first of the emotive attributes within Creation.

Gevurah: Might is the second of the emotive attributes within Creation.

Tipḥaret: Beauty is the third emotive attribute within Creation.

Netzach: Victory is the fourth emotive attribute within Creation.

Hod: Splendour is the fifth of the emotive attributes with Creation.

Yesod: Foundation is the sixth of the emotive attributes within Creation.

Malkut: Kingdom is the seventh and final emotive attribute within Creation.

Sequentially from Keter down to Malkut, the Sefirot together represent the various stages of the creative process of the Universe. Note that this is the same process as independently described in the Emerald Tablet of Hermes Trismegistus.

This is the true solution to the origin of the "big bang" as sought by astronomers and astrophysicists. However, as previously mentioned, the "big bang" did not originate from a point within the narrow confines of the three-dimensional Universe which represents only miniscule fraction of the entire Universe, but rather originated beyond all space-time as a Though Form sent forth from the Logos by The Source, The First Cause, God.

According to the Kabbalah, the primordial Light of God progressively manifested down through sequentially lower dimensions or levels of Energy and vibration, analogous to the realms of the ten Sefirot, until finally achieving a low enough vibrational rate to differentiate into matter, thereby achieving material density in the form of the physical Universe. Again, as previously mentioned, quantum physicist David Bohm most appropriately described the physical Universe of matter as “frozen light”.

The interaction between the ten Sefirot is depicted in the Kabbalistic tree of life by a network of connecting channels or “tzinorot”, which serve to illustrate the flow of Divine Energy. Following is a short description of the meaning of each of the ten Sefirot. (Note that the Tree of Life and all it represents is an extremely large and complex subject that could easily form the subject matter of an entire large book).

Each Sefirot of the Kabbalah consists of both an external as well as an internal dimension of reality. The external dimension is associated with its function in the process of creation. The internal dimension is associated with the hidden “motivational force” inspiring the activity of that particular Sefirot of creation and serves to describe how it manifests in the individual Soul. “Chassidut” describes the inspirational force behind each Sefirot, while the individual names of the Sefirot describe the Divine effect of each of these individual powers upon the creative process.

The Kabbalah also describes the actual stages of the entire creative process, beginning with the very highest, The Source, all the way down to the physical world of matter. These stages can be summarized as follows:

Or Ein Sof: “God’s infinite Light”. The ten stages of God’s Infinite Light.

Sod Ha’Tzimtzum: “The secret of Contraction”. The three stages of the secret of Contraction, the “removal” of God’s infinite Light.

Adam Kadmon: “Primordial Man”. The two stages of Adam Kadmon. God’s specific will and plan to emanate the Worlds, the Lights emanating from Adam Kadmon.

Akudim, Nekudim, Brudim: “Binding, Points, Connection”. The tree stages of “vessels” originating from the lights that emanated from Adam Kadmon.

Keter D’Azilut: “The Crown of Emanation”. The eight stages of the rectification process of the World of Atzilut, beginning with the rectification of its Crown.

Olam Ha’Atzilut: “The World of Emanation”. Ten stages of the World of Atzilut, the exclusive Consciousness of Divine unity.

Worlds of ABiYA: Atzilut, Beriah, Yetzirah and Asiya. Four stages, which emerge out of the infinite Light of God.

The last of these, the Worlds of AbiYA; Atzilut, Beriah, Yetzirah and Asiya, are extremely important in the understanding of the mechanism of all creation from the perspective of Kabbalah. Atzilut is the world of Emanation, Beriah is the world of Creation, Yetzirah is the world of Formation, and Asiyah is the world of Action. All of these emanate from the Divine, primordial Light of God, the Prime Creator, The First Cause, resulting in the sequential process of creation and ultimately culminating in the Mental, Astral worlds and finally the physical Universe as recognised by science.

Again, it is important to note that the creation of the multi-dimensional Universe is exactly the same as that detailed completely independently by the words of the Emerald Tablet of Hermes, both of which are in full accordance with the wisdom of the ages, and also of modern quantum physics.

Notwithstanding the Hebrew names and descriptions which are necessarily used, the description of the creation and nature of the Universe as depicted in the Kabbalah is in accordance with other world wisdoms and knowledge of the ages, but is expressed in a way appropriate to its particular tradition.

Chapter 16
The Wisdom of Quantum Physics

From the second half of the seventeenth century until the late nineteenth century, the mechanistic model of the Universe based on the theories of Isaac Newton dominated science, and especially physics. This Newtonian view of the Universe was accompanied by the popular religiously motivated and orthodox concept of an archetypal, patriarchal God, Who is completely separate from the Universe, ruling from above by imposing "laws" as recorded in the various religious texts.

This inflexible, mechanistic, and three-dimensional view of the Universe suited the aspirations of most people very well and dominated all scientific thought until the early twentieth century. Indeed, it still dominates scientific thought even today.

The Newtonian model of the Universe and the popular perception of "God" were so convenient for all branches of science, religion and the population at large that to challenge it was largely unthinkable. Even now in this early part of the twenty-first century, most areas of science still think exclusively in terms of physical units known as atoms, molecules and subatomic particles forming the basis of solid three-dimensional matter. This matter, in turn, supposedly constitutes the physical universe as perceived by science and experienced through the mediation of the five physical senses.

During the first three decades of the twentieth century, two emergent theories of relativity and atomic physics began to shatter the traditional Newtonian view. The fundamental concepts of absolute space and time, of solid particles, and the causal nature of physical phenomena could no longer be sustained by these new theories, and in particular those of one man—Albert Einstein.

In 1905, Einstein published two articles, one of which was his special theory of relativity, and the other was a new way of looking at electromagnetic radiation, which was a precursor to what would later become known as the "quantum theory" adapted by a team of physicists twenty years later.

According to Einstein's theory of relativity, space is not three-dimensional, and time is not a separate entity, both of which are extremely important realizations. This theory, of course, is in accordance with the true nature of the Universe as has always been known and taught throughout by the ancient wisdoms of the ages.

Einstein postulated that both space and time are connected by a fourth dimensional continuum known as "space-time". Accordingly, space and time could no longer be considered to be separate from each other as was commonly believed in accordance with the Newtonian mechanistic concepts of absolute space and absolute time existing as separate entities.

The theory of relativity arrives at the extremely important realization that mass is in fact a form of Energy. Again, this realization is in full agreement with the teachings of the wisdom of the ages, which has always taught that the Universe in all of its dimensions or spheres is pure Energy, or more specifically Energy in the form of vibration at progressive degrees ultimately originating from The Source, and progressively descending down to the physical world of matter.

During the early part of the twentieth century, scientists observed the effect on atoms when they were bombarded with x-rays. This led to another famous scientist, Ernest Rutherford, bombarding atoms with alpha-particles, which led to the astounding discovery that rather than being solid, as traditionally believed, atoms were, in fact, comprised of vast regions of space in which extremely small particles known as electrons moved around the centre of the nucleus bound by other forces.

Soon after the discovery of this "planetary model" of the atom, it was further discovered that the number of electrons in the atoms of a specific element determined the chemical properties of that element. This later became the basis for the periodic table of elements as is still used today in modern chemistry.

It came to be understood how the interactions between atoms resulted in chemical reactions forming molecules and, therefore, the many chemical compounds known to science today. This resulted in the realization that the Principles of chemistry could be entirely explained in terms of the laws of atomic physics. It would later also become apparent, as the ancient wisdoms of the world have always taught, that matter—whether in a form which is readily apparent to the five physical senses, or in the form of molecules, atoms or sub-atomic particles—is pure Energy manifesting as rates of vibration. This is the very same Energy manifesting vibration of which everyone and everything in the Universe is an integral and inseparable aspect—the very highest vibration and manifestation of Energy of all being God, The Source, The First Cause.

In the 1920's, an international group of scientists gathered in order to progress these discoveries. This eminent team included Niels Bohr, Werner Heisenberg, Paul Dirac, Erwin Schrodinger, Wolfgang Pauli and Louis de Broglie. They worked together on the then emergent field of the exploration of sub-atomic particles and were faced with paradox after paradox as they came to realize from their experiments that nothing could be explained in terms of traditional physics. The real breakthrough came when they set aside their traditional way of thinking and viewed these recently discovered phenomena in a completely new way. As Werner Heisenberg said, "they somehow got into the Spirit of the quantum theory". These revelations initially came as quite a shock to these distinguished scientists as concepts of quantum theory were not at all easy to accept after years of acceptance of conventional

Newtonian physics. This was particularly evident when the realization came, due to the work of Ernest Rutherford, that atoms actually consist of vast regions of space in which extremely small particles move. The physicists were now able to further postulate that even these subatomic particles were not solid in and of themselves. This led to the beginning of the extremely important realization that molecules, atoms and subatomic particles are ultimately pure Energy vibrating at extremely high but varying frequencies, and in fact not solid at all. This led to the further realization that subatomic particles have no meaning whatsoever in the context of existing as separate entities, but are rather part of an intrinsic oneness with the entire Universe.

By the 1930's, scientists were beginning to believe they had finally discovered the building blocks of matter and, in particular, that atoms consisted of protons, neutrons and electrons—the sub-atomic particles. As experiments proceeded and became progressively more sophisticated, more and more subatomic particles were discovered. By 1935, six such particles had been discovered, and by 1955, eighteen particles had been discovered. Modern science has since identified the existence of over two hundred subatomic particles.

The theory of relativity of Albert Einstein also had a profound effect on the concept of matter around the time of the early discoveries of subatomic particles. The relativity theory clearly demonstrates that mass is not related to substance, but is rather a form of Energy in and of itself. However, Energy is dynamic in nature and is associated with activity or vibration. The mass of a particle is directly equivalent to a certain amount of Energy, which proves the particle cannot be considered to be a static object. Instead, it involves Energy, or vibration, which, in turn, constitutes the mass of the particle.

These discoveries were pivotal to the understanding of quantum mechanics and quantum physics to the stage it had progressed and formed the basis for considerable future ongoing work in these important areas. Today, these theories are taking the entire range of sciences to new levels and, indeed, to a new understanding of the true nature of the Universe.

A further and extremely important breakthrough in the quantum sciences arrived due to the work of physicist David Bohm, a protégé of Albert Einstein. David Bohm is the physicist who first realized the entire Universe can be metaphorically likened to an infinite, magnificent hologram of which everyone and everything is a constituent component. Note that any portion of a hologram reflects the totality of the hologram, and this reflects the reality that everyone and everything in the Universe is an integral aspect of the whole or of God.

David Bohm attended Pennsylvania State College where he became fascinated by quantum physics and began to study the work and discoveries of the pioneers in this area. One of the most important discoveries of quantum physics is that an individual electron can manifest either as a wave or a particle, a characteristic of all subatomic particles. The electron also includes frequencies that were once thought to only manifest as waves, such as light, gamma rays, radio waves and x-rays, all of which can alter form from waves to particles and back to waves again.

Physicists came to believe that these particles should not be classified simply as waves or particles but as a single, all-encompassing classification, which later came to be known as "Quanta". Most importantly, scientists came to agree that the entire Universe is constituted entirely of Quanta. "Quanta" in turn constituting the primordial Light as has always been known about and taught through the wisdom of the ages.

It is very interesting to note how the various pioneers in the field of quantum physics were, even by this stage, inexorably arriving at a wide range of conclusions confirming the integral and inseparable nature of the Universe—again facts that had been taught all around the world for many thousands of years by the great masters and teachers of the ancient knowledge.

One of the discoveries that proved to be most astonishing to physicists was the observation that the only time Quanta ever manifest as particles are when people are actually observing them. The significance of this realization alone is extremely profound in terms of our understanding of the material world. The wisdom of the ages has always maintained and taught that everything within the physical world of matter is nothing but an illusion, with all non-natural things, in other words those things that were not originally thought into existence by The Source, The First Cause, God, being in reality the projections of the minds of humans, only perceived by most as "reality" through the mediation and perceptions of the five physical senses. Quanta, now established by science as a fact, clearly demonstrate this sensory illusion of manifestations within the physical world. Those things which humans perceive as "solid objects" are only reality in the context of those experiencing those same through the mediation of the five physical senses.

During this chapter and in other chapters of this book I will frequently refer to the physical world as an "illusion", mystically referred to in the East as "maya". I need to make it absolutely clear at this stage that the illusions referred to in this context are not the natural, untouched by human hand, characteristics of planet Earth Herself with all Her glorious, beautiful and varied features and landscapes, or of all life on Earth including humans—these are all projections of the Mind of The Source, the First Cause, God, and are therefore very real manifestations of Spirit, although of course still ultimately composed of Energy. I rather refer to the multitude of illusions created by the Minds of humans living on Earth including all material "things" which are only "real" to the extent they are observed at either an individual or consensual level. These material "things" are not "real" in a Universal sense, but are transient and in the context of eternity ephemeral, only perceived as having such characteristics as "solidity", "liquidity", "form" and other physically discernible characteristics through the mediation of the five physical senses, which in turn perpetuate these illusions.

Earth Herself, the suns, planets, galaxies and other creations in the physical Universe were created by the Mind of The Source during an act of creation that commenced with The Source, The First Cause, God, projecting outwards with ever decreasing vibration and increasing density, until finally differentiating into matter, finally resulting in the formation of the physical Universe. Nevertheless, the physical Universe is still transient to the extent they can only exist in its present form while The Source chooses to continue to maintain the Thought Forms that constitute the physical Universe and all its manifestations.

The discovery of the characteristics of Quanta further underlines the extremely important fact that everyone without exception creates their own reality. These factors equally apply to the inner worlds, including the Astral worlds to where most people will transition after physical death, and where anything can be manifested instantly through the focused powers of the Mind in the form of thoughts, intent and imagination. We will discuss manifestation with the power of the Mind in much more detail in later sections of this book.

The Astral and inner dimensions or spheres of reality exist at a much higher level of vibration or Energy than the physical world, and Quanta of Energy, identical to vibration or Light in the Universal sense, are much more easily influenced by the power of the Mind—the inner spheres of life being "Mind worlds". Physicist Nick Herbert likened the behaviour of Quanta to "a radically ambiguous and ceaselessly flowing quantum soup". Nick Herbert goes on to observe that "humans can never experience the true nature of quantum reality, because everything we touch turns to matter". In fact, this could be more appropriately stated that everything we "observe" turns to matter.

David Bohm was particularly interested in the observation relating to the strange state which seemingly existed between apparently unrelated subatomic events, an area most scientists had hitherto seemed to disregard. This disregard was due in part to the views of physicist Niels Bohr, who maintained that if subatomic particles only came into existence in the presence of an observer, it is also meaningless to speak of a particle's properties before they are actually observed.

David Bohm became increasingly dissatisfied with the views of his peers in these areas and in particular those of Niels Bohr. Bohm eventually wrote a paper on the subject with a view to increasing his own understanding, copies of which he sent to both Niels Bohr and Albert Einstein for their opinions. Niels Bohr failed to respond, but Albert Einstein suggested that they meet at Princeton University where they were both located at the time in order to discuss the paper. Over the course of time, these two great physicists met frequently to discuss quantum physics and gained considerable mutual respect in the process. In due course, Bohm published a work entitled "Quantum Theory" in 1951, and it was hailed as a classic. However, Bohm later became increasingly disenchanted with the theories he had put forward in his own work and continued searching for a better way to describe Universal reality.

During the next few years, Bohm continued his work, but constantly finding himself at odds with the theories of the highly respected physicist, Niels Bohr. Among the issues in question was that of Cause and Effect, where Bohm postulated that any particular effect could have an infinite number of possible causes behind it. Bohm's position was based on the assertion that any particular effect was the result of a cause, and the cause was an effect of a further preceding cause and so on. No single Cause and Effect relationship can be separate from the entire Universe as a whole. Once again, the position of Bohm is totally consistent with the Universal Principles of Cause and Effect and karma and of the ancient knowledge.

Bohm continued to refine his theories and research, looking more and more deeply into the meaning of the "quantum potential" he had discovered. One of the most important aspects of his quantum theories was that of "wholeness", which, probably unknown to him at the time, has also long been taught through the ages by the teachers of the ancient wisdoms.

In the late 1950's, Bohm moved to England where he continued his research at Bristol University as a research fellow, where he met another research student, Yakir Aharanov. Working together, they discovered another important example of non-local interconnectedness when they found that under the right circumstances, an electron can sense a magnetic field in an area where there would otherwise be no chance of finding the electron. These findings became known as the "Aharanov-Bohm effect". Even though this phenomenon has been proven time and again in subsequent experiments by several different scientists, many scientists still do not believe it to be possible, preferring to remain with the traditional Newtonian models of physics, simply because they feel comfortable with that framework, not challenging their own traditional scientific perspectives.

To his immense credit and the future integrity of all areas of science, David Bohm stood firmly by his work, stating most appropriately, *"in the long-run it is far more dangerous to adhere to an illusion than to face what the actual fact is*". The "illusion" to which he refers is the illusion that traditional Newtonian theories are still the truth, even though they had, by that time been proven by Bohm and others to be erroneous.

Eventually Bohm's attention moved to the matter of "order", where he began to realize that there are different degrees of order and that some things are more ordered than others. This led to the realization that there are an infinite number of "orders" in the Universe—indeed an entire hierarchy of orders. In the context of the Universe as a whole, there is positively no disorder. The Universe eternally exists as a perfect hierarchy of orders from the very highest order of The Source, The First Cause, God, the order of absolute Perfection and Unconditional Love, to the very lowest order of vibration that we know as matter. This is again fully supported by the ancient wisdoms of the world, which have always taught that the nature of the Universe is ordered by Divine perfection. Otherwise, the entire Universe in all dimensions would instantly collapse into chaos.

Bohm later experienced a major breakthrough in the progress of his theories while watching a television program where a demonstration was being shown of a large transparent container with a rotating cylinder connected to an external handle. This container was filled with glycerine with a single drop of ink was suspended within it. When the handle of the drum was turned, the drop of ink appeared to disperse throughout the glycerine and disappeared completely. However, when the handle of the drum was turned back in the opposite direction, the droplet of ink reappeared, collapsing upon itself and reconstituting as the original drop of ink in its original form. Bohm immediately realized the significance of this phenomenon when he wrote:

"This immediately struck me as being very relevant to the question of order, since, when the ink drop was spread out, it still had a hidden order that was revealed when it was reconstituted. On the other hand, in our usual language, we would say that the ink was in a state of disorder when it was diffused throughout the glycerine, this led me to see that new notions of order must be involved here".

This enabled Bohm to bring together the various threads of his previous theories with considerable clarity. It was the beginning of his "holographic" perspective of the Universe and a new method by which "order" could be understood. Like the metaphor of the ink drop in the cylinder of glycerine, it became highly evident to Bohm that the Universe possesses complete orders which can manifest in either a folded or unfolded form, only the latter of which is the more immediately apparent when observed. The folded orders are still a completely integral aspect of the order of the Universe as a whole, and unfolded orders are in the totality of order, thereby illustrating the absolute order of the Universe in all its completeness and perfection. This led Bohm inexorably to the realization that the Universe could, in and of itself, be likened to an infinite flowing hologram which he termed "holomovement". This is again is totally consistent with the Principle of rhythm we discussed earlier. Everything from the very highest to the very lowest, or more correctly the very inner to the very outer, ultimately flows from the infinite Mind of The Source, The First Cause, God. Nothing ever rests in the Universe with everything always flowing and in motion. Folded or unfolded orders reveal the order and perfection of the Universe as a whole.

During the early 1970's, Bohm published his first papers on the "holographic universe", which eventually led to the publication in 1980 of an extremely important, and indeed groundbreaking book entitled, "Wholeness and the Implicate Order". This book not only crystallized the life work of Bohm to that point, but it was a brand new and highly revolutionary way of perceiving the reality of the Universe in all realms, spheres and dimensions in scientific rather than esoteric terms.

One of Bohm's most startling conclusions was a fact that has always been taught by the wisdom of the ages—the truth that the everyday life that most people know as "reality" is nothing more than an illusion, a holographic projection of the greater multidimensional Universe as a whole. On a deeper level there exists an infinitely larger reality where the entire Universe, including the physical world perceived by people with the five physical senses, actually exists as individual units of a hologram, each of which is also identical to the hologram as a whole.

David Bohm calls the level of reality which is perceivable by the five physical senses the "explicate order" or the "unfolded order". He calls the deeper level of reality "the enfolded aspect of the Universe" or the "implicate order". As we will see later in this book, the Universe has many levels of reality beyond those merely apparent through the perception of the five physical senses. This also explains the truth that the Universe is constantly in motion, manifesting as an infinite number of "foldings" and "unfoldings" occurring between the implicate and explicate orders. The very existence of a deeper order explains why reality becomes non-local at a sub-quantum level.

Bohm further demonstrates the Universal reality of "wholeness". Everything in the Universe is constituted by the seamless holographic material of the implicate order, and cannot, therefore, be properly viewed in terms or parts or separateness. These realizations again are fully consistent with ancient knowledge which teaches that everything in the Universe is an integral aspect of everything else in the Universe, and ultimately everything is an aspect of the Whole. The concept of separateness then simply cannot and does not exist except as an illusion, albeit a persistent illusion, perpetuated only through the mediation of the five physical senses. This is also fully supported by Albert Einstein's theory of relativity, which states that space and time are not separate entities, but components of an infinitely larger reality known as the "space-time continuum".

Bohm extends this to include that everything in the Universe without exception is a continuum, including space-time and implicate and explicate orders. Most people today, including most of the sciences, view their own "reality" purely at the explicate level (the physical level), which gives rise to the illusion of separateness. This illusion is sometimes known in the East as "duality" and is one of the major reasons why the human race still finds itself in such a chaotic state today.

Everything then is a seamless aspect of everything else, and even the implicate and explicate orders ultimately blend into each other to include the ultimate Whole. Once again, this same reality has always been taught by the ancient wisdoms of the world. Bohm also realized that the illusion of separateness is not only directly responsible for the misdirection of much of science today, but is responsible for most of the social problems currently facing humanity. He stated that continuing to fragment the world into parts could ultimately lead to extinction—an extremely important and justified observation.

These are the major reasons why mankind absolutely must come to understand the true meaning of reality, its purpose and ultimate destiny, and, therefore, the very meaning of life. This emphasizes that whenever man harms or destroys anyone or any part of the environment whatsoever, whether it is another human being or any creature, however large or small, he equally destroys a part of himself. The importance and significance of this profound truth simply cannot be overstated.

Additionally, David Bohm recognized Consciousness as a more subtle form of matter. The entire Universe is both "mental" and infinite Consciousness. Because the Universe is not static but in a perpetual state of movement, Bohm began to use the word "holomovement" in order to more accurately describe the dynamic nature of the Universe. Because therefore everything in the Universe is an integral aspect of the same "holomovement", Bohm believes the relationship between matter and Consciousness exists deep in the implicate order rather than at the explicate level of the human perception of reality. Therefore, this relationship is present in the various degrees of the foldment and unfoldment of matter.

As we will see later in this book, thought itself is Energy in the form of degrees of vibration and can therefore directly influence other Energy to bring about non-physical and physical manifestations of Energy. Thought is an aspect of individual Consciousness which in turn is an integral aspect of Universal Consciousness, and accordingly thought is an integral aspect of the implicate and explicate orders. Consciousness, therefore, pervades everything in the Universe.

Bohm realized that dividing the Universe into living and non-living, animate or inanimate, is completely meaningless in the context of an integrated quantum reality. Everything in the Universe is an inseparable aspect of everything else in the Universe, interwoven and enfolded into the fabric and totality of the Universe. He also unknowingly agreed with the ancient wisdoms when he stated that everything in the Universe is life to some degree, even those things appearing to be solid and inanimate to the perceptions of the five physical human senses such as a stone, a mountain or a grain of sand. He said that life and intelligence exists not only in matter, but in fact exists within the very fabric of the entire Universe as a Whole.

Like a hologram, every single cell in a human body contains the entire Universe, as does every flower, rock, flake of snow, grain of sand, or atom. Mankind and everything else in the Universe can be likened to an infinite, magnificent hologram or holomovement projected from the infinite Mind of our Prime Creator, “The First Cause”, “The Source”, “The All”, “Spirit”, “God”, The Universal Mind.

As the work of David Bohm progressed, he came to realize that the metaphoric hologram or holomovement only provided for a relatively limited view of the implicate order, and to penetrate more deeply, he later developed a causal interpretation of the quantum field theory. Primary physical reality is assumed to be a continuous field, and discreet Quanta are viewed more in terms of a secondary symptom. Therefore, instead of taking a particle as a starting point, the field is accepted as a fundamental reality. At the same time, rather than view quantum potential as influencing a particle, Bohm postulated a "super-quantum" potential acting on a field. Now, the super-quantum potential assumes responsibility for the perception of discreet Quanta, thus creating the appearance of a particle in its Energy state, causing it to behave as if it was constituted by discrete elementary particles. This implies that wave-particle duality is an effect of the super-quantum potential on the continuous field. This later lead to the theories presented in a book published by Bohm in 1987 entitled, "Science, Order and Creativity", where he put forward the theory that above and beyond the implicate order, there is also a super-implicate order, postulating that in accordance with quantum field theory, the implicate order is the field itself and it is the super-implicate order that has the super-quantum potential. This lead to the conclusion that the particle itself is not a fundamental concept, as the primary realities are in fact the implicate and super-implicate orders.

In the super-implicate order, a particle does not exist except as a creation of the Mind or as a secondary symptom that can be perceived by instruments. What is actually present here is the holomovement consisting of a continuously changing quantum field of the implicate order, and the super-quantum potential of the super-implicate order, the particle, and the explicate order have a discontinuous ripple effect on the super-quantum potential of the field, thus providing for the existence of the second implicate order.

It becomes apparent that if a second implicate order exists, there could also be a potentially infinite number of successive inner implicate orders above the first and second implicate orders, giving rise to a whole hierarchy of inner super-implicate orders. The effects of these inner super-implicate orders would be progressively more subtle, and well beyond the range of measurement by any human instrumentation.

Once again, the ancient knowledge of the world has always fully supported the existence of a hierarchy of successively inner and more subtle super-implicate orders, often known as "planes", "realms", "spheres", "worlds" or "dimensions". An excellent ancient illustration of the hierarchy of super-implicate orders is "the Tree of Life" of the Kabbalah as previously discussed, where each Sephirot could, in this context be considered equivalent to a super-implicate order. Similarly, the various planes of correspondence which will be discussed later in this book are also super-implicate orders, all existing beyond the explicate order of the physical world of matter.

As the order of these super-implicate orders, planes or spheres of reality move progressively more inward, the "ether" or "fabric" of these planes becomes progressively finer and more subtle with increasing vibration and reducing density. The more inner the plane or super-implicate order, the more readily the Quanta of the ether are influenced by the Mind. As we will see later in this book, everything in the Universe is created first by Mind, thought which is Principle. Thought then materializes in the physical world as "something" observable and which can then be experienced through the mediation of the five physical senses.

David Bohm's theories postulate an ultimate reality comprised of a dynamic holomovement with three fundamental levels of manifestation—the explicate order (physical "reality"), the implicate order, and the super-implicate orders. The realms of the implicate and hierarchy of super-implicate orders comprise absolute reality, the remainder, for the most part consisting of the explicate order, the physical Universe.

Bohm goes on to speak of an "eternal order" that is neither static nor permanent and is in a perpetual state of creation. As the eternal order progresses down through the succession of implicate orders, when it reaches a level of implicate order bordering on the explicate order, it enters the realms of time, becoming manifest in the temporal realms of the Etheric plane and, in turn, the physical world, then becoming subject to the three-dimensional laws of "space" and "time—the space-time continuum.

The quantum potential, super-quantum potential, implicate and super-implicate orders are the names equivalent to the spheres manifesting beyond the perceptions of the five physical senses and are, therefore, unperceivable to humans. For David Bohm, however, as well as the ancient teachings and wisdoms of the world, these orders represent true reality. The implicate and super-implicate orders are the primary structure, and the explicate order of the physical Universe is the superficial projection or illusion, often known in the East as "maya", ultimately responsible for duality as unknowingly experienced by most human Beings.

Mainstream sciences remain very much steeped in the minimalistic Newtonian three-dimensional view of the world of matter and refuse to acknowledge the existence of the much greater inner spheres of life and reality despite the globally consistent teachings of the ancient wisdoms of the world and the compelling and pioneering work of David Bohm.

By denying the existence of these inner true realities simply because they cannot be observed or measured by physical scientific instruments, empirically based science can still justify continuing to work within the confines of this persistent illusion. This highlights the relative absurdity of the trillions of dollars spent on the exploration of the temporal, physical three dimensional Universe, when true exploration of the real Universe, our real home, costs absolutely nothing, and "space" and "time" present no barrier. The true pioneers and greatest explorers are those who recognise these truths, and courageously explore the true inner worlds of life and reality.

The future and destiny of all mankind is not to be found within the space-time bound limitations of the three-dimensional Universe, but within the inner spheres of reality beyond the temporal nature of space and time. As we will discuss later, exploration of the inner spheres is within the ability of everyone. Exploration of the true reality of the Universe by means of Astral and Mental projection and other natural abilities is the true future.

Bohm later began to consider the position of Consciousness relative to the implicate order, stating:

"Consciousness is much more of the implicate order than is matter". He also concluded: *"Deep down, the Consciousness of mankind is one. This is a virtual certainty because even in the vacuum of matter is one; and if we don't see this, it's because we are blinding ourselves to it*".

Here again, Bohm has arrived at a profound conclusion that has always been known and taught throughout the ages—all humans, as with life itself, share a common level of Consciousness at a inner level, specifically at the level of the group Consciousness of the human Mind, which level is equivalent to a super-implicate order of Bohm. It is this super-implicate order of the plane of the collective Consciousness of the human Mind that explains many so called "phenomena" often regarded as "supernatural", such as telepathy, telekinesis and remote viewing. Mind is Principle, experienced in physical human form as conscious, Subconscious and Universal, all levels or states of Mind manifesting within Universal Mind as one, separation being simply an illusion of the physical senses.

The work of David Bohm and his holographic view of the Universe is in no way representative of the totality of the ongoing work in the field of quantum physics. However, all of his theories have been rigorously tested against all known principles of quantum theory as well as in the laboratory. Bohm approached all science not merely as an academic endeavour, but as a quest for the absolute truth. He also remained true to his discoveries despite pressure from the more academic and theoretically inclined members of his profession. Bohm's work in quantum physics and quantum mechanics realized and affirmed a single ultimate reality—the true nature of the Universe. Time will inevitably show the Universal explicate, implicate and super-implicate orders as conceived and named by David Bohm are truth, however they are described, and will eventually have profound implications for humanity which all science will have to accept sooner or later. This will then show conclusively that the Universe is actually a magnificent unbroken wholeness, a continuum, an infinite flowing movement of Energy or vibration—the holomovement.

Bohm also conclusively demonstrated that there is absolutely no real evidence of a fragmented, chaotic, disparate Universe of separateness. He said:

"What is needed today is a new surge that is similar to the Energy generated during the Renaissance but even deeper and more extensive; the essential need is for a loosening of rigidly held intellectual content in the tacit infrastructure of Consciousness, along with a melting of the hardness of the heart on the side of feeling. The melting on the emotional side could perhaps be called the beginning of genuine love, while the loosening of thought is the beginning of the awakening of creative intelligence. The two necessarily go together".

Whenever you look at a material possession, such as a home, a car, a television set, they are nothing more or less than an arrangement of vibrating Energy or Quanta, Thought Forms created by thought processes and the powers of imagination of the Mind. If these objects were to be inspected very closely, it would be apparent that they are not solid at all but are rather composed of Quanta of Energy vibrating and moving at extremely high rates in and out of the object being observed.

Nothing can exist permanently unless it is observed because it is Mind that influences and shapes Quanta of Energy, without which Quanta would once again become a "potential" for something else. If, for example, everyone in the world were to cease observing everything in the world that was created by humans by ceasing to focus on its perceived existence, then everything on Earth that was man-made would cease to physically exist and would dissipate back into formless Energy. There would be no thought Energy to perpetuate the illusion of its existence. This is why everything on Earth and indeed the Astral worlds are referred to in some cultures as "maya" or illusion, due to its inherent transient and ephemeral nature.

Quantum physics completely confirms this by recognizing the fact that a "thing" can only come into "existence" when it is observed and Quanta arrange themselves according to the influence of Mind Principle of the observers. Of course, "existence" is a term relative to the five physical senses. It is only the illusion of form that changes in response to thought (Mind). When something is observed, Quanta coalesce to form subatomic particles, and, in turn, atoms, followed by molecules, until some "thing" finally manifests in the physical world as a localized temporal space-time event that can be perceived through the mediation of the five physical senses, giving rise to something that appears to be "solid", and part of that which physical humans usually perceive as "reality".

This process is the very basis of how each and every person creates his or her own perceived individual reality. Every single thought, as Energy, directly and instantly influences the quantum field causing Quanta to arrange and coalesce into a localized, observable, experiential event, object or other influence. This is also the basis of true "Magic". Those who understand and are in harmony with Universal laws are conscious creators, while most people are unconscious creators, constantly and unconsciously creating their own reality by means of their own un-ordered thoughts without ever being aware of these creative processes. As a result, they ascribe everything experienced as a result of their own unconscious thought to such superstitious notions as "luck", "chance" and "fortune". Conscious creation is also the basis of the Law of Attraction, which will be discussed in depth later in this book.

People might ask how things appear to be real, tangible and solid when they are not solid at all. The behaviour of Quanta can be likened to a reel of film. When the reel of film is played, thousands of frames of individual images are passed over a light projector and onto a screen, thereby giving the illusion of a solid moving scene. Quanta operate in exactly the same way. Countless Quanta of Energy constantly move in and out of an area of focus, coalescing to appear to the perceptions of the five physical senses as a "solid object". Like the movie, however, this is only an illusion that has been constructed from much smaller components, in this case Quanta of Energy. In the case of the movie, the visual image is created by the influence of the projector mechanism, analogous to the Mind principle, as individual "frames" of still images, analogous to Quanta, are passed in front of a strong, focussed light projection analogous to the process of thought. In the case of objects appearing to be solid, the illusion is further perpetuated by the Mind through the act of observing the objects. Due to the high density, low vibration of Energy in the form of physical matter, "objects" can exist for even millions of years, but we must also take into account that "time" is also an illusion, and one which is inseparable from "space".

As we will see later in this book, understanding these fundamental factors is the way toward consciously creating the reality you desire rather than unconsciously attracting that which you do not desire. Quanta never, ever differentiate between what you desire and what you do not desire. They merely obey Universal Laws as perpetuated by thought, in immutable accordance with the Mind Principle.

Everything that can be observed is a result of a mental focus or a decision at some level of Consciousness that it should be in the place it is expected to be. Without that level of focus and expectation, the object simply could not exist. This also applies to things that we have never seen before as for example when going shopping. When we take a trip to the shopping mall, there are thousands of "things" that we have never seen before on display in the shops. They exist as conscious creations of someone else. When we observe that creation and acknowledge its existence, it instantly becomes a part of a greater "consensus creation" that further perpetuates its own existence. Reality can either exist at a personal level or a transpersonal, consensual level. In other words, if enough people believe that something exists, such as a park, and they focus on the belief of that existence, it will continue to exist in accordance with the consensus expectation. If people cease to focus on the object, the Quanta become less concentrated, resulting in decay until eventually the object no longer observably exists. At that point, the Quanta of Energy that originally comprised the object will have dissipated back into the Universe in the form of pure Energy, again though, depending on the number of people focussing on this object, and the amount of focus or "attention" given to it, the object might continue to exist in physical form for a time period, relative to the human concept of "time", for a very short or very long period.

The Astral worlds, often known as "the beyond" or "the afterlife" are also the consensus creation of mankind based upon perceptions learned during physical existence on Earth, and based upon what the inhabitants of the Astral world perceive as "reality". So, the Astral worlds include every possible consensus reality for every culture, race and tradition that exists now, has ever existed and will ever exist relative to the human perception of "time"—all created by the Mind of humans and other Beings existing at that level of vibration, and fashioned upon their corresponding desires, expectations and experiences. The Astral worlds are therefore every bit as much of an illusion created by humans as the physical world of matter. Eventually, as mankind leaves the created illusion of the physical and Astral worlds behind to enter the realms of true reality, beyond all concept of physical form, all manifestations within the physical and Astral worlds, no longer being observed, will once again dissipate back into the Universe of Energy, the illusions no longer being perpetuated.

Each culture, race and society has its own "belief" of what represents "reality", and therefore what things should "look like", so when people pass on from any particular Earth culture, tradition or belief system, including dogmatic religion, they naturally create with the Mind an environment in exact accordance with those expectations. This can be at a group level where entire cities, towns, villages and other environments are created by the consensus group Mind, fashioned after their equivalents on Earth or at an individual level. People with strongly held beliefs, such as religious beliefs, will find themselves, after passing, in a realm of like-minded religious people where the emphasis is on religious activities—again a self-perpetuating illusion. These lower areas of the Astral are known as the "belief system territories", existing "lower", in other words at a lower vibration than the mid-Astral worlds where most people transition upon the transition to the non-physical worlds after the change known as "death".

The Astral worlds exist at a much lower density, much higher vibration than the physical world of matter. As a result, Quanta are influenced much more quickly so that thoughts manifest as their observable equivalent immediately, no matter how large or small. This is instant creation of any desire.

There is only one set of immutable laws, and they apply to all planes of life and reality. The same laws apply in the physical world, but the higher density and lower vibration characteristics of Energy manifesting there require more focused thought over a longer period of time in order to overcome the lower vibration, higher density environment of the physical world, before the Thought Form can manifest as an observable experience in the density of physical reality.

The continued existence of the creation depends on the degree of ongoing focus and observation both on an individual and consensual level. If a house was created, it will continue to exist for as long as the creator or consensus group focus on its perceived existence, thereby providing the Energy for its continued existence. The same applies to the entire physical world, but the process requires concentrated thought over a sustained period. This, of course, is an important reason we are here in the physical world—to learn how to control our thoughts and therefore individual reality. Only when these and other important lessons have been learned, taken to and assimilated by the Higher Self can true Spiritual progression be attained beyond the cycle of reincarnation of the Higher Self.

The entire Universe is Mind Principle, "infinite intelligence" existing in the Mind of The Source, The First Cause, God. Quanta are also intelligent, as they are controlled by the Mind of God. Not only are Quanta capable of making decisions, but they also know what decisions other Quanta are making anywhere in the Universe. This, of course, is due to the inseparable and integrated nature of everything in creation. Everything is connected by this same ultimate, infinite, Divine intelligence, the very same intelligence of which we are all integral aspects and in Whose image we are made.

In quantum terms, Quanta can also be regarded as "packets of probability". Every Quanta of Energy has a "potential" or "quantum potential" to manifest anywhere at any time and can be influenced by thought or other Quanta which in turn are influenced by other thought. For example, if you wish to meet someone for the first time, that person has the potential to exist anywhere in the world. When you make the conscious decision to meet with this person in a particular place, he or she has actually manifested as a physical reality into your life in accordance with the mutual consent of both people. Once your meeting has concluded, the person will leave and become a "potential" person once again.

Quanta are not bound by space or time. Quanta are spaceless, timeless and exist everywhere concurrently. The Source, The First Cause, God is at once omnipotent, omniscient and omnipresent, and Quanta are a fundamental aspect of God in Whom we have our Being. Therefore, as aspects of the Universe, we are also boundless, spaceless and timeless Beings existing concurrently everywhere in the Universe. We have no true form, limits or boundaries, and no specific "point" of existence. Form and "location" are all illusions created by the Ego and perceived by the conscious Mind through the mediation of the five physical senses. Everyone is an integral aspect of the same infinite field of Mind, Energy and vibration, much bigger and more powerful than most people can possibly realize or have the Earthly capacity to comprehend at this stage of their evolution.

We already have everything in the Universe that we could possibly need. Infinite abundance is our heritage. All anyone has to do is bring the object of desire into their local observable reality by focusing on it, thus experiencing it as a localised temporal space-time event. Ask, and it is given—instantly, always, and with no exceptions. There is no poverty in the Universe. Everyone has infinite abundance if they only realized it. There is absolutely nothing that we cannot be, do or have.

The entire Universe is a vast expanse of Energy vibrating at different rates from the lowest vibration of matter to the highest vibration of The Source, The First Cause, God. The illusion of separation is perpetuated due to the way in which Mind perceives and decodes vibrations in the form of sound, light Things" only exist because we observe them, and the Mind decodes the vibrations of the "thing" being observed. So, everything in the Universe is a probability of existence until it is observed, and its Energy is decoded by the Mind, at which point the quantum probability becomes an quantum actuality while it is being observed, after which, when observance ceases it becomes a quantum probability once again with the quantum potential to manifest in another form.

Everything within the Universe manifests in the direction of life, evolution and growth. Nothing ever stands still or fails to evolve. Abundance and growth are Universal principles. In order to perpetuate growth in a Universe where All is intrinsically One, a differentiation is required into the "observer" and that which is being "observed", otherwise there would be no point of reference by which to measure growth.

It has also been demonstrated by quantum physics that there are an infinite number of parallel "worlds" or Universes. Quanta have the potential to manifest in any parallel existence, but once observed in one locality, the same Quanta will not be observable in other localities, so Quanta, although non-local in a native form, can only manifest as a localised event at the point of observation within the space-time continuum where the resultant event can be experienced as a physical event.

At the quantum level, however, everything is "non-local". Beyond space and time, everything can and does exist concurrently as an infinite number of parallel realities. This gives rise to the "holographic" model of the Universe as postulated by David Bohm and other quantum physicists. It is this holographic model of the Universe that explains parallel realities, and how we concurrently exist as integral aspects of all realities as One with The Universe, The Source, God.

As body, Soul and Spirit, our ultimate reality is infinite Energy and intelligence beyond the boundaries of space and time as a true Son or Daughter of God, existing infinitely and concurrently across the entire Universe in all spheres of life and reality. Our localized reality as perceived in our human form is simply our point of focus or point of conscious awareness in accordance with our level of Spiritual evolution, which, for most people, for the time being, is focussed within the physical body, within the physical world. Only when everyone fully understands their own nature as infinite Spiritual Beings of the magnificent multi-dimensional Universe, can the human race turn towards its true purpose—to evolve back to the First Cause, The Light, The Prime Creator, The Source, God in a state and therefore vibration of perfection.

From time immemorial, the greatest teachers who came to Earth made the point that we "came from the Light". The "Light" to which they refer is not some physical light, but rather the eternal, infinite Primordial Light of The Source, The First Cause, of God. In that context, as Energy, Consciousness and integral aspects of The Source, we are, always have been and always will be Beings of The Light, but most still having to realise this glorious truth.

The nearer to The Source we reach through the process of perfection, the more we experience the glories of The Light until ultimately we can reunite with The Light from whence we first came in the beginning, once again with the potential to cease existing as an individuated Being, and to become consciously One with The Source, The First Cause, God. This is the ultimate meaning of life, our ultimate destiny, Our Ultimate Reality.

Chapter 17
The Wisdom of the Ages

As can be clearly witnessed from the collective knowledge and wisdoms of the varied traditions of the World, taken together with conclusions of quantum physics, the basis of all philosophies as to the creation and nature of the Universe, as well as the true purpose and destiny of all mankind, are extremely similar. The age-old cultures teach these same Universal and Spiritual truths through deep philosophies, colourful stories, plays, rituals and practical exercises specific to each culture. All traditions teach the true meaning of life, and how life should be lived for the ultimate good of all humanity, of the planet and of the Universe. Clearly, this is no coincidence.

Although these cultures have acquired true Universal knowledge from quite separate sources dating back many thousands of years, the inner sources of knowledge have always connected with the Beings of the physical world for the ultimate progress of mankind. If mankind is to fulfil its true, ultimate, Divine purpose and destiny, it needs to fully understand the true nature and truth of that Divine purpose and destiny—the truth of its own Spiritual nature as inseparable aspects of God and All that Is. Mankind needs to understand the glories of the Spiritual worlds which will be experienced by each and every person during the onward journey through the inner spheres of life and reality on the return to God.

As a direct result of this current lack of awareness, the world has been heading into darkness, driven by the insidious forces of creed, dogma and materialism, as well as various factions who seek only power and control over others, compounded by the very negative Energy these destructive forces generate.

Since modern quantum physics is a science deriving its information by experimentation, theory and practice, it does not as yet seek to explain the actual meaning of the Universe as a complete picture as it relates to everything and everyone in existence. Rather, it puts forward scientific theories and perspectives as to the structure and characteristics of the Universe in absolute terms. While the scientific approach and phraseology is vastly different from that of the ancient wisdoms of the world and is approached from a completely different direction, the conclusions of quantum physics remain remarkably similar, if not identical, to the ancient knowledge.

Quantum physics has determined that the entire Universe, including the physical Universe, is comprised of Energy vibrating at progressively higher rates and lower density. Quantum physics also acknowledges the fact that the familiar physical world of matter is not true reality at all, but is rather an elaborate "illusion" perpetuated through the mediation of the five physical senses. Quantum physics has also concluded, just as the ancient wisdoms have taught through the ages, that the inner states of Energy and vibration, known as spheres, worlds or planes, are true reality, and that the physical world, and we may also include the Astral worlds, are simply illusion.

After a lifetime of work, David Bohm reached the realization that the entire Universe from the very highest to the very lowest can be likened to a grand holographic projection, the holomovement, originating from the very highest—God, The Source, The First Cause—descending down to the physical world of matter of which everything and everyone in the entire Universe is an integral and inseparable aspect. Further, each and every discreet "unit" of the Universal hologram includes precisely the same detail as the hologram as a whole.

Nothing whatsoever can exist separately from the ultimate whole of the multi-dimensional Universe. Quantum physics is putting forward exactly the same concepts and conclusions as the wisdom of the ages as to both the true nature of the Universe and the relationship of everything and everyone within the Universe—that of a totally integrated multi-dimensional continuum of conscious, vibrating Energy, of which everything and everyone is, always has been, and always will be an inseparable and Divine aspect.

Throughout the ages, theologians have attempted to ascribe human-like qualities to the inner nature of God. These can only be regarded however as feeble attempts by human Minds to grasp the secrets and nature of the infinite. Some religions have even attempted to ascribe typical human characteristics to God, even going as far as to include such extreme, shallow and negative human traits as jealousy, anger, caprice, desire, the need to be worshipped, the desire to receive offerings, the desire to be flattered, "praised", etc. These perceptions simply do not and can never do justice to the true and infinite nature of God, the Supreme Creator and Master of the Universe.

God is immutable and not subject or open to any sort of change. God cannot be divided, added to or subtracted from in any way and can never be increased, decreased, diminished or become lesser or greater than God's Self. God is "Infinite Living Mind", the Universal Mind, the Macrocosm in which everything and everyone has its Being. The human Mind, the Microcosm, is an extension and integral aspect of the infinite Universal Mind, and creator in the Microcosm just as God, the Macrocosm is the First Cause, creator of the entire Universe.

The "Infinite Living Mind" is the living "essence" of that which everything and everyone in the entire Universe in all of its spheres or "dimensions" are a completely integral and inseparable aspect. This living essence has been known from time immemorial as "Spirit". "Infinite Living Mind" also fully explains so-called "supernatural phenomena". When placed in context, these become recognized for what they truly are—completely natural aspects of the Universe of Consciousness and Energy, which should never be a surprise to anyone.

The Universe and everything and everyone contained therein are mental creations of God. Everything and everyone in existence is a Thought Form, an "idea" in the infinite Mind of God—a God who has the unlimited capacity to hold an infinite number of such Thought Forms in the form of unique Energy fields within the infinite Mind of God.

Since something can never be created out of nothing, from what could the Infinite Mind of God have created the Universe? Some might speculate that God created the Universe out of God's Self. This cannot be the solution however, because we already know that God cannot be added to, subtracted from, or otherwise divided in any way. How then could God have created the Universe? The ancient knowledge tells us that the entire Universe is purely a mental creation within the Infinite Living Mind of God, the Macrocosm, in exactly the same way that human Beings, the Microcosm, are made in the true image of "God" and who create mentally within individual Mind. The human Mind is a Microcosmic reflection, image and integral aspect of the Macrocosmic Mind of God, the Supreme Creator.

This view of the Universe is also entirely consistent with the holographic view of quantum physics. A hologram is ultimately a projection where each of the parts is equal to the whole, and the whole is also equal to the sum of all of its parts. As discussed previously, quantum physics has also demonstrated that "Quanta" only come into existence in the presence of an observer. This is equally true of the physical world of matter, which only exists when observed through the mediation of the five physical senses.

Within the true realities of the inner worlds or "planes", everything is instantly created by means of the imagination. Later in this book, we will see exactly how we create and control our own realities both in the physical world and inner worlds, in exactly the same way as the ultimate reality of the entire Universe was created within the Infinite Mind of God.

There is no difference between the act of creation by the human being and that of God. It is merely a matter of scale. At the most fundamental level, the entire Universal Mind and, therefore, "God", is pure Energy. As Spirit, immortal Sons and Daughters of God, we are all manifestations of that very same infinite, Divine, Conscious Energy and we are all, as with all creation, individual, immortal aspects of "God", the very highest manifestation of Energy, vibration. Spiritually, we are all made in the true "image" of God. This can be seen in all of the religions of the world, notwithstanding their doctrines or whether or not they choose to accept this great truth:

Christianity: *"Neither shall they say, lo here! or, lo there! For, behold, the kingdom of Heaven is within you"*. -- Luke 17:21

Islam: *"Those who know themselves know their God"*.

Buddhism: *"Look within, thou art Buddha"*.

Vedanta, part of Hinduism: *"Atman (individual Consciousness) and Brahman (Universal Consciousness) are one"*.

Upanishads, part of Hinduism: *"By understanding the self, all this Universe is known"*.

Yoga, part of Hinduism: *"God dwells within you as you"*.

Confucianism: *"Heaven, Earth and human are of one body"*.

Christianity: *"On that day, you will know that I am in my Father, and you in me, and I in you"*. -- John 14:20

Chapter 18
Wisdom from the Inner Spheres

In addition to the ancient wisdoms of the world and the recent conclusions of modern quantum physics, the same knowledge is constantly confirmed from Beings of the inner spheres in our current century. Thousands of people are now actively pursuing Astral Projection, thereby visiting the Astral worlds, the "afterlife" where most people transition to after the change known as "death", obtaining knowledge first-hand from the people, Beings and vast record resources which exist there in the form of Astral libraries and other resources. Others are able to employ the process of mental projection in order to obtain information from high Spiritual intelligences, whose mission it is to progress the development of mankind.

Many people are now, from altered states of Consciousness and meditation, accessing the vast and infinite source of all Universal knowledge known as the "Akashic Record". Others are receiving information by various inner other means.

It should be readily apparent that it is no longer necessary to rely upon "belief systems", creed, dogma, doctrines or other sources of questionable origin. The truth and the knowledge required for individual evolution, the progression of the human race and future of the planet Earth has always been available and is readily available today for those who seek such knowledge with absolute sincerity and completely open Mind.

Those who seek their own true destiny, which is the same destiny of all mankind, will discover spheres of glory, splendour and bliss far beyond the comprehension of those still living solely in the physical worlds. These people possess abilities that will be used for the ongoing evolution of mankind.

Chapter 19
The Universe of Vibration

Vibration of the Energy of which all things are made is one of the most fundamental characteristics of the entire Universe in all spheres of life and reality. Energy is the very fabric of the great continuum of the Universe, manifesting an infinite number of characteristics in accordance with the influence of Mind Principle and therefore of thought, emotion, imagination and other qualities of Mind. Human Beings consist entirely of pure Energy in a state of vibration inhabiting a physical body through which to experience the physical world at the same level of vibration, which appears "solid" due to the comparatively low rate of vibration relative to the more subtle Energy of the inner nonphysical worlds of life and reality.

As we discussed in the context of quantum physics, what we know as "matter" comprises smaller units known as molecules and still smaller units known as atoms. Smaller still are the subatomic particles made up of still finer particles and so on, until the ultimate constitution of everything is pure Energy vibrating at specific rates according to individual characteristics of the form in which the Energy is manifesting under the influence of Mind Principle. From the highest vibration of The Source to the lowest and densest vibration of the outer Universe of differentiated matter, there are an infinite number of degrees of vibration. As quantum physics has discovered, subatomic particles are not "particles" at all, but are rather more subtle forms consisting of vibration of pure Energy and are, ultimately, units of quantum probability with quantum potential to manifest in an infinite number of ways.

This Energy is also known as "Light". This is not the light commonly known in the physical Universe in the form of photons emanating from The Sun or a lamp for example. It is rather the Primordial Light from Which everything in the Universe was created—the Primordial Light of God. As observed by quantum physicist David Bohm, the physical Universe of matter can be considered to be “frozen Light”.

So, how do we reconcile this with multi-dimensional reality? We first need to look at vibration much more closely in order to understand what multi-dimensional reality really is. Most people know that sound is vibration. For example, a loud noise at a high enough pitch, or vibration, can cause windows and other structures to vibrate very rapidly until, at a high enough amplitude can cause fragile objects to shatter completely.

The frequency range of the human ear, depending on age, is from around twenty vibrations per second up to around twenty thousand vibrations per second, sometimes measured in “cycles” or “hertz”. Moving up the vibrational scale, we reach electricity at around one billion vibrations per second. Moving further up the vibrational scale, we encounter heat at two hundred billion vibrations per second. Further up the scale, the spectrum of visible colours vibrates in a range of around five hundred billion vibrations per second. Higher still is the invisible spectrum of colour including infrared and ultraviolet. We can move further up through the levels of vibration until we reach the higher levels where we encounter x-rays, which vibrate at around two trillion vibrations per second.

Eventually, we reach levels of vibration that do not manifest any characteristics yet known to modern science. Therefore, they are overlooked or very often deemed not to exist at all. In other words, vibration is often deemed by science to be finite, existing only to the degree that it can be measured by scientific instrumentation.

The reality, however, is very different indeed. It is completely erroneous to conclude that progressively higher levels of vibration do not exist simply because they cannot be measured by scientific instruments, when such scientific instrumentation can only hope to measure the very lowest manifestations of vibration, at the very outer extremes of the frequency range of vibration as a whole, a range that represents only a tiny aspect of the entire frequency spectrum of vibration between The Source and the outer shell of the Universe of matter.

Vibrating at speeds completely beyond the comprehension and observation of science are the inner dimensions of the planes of correspondence, The Astral, and inner still the Mental and great Spiritual planes. When something raises its vibration to a high enough level, it has the potential to rejoin The Source, God, The First Cause, and indeed this is the ultimate destiny of every human being, the raising the vibration of the Soul and Spirit through the process of perfection, ultimately realizing the potential to achieve vibrational harmony with God. The raising of the vibration of our Spiritual bodies during the process of perfection, ultimately approaching the vibration of God, The Source, The Prime Creator, is the fundamental and true meaning of life.

In addition, all life manifesting at any specific level of the continuum of the Universe vibrates at exactly the same level as the plane or sub-plane it occupies. Because everything vibrates in harmony, the physical world appears to be solid and real only through the mediation of the five physical senses. Everyone and everything "tunes" into the plane, world, sphere, dimension corresponding to its own unique vibration. This is analogous for example to tuning a television receiver to a specific channel. While although there are thousands of programs broadcasted into the ether concurrently, it is only possible to tune into one program at its own unique frequency at any one time. Likewise, human Beings and indeed all life, although existing at every level of the Universe concurrently, is always tuned into just one very specific frequency, corresponding with one of an infinite number of bodies and level of Consciousness, at any moment. As we perfect ourselves our vibration increases, and we transition to the corresponding vibrational level of Energy within the Universe.

Beyond the confines of the physical world of matter, Energy is the means by which all life manifests and exists within its own unique, individual, corresponding level or plane of reality. This also fully explains why humans, and all forms of life upon passing on to the Astral worlds after the "death" of the physical body find a world which is every bit as "solid" and "real" as the physical world. In fact, the Astral worlds seem, to the residents, to be much more "solid", and much more "real" and vibrant than the physical world, and this becomes progressively more the case as we progress towards the inner spheres of life and reality. The higher the level of Energy, the finer are the corresponding vibrations, and everyone and everything within that level of Energy or vibration will be much more "finely tuned" with it. Physical matter manifests at the very lowest level of vibration and is, therefore, extremely coarse, differentiating into matter or "frozen light".

So, everything in the Universal Mind, The All, God is in a perpetual state of vibration, up to and including The Source Energy, Who exhibits a level of vibration of such an infinitely high degree and intensity that God, The Source, The First Cause can almost be considered to be at rest. Such levels of vibration are far, far beyond any current human comprehension. This can be conceptualized by observing a spoked wheel, for example a wooden cart wheel, from a sideways perspective spinning ever faster. First the wooden spokes appear to fade away and vanish and then the wheel achieves such a high rate of rotation as to appear stationary and not spinning at all, its spokes being invisible to the human eye.

As discussed earlier, science now recognizes the fact that the "phenomena" with which everyone is so familiar, such as heat, light, temperature and magnetism are all differing degrees of vibration, each exhibiting unique characteristics and each of which can be experienced through the mediation of the five physical senses. Modern science is nevertheless still struggling to fully explain such important characteristics as cohesion, molecular attraction and affinity, and the very force which keeps everything rooted firmly on the on Earth ground—gravity.

Vibration plays an extremely important part in our everyday activities. Thoughts, emotions, desires, temperament and any mental state of Mind are all degrees and aspects of Energy manifesting vibration. This is just one reason why thoughts can often unwittingly affect other people through projection and mental induction. These are major factors in so-called "paranormal phenomena", which people recognize as "telepathy" and other forms of Mind power. It is also the reason why a person's mood can affect the moods and temperaments of others, because a mood is simply an energetic state of vibration, which can be transmitted, just as a radio wave can be transmitted and received by a radio receiver which subsequently converts the vibration into sound Energy which can be heard by physical ear. Different life-forms, for example the different varieties of animals including bats, dolphins, and also different varieties of fish and birds as well as other life-forms, all have different thresholds of detecting vibration both in the form of physical sound, and in the form of vibrations of Energy in the form of thought and other projections of the Mind. This is one reason why many groups of life-forms, for example large flocks of birds or shoals of fish, sometimes comprising many thousands or even millions of individuals can appear to behave as one, instantly moving in a different direction as if a single Mind, which indeed they are upon the Mental Plane of the Mind of that particular species.

It is a most important fact that every single thought, every single state of Mind and every single emotion is characterized by its own unique vibration. In the physical world of matter, these vibrations and "Thought Forms" are not readily apparent to the physical senses. However, as we will see later in this book, in the infinitely finer degrees of the Astral worlds and beyond, thoughts and Thought Forms are instantly created and projected, where as a cause, will exert a corresponding effect.

As we will also see later in this book, those understanding these laws of vibration and mentalism can exercise a high degree of control over their own individual thought processes, thus gaining a high level of control over their own states of Mind, moods and emotions. In the same way, a person who is well practiced in these disciplines can affect the Minds of others by applying these same laws. Very often, people do this without even realizing it. On the Mental plane, therefore, people produce thought Energy or vibrations which can affect themselves and the people around them by induction, either unintentionally or at will. It should be pointed out that conscious and effective use of these abilities can usually only be acquired by the means of dedication and practice over some period of time, although there are a few people in existence who can command these powers as a natural ability from birth.

The Principles we have discussed so far will explain many of the so-called "phenomena" that have been demonstrated over the ages by the great masters, adepts, magicians and others, which have often been called "miracles". All these people are doing in fact is to consciously control Universal principles. In the case of physical manifestations, they are controlling the law of vibration in order to alter or transmute one form of Energy into another form of Energy, which then alters the form of physical objects. This would appear miraculous to those who have yet to fully comprehend the law of vibration or other Universal laws, but nevertheless these are abilities that everyone has the potential to realize.

Chapter 20
The Principle of Cause and Effect

The Principle of "Cause and Effect", sometimes referred to as "Causation", is an immutable Universal Principle, encompassing the truth that nothing in the Universe can ever happen by "chance". For everything that happens—for every effect—there is always a corresponding cause preceding it, without exception. The Principle of Cause and Effect is and always has been widely accepted throughout the ages as a most exalted Universal Principle.

To not fully accept the Principles of Causation would be to suggest that everything happening in the Universe is chaotic, random and occurs by pure "chance", "luck" or "fortune"—an unthinkable notion. If this were the case the entire Universe would instantly collapse into a state of utter chaos, and in fact could not exist at all.

The Principle of Cause and Effect has often caused confusion. How can one "thing" be the cause of or the "creator" of a second "thing"? This is however actually an erroneous way of viewing this Principle, because no "thing" actually "creates" any other "thing". Cause and Effect is a whole "chain" or series of unique events, causes, and their corresponding effects, one following the other in immutable succession. In this context, any "event" may be defined as something occurring as a direct result of a preceding event and is part of a flow and succession of such events, all of which are ultimately linked to The Source, The First Cause, God. Therefore, there is always, without exception, a relationship between a specific event and everything preceding it, the corresponding cause, as well as everything that follows. A graphic example of the Principles of Cause and Effect would be to consider your own existence. If a certain male had not met a certain female some hundreds of thousands of years ago, way back in the earliest times of mankind, then you simply would not exist today in human form. The cause in this particular case is the male and female getting together and subsequently reproducing, and you, along with countless millions of other people, are the corresponding effects many millennia later of this one single originating cause. No person or indeed any manifestation of life is therefore merely a product of "chance".

Absolutely every action we take, including every single thought, has its corresponding effect at some level of vibration within the greater Universe. In part, it is due to the lack of understanding of this Principle that most people have no control over their existence on Earth and, accordingly, exhibit very little freedom. People are swept along with events in accordance with the Principles of Cause and Effect, influenced by situations and other people, often in endeavouring to conform to the expectations of family, friends and society generally. People might well protest at this assertion, claiming they are free to "do as they please". Indeed, they are certainly blessed with freewill, but how many people really take advantage of freewill? Yes, they are free to do as they please, but what makes people "want" to do what they "please"? These "wants" and "pleases" are actually all relative. What causes someone to "want" to do a particular thing in preference to another, or "please" to do something else? These "wants" and "pleases" are, therefore, entirely dependent upon each other.

Those who can control their own lives are never carried along on a succession of "wantings" and "pleasings". They rather exert genuine, conscious will and focus in order to proactively determine precisely what they need to accomplish, and set about creating the corresponding causes that will result in the desired effects by use of the powers of the Mind, for example by the Law of Attraction. This then becomes a predetermined act of creation rather than simply a chain of random events.

Most people are carried along in life from the moment they are born, swept through the "game of life" as pawns on a chessboard. People are influenced by and obedient to families and friends, their environment, socio-economic pressures and many other factors depriving them of freewill, often wishing only ever to conform to the expectations of others, without ever exerting any conscious control over their own futures, life and destiny. People often simply do things simply because "it is the way things are done", usually conforming to the expectations and aspirations of family, friends and "society". Cause and Effect is prominent in these situations, each person unwittingly enacting the effect of a preceding cause without ever thinking twice about it.

People remain oblivious to this exalted Principle and the inexorable influence it exerts upon their own lives. We will see later in this book how this Principle can be put to positive effect. Rather than merely being a pawn in the game of life, anyone can become their own king or queen or master-piece with total control over the entire "game". This is not to say that a person with such control is no longer subject to the immutable Principle of Cause and Effect, but such a person is now making conscious and positive use of this Universal Principle to further their own state of health, happiness, abundance, well-being and of course Spiritual evolution.

So, there is no such thing as "chance". The Principle of Causation, "Cause and Effect", is always present and always in operation, both in your life and everyone else's life, effect following cause in perfect immutable sequence. Nothing is "chaotic" or ever happens outside of Universal Principle, and nothing ever acts contrary to Universal Principle. Mankind should never be a pawn in a game of life, but should master and work with these Principles, such is the path to mastery itself as we evolve beyond the kindergarten of the Universe, the physical world, and onwards towards more glorious spheres of life and reality on the path to perfection and God.

Chapter 21
The Universal Elements

We have already discussed how the entire Universe consists of vibration from the very highest vibration of The Source, The First Cause, God, to the very lowest vibrations comprising the physical world of matter. We have also discussed how all vibration is Energy and how vibration can manifest an unlimited number of unique characteristics. Another of the many names for The Source, The First Cause or God is the "Ether". This is not necessarily the "ether" referred to in science, but rather the Universal Ether, also known as "Spirit".

The very beginning of the creation of the Universe within the Mind of The One is symbolically identified with those well-known words "*Let there be Light*", Fiat Lux. At that point, the entire Universe was created as a glorious Though Form within the Infinite Mind of God. God then became The First Cause for the Universe and The Source of All that Is as the entire magnificent Universe in all of its spheres then came into being.

It should also be noted this does not only apply to the physical Universe according to science's own "big bang theory. It applies to all of the Great Planes of life from the very highest vibration of The Source, The First Cause, God, descending all the way out to the physical world of matter.

This process symbolically began with "The Word". As we have said, "The Word" is not the same as a word in physical language. "The Word" is the sending forth from The Logos, of vibrations of Energy within the Mind of God in the form of images, the great Thought Form, giving rise to the constituents of the Ether and, ultimately, the creation of the entire Universe.

The Ether is symbolically comprised of the four Universal "elements" from which everything in existence came into being upon The Word. These are the Universal elements of Fire, Air, Water and Earth, of which the Ether, The Source, God is the very finest—the Quintessence of the others, the primordial Light. It should be made clear from the outset that the elements are not in any way separate from Energy or vibration, but are rather configurations of Energy and vibration constituted in a specific way. Each element has its own unique characteristics in accordance with its Energy configuration.

Each element, as a configuration of Energy, influences corresponding Energy just as all Energy has the capability to influence any other Energy. In this way, the elements, under the influence of the Infinite Universal Mind of God, are Energy "building blocks" configured during the initial act of creation.

It must be stressed once again that these are not the commonly recognized fire, air, water and earth of the material world. These elements are rather the Universal attributes of configurations of Energy that are analogous to the physical elements, having similar but non-physical characteristics.

Everything that has ever been and ever will be created was as a direct result of the interaction between the Energy configurations or vibrations of these four Universal elements. The characteristics of each the four Universal Energy elements are as follows:

The Element of Fire:

This was the first element to descend from The First Cause, the fundamental attributes of which are light, heat and expansion. All of creation began with these Universal attributes radiating and expanding outwards from The Source until finally reaching the very outermost levels of vibration, at which point the physical Universe of matter was formed. The Emerald Tablet of Hermes is an ancient account of this event.

It follows, therefore, that everything without exception in the entire Universe in all planes of life contains the Universal element of Fire. In accordance with the Universal Principle of polarity, the Fire element, as with all of the elements, is bipolar. In other words, it has two poles that are respectively active and passive in nature. The active or positive pole is creative, and the passive or negative pole is destructive.

The Universal attributes of the Fire element as relates to the Macrocosm have a profound influence over human Beings, the Microcosm. As already mentioned, everything in the Universe contains all four elements, and human Beings are no exception.

The action and balance of the elements in the subtle bodies, and most notably the Astral body, the Soul, has a very considerable influence over the emotions, temperament and all other mental attributes of human Beings. In addition, imbalances in the elements will often result in a physically manifested illness, usually diagnosed by doctors as originating from a physical medical origin. Of course, it is not possible to fully heal such ailments by physical, somatic means but only to mask the manifesting symptoms. In accordance with Universal laws, and in particular the law of Correspondence, all diseases first originate within before manifesting in the physical body as a physically observable disease.

The elements also correspond to the five physical senses through which the physical body experiences the physical world. The Astral body, or Soul, experiences the physical world through the mediation of the five physical senses and is a primary reason why the Astral body is so fundamental to the balance and well-being of the physical body. The Energy body is the Energy interface between the physical body and the Astral body.

In the Mental Body, the Fire element gives rise to the emotional attributes of Energy, might and passion. It is ultimately the Mental Body or the Immortal Spirit that actuates the five physical senses through the mediation of the inner senses of both the outer Astral and physical bodies.

The Fire element, in recognition of its fundamental property of expansion, is also known as the “electric fluid”.

The Element of Air:

The next element to descend from The First Cause was the element of Air. Air is not a true element in the same way as Fire and Water, but it is still fundamentally important to the balance of the Universe.

The function of the Air element is to act as a Universal Energy mediator between the Fire and Water elements. In the course of this mediation, the Air element acquires the attributes of warmth from Fire and moisture from Water. These are Universal Energy attributes—configurations of Energy present in all planes of life.

The Element of Water:

Water was the third Element to descend from The First Cause. The element of Water has exactly the opposite properties to those of Fire, its Universal Energy characteristics being principally those of contraction and coldness.

As with all of the elements, Water also has its two polar opposites, the actions of which are vital to the great Universal scheme of things. The active or positive pole of the Water Element is nourishing, preserving, and life-giving, while the negative pole is decomposing, fermenting and dispersing. The Fire and Water elements are interdependent upon each other, being both equals and opposites from a Universal polar perspective.

The Water element represents the Astral body, just as the Fire element is also analogous to the immortal Spirit. The Electric fluid, the element of Water is also analogous to the "Magnetic fluid" in recognition of its fundamental property of contraction.

The Element of Earth:

The fourth element to descend from The First Cause, like Air, Earth is not a true element but is the result of the interaction of the other three elements—Fire, Air and Water. The main characteristic of Earth is the property of solidification. As this occurs, the Earth element assimilates the other three elements from which it is constituted, thus providing them with a solid form. It is due to the activities of the elements during this process that the material Universe of physical matter came into being during the great act of creation, along with the physical world attributes of measure, space, weight and time as they are known to us.

All life came into being as a direct result of the interaction of Energy analogous to the properties of Fire, Water and Air expanding from The Source, The First Cause, God, eventually resulting in the physical, solid Universe analogous to the element of Earth.

Again, the Earth element has, like the other elements, unique characteristics of vibration or Energy and is not, therefore, merely the physical Earth of solid matter as constituted by the elements at the lowest level of Energy vibration and highest density. It is also important to note that we are not merely referring to the planet "Earth", but rather to the entire physical Universe as known to science, the creation of which is analogous to the "big bang" theory of the astrophysicists.

Science is constantly seeking the origin of the "big bang" in the physical Universe. However, as we will discuss later in this book, science will never find such a single origin within the physical Universe for the "big bang" or the start of creation, because in the beginning, the Universe was created out of and by The Source, The First Cause, God beyond the confines of space and time—a place where all exists in the Eternal Now.

The descent of the elements commenced beyond space and time, expanding outwards through the Ether with progressively lower vibration and increasing density, until finally resulting in solidification by way of differentiation into matter in the form of the physical Universe, the existence of which science attributes to the event know as the "big bang".

The solidification process analogous to the Earth element is still subject to the laws of vibration, which is why all matter is ultimately constituted of subatomic particles, atoms and molecules of unique properties, together giving rise to the chemical elements and compounds as recognized by science.

Again, however, chemical elements should not be confused with the Universal Elements of Fire, Air, Water and Earth, and neither should they be confused with the physical fire, air, water and Earth of the same name. The Universal elements, like the entire Universe in all spheres of life and reality are pure Energy with unique characteristics ultimately under the influence of the power of Mind Principle, either the Infinite Mind of God or of human and other Beings.

The "big bang" theory is to scientists as Genesis I is to the biblical scriptures. The story of Genesis, like almost all of the biblical accounts, is very deeply symbolic, intended for those who would understand its true meaning. Over the millennia, these accounts have all been interpreted and translated in material terms, and the true meaning has long been lost to most. Genesis is in fact an account of the greater act of creation in all planes of life and not merely of the physical planet Earth as is generally supposed by religions.

One of the key Principles in the health and well-being of all tetrapolar life (life which is constituted from all four of the elements of Fire, Air, Water and Earth) is in maintaining a fine balance of the Energy and vibration of the elements.

Within the Astral worlds, there are various degrees of Beings existing as configurations of Energy comprising a single element. Some of these Beings are fairly advanced in nature, including such creatures as are more commonly associated with "fairytales", and some of which are much more basic in nature. The more basic Beings of the single elements are known as "elementaries" when they exist in the Astral planes and "elementals" when their principle habitat is within the Mental planes. Despite their comparative simplicity, these Beings are nevertheless very important in the grand Universal scheme of things. We will discuss these and the more advanced Beings of the single elements later in this book.

The Universal elements of Fire, Air, Water and Earth are configurations of Energy that are analogous to their Earthly recognized counterparts, each of which exhibit unique characteristics, forming Energy building blocks within the Universe. These elements not only exert a profound effect over human Beings at all levels, but also within the Universe as a whole.

As previously mentioned, many human diseases are a direct result of an imbalance of the Energy of the elements within the inner Energy, Astral or Mental bodies, which, in turn, manifest in accordance with the Principle of Correspondence as a physically observable ailment. The elements also have a profound effect on human emotions and mental states, giving rise to psychological imbalances and observable mental illnesses. Equilibrium of the elements within the human body is a fundamental aspect of the ongoing process of evolution and perfection that is the destiny of every single human being without exception. It should be noted however that all such imbalances, however they manifest ultimately originate from one source—Mind. In the case of diseases therefore these imbalances have been caused by the thought processes of the person experiencing them.

Full elemental equilibrium and harmony of the elements at all levels can be controlled and maintained by the Mind. Balancing of the elements comprising the human being at all levels is an important aspect of progression, and one which we will accordingly discuss in detail later in this book.

Chapter 22
Vital Energy

All life is sustained by means of conscious, intelligent, vibrating Energy, the "Life Force" that pervades and sustains the entire Universe in all spheres, dimensions or planes of life and reality. This unseen Energy has many names according to the various cultures, traditions, practitioners, healers and sciences including, "Prana", "Chi", "Ki", "Psi", "Ruah", "Breath of Life", "Bioplasma", "Manna", "Life Force", "Orgone", "Odic Force", "The Force", and "Quanta". Ultimately however, everything in the Universe, without exception, is a manifestation of the very same Source Energy, often known as "Spirit", but known by most simply as "God".

Energy can manifest an infinite number of characteristics under the influence of Mind, the collective thought projections of which creates and in turn determines the unique characteristics of an "Energy Form", or "Thought Form" including its vibration. Throughout the course of this book we will discuss Energy in the proper context of the subject of each chapter.

Energy is also known as "Vital Energy" in recognition of its status as the force that sustains all life in the Universe, and the force approached by healing, esoteric and occult practitioners of all kinds in pursuit of their traditions, practices and abilities.

Vital Energy has powerful characteristics when utilized in the context of "alternative healing", for example "Pranic Healing", which is well-known in eastern countries and now increasingly practiced around the world.

When a person becomes ill, the origin of the disease is never within the physical body itself but rather originates within, under the control and influence of the Subconscious Mind, always in turn under the control of the conscious Mind, the thought processes of which originate the disease at some level.

The process of Pranic Healing in all of its variations involves the accumulation of "Vital Energy" by a Pranic Healing practitioner, who then directs that accumulated Energy towards the location of the disease within the Energy body, at the same time using the power of the Mind to imagine the perfect health of the person being healed, particularly at the site where the ailment exists. The Energy body has several main "centres" known as "chakras" in eastern terminology.

There are seven main chakras, each of which has a very specific purpose, and all of which are connected to the vastly complex energetic system of the subtle Energy body. Bioplasmic disturbances in any part of the Energy body, as a result of the thought processed of the person afflicted, will usually manifest as a physically observable illness. Of course, doctors will attempt to "cure" these illnesses by the use of medicines, surgery, therapy and so on, but the only real and enduring cure is entirely non-physical and firmly rooted in the inner bodies of the patient. In these cases, no amount of medicines or surgery will bring about a cure. We will discuss Pranic Healing in more detail later in this book.

Another "alternative" and often highly effective form of treatment is Acupuncture. This is an ancient but increasingly popular Chinese procedure whereby sharp, very fine needles are inserted at critical points of the physical body. These points correspond to important paths of Energy within the Energy body. The needles are not, therefore, affecting physical nerves as some doctors might suppose, but are acting upon the balance and flow of Vital Energy within the Energy body. In this way, Acupuncture can bring relief and often a complete healing.

Acupuncture is a highly skilled profession requiring a detailed knowledge of the Energy body, its balancing points or "meridians", and of the control of Vital Energy itself, known as

"Chi" in China. Acupuncture also makes use of the Principle of polarity, where Energy points can be subject to opposite poles of balance known in Taoist terms as "Yin" (the negative polarity) and "Yang" (the positive polarity).

"Tai Chi" is another well-known and extremely popular exercise in Chinese cultures involving Chi (pronounced "chee"). Tai Chi exercises balance the flow of Vital Energy in the body, facilitating a better state of health and well-being.

Yet another form of healing which makes use of Vital Energy is known as "Reiki", a Japanese word meaning "Universal life-force". "Rei" means "Universal" and "Ki" means "life force". Like most other forms of healing practice, Reiki can take place with the patient in the same room as the practitioner or at any distance, time and space not presenting any sort of barriers.

It should be pointed out that ultimately the Source of all healing is the Subconscious Mind, either at an individual level in the case of a personal healing, or a collective level in the case of remote healing. The fundamental source of all healing power is therefore the Subconscious Mind of the healer, who is able to succeed in healing due ultimately to their own faith in the power of their chosen healing process. The action of the projection of Energy provides a channel to which to which the faith is Energised, in exactly the same way as all faith healing.

This of course is to take nothing at all away from healers and healing professions of all types, all of which provide an exceptional and most valuable, often unselfish service to humanity. It matters not what modes of the powers of the Mind are behind the process, only but that it is possible at all.

Chapter 23
Psychic "Phenomena"

In recent years, so-called "psychic phenomena" have become increasingly high profile, due in part to the popularity of "psychics" and "mentalists" on television. The recent revelations of the use of "Remote Viewing" by the secret services of various governments has also brought psychic potential very much to the attention of the world.

The most notable remote viewing situation was a program instigated by the United States government known as "Stargate". This was a covert "information-gathering" operation in which highly trained "remote viewers" were able to obtain often very accurate information about anything or anyone, including government and military activities, regardless of the physical distance or even time involved.

In addition to remote viewing, most people have heard of abilities such as telepathy, Telekinesis and divination by means of tarot cards, runes and many other instruments. Most people will also be aware of the multitude of personal "psychic services" on offer today, especially on the Internet. Although psychic abilities are not strictly necessary during the course of everyday life, such abilities can and often do arise spontaneously with Spiritual growth. This certainly does not imply that those people who already have psychic abilities are Spiritually more advanced than anyone else, often the contrary is true, but rather that some people are born with such abilities, sometimes due to physical irregularities or differences within the physical brain. The following chapters are a summary of a few of the better known psychic abilities.

Chapter 24
Remote Viewing

There are many different methods of remote viewing, including Ganzfeld, Outbounder or Beacon, Associative, Coordinate, Controlled or CRV, Extended or ERV, and Scientific or SRV. Although all of these methods vary to some degree, remote viewing can be defined as the ability to obtain information on an object or "target" in a remote location across both space and time as it relates to the physical world. Distance and time are no barriers to remote viewing, and the object or event can be anytime in the past, present or future relative to physical time. It should be mentioned from the outset however that the "future", as relates to the Earth concept of "time", only exists as quantum potential, or probabilities, and not as fact.

Unlike some psychic abilities which require entering into a trance state, remote viewing is a controlled shifting of awareness performed from the normal waking state of Consciousness to achieve a slowing down of the brainwaves to what is known as the "alpha" frequency state. As we will discuss later, we are all aspects of the same Universal Mind existing beyond the limitations of physical space and time. Anyone who is focused in this physical "dimension", which is a level of Energy or vibration, can potentially project their Consciousness anywhere in the world or even the physical Universe in an instant. Remote viewing works by means of the "remote viewer" projecting or tuning his or her Consciousness into this spaceless and timeless aspect of the Universe, enabling the remote viewer to obtain information in accordance with "coordinates" they have been given by their "tasker".

These "coordinates" are not the same as those on the grid reference of a map, but are a group of random numbers created by the "tasker" and assigned to the "target". The remote viewer has no prior knowledge whatsoever of the target, thus preventing the remote viewer's Subconscious interpretation or bias relative to the "target" assigned by the "tasker".

In this spaceless, timeless environment, the remote viewing coordinates are associated with the target by the tasker, and these coordinates are all the remote viewer requires in order to obtain the information they have been assigned to "view". It should be pointed out, however, that the term "remote viewing" is somewhat misleading in that there is usually no "visual" aspect at all. The remote "viewer" receives "impressions" from the target through a sort of intuition and very quickly writes these impressions down in a type of symbolic shorthand, thus building up a complete picture.

Very often teams of professional remote viewers work together towards a common objective. In these cases by comparing the notes of several viewers, a more accurate picture emerges, and any individual bias of the conscious Mind can be filtered out, thereby only focussing on the factors common to the information received by all the remote viewers in the team.

Remote viewing can without doubt very accurate indeed, and one of the most accurate of the "psychic" abilities, but nevertheless still relies heavily on the ability, commitment and focus of the remote viewer. Nevertheless, of all of the abilities that comprise the general group known as "psychic abilities", remote viewing is the one that is probably the easiest to learn for most people, and the one likely to be of most benefit.

Chapter 25
Telepathy

Telepathy may be defined as the transference of thoughts from the Subconscious Mind of one person to the Subconscious Mind of another person or several other people or even to a large crowd of people, where the thoughts surface within the conscious Minds of the participants and subsequently received as discernable messages in forms including voices, imagery or feelings. Although this process is usually a Subconscious process, in those with higher than normal telepathic abilities thought transfer can be continued consciously as a form of communication. Telepathy often occurs and is experienced spontaneously when, for example, a person suddenly receives a "thought flash" from another person standing nearby, who might in turn even respond to that thought verbally believing it to have been a spoken communication—much to the surprise of the originator of the thought. This happens much more often than most people realize, but such received thoughts are usually simply dismissed as a "figment of the imagination".

There are people, however, who can consciously communicate telepathically over great distances and with complete accuracy. As with remote viewing, space and time are no barriers to telepathy as the communication process is taking place beyond the temporal confines of the physical world of time and space.

Although telepathy is an ability that can be learned, there are people who inherently exhibit a natural ability to consciously communicate in this way, as sometimes happens in the case for example of identical twins.

Within the Astral planes and beyond, where most people arrive after physical "death", communication is almost the same as telepathic communication would be on the physical plane, in the form of a stream of thoughts, but as a person progresses, telepathic communication becomes much more sophisticated and “compressed” so that vast “packets” of information can be transferred between two or more people, or indeed any Beings almost instantly. This is a subject for discussion later in this book, but such communication in the inner planes is almost entirely symbolic—a sort of “picture language”, where words as known in the physical world do not apply. Likewise, languages spoken in the physical world are not relevant within the inner planes, and are no barrier to communications in the inner spheres of life.

Everyone in the Astral and inner worlds can, therefore, communicate regardless of the country or even planet from which they originated before their transition to the non-physical worlds. Indeed, among humans still living on Earth, telepathy can be much more subtle than the transfer of words or sentences. People frequently influence each other at a much more Subconscious level. For example, when a person is in a good mood, that mood can be transferred by mental induction to people around him or her or even at a great distance. Whole crowds of people can influence each other in this way, and it can often be noted that whole families or groups of office workers might be feeling happy or depressed at exactly the same time. This is a more subtle aspect of telepathy, where emotions are being transmitted in the form of vibration.

So, how exactly does telepathy work? There are several principles in operation during the telepathic process, in particular the great Universal principles of Mentalism and Correspondence. We already know from the Principle of Mentalism that the entire Universe is mental in nature with everyone being a seamless part of the whole, with the Subconscious Mind being that aspect of our Being that sends, originates and processes telepathic communications. Therefore, an infinite possible number of direct lines of communication are possible. Since thought transference is a mental process, it takes place between the Subconscious Minds of two or more people upon the level of the Mental plane, at the level of the group Mind of the communicators. Ultimately telepathy takes place through vibrations originated by thought with Energy as the Universal medium of propagation.

It is quite likely that as the human race evolves, telepathy will become increasingly commonplace as a means of communication on the physical plane, and ultimately the de-facto way of communication, as humans finally realise their own true nature as Beings of the Mind, not the physical Body.

Chapter 26
Karma

We have already discussed the Universal Principle of Causation—Cause and Effect. Later, we will discuss reincarnation and its significance to all human Beings. Karma operates within the laws of Cause and Effect. For every "bad" or negative action, a "bad" or negative result will occur, and for every "good" or positive action, "good" or positive result will occur. Of course, in accordance with the Principle of polarity, there is no such state as "absolute bad" or "absolute good"; there are only degrees of "badness" and "goodness". Every deed or "cause" will bring about its corresponding "effect". It should also be noted that Cause and Effect and, therefore, karma are still functions of Universal Energy and therefore of vibration. Everything in the Universe is subject to the law of Cause and Effect—every person, animal, fish, insect, plant, mineral, etc. There are no exceptions to this Principle.

Karma literally means "action", but an action need not only be physical. It can be a thought. A "bad" thought will cause a corresponding "bad" effect at the Mental level, and a "good" thought will cause a corresponding "good" thought at the Mental level. This is also in accordance with the laws of Vibration and Mentalism, whereby a thought is a cause in the form of vibration.

Although the entire Universe is subject to the immutable laws of Cause and Effect, the aspect of Causation known as karma is of fundamental importance. In order to progress along the path of perfection through the Astral and great Spiritual planes on the journey back to our Creator, it is vital that all bad attributes and deeds are balanced, transmuted and completely cancelled. Due to a general lack of the understanding of the Principle of karma, most people continue through life causing "bad" effects or “bad karma” without ever realizing it, often ascribing their experiences to such things as “luck”, “fortune” or “chance”.

There is simply no escape from karma. Sooner or later, karma has to be balanced within each and every person. Fully understanding the laws of karma will not only assist you on your path, but it might save you considerable pain, suffering and discomfort in this life, as well as past and future lives.

Within the multi-dimensional reality of the inner spheres, all lives are non-sequential. They are rather “simultaneous” or “concurrent”. So, there are no such things as a “previous life”, “this life”, “the next life, “the life to come” or “the life after that”. All lifetimes are experienced concurrently as a fully integral aspect of the Universal continuum beyond the space-time level of reality, and where the individual Spirit is immortal. Each “life” is, in reality, a temporal, physical manifestation of the Higher Self, each of which gains unique experience to contribute to the Higher self in the process of attaining such a state of perfection as to transition above the cycle of reincarnation, whereby some “time” as measured in physical terms is spent in the physical world living within a physical body. Such “time” has no meaning, however, in the context of the Higher Self, or of Universe and all eternity.

Karma also conforms to no time limits. Sowing a “seed” of karma creates a certainty that at some point in the future as measured by physical time, the seed will sprout, grow and bear fruit as a corresponding effect. This point in the future might be the current physical life, the next physical life or any future physical life. It is even possible that the “effect” might manifest between physical lives while living in the Astral world if the cause can be balanced within the Astral planes.

Even our personal thoughts are subject to karma. So, for example, if a person thinks “badly” of someone else, sending out aggressive or vindictive vibrations, those same vibrations will eventually return to the originator. There is a saying highly appropriate to karma—that people can be their own worst enemies.

Individual karma can be accumulated over many lifetimes, so when a "bad" thing happens, it will not be by mere "chance" or due to "bad luck" (notions which are impossible in accordance with the law of Cause and Effect). The cause of the bad effect may even have originated many lifetimes ago.

According to Hindu philosophy, there are three manifestations of karma. The first is called "Sanchita karma", which is caused by a past situation still awaiting its corresponding effect or reaction. This is in effect "latent" karma.

The next consists of "past causes", including those from "past lives" relative to the Earth concept of "time", the effects of which are still manifesting in the current, temporal lifetime. This type of karma, called "Prarabdha Karma", is a manifestation of karma that shapes our current experience.

The third level of karma is known as "Future karma". This is where the causes are created in the current temporal lifetime but will manifest in the "future", either later in the current lifetime or in a future lifetime.

Again it must be noted that in reality all karma is caused and reconciled in the same eternal moment of Now—it is only experienced as "past", "present" and "future" in the context of the Earth concepts of "time" and "space".

It is also important to note that a sequence of causes do not necessarily give rise to "effects" in the same order. This is largely due to the differences in the magnitude of each original cause and the fact that it is not subject to the confines of physical space and time. A large karmic event might not be able to balance itself as a corresponding effect until much later in a lifetime or perhaps not until a "future" lifetime or even in a "past" lifetime, again due to the fact that "space" and "time" are not really factors in this process, and life itself is a continuum. On the other hand, a small karmic event—a thought, for example—might well yield a corresponding effect within seconds, minutes or hours of the original cause. There are no hard and fast rules with regard to this, the only certainty being that the law of karma will inexorably exert itself throughout and beyond space and time. Everyone should always be consciously aware of karma and live accordingly, ensuring that no bad actions or thoughts are allowed to occur.

It should be stressed at this point that karma is not a "punishment" and "reward" system. Everyone is provided with the freewill to do as they please, and everyone is responsible for their own actions by virtue of the freewill provided by our Creator. Karma is not therefore a court of justice type scenario— there are no judges or juries, only Energy, vibration and the immutable Principle of Cause and Effect unfolding perfectly throughout space and time as experienced on Earth, and throughout all spheres of life in the Eternal Now.

As the well-known and highly appropriate saying goes - "as you sow, so shall you reap". Problems arise when people do not understand or choose to ignore this immutable and exalted Principle. Ignorant of the laws of Cause and Effect and of karma, people continue to sow negative seeds throughout their lives, remaining completely oblivious to the fact that sooner or later, the price will have to be paid when these karmic seeds sprout, grown and always finally come to fruition. On the other hand, those who fully understand these great and immutable Universal laws will always be most careful and diligent about what they think, say and do in order to ensure no seeds of negative karma are sown. They will strive to sow only the seeds of positive karma that will be of equally positive benefit in the future. The importance of conscious living is discussed more fully in the final section of this book.

People who create negative karma over many physical lifetimes often wonder why negative things happen to them in their current lifetime. They will typically say things like "what have I done to deserve this?" or "why do I always have bad luck?" Until they come to fully understand these great Universal laws, they will continue to create negative karmic causes which will create corresponding negative karmic effects over many lifetimes, until all karma has eventually been fully balanced. Karma is a very important aspect of individual evolution and progression back to The Source, The First Cause, God, Who is absolute perfection, and Who must therefore be approached in a state of absolute perfection as characterized by the Energy vibration of the Spirit of each individual person.

Although an aspect of the great Universal law of Cause and Effect, karma is also a "tool" for learning. We incarnate into the physical world to learn, evolve and balance karma. As we will discuss in the next section, this planet Earth is not our true home. It is not reality. The entire physical Universe of matter is not reality but rather an illusion experienced and perpetuated by the five physical senses. Our true home as immortal Spiritual Beings is within the great Spiritual worlds, including the great Celestial and Cosmic planes of life beyond the illusion of the Astral worlds. Life in the physical world is, therefore, intended to be as a schoolroom in which we learn the lessons required to progress to our true home—the glories, splendours, peace, harmony and Light of the Spiritual worlds. Therefore, karma is one of our greatest teachers. Like all teachers, karma should be afforded the greatest of respect. Those who do not learn these lessons will continue to suffer at the hands of karma year after year, lifetime after lifetime, past, present and future, all still relative of course to the physical Universe space-time continuum, until the lessons are finally learned, and the Higher Self can move on to greater and more magnificent adventures of evolution within the inner spheres, of life and reality in the great process of ultimate perfection.

Chapter 27
The True Nature of God

Many of the belief systems of the western world are based upon Christianity and Judaism, with Islam being prevalent in the Middle East, and Hinduism and Buddhism prevailing in the Far East. Islam and Christianity in all of their forms rely heavily on the words of their respective "holy books" or texts.

A major issue today, however, is that many people still live their lives by the literal word of these ancient books, many of which have often been misinterpreted, misunderstood and often mistranslated, and by the word of the churches and their representatives, without ever thinking to question it. Often, of course this is due to strong, historical family beliefs and traditions, handed down through generations, which people accept and follow out of trust and respect, without questioning whether these doctrines are true, simply being accepted as such without question. In other cases, the very high profile and often psychological power and control over people through the invocation of fear and guilt, the orthodox churches have led people to believe that these churches must represent reality.

Orthodox religions package a belief system, offering people the comfort and convenience of not having to think for themselves, often suggesting that anyone adhering to this system will be assured of a ticket to "Heaven" providing only that they follow the creeds, dogmas and doctrines of that religion. While we must all maintain absolute respect for the beliefs of others and their absolute freewill to subscribe to these beliefs and doctrines, they will soon discover that everyone, without exception, are subject to the immutable the Universal Principles of Spiritual evolution, not subject to any form of creed, dogma or indoctrination, being dependant entirely upon the efforts of each individual. These are the only principles governing progression to levels and states of existence which truly are the "Heaven worlds", the glories and splendours of which transcend all religion, dogma or any belief system.

We are all integral aspects of the same God, The Source, our Prime Creator from whence we came in the beginning, and it is the true destiny of every single human being without exception to truly become a "God man" or "God woman", with powers far beyond the comprehension of Earthly man at this stage of his or her development. This destiny can only be fulfilled however with ongoing true, sincere, individual progression and evolution based only upon true Universal knowledge and absolute Spiritual Principles and truths as the basis. These can never be fulfilled by accepting mere creed, dogma and indoctrination demanding conformance through fear, guilt and oppression as the basis for true, happy and abundant living.

Our true God does not in any way conform to the popular religiously motivated vision of an elderly, stately looking gentleman with a white beard, adorned in long flowing white robes, sitting on a golden throne flanked by choirs of Angels, while directing and judging the affairs of Earth and mankind. The One true God is not a judgemental, tyrannical, vengeful, jealous, or angry deity. The true God has no need or desire to be "worshipped" or to receive offerings of any sort, and is most certainly not influenced in any way by flattery or "praise".

The true God does not punish people for failing to believe in Him/her, for failing to attend a church, or for failing to accept a historical person as their "saviour". This same true God does not in any way require intermediaries or "go-betweens" to interpret, represent and convey the "will" of God. No such intermediary has ever had the ear or authority of God or has ever possessed any sort of special connection with God. No such self-appointed representative of God can possibly know "God's will" or convey the wishes of the people back to God. All of these are human concepts based only upon human attributes and the inability to comprehend anything greater, leading people to view and judge God as existing by Earthly human characteristics, attitudes and values.

Above all, God is neither separate from the Universe or from anyone or anything within the Universe. God is at once Omnipotent, Omniscient and Omnipresent. Every human being, all life and everything within the entire Universe, has its Being within the infinite Mind of God. God is within, through, and encompasses every human being, all life and everything in the entire Universe without exception. We are God.

Everyone is a totally equal and integral aspect of God, the Supreme Universal Consciousness, The Source, The Prime Creator, The First Cause, The One Universal Mind, Who in turn is the same absolute, total and complete perfection that every human being, and all life is striving to achieve during the journey of evolution and ultimate perfection back to God.

Everyone is the master of their own destiny by virtue of the Divine freewill conferred upon each and every individual by our Creator. We all, without exception, create our own reality. The One True God, The First Cause, The Source of All that Is ultimately sustains everything in creation with the most powerful force, vibration and Energy within the Universe, in all spheres of life and reality—Pure Unconditional Love.

Part 2

The Inner Realities

Chapter 28
Truth About the Change Known as "Death"

I wish to emphatically commence this chapter with what might, for many people, seem to be a surprising or even shocking statement—**there is, in reality, no such condition as "death".**

What many people believe to be the finality of "death" is in reality no more or less than a transition, or change, from one state of life, a physical state of life characterised by the physical body, to a nonphysical state of life within a much finer, more subtle, non-physical body, existing at a much higher vibration and lower density sphere of the Universe known by many names, but often known as "the afterlife", "Astral planes" or "the beyond". The name is of no consequence however. The fact is, this phase of life really does exist and becomes the new home for most people after departing the physical phase of life of that Higher Self incarnation. Some people, will, their Higher Self having completed the cycle of physical incarnation, or who came to Earth on Earth on a special mission from the inner spheres of life and reality, the true realms of Spirit, will transition beyond the Astral planes, inwards to their rightful place of residence in accordance with their current state of Spiritual evolution.

We will discuss the nature of the Astral planes and the Spirit worlds later in this book, but first, we must take a closer look at the change erroneously known as "death". We are all multi-dimensional Beings, each of us having infinite "bodies" corresponding to our many states of "Being" within the multi-dimensional Universe. Although we have an infinite number of "bodies", we are only "focussed" in one body at a time in accordance with our state of evolution, and therefore vibration. These bodies very broadly consist of the physical body, the Etheric or Energy body, the Astral body and the Mental bodies. We have an infinite number of Mental or Spiritual bodies, all relating to the infinite degrees and states of vibration, density and Being, ranging from the very lowest to the very highest approaching the highest vibration of The Source. The Astral body is often referred to as the "Soul", and the Mental Body is often referred to as the "Immortal Spirit". It is the Immortal Spirit that is "made in the image of God", not the physical body is commonly supposed.

God is pure Spirit, and ultimately every single person exists as pure Spirit beyond all concept of form—an illusion of the physical and Astral worlds. The seat of our very "Being" or Consciousness is the Immortal Spirit. The Astral body or Soul actually consists of both the conjoined Astral and Mental bodies and can, therefore, be more accurately referred to as the Astra-Mental Body. These subtle bodies are composed of Energy vibrations which are completely unique for everyone, each individual possessing a particular Energy signature. Within the inner spheres of reality or the Astral and Mental planes, people exist at the level of vibration of the Universe corresponding precisely to the level of vibration of their Astral and Mental bodies, respectively. The level of vibration of the Astral and Mental bodies depends in turn upon many factors, including the individual degree of ennoblement or perfection, the degree to which the Ego has been subjugated, the realization of Spirit or "God" within and of the oneness of All, unresolved karma, and the realization of the most powerful force in the Universe—Unconditional Love.

It should be briefly discussed at this stage where the Higher Self fits into this picture. Our Higher Self is the "base" of all physical incarnations on Earth. Because most people cannot gain sufficient perfection in one single incarnation, the Higher Self, our "Complete Self" in the world of Spirit, representing the totality of all incarnations, sends numerous aspects of Him-Her Self to Earth until sufficient experience, perfection and wisdom is attained, at which point the Higher Self assumes the identity of the final incarnation, and moves on to greater things. The Higher Self is therefore also made in the Spiritual image of

God, in that God is also experiencing by means of the same process, but as the ultimate Creator as we will be discussing during the course of this book.

So, what actually happens when people experience the change known as "death"? Regardless of the precise circumstances at the end of physical life, what follows is substantially the same in all cases. At the instant when the physical body ceases to function, a large amount of Energy is transferred to the Etheric body, also known as the Energy body also including the Astral and Mental bodies. The Etheric body will usually then become the new "temporary" body of the recently "deceased" person. Sometimes, however, the recently deceased person will transition directly to the Astral worlds. It is the Etheric body that some people, in particular those with psychic or clairvoyant abilities, can "see", and is the basis for the "paranormal" phenomena known as a "ghost".

What happens next varies from person to person. Those who do not transition directly to the Astral worlds will, immediately after physical death, find themselves very much "alive" in their Etheric body, feeling more "alive" than they ever did in their physical shell. A person after "death" will often fully observe everything happening around them, including all people present. What the person is actually "seeing" is not their physical surroundings as such, as they no longer have any physical senses. What they "see", now through the mediation of the Astral senses is a very close Etheric "reflection" of those surroundings which, for all intents and purposes, are identical.

If other people such as doctors are present, the person might well see and hear himself or herself being pronounced "dead". The "deceased" person can then, if desired, stay and watch what happens to their "old body", observe the actions of the people present or immediately go elsewhere. In this much finer state of existence as pure Energy, it is quite possible to travel anywhere in the world or the entire Universe in an instant—

literally at the speed of thought. The Etheric plane, like the Astral and Mental planes is a Mind world, an extension of the Astral planes and of the Universe as a whole, existing beyond the boundaries and restrictions of physical space and time.

The "deceased" person often remains very close to the physical world while the level of Etheric Energy in their Etheric body remains sufficiently high. They will very often make the most of this opportunity to visit and say goodbye to family and friends and perhaps to visit their old home and favourite places from their physical life. Of course, living people cannot, with the exception of psychics and clairvoyants, usually "see" the "deceased" person, and any attempts by the deceased person to communicate with living people usually fail, often becoming a source of frustration. Very often, the "deceased" person will also attend his or her own funeral, not only to "see" all family, friends and other people they knew and loved in physical life gather to pay their last respects, but also to realize the finality of that particular physical life on Earth. Soon after this their reserves of Etheric Energy will dissipate, and they will make the transition to the level of the Astral worlds corresponding to their own unique vibration, being dependant on many factors including Spiritual evolution, character, materialism etc., and where very often previously deceased relatives will be waiting to greet and assist the new arrival in their latest home.

The deceased person can make the decision to transition to the Astral worlds at any time simply by desiring and willing it to happen and by thinking of being there, but only if they realize the possibility exists, otherwise, the transition will usually take place naturally once the supply of Etheric Energy in their Etheric body is depleted, at which time it will dissipate, giving way to the finer vibrations of the Astral body.

The other extreme occurs when a newly deceased person transitions directly to the Astral world almost immediately after physical "death". Sometimes, they will be aware of their physical death, but very often, the first thing a deceased person will be aware of is what is often described as a "tunnel of light" into which they are "pulled" at great speed before emerging at the other end within the Astral worlds, often to be greeted by family and others with an interest in the newly "deceased" person. In other cases, the scenery will simply seamlessly fade away from the physical world and "melt" into the Astral world.

There are however cases where for example people "die" very suddenly, or are bound to Earth by strong emotions such as guilt, or by grossly material attraction, when the person does not realise they no longer inhabit a physical body, and will linger around their familiar surroundings, not understanding why they cannot communicate with anyone. This individual is often known as a "ghost", which we will discuss later in this book.

Irrespective of how the deceased person arrives in the Astral worlds, they will never be alone. Other Astral residents, frequently previously deceased relatives and friends, will be there to greet and help them to settle into their new home. Very often, the newly deceased person will be taken to a place in the Astral world which is effectively a "reception area" for newly arrived Souls where, they will be met by a host of helpers with the task of assisting new arrivals. Such helpers specialize in all manner of cases and are able to assist with the transition process regardless of the circumstances surrounding physical death, having experience with a wide range of conditions associated with transition, ranging from the natural to the traumatic. There are billions of people living within the Astral world, having previously experienced physical life in the past, present and future of Earth, in fact each person may well have hundreds or even thousands of him or herself living in the Astral worlds concurrently, each of which is an individual incarnation of their Higher Self that has not yet evolved sufficiently to leave the Astral to return to their Higher Self.

Every eventuality is fully accounted for, and no person is ever left alone in the Astral worlds after physical death. For most decent people who have led a life with no strongly held religious or other strong beliefs, the environment is always extremely peaceful and harmonious and otherwise quite similar to Earth. If the physical death was sudden, violent or due to some self-inflicted disorder such as alcoholism, or if the person was ill for some time before physical death, there will be the Astral equivalent of hospitals with doctors and nurses on hand to assist, people who might well have been doctors and nurses in their own previous physical life. At these levels of the Astral everyone contributes out of a desire for service, and, unlike the physical world, with no expectation of reward. As mentioned before, in the Astral worlds anyone can create anything they wish for, so the concepts of "work" and money do not exist, and the people living there accordingly have no need of it.

Because the Astral worlds can appear to be almost identical to the physical world in appearance, some people do not believe they have actually "died". Such people can become confused and disoriented and might require attention by specialist helpers until they can come to terms with their new non-physical existence in the "afterlife" of the Astral worlds.

Children and infants especially require a great deal of care from Astral specialists. In these cases, a nurse or designated helper, often a previously transitioned family member if available will look after the child until he or she is old enough to join a family or make their own way in the Astral worlds. There are many such families who will gladly take on the responsibility of looking after young children or children in need of guidance who arrived before their own Earth based parents. Older children will often join a family as soon as they have come to terms with their new home in the Astral worlds.

Children can usually adapt to the Astral worlds much more quickly than adults, largely because they had not yet been fully indoctrinated into the ways of the physical world, and children are generally much more adaptable than adults.

Upon arriving in the Astral world's most people settle into their new home very quickly and create a new "life" for themselves. They will, sooner or later, completely lose interest in the physical world and their previous physical life. However, people living in the Astral worlds can, and very often do "visit" the physical world whenever they feel the need to, often to visit loved ones left behind. There are numerous cases of bereaved family and friends suddenly feeling the "presence" of their loved one, and in these cases, it is very often truly their loved one visiting for a time from the Astral worlds.

It should be mentioned that "deceased" people living in the Astral worlds will often watch over their loved ones still living in the physical world, guiding them by mental influence and protecting them from inner dangers whenever possible. Because the Universe is Infinite living Mind, thought is a very powerful primary Energy. Therefore, it is relatively easy for people in the Astral worlds to influence or "impress" the Minds of people still living in the physical world. Such influence can suddenly arrive in the Minds of people on Earth as intuition, inspiration or ideas that appear to come from the individual's own Mind. Pets, such as cats and dogs, can often sense the presence of their deceased owners in a very powerful way.

It is also possible for people living in the Astral worlds to visit people in their dreams. This happens more often than people realize. Dreams of meeting deceased people are often very real, and such contacts should always be taken very seriously and any messages remembered. Everyone in the physical world leaves their body at night while in deep sleep, and Astral residents sometimes take this opportunity to meet with their loved ones "face to face" in the Astral worlds. These meetings are then often remembered in the morning as a vivid lifelike dream. Again, these meetings are often very real indeed and should be remembered to the best of your ability. This can easily be accomplished by keeping a dream diary by your bed, and writing down everything you remember about your dreams as soon as you awaken in the morning. Sometimes, important information is passed along this way, as well as reassurances that the "deceased" person is very well, happy and content in their new Astral home.

Although it is perfectly natural and healthy to grieve for a deceased loved one, it is important to realize that these people are not really "dead" and have not "ceased to exist". The loved one is now living in what is actually a truer reality than the physical world. Assuming they are living in the mid to high Astral worlds or within the Spirit worlds, they will be experiencing an existence of pure love, light, bliss, peace and happiness on a level beyond the comprehension of most people still living on Earth. They can and do often visit loved ones still living on Earth, often endeavouring to make their presence felt in order to reassure the grieving loved ones that they are happy.

Whilst grieving for people who have "passed on" is understandable, it is also important to understand that the "deceased" person can feel these emotions and "hear" the thoughts of those grieving in a very powerful way. It is best therefore to feel happy for the "deceased" person for completing their life on Earth, and to send them Love and understanding in the knowledge they live on, and you will be reunited.

One of the benefits of Astral Projection, which will be discussed later in this book, is the ability to visit and explore the Astral worlds and to meet deceased loved ones and friends in person. To Astral projectors, death holds no fear because they have had some experience of the glorious life waiting after the final release from the restrictions of the physical body.

As we will also see later in this book, everyone in the Astral worlds lives at the same level, the same realm, sphere or plane as people who were of similar characters, beliefs and levels of Spiritual development. In the mid-Astral worlds where probably around fifty percent or more people transition after physical death, there is no work, money, or unhappiness. Everyone lives together there in perfect harmony. People who were disruptive in the physical world live in the lower Astral worlds with like-Minded, similarly disruptive people, thus always preserving the complete peace and harmony of the inner Astral worlds, although eventually, lessons learned, they too can move on to the pleasanter levels of Astral life.

People who have left the physical world of matter have been liberated once again and will live and rest for a time in the Astral and Mental worlds before returning to their Higher Self with their own unique package of experience to contribute to the Whole Higher Self. Friends, relatives and loved ones should celebrate this joyfully. Death, however sad, tragic or unexpected it seems to those left behind on Earth, the change known as "death" means the liberation of a Soul from its physical body, and the completion of another mission.

Although people still living in the physical world regard those living in the Astral and Spirit worlds as "dead", to those people who passed on to the Astral and Spirit worlds, it is the people still living in the density of the physical world, with all of the trials and tribulations it brings, who actually appear to be "dead" by comparison, dead to the splendours, glories, peace, harmony and liberation of the inner worlds of life and reality.

"Death" should never, ever be feared. It is rather something to anticipate and celebrate when the time comes as a completely natural aspect of individual evolution and a transition to glorious worlds of pure harmony, bliss and beauty where no hardships, trials or misery exist. The transition of passing to the inner, Astral and inner worlds is a joyous time for celebration.

Chapter 29
Animals after Passing

All too many people still believe that human Beings are superior to animals. This is an entirely erroneous perception, due in part to the dogma of orthodox religions who believe that humans are in some way "chosen" by God to be superior, and the Ego of human beings generally. It should be noted that most orthodox religions, even today, still do not even acknowledge the equal status of female human beings to their male counterparts, much less of members of the animal worlds.

This perceived superiority of humans over animals is also responsible for the way humans treat animals including the use of animals for food, labour, entertainment and hunting. Animals as pets, are of course generally treated very well, and are usually very much loved, cherished and often respected by their human companions.

All life, without exception, whether animal, vegetable or mineral is Mind and Spirit, and a completely equal aspect and expression of God. The meaning of the words "God made man in his own image" has been drastically misinterpreted by orthodox religions, leading many humans believe they hold some special position in the Universe, with all other forms of life being subordinate and therefore inferior to the human race.

As previously mentioned, the true "image" of God is pure Spirit—formless, vibrating, conscious, intelligent Energy, the very same pure Spirit of which everything and everyone, including all animals and all life generally, whether animate or inanimate, are equal aspects. No animal life, from the smallest single celled organism such as the amoeba, to the largest whale is in any way inferior to human Beings because animals are simply other aspects and expressions of God, differing only in form, abilities and priorities, but nevertheless still on their own path back to God.

Because many humans are governed to varying extents by the Ego, they tend to perceive all other forms of life as inferior. After evolving to much higher levels of Spiritual life, people will discover that mankind is in fact today equivalent to what humans on Earth now perceive to be the very lowest forms of single celled organisms. To the advanced Beings of the inner spheres of life, Earthly man seems barely capable of any sort of thought processes by comparison. Yet, these inner Beings do not make such comparisons, or in any way perceive Earthly man to be inferior or subordinate to themselves, knowing the unconditional Oneness, Unity and Equivalence of All. They perceive Earthly man with Unconditional Love as equal aspects of God who are simply further down the path of evolution on the journey back to God, knowing that one day even those on the lowest stages of the path will be as them, and still greater. All life is in a perpetual state of evolution on the Divine path of return to The Source, our Creator, The First Cause from whence we came, and Who gave us the most precious and Divine gift of eternal life in the beginning.

Because animals are equal aspects of God, their progression after physical death is no different in most respects to that of humans. Like humans, all animals survive the death of the physical body. For all those who mourn the passing of a beloved pet, please be absolutely and completely assured that your pet is safe and well, enjoying the peace, harmony and happiness of the inner worlds, often with their own species, and in the case of loved pets such as cats and dogs with humans who will love and care for them until their owner makes the transition and both are reunited. Please also be absolutely assured that your pets will never forget their human companions. "Deceased" animals visit loved ones who remain in the physical world just as humans do. Your pets will most assuredly still be with you in Spirit and will continue to express their love for you from the inner worlds, often visiting and behaving just as they did in physical life. Very often cats and dogs can be heard and even felt to jump on to a bed at night, continuing life as though they were still in a physical body. Unlike humans, animals have no fear or even concept of "death", which is a human contrivance, for which they are truly blessed. If only the same were true of humans— another reason why animals may be considered to be no less advanced than humans, in fact often being more advanced in many respects.

Different species of animals progress in different ways after physical death. Animals who were particularly close to humans in physical life, for example, such as dogs, cats, and other pets, assume a special affinity to the human Spirit, increasing the vibrations of their Astral body, elevating and enabling them to retain a higher level of individuality and closeness to their human companions with the bond of Unconditional Love, again, the highest and most Divine vibration in the Universe. Animals who were not particularly close to humans, such as so called "wild animals", continue to survive after physical death within a group Soul of their own species, in a very similar way as in their physical life on Earth, and will continue to evolve in the context of a group Soul, just as human Beings evolve as a group centred on the Higher Self. Group evolution is an important Universal Principle with individual evolution, further highlighting the intrinsic Oneness of All.

There is a vast amount of evidence to prove the continuity of life after the physical death of animals, and particularly pets. For example, during séances, pet cats and dogs frequently appear before their human companions, during which they make every possible effort to make their presence known. Just as with human Spirit communication, the way in which the pet makes its presence known can vary considerably, but it may make its usual characteristic noises in a "direct voice" method of communication, it may brush against the human companion with its Etheric body, or it may even materialize visibly. Very often during a séance, a human Spirit will appear accompanied by the pet of one of the attendees of the séance. The Spirit will provide complete assurance that the pet is being well taken care of. Of course, a séance is not at all necessary for these visitations to occur. All these methods of Spirit communication will be discussed in more detail later in this book.

Other animals who are still physically living, can also "see" or perceive deceased animals with their natural inner Spiritual abilities, and very often react to the Spirit of the animal in exactly the same way as they did when the animal was still physically alive. Cats and dogs have highly developed psychic and clairvoyant abilities, unspoilt by materialism, and "seeing" their former living companions seems perfectly normal to them, as indeed it is and should be for humans, thus once again highlighting the superiority of animals in these respects.

As previously mentioned, pets are never alone after passing from the physical world. Apart from their ability to visit human companions whenever they wish to do so, they are also often befriended by a human Soul within the Astral worlds who will happily look after the pet on behalf of the human companion still living on Earth. This is exactly the same situation as occurs when a child passes on before his or her parents. There are always plenty of people within the Astral worlds who will happily look after children and pets.

You can be absolutely sure that pets will be waiting in the Astral Worlds to be reunited with their human companions. As we will discuss later in this book, Unconditional Love is the most powerful vibration in the Universe—a force binding the Spirits of both humans and animals alike. The Love between an animal and a human companion is totally unconditional and does not diminish when the time comes for the physical passing of either, an Unconditional Love that crosses all boundaries of the human concept of "species" abilities or form.

Chapter 30
"Ghosts"

A "ghost" is a person who, after the change known as "death", remains firmly attracted to the physical world, from which they originally departed, having for some reason been unable to make the transition to the next phase of life. This attraction to the physical world motivates and enables the "ghost" to draw Etheric Energy from their surroundings at will, thus keeping them grounded in the Etheric body rather than making the full transition to the Astral worlds. The reasons for this apparent preference of some "deceased" people to remain close to their previous Earthy environment are many and varied.

Very often, a person simply cannot accept the fact that he or she has "died" and no longer has a physical body. Such a person continues to live in their familiar environment, such as the home in which they once lived, as if nothing had happened, often believing that they are still living in a physical body. A house where such a person lives is often considered by paranormal researchers to be "haunted". In other cases, the person is so engrossed and attracted to the material things they enjoyed during physical life that they simply cannot stand the thought of leaving those physical addictions behind. Such addictions might include power, drink, drugs, food, or sex.

In other cases, the person might harbour guilt over some aspect of their past life, lingering around to reconcile the situation, but which is simply not possible in a non-physical state, leading to a situation where the person becomes trapped in a "loop" where they continuously endeavour but fail to correct the perceived situation that concerns them, but are unable to do so. The "ghost" will have no concept of "time", and this behaviour can continue for centuries relative to the Earth concept of time.

Sometimes, a ghost is a newly deceased person who is frightened by the unfamiliar circumstances and does not want to move far from the familiar environment they once knew. Other recently deceased people might wish to stay close to their loved ones, believing that remaining close to the physical world is the only way by which to accomplish this.

If the "death" of someone was particularly violent and sudden, the deceased person may also become trapped in a "loop", continuously enacting the same sequence of events leading up to his or her untimely death. Frequently, such people do not even realise that they are "dead" and therefore simply cannot understand why living people cannot see, hear or communicate with them.

The Etheric plane is an extension of the Astral plane where space and time simply do not exist. Some "ghosts" will play out exactly the same sequence of events leading up to physical death until they can be rescued. Such rescues are often carried out by people residing in the Astral worlds, sometimes with the help of Astral projectors who are still based within the physical world. When rescued. the "ghost" will be escorted to the Astral worlds where they can finally come to terms with their new situation. It should be noted however that this must happen in accordance with the freewill of the "ghost". The rescuers cannot force the "ghost" person to go anywhere against their will.

Sometimes a person trapped at the level of the Etheric plane close to the physical world will eventually arrive at their own realization that they are no longer living within a physical body. Others will eventually come to realize the folly of their actions in remaining close to the physical world, and then willingly make the transition to the Astral worlds without any assistance, simply by deciding and intending to do so, resulting in a raising of their vibrations making the transition possible.

When the Soul of a deceased person remains in a particular locality, the Soul is known as a "ghost", and the location inhabited by the ghost is considered to be "haunted". To a physical person living in a "haunted" house, the "ghost" will often seem to carry out exactly the same series of actions every time it makes an appearance, such as "stepping" on a creaky floor board, walking up the stairs, rattling door handles, moving items around, and even switching lights and other electric appliances on and off. This is possible because the Etheric body is relatively dense by comparison to the inner Astral and Mental bodies, and a ghost can sometimes achieve the necessary density required to influence physical objects.

There have been numerous cases throughout history where ghosts have actually been "seen" with physical eyes, often as a billowing white shapeless cloud or even in the form of a cloudy human shape. This is possible due to a particularly high concentration of a substance known as "ectoplasm". Ectoplasm is produced by the Energy body of living humans and is normally exuded as a completely natural process of living. All humans living in the physical world continually exude ectoplasm to some extent. Many mediums, particularly during a séance, are able to produce particularly high concentrations of ectoplasm, often with the assistance of the Spirits present. Very often, the "sitters" present at the séance also produce ectoplasm to some extent under those same conditions, thereby creating the ideal situation for Spirit communication and perhaps even full materialization to take place in the presence of the ectoplasm. A characteristic of all mediums for materialisation and the direct voice séances are the natural ability to exude a high volume of ectoplasm in the séance room through which the Spirit communicators manifest to the sitters.

The concentration of ectoplasm in any particular location is not particularly high, especially in relatively new buildings. Very old houses and buildings where many people congregate over long periods of time, for example old theatres have concentrations of ectoplasm that are much higher than normal. In such circumstances, the Etheric body of a "ghost" can interact directly with the high density of the whitish-coloured ectoplasm, bringing about a partial or even full manifestation in the form of a visibly discernible "apparition". This is why "apparitions" are frequently seen in old, public buildings.

Although ghosts are very real, they are almost always completely harmless. A ghost is simply a normal but deceased human being living within a more subtle non-physical body after having experienced the change known as "death". A ghost can often be assisted by people still living within the physical worlds who are expert in these matters. As previously mentioned, such help is often by Astral projectors who can actually meet the ghost "face to face" in the Astral Worlds, or by psychic mediums or clairvoyants who can "see" and communicate directly with the "deceased" person. There are whole bands of people living within the Astral worlds who make it their mission to rescue Souls who are trapped near to the physical world, as in the case of a ghost, or within a lower Astral plane, such as a "belief system territory". This process is known as "Soul retrieval" and broadly involves bringing the Soul from the low level of vibration where the Soul was trapped, to their new and rightful home in the Astral worlds.

There is another class of "ghost"; a person who was very religious during physical life, who becomes trapped near to the physical world due to the misinterpretation of the Christian Bible—here is just such a case:

"Behold: I show you a mystery; We shall not all sleep but we shall be changed.

In a moment, in the twinkling of an eye, at the last trump: for the trumpet shall sound, and the dead shall be raised incorruptible, and we shall be changed.

For this corruptible must put on incorruption, and this mortal should put on immortality".

So when this corruptible shall have put on incorruption, and this mortal shall have put on immortality, shall be brought to pass the saying that is written, Death is swallowed up in victory". -- 1 Corinthians 15: 51-54

It is highly ironic that a passage in the Bible intended to teach the truth of what actually happens at the time of physical "death" should cause so much misery to so many recently deceased people. Those who feel strongly about these words and have misinterpreted them will usually await their "judgement day", expecting an Archangel to arrive and blow a "trumpet", thus signifying their "right" to proceed to "Heaven" if it is judged that their life has been a "good" one. Of course, the Archangel never arrives and the deceased person often continues to wait close to their body, potentially for all eternity. This is one reason why there are so many "haunted" cemeteries, with Souls awaiting their "judgement day.

The strength of belief in this passage in the Bible is usually sufficient to allow the deceased person to draw enough Etheric Energy from their surroundings to stay in an Etheric state very close to the physical world indefinitely. These people become "ghosts", often "haunting" the cemetery where their physical body has been laid to rest. However, as with other types of ghost these people are often rescued people living within the Astral worlds specializing in "Soul retrieval", sometimes with the help of Astral projectors still living in the physical world.

The words from the Bible actually describe the true mystery of what happens at the time of physical death and are evidently intended to remove the fear of this completely natural process:

"Behold: I show you a mystery; We shall not all sleep but we shall be changed".

This confirms that there is no such thing as "death", that we shall not be faced with oblivion, but instead will "be changed" into another more subtle form to another life in the Astral body.

"In a moment, in the twinkling of an eye, at the last trump: for the trumpet shall sound, and the dead shall be raised incorruptible, and we shall be changed".

The "trumpet" referred to in this part of the passage is a symbolic trumpet and not an actual Earthly musical instrument. It symbolizes the "trumpet" of liberation of the Soul from the physical body. These words go on to reiterate the truth that a person shall rise as the same person from the physical body and shall be "raised" or "changed" to the Light body, Astral body.

"For this corruptible must put on incorruption, and this mortal should put on immortality, shall be brought to pass the saying that is written, Death is swallowed up in victory".

This says that the temporal, corruptible physical body and the person who inhabited that mortal Earthly body shall become immortal in his or her inner Spiritual bodies. This underlines once again one of the most fundamental important truisms—that every single one of us is an immortal Spirit, an integral aspect the Great Spirit, The One, made in the true image of God, who lives on once the temporal Earthly existence is over.

Chapter 31
Reincarnation

Reincarnation is truly one of the greatest mysteries confronting mankind. Do we really "return" for further "lives" on Earth? If so, how many times? Why do we reincarnate at all? Do we have any choice in the matter?

To "Re-incarnate" literally means to "come back in the flesh, "carne" meaning "flesh" in Latin.

Before looking at reincarnation in greater depth we need to clarify some important facts that we will discuss in detail later in this chapter.

There is reality no such state as "past" lives or even "lives". All those experiences we know as "lives" are in fact the continuum of a single collective experience of the Higher Self, concurrently experienced across all what we know as "time zones" or "periods in history" relative to the human concept of what we call "time", concurrently encompassing all Higher Self incarnation experiences. In the realm of the Higher Self "time" does not exist as is not therefore experienced. When people talk of "past lives" therefore, it is simple relative to a linear perception of incarnations within the confines of space-time in accordance with the perceptions of the physical brain and five physical senses.

A convenient way of looking at this is by using the metaphor of a cart wheel. The cart wheel consists of a hub, which represents our Higher Self, spokes, which represent "timelines" relative to the earth experience of "time", and the rim of the wheel which represents the space-time continuum of Earth, and indeed the physical Universe. Each separate incarnation of the Higher Self, "descends" from the Higher Self along its "time spoke" until being physically "born" into a physical body on Earth. From a physical perspective the point where each spoke meets the rim is a "timeline" or "time zone" on Earth, but from the perspective of our Higher Self it is all concurrent and with no concept of "time" which is a human construct.

When each physical life on Earth has been completed, after the change known as "death", that aspect or "fragment" of the Higher Self travels back up the spoke to the Higher Self with its own package of experience which contributes towards the whole. As it does so it passes through the realms of the collective Mind known as the Astral planes and the Mental planes where further experience is gained on the return back to the Higher Self, increasing its vibration as it does so.

It should also be mentioned that it is erroneous to think in terms of "bodies". We have only one Spiritual "body" which extends from The Source, The First Cause, God. What we therefore experience as a physical life, Astral life, Mental life and so on is therefore simply a state of conscious focus at that level of vibration. What we know as "Astral Projection", Out of Body Experiences and even dreams are therefore simply an inner projection of Consciousness within the continuum of Consciousness extending to our Higher Self and on to The Source, and not in any way a physical movement of a discreet physical or non-physical "body", although it is often useful for the sake of understanding to think in those terms.

As the cart wheel representing all physical incarnations of the Higher self revolves, the Higher Self experiences cycles of experience, just as the Universe itself, God, the Universal Mind experiences cycles, everything in creation being a reflection of the whole.

So again, when discussing "past lives" or "previous lives" or "incarnations" within this chapter and book as a whole, in the interest of understanding, we are referring exclusively to the physical linear incarnation experiences of the Higher Self relative to the space-time continuum of Earth and the physical

Universe, and not of “past” or “previous” lives in absolute terms, which in reality simply do not exist. That said, let us now take a closer look at this process we know as “reincarnation” and erroneously as “past lives”.

In order to understand reincarnation, we first need to understand the true destiny of mankind. Each and everyone one of us from the moment of our very first physical “life” on Earth, our very first “incarnation”, has the most sacred mission to ultimately reunite with our Divine Creator, The First Cause, God by the process of raising vibration through the process of perfection. This is the true and ultimate meaning of life. Upon reaching this most exalted and sacred stage in our Spiritual evolution, we will all have the option of either relinquishing our individuality and merging with The Source—an act often known as “Unity”—or retaining our individuality for as long as we wish to do so. Those who choose to retain their individualities at these highest and most exalted of levels are “God-people” residing in the very highest, most glorious Cosmic spheres of life, usually concerning themselves with the ongoing evolution of other Beings throughout the Universe.

So, where does reincarnation fit into this process? The physical world (in our case, the planet Earth) can be likened to first year at kindergarten, and the very highest spheres of reality (the Cosmic spheres) can be likened to post-graduate University. It goes without saying that no one can even think about attending University without first having progressed through all necessary levels of primary and higher education, thus achieving the necessary levels of attainment.

The inner spheres beyond the physical planet Earth are “Mind worlds” where anything desired can become an instant reality through the powers of thought, imagination, emotion and other powers of the Mind. The environments most people will find themselves residing in after “death” are the Astral worlds, often known as “the afterlife”. Wonderful though these inner spheres surely are to the people living there, they are not an environment where important lessons can be easily learned due to the lack of physical world type challenges. These initial lessons require the characteristics, density and challenges of the physical world of matter in order to be effective. As we all know only too well, the planet Earth is populated by people with an almost infinite number of characteristics; temperaments, characters, Egos, personalities, beliefs and so on, a situation which does not exist in the Astral and beyond.

Everyone on Earth lives within a material body subject to the rigors of the physical environment, not the least of which is health, the need for food and shelter, and co-existence with other people. The physical Universe is a school of learning where the Higher Self of every person must first attain the necessary degree of perfection in order to graduate and progress to the inner, more blissful, glorious worlds of Spirit, spheres beyond the form of the material and Astral worlds. Only when such a level of perfection and ennoblement is achieved can true progress be made on the path back to God.

Again, it must be stressed that there is no way to avoid this progression of events. It is the absolute and most sacred destiny of every single individual, a process which could take aeons upon aeons as measured in the linear concept of Earth time, but which in reality is experienced beyond time as all incarnations take place concurrently. Each separate incarnation on Earth adds to the pool of experience and knowledge required for the completeness of our Higher Self in order to progress to the inner spheres of the Universe and thus to transcend the cycle of physical reincarnation.

Each life experience on Earth provides a vehicle of expression and personality, the sum of which contributes to the total individuality. Memories and experiences of all lives on Earth and beyond are "stored" perpetually within the Higher Self or "Inner Self" and become an aspect of who we are in total. In other words, the Higher Self is the sum of all of our physical experiences on Earth or even on other planets.

Each individual lifetime can be likened to a facet of a diamond. The full sparkling diamond with all of its many facets represents the complete Self, The Higher Self, while each facet of the diamond represents each separate life. A diamond has many facets, the total of which constitutes the whole glittering gem of our Individuality. Each lifetime will add a new facet to the diamond until the whole diamond is ultimately complete in all of its sparkling splendour. The Higher Self, or "Inner Self", finally assumes the characteristics of the final incarnation, after which life continues within the inner spheres of life and reality as a complete glistening diamond, an eternal Spirit, becoming ever brighter and perfect as the ascent back to The Source, The Prime Creator, God progresses. The Higher Self requires a number of physical lives due to the mortality of the physical body, which means that each life on Earth is, in the context of eternity, just a temporal blip in eternity. Numerous physical lives are often required therefore in order to gather all of the necessary experience though a wide range of physical personalities.

Throughout all lives, everyone will retain full conscious awareness and all other fundamental attributes of the immortal Spirit such as intelligence. Each physical life, however, results in a new personality and a correspondingly new Astral body and Etheric body. Only the Spirit, "made in the true image of God" is truly immortal. We should also differentiate between "personality" and "individuality". Each incarnation is characterised by a different personality, in male or female form, but our individuality, our true Spiritual identity is eternal.

Reincarnation is not a random process. The Higher Self will to select the next life on Earth in accordance with the lessons that need to be learned and experience gained for progression, and to balance accumulated karma. It is then for each individual to make the most of each individual lifetime by living a life of complete inner awareness and making the most of opportunities as they arise. If any particular lifetime is partially or fully wasted, it will be necessary for the Higher Self to send another, similar personality to Earth again for a further physical lifetime of similar circumstances in order to complete the lessons previously left unlearned. This is just one reason why everyone should have full conscious awareness of the ultimate significance and importance of each individual life on Earth.

Everyone knows from personal experience just how hard and sometimes seemingly “unjust” life can seem. Physical existence depends on basic material things such as the need for food, shelter and warmth. During each life, everyone interacts with a wide variety of people, often in the course of obtaining the money with which to purchase the things that are perceived to be required for physical existence. Physical life brings obstacles which need to be recognized, faced and overcome. Of course it is also true that The Source, The Universe, God will provide all of our needs to survive on Earth for the asking, leaving only the lessons to be learned. But, as we will see later in this book, most people remain oblivious to this, erroneously believing they must force the physical world into submitting to their demands.

During the course of each lifetime, everyone is presented with all manner of trials, tribulations, challenges, situations and temptations, all of which are valuable lessons presented in order to potentially assist in ultimate progress on Earth, contributing to the completeness of the Higher Self. Very few people at this time recognize these valuable lessons for what they really are, simply ascribing them to “chance”, “luck”, “misfortune” or any number of other dismissive or superstitious explanations, not knowing that we all create our own reality and must accordingly accept the consequences.

In order to progress, as everyone must eventually do, all life situations must be recognized both as valuable lessons and opportunities to equalise karma. As previously mentioned, it is very difficult to achieve these things from within the inner spheres of life, particularly the mid-Astral where materialism still prevails, and where everyone is at the same level of progression, and where the physical density of matter does not provide any sort of challenge.

As we will see later in this book, within the Astral worlds, also known as the "desire worlds", everything desired can become an instant reality without the need for effort, work or money. As we will also see later, however, all needs in the physical world can also be realized by using the power of the Mind and a Universal Principle known as "The Law of Attraction". This applies just as much in the physical world as it does the inner worlds, but even using the Law of Attraction does not remove people from the need to survive, interact and thrive within the physical world of matter. The lessons everyone needs to learn include subjugation of the Ego, balancing of the inner, subtle bodies, the Soul and Spirit, and the development of the Divine "spark" of "God" within until it becomes the very brightest Light and highest vibration. This is to fully realize God within.

Selfless service is also extremely important, as is living in harmony with the most important and powerful force in the Universe—Unconditional Love. Every single situation which presents itself in life should be considered as a valuable opportunity for personal evolution, and we should all acknowledge and embrace these opportunities. No opportunity for personal evolution and progression should ever be wasted.

Most people prefer to complain, blame others or such superstitions as "luck", "chance" and "fortune", and often carry on through life with a material, vain and often selfish outlook, with everything revolving around temporal material possessions, in an effort to satisfy the relentless demands of the Ego and to perpetuate the illusion of superiority over others. One day, whether in the current or a future lifetime, every single person must awaken to the realization of the true purpose and value of life in the material world and to live each moment accordingly. This realization might well take some people hundreds or even thousands of years of incarnations of the Higher Self as measured in Earth time. The vast majority of mankind has yet to reach such realization, continuing to live in the belief that their current "life" is the only life they will ever get before being "sent" to either a "Heaven" or "hell" or even to face "oblivion".

Just as the Higher Self of many Spirits currently in incarnation have experienced numerous previous physical lives over aeons of time, others are being born today into their very first Higher Self experience on Earth. One day, after the cycle of reincarnation is finally complete, the Higher Self, now as a integrated and realised Spiritual Being, with the benefit of numerous physical lives, will move on to further experiences within the inner realms of the Universe at an ever higher vibration, ultimately becoming a true "God person", residing deep within the exalted inner spheres of life, but still always of service to those who are not so far along the path.

All life is Spirit, equal aspects of God, our Prime Creator, The Source, so the human concept of "aliens" or "extraterrestrials" is erroneous. It might well be that an incarnation as a personality on another distant planet might be more appropriate for progression than a life on Earth. Likewise, it is believed that many Spirits originating from distant planets also incarnate as Earth humans in order to gain that particular physical experience. The whole meaning of incarnation throughout the Universe is for individual evolution in order to facilitate onward progression through the inner spheres of life and reality, all of which lead ultimately to the very same God, irrespective of which planet a Being was originally born, or "race", creed or religion the person belonged to while on Earth. Once a person achieves an understanding of the true meaning of physical life, that person will joyously and enthusiastically embrace it and begin to learn the lessons necessary to balance karma, to create their own reality and to evolve.

After each physical life, a person usually progresses to the Astral worlds, and thereafter, in due course, keeping in mind that "time" does not exist, evolve through experience back to their Higher Self, bringing with them their individual package of experience that contributes towards the totality of the Higher Self.

The Soul, Immortal Spirit and Higher Self exists in the inner spheres of life beyond space and time and will know exactly what sort of individual physical life is needed in order to progress. The Higher Self will choose the precise location in the world where the next incarnation will take place, who the parents will be, and the conditions to be faced, including even the circumstances of the next physical death. While many people complain about their "lot" in life, the Higher Self of that person actually chose their "lot". Rather than complaining, they should determine the reasons for that particular life and make the most of it by learning the lessons that need to be learned. Of course, once on Earth, a person's "lot" is further determined by the life they create with their Mind, either consciously or unconsciously, in accordance with the truth that we all create our own reality, not through actions but by and through Mind. Again we should know, beyond all doubt that Mind is the only fundamental Principle of Life, and that in human form we experience Mind as conscious, Subconscious and Universal.

Until people begin to understand these realities, they will continue to stumble through life, complaining about everything that does not agree with their status and Ego. It is not until such a person eventually passes to the Astral worlds will they see and understand the true meaning of the life just past and have the opportunity to reflect upon any opportunities not taken. Of course, another life, another representative of the Higher Self on Earth will be necessary to complete the unlearned lessons.

One of the most frequently questions asked about reincarnation is: "How long do we live within the inner worlds before returning for another physical life?" Beyond the physical, temporal realm we call "Earth", time does not really exist. It is but an illusion, so each Higher Self will experience every physical incarnation concurrently in different "time zones".

The Higher Self will decide what additional experience is required in order to become a complete and perfect Higher Self in readiness for the next phase of evolution on the return to The Source, and will determine what "time-zone", circumstances and parents will be optimal. Once incarnated on Earth, the personality has no memory of previous incarnation of the Higher Self and has the freewill to live and gain experience on Earth, unrestricted by memories of previous incarnation of the Higher Self.

As with many things, it is the cynical nature of mankind to demand proof of everything, and reincarnation is no exception. Many people are still under the influence of the churches, which have taught since the 6th century CE that reincarnation does not exist. This is when references to reincarnation were officially removed from the church doctrine to maintain control over their own congregations through instilling the fear of a "hell" or "purgatory" where non-believers or non-followers, or "evil" people will go after death.

Others, quite understandably, make the point that if they have lived so many previous lives, why can't they remember those lives? The brain is not the Mind. Memories are not permanently stored in the physical brain. The physical brain is simply a temporary storage device, like the flash memory card in a digital camera, and an organic interface between the physical body and the Etheric and inner bodies. As already mentioned, memories of both the current, past and future lives are all stored in our Higher Self as a "causal body" existing within the causal sphere of the Universe. The organic brain can also be likened to a super-computer, responsible for controlling the physical organic body and acting as a filter and "receiving station" for thoughts originating from the inner spheres.

As previously discussed, in addition to the physical body, everyone also has an Etheric or Energy body, an Astral body also known as the Soul, and Mental bodies. Humans are multi-dimensional Beings with a potentially infinite number of "bodies" existing concurrently in all spheres of Energy and vibration of the Universe, from the physical to Etheric, the Astral and Mental, Higher Self, Celestial and Cosmic planes, all the way to The Source, The First Cause, God. A thought originating in the Mental plane in accordance with the Principle of Mentalism, is first received by the Mental Spirit body where it proceeds through the Mental matrix connected to the Astral body and from there through the Astral matrix connected to the Etheric and physical bodies where the thought arrives and is received and interpreted in Consciousness.

The organic brain can, in the context of receiving thoughts and ideas, simply be likened to a receiving apparatus such as a television set. Just as a television is designed for receiving radio waves, the physical brain has the function of receiving "Mental waves" in the form of vibrations. By nature of its design, the brain filters out everything that is not required to avoid interference and lack of clarity. If this were not the case, humans would know the details of all past and future lives and would, therefore, be deprived of freewill and the ability to evolve. Instead of living spontaneously based upon physical life circumstances as they arise, a person would be heavily influenced by all past and potential future incarnations of the Higher Self. Therefore, rather than learning the lessons as they are presented in the current incarnation, the person would endeavour to re-live and compensate for the other incarnations. No beneficial progress would then be made. This does not mean, however, that we incarnate without the benefit of past lives. The lessons have to be based upon something. The solution to this is within the realm of the Subconscious Mind, which exists beneath the level of normal conscious awareness of daily life, and which in turn has full access to the realms of our Higher Self, which is who we are—the totality of all our incarnations into the physical Universe.

Clearly then, being consciously in control of the Subconscious Mind is most important. Often, people wisely wish to cease an addiction or other harmful habit such as smoking, drinking alcohol, the wrong foods etc., and it is the Subconscious Mind, together with the Ego, that will relentlessly urge the continuation of the habit. It should be pointed out that this is not due to any "intent" on the part of the Subconscious Mind per se, but rather the Subconscious Mind immutably fulfilling its task of manifesting everything the conscious Mind has impressed upon it by the conscious Mind into physical experiential reality.

It is possible for example to enlist the assistance of a hypnotist, to give up smoking. The hypnotist is actually addressing the Subconscious Mind and reprogramming it through suggestions. It is infinitely better however for a person to become the master of their own Subconscious Mind using the entire power of the Mind, rather than to rely on the services of a hypnotist.

Mastering the Subconscious Mind then is extremely important for progression, and this subject will be addressed more extensively later in this book. As the Higher Self has full knowledge of all past and future lives, the Higher Self always provides guidance and direction whenever appropriate. This is why it is so important to recognize communications from the Higher Self and to always act upon them immediately. The Higher Self can influence the conscious Mind through the Subconscious Mind and will do so whenever the need arises.

Ultimately, the Immortal Spirit of the Higher Self is not concerned with previous "lives" or personalities of the Higher Self, all such lives being experienced as a continuum of the

Immortal Spirit beyond the physical confines of space and time. All physical incarnations are, therefore, important aspects of the totality comprising each "higher" individual, but the real essence of the Immortal Spirit is ultimately concerned with the process of ennoblement and perfection during the progression along the sacred path back to our Divine Creator.

There is considerable evidence as to the truth of reincarnation. Many thousands of people have experienced recollections or "flashes" of a previous life or "lives" through dreams, when facing life-threatening situations, or by past life regression methods. These "connections" to past lives are actually connections to the Higher Self through the Subconscious Mind where every detail of "past lives" are recorded and assimilated. People who understand reincarnation are often curious to discover who they were in "previous lives", how and where they lived, and how they "died". Again, there is in reality no such thing as "previous lives" all lives being experienced concurrently relative to the Higher Self, so any past life regression is in fact communicating directly with the Higher Self through the Subconscious Mind in order to retrieve information on another aspect of the Higher Self as it is actually experienced.

For those not having the necessary meditation or trance abilities to obtain past life information for themselves, an alternative is to seek the services of a hypnotist who can facilitate the necessary altered state of Consciousness and ask the appropriate questions. In this case the hypnotist is carrying out exactly the same process as a person who directly accesses "alternative life" information in a trance state, except that the subject under hypnosis may not have fully recalled what transpired during the session. The information will have been recorded for the subject to listen to afterwards. This entire process is known as "past life regression".

Children are particularly excellent at recalling "alternative incarnations, even in a normal state of Consciousness. The reason for this is because a child is much more "in touch" with the Higher Self, having not yet been programmed and indoctrinated into the ways of the physical world, often being taught that "imagining things" or talking with "imaginary friends" is "bad". As this process of programming and indoctrination continues and the child becomes older, the child's contact with the Spirit worlds and the Higher Self gradually fades until the memories become subsumed below the level of normal waking Consciousness.

Children up to the age of seven years, and certainly before the age of five years, usually maintain close contact with the inner realms of life in normal waking Consciousness and frequently interact with their friends and other Beings in the Astral worlds during the course of play. Of course, adults assume their children are simply "pretending" to play with "make believe" or "imaginary friends", but these friends are often very real. Likewise, children are often so much in touch with their previous Higher Self "life" that they have problems distinguishing it from their current physical "life". Children will sometimes talk of their "other mummy" or "other daddy", or their "other house" or "other friends" or "other school". These are most certainly not the fantasies of a child but are very real and vivid memories of a previous life, which, as discussed at the beginning of this chapter, are not really "previous" at all, but being experienced Now. They are in fact connecting with a concurrent life through the Subconscious Mind.

Some children have quite extraordinary natural memories of other Earth lives. Some of the most remarkable situations arise when children spontaneously speak in a foreign language, which they could not possibly have learned during their present life. Sometimes these are very ancient languages and dialects that are now and have long been extinct and are no longer spoken in the modern world today. In other cases, children can describe their previous homes and lives in considerable detail, including the town or area in which they lived in a "previous" or more specifically alternative life. Sometimes, a child will say to a parent, "please can we go and visit...", and then mentioning a name completely unknown to the parents.

There are also many documented cases where a Higher Self has reincarnated a personality very close to a previous physical incarnation on Earth. In some cases, there are people still living from the previous life of the child who can verify the accuracy of the information provided by the child. This especially occurs when the incarnation of the Higher Self was terminated abruptly before it was due to end and immediately sends another aspect to Earth under similar circumstances to continue with the incomplete experience from the previous incarnation.

There are researchers who have devoted a considerable amount of their own lives to the verification of past lives, particularly of children. Probably the most well-known and respected of these researchers is Dr. Ian Stevenson, who is very widely recognized as a most important pioneer in this field.

Over the course of 40 years, Dr. Stevenson meticulously documented more than three thousand cases of children's past life memories, presenting irrefutable proof as to the truth of reincarnation. In all of these cases, the children were able to recall "past" physical lives of their Higher Self spontaneously in considerable detail and clarity without any prompting whatsoever and without being subjected to any form of hypnosis.

Dr. Stevenson took whatever action is necessary to verify the facts of each child's memory and was able to even match birthmarks and birth defects to the wounds and scars of the deceased person from the child's previous life, all verified by medical records. His strict methods systematically rule out all possible "normal" explanations for the child's memories.

There is a dramatic example of reincarnation involving a Turkish bandit. A boy claimed he was formerly a Turkish bandit, who was cornered by the authorities and shot himself through the lower jaw to evade capture. Upon medical examination of this boy, they found a large mark in his jaw where the bullet would have entered in a previous life, and there was hair missing from the top of his head where the bullet would have emerged. A witness to this incident is still alive today and was able to confirm the precise details given by the boy. In this case the Higher Self of the boy incarnated a similar personality in similar circumstances soon after the previous life had been prematurely terminated.

Many people, including sceptics and scholars, agree that these cases offer the best evidence yet for reincarnation. Dr. Stevenson's credentials are impeccable. He is a medical doctor and had many scholarly papers to his credit before he began his past life research. It is believed that the cases researched by Dr. Stevenson have been instrumental to the widespread acceptance of reincarnation in the West.

Dr. Stevenson is absolutely meticulous in his research, apparently taping interviews with up to 25 witnesses for each individual case. His researchers checked medical records and compared the character of the child with the character of their previous life personality. As mentioned before, "individuality" is an aspect of the Immortal Spirit, and who a person "is" remains infinitely constant.

If only more people knew of these scientifically documented cases of reincarnation, they might be more likely to listen when their own young children talk about when they "died" before or their "other home", etc. When children are not taken seriously, they begin to doubt themselves, becoming self-conscious or even feeling guilty about their past life memories. After several years of indoctrination into the physical world and not being taken seriously when they talk of previous lives, children lose their connections with past life memories by consciously disconnecting the link through the Subconscious Mind. It should be mentioned that everyone is intended to maintain the connection with the Higher Self and the completeness of our true Self. It is the loss of this connection that has contributed to the state of the world as it is today, thus highlighting the importance of the work of Dr. Stevenson and others who are continuing similar most important research.

We will now take a closer look at just a few examples of past life recollections by children.

Reincarnation Case 1.

This case involves a young girl who was able to recall considerable details of her previous life at age three. So detailed was the information she provided that Dr. Stevenson was able to locate the family of the girl in her past life experience. It started when her family travelled approximately 100 miles from their home. The girl suddenly asked the driver to go down a road to "my home", saying they "could get a better cup of tea there".

Soon afterward, she started to relate numerous details of her past life associated with her previous family living in this home, including her previous name and that she had two sons. The little girl also provided precise details of the home, including its location relative to other landmarks in the area and numerous details regarding the interior. The little girl said she had died after experiencing a pain in her throat.

Some years later, news of this case reached a local professor, who was a paranormal researcher. He subsequently interviewed the girl's "previous" family at great length, and they confirmed every single detail provided by the little girl, including that she had died very suddenly leaving behind a grieving husband and two young sons. The two families lived one hundred miles apart and had certainly never heard of each other previously.

Sometime later, members of the girl's previous family journeyed to the town where she now lived in order to test her memory. The girl immediately recognized her former brother and called him by his pet name. She then went around the room and identified the men she knew from the town in her previous life. She then came to the man who had been her husband in her previous life. She lowered her eyes and looked bashful in the tradition of the religion they had shared. Then, she spoke his name. She went on to correctly identify her son from her past life, despite numerous efforts by the boy to mislead her.

The girl later visited the home of her previous life and provided numerous little known details about her home, her previous family and her life. Many of these details would have been impossible to know unless she was actually who she claimed to be in her previous life.

The two families became very close, and the previous family of the little girl accepted her as part of their own family just as she had been in the previous life of not too many years before.

Reincarnation Case 2.

This Dr. Stevenson case involves a young two and a half year old boy who suddenly began to talk to his parents about his "other life". He said he had been the owner of an electrical appliance shop that sold TV's and radios. He knew his previous name, as well as the names of his wife and two children. He was able to recall the end of his previous life in great detail, specifically how he had been shot, cremated and his ashes thrown into the river. Note that this is in accordance with what we discussed previously about how a "deceased" person can remain in their Etheric body close to the physical world for quite some time until the supply of Etheric Energy is exhausted. This provides the deceased person with the opportunity to visit loved ones and friends, as well as observe the destiny of their physical body. Acts of love and remembrance do not go unnoticed by the deceased person and are very much appreciated.

The boy's parents did not take him seriously at first, but his behaviour puzzled them, and he often behaved as if he was not part of his current family at all. He would tell his parents that he was homesick and wanted to go back to his home. He became so insistent about this that he even rolled up his clothes and threatened to leave home.

The elder brother of the boy decided to check out his brother's claims for himself. He travelled to the town named by his younger brother and soon found a radio shop that was managed by widow whose husband had been shot some years previously. The lady was understandably curious and decided to meet the family of the boy to investigate it further. When she arrived, the boy shouted to his parents that his "other family" had arrived. When both families were together for this most unusual meeting, the boy stunned the widow (his wife in his previous life) by recounting full details of a family outing to a fair in a neighbouring village where he had bought some sweets. This was an occasion that only the widow and her husband would have known about. The boy also amazed his wife from his previous life by accurately describing where he had buried some gold in a hole in the home.

Later, it was arranged for the boy to travel to the town where his former wife lived. As a test, the widow arranged for her sons, previously the sons of the boy, to be playing in the neighbourhood with many other children of the same age. Upon his arrival, the boy was immediately able to pick out his former sons from the crowd of children. He also recognized the changes that had been made to his former shop after his death.

The boy recalled the full circumstances of his "death", how he had been shot in the head while sitting in his car after arriving home from work. The autopsy report, which was filmed, confirmed he had been shot in the head and had died as a result of a bullet wound to the temple. The autopsy showed the exact size and location of the entry wound and also of the exit wound on the opposite side of the man's head. It was later decided to shave off some of the boy's hair around the region of the fatal wound inflicted in his previous life. The boy had a birthmark at the same location as the bullet entry point of exactly the same size and shape as the bullet that killed him in his previous life. He also had a second birthmark on the opposite side of his head corresponding to the exit point of the same bullet.

This case later attracted so much interest that it was presented in court to conclusively prove that the boy was the reincarnated former husband of the widow. As a result of this case, a professor at a major University was quoted as saying that due to the police involvement, "this is one of the best documented cases of reincarnation he had ever seen".

Reincarnation Case 3.

This is a case from the portfolio of Peter Ramster, a psychologist and past life regression expert from Sydney, Australia. In 1983, he produced a television documentary in which four women from Sydney that had never before left Australia gave details under hypnosis of their past lives. Then, complete with television crews and equipment, they were taken to the other side of the world.

One of the subjects, until then a staunch sceptic, was a lady by the name of Gwen McDonald. She remembered a life in Somerset, England that would be impossible to obtain from a book, but which was subsequently confirmed in front of witnesses when she was taken there.

She was blindfolded and taken to a particular place in Somerset, after which she was able to find her way around perfectly and correctly point out the location of three villages she had known in her former life. She was able to direct the film crew to various destinations far more accurately than the maps they had with them. She knew the location of a waterfall and the place where stepping stones had previously been located. The locals confirmed that the stepping stones had been removed about forty years before. She pointed out an intersection where she claimed there had been five houses, and inquiries proved this was accurate. The houses had been demolished some thirty years before.

She knew the names of the villages as they had been two hundred years ago, even though the names do not appear on modern maps. People she claimed to have known were proved to have existed, one of whom was listed in the names of the regiment to which she apparently belonged. She knew many local legends, all of which were confirmed by Somerset historians. She correctly used obscure West Country words that were no longer in use and did not even appear in dictionaries.

In Sydney, she had described carvings that had been in an obscure old house twenty feet from a stream in the middle of five houses located about one and a half miles from Glastonbury Abbey. She knew the local people called Glastonbury Abbey "St. Michael's", a fact only proven by reading an obscure two hundred year old history book not available in Australia. She was able to draw (while still in Sydney) the interior of her Glastonbury house, which was subsequently proven to be completely correct. She described an inn on the way to her house that was found to exist and was able to lead the team directly to the house, now a chicken shed. After cleaning the floor, they discovered the stone carvings she had referred to in Sydney. The locals came every night to quiz her on local history, and she knew the answers to all of the questions asked including a problem with a big bog where cattle were lost.

These are just a few of the numerous cases proving reincarnation which have been documented by Dr. Stevenson, Peter Ramster and other dedicated researchers based upon cases gathered from all over the world. There are possibly many millions of such cases of past life recollection which have simply never been documented. In most of these cases, the parents of the child simply ascribe the child's claims to fantasy or the product of an overactive imagination. There might be other situations where the parents take the child seriously but prefer to keep the recollections to themselves for fear of being ridiculed by others.

We can justifiably say that not only can reincarnation be proven to be very real, but it is an integral aspect of the evolution of the Higher Self of human Beings as a necessary aspect of the ongoing journey of perfection back to our Creator from Whence we came in the beginning. Graduation of the Higher Self from "lives", which, as discussed at the beginning of this chapter are not really "past lives" at all but rather concurrent Higher Self experiences, in the physical Universe, can then finally take place. From the kindergarten environment of the planet Earth the Higher Self can progress to further education, experience and progress as a powerful co-creator within the inner realms of the Universe and of life and reality, within the great worlds of Spirit, leading onwards and inwards to the Celestial and Cosmic spheres, and eventually the return in a state of perfection to our Divine Creator, The First Cause, to God from Whence we first came in the beginning.

Chapter 32
Suicide

Suicide is without doubt one of the most tragic situations, not only for the shocked and bereaved love ones left behind, but also for the person who took his or her own physical life. When a person takes their own life, contrary to what they might believe at the time, they do not escape from anything at all except the physical world, and any chance of resolving the problems from which they sought refuge are lost. The issues that caused the person to terminate their physical life in all of their original magnitude are brought to the Astral worlds where they still have to be fully faced and reconciled. Sometimes, as discussed previously, sometimes a person who has terminated their physical life is so shocked to find they are still very much "alive" but in a non-physical body, and with all of their "problems" still with them, that they remain close to the physical world and become what is known as a "ghost".

Bereaved friends and relatives are left agonizing and confused as to why their loved one felt so compelled to undertake this seemingly final act. Frequently, they will feel guilt, believing they might have been able to "do something" to prevent the tragic situation if only they had been more diligent about watching out for and recognising the "signs".

However, Souls who takes their own life do so of their own freewill regardless of the circumstances prevailing at the time. Often, the focus of the deceased person might well have been on suicide for quite some time. When a person focuses sufficiently on something, the focus will be impressed upon the Subconscious Mind of the person, and will sooner or later inevitably manifest as a reality unless it is changed. Tragic though these situations are, there is little friends, relatives or anyone else could have done to prevent it.

The reasons for suicide are many and varied. Suicide rates have been increasing over the last few decades due to the perceived and increasing pressures of life and the current state of the world humanity in general. Only when mankind fully understands the true meaning and purpose of each life on Earth and the true destiny of all mankind can these events cease.

When a person takes their own life, it is extremely important for family and friends to realize that, understandable though it is, grief and emotions can have a profound and detrimental effect on the transition of the Soul of the deceased person to the Astral worlds, the afterlife, and new home. The greater the grief and emotion projected by those left behind, the more difficult it will be for the Soul to fully transition to their new home. The Soul of the person who has "passed on" will receive the full effect of these emotions and will know exactly what family and friends are thinking and experiencing. Although entirely understandable, these emotions will weigh heavily on the Soul of the deceased person, often bringing about intense emotions of guilt and regret. This will sometimes cause the Soul to remain very close to the physical world effectively as a "ghost", rather than transitioning to the Astral worlds where they can rest in peace and harmony, and receive assistance in their transition from the Astral residents, some of whom specialise in assisting people to make the transition from the physical to the non-physical life.

Even when the Soul does successfully transition to the Astral world, strong emotions emanating from the people left behind can be felt in a very intense and direct way, often making the transition difficult. Bereaved family and friends should always endeavour to send the most positive feelings possible of understanding, compassion and pure Unconditional Love to their deceased loved one, knowing that they are actually "alive", safe and happy in their new home.

The need for stability is particularly important for the newly deceased person in the case of suicide. They believe they will escape the physical world forever, including all of the trials, tribulations and what they perceived as misery. In accordance with the religion or "belief system" of the person, they will anticipate either a complete escape into oblivion, thereby ending everything, or might believe that, they go to "Heaven" for all eternity, escaping the trials of the physical world.

The reality, however, is very different. As we have already discussed, memory is not a function of the organic brain. Memories of all physical lives past, present and future are eternally stored within the Higher Self of the person, the Higher Self being the total experience of all physical lives. When transitioning to the Astral world, there will be a full and vivid memory of every aspect of the previous life, memories that will be much more vivid than they were while still inhabiting the physical body, due to the fact there is no longer a physical, organic brain to filter these memories which are now experienced directly within the Mind connection with the Higher Self. People in the Astral worlds have a full understanding of the meaning and purpose of the physical life recently left behind and can review the experiences and lessons learned or otherwise. This knowledge is absolutely necessary to begin the process of understanding the significance of the previous life, and thereby to reconcile the lessons learned or not learned, experience gained, and Spiritual progress made.

As we will discuss later in this book, there will always be the Higher Self of a person who, having completed their "kindergarten education" with their final incarnation will never need to send another representative to Earth again. This might not however apply to those who took their own lives if their "mission" on Earth was not fully completed. The only solution for the Higher Self of such people is to send another representative to Earth once again in order to complete the mission necessary for their overall ongoing evolution.

The newly transitioned Soul who took his or her own life before their mission was completed will be fully aware of this, and the fact that they have now lost a valuable opportunity to resolve the very problems that caused them to make the decision to "call it a day" on Earth. There is absolutely no escaping these lessons and responsibilities. The Soul who took his or her own life will often feel deep regret for the valuable opportunities missed, the lessons they failed to learn, and the karma they failed to balance. As one Soul who recently arrived in the Astral world having took his own life said to a person who was visiting by Astral Projection:

"I now realize that I suicided because there were things I couldn't deal with, emotional things, things between myself and others. I was in so much pain. That pain didn't go away after I killed myself, and I now realize that the one thing I need to resolve the pain is hanging from the rafters in the garage".

The person quoted above now knows only after it is much too late that there is nothing that can be done to correct this situation from his new home in the Astral world, and the only solution is to face and reconcile all perceived difficulties in the physical life within the physical body.

The person will however eventually transition back to their Higher Self, with their often incomplete package of experience, which will go towards the completeness of their Higher Self. Ultimately no physical life is wasted, each bringing to the Higher Self its own unique experiences and knowledge, which will go towards the whole.

Above all, although temporarily separated by physical death, it is very important to know beyond doubt that there is no separation between people in the physical world and people in the inner worlds, but merely different states of being at differing vibrations and density. One day, everyone will be reunited in Love once again in the inner spheres.

Chapter 33
The Etheric Body

In addition to the physical body, there are also a number of much more "subtle" bodies existing at much higher levels of vibration which usually cannot be perceived by the five physical senses. It should be noted however that these are not "bodies" in the physical sense, or are they separate from each other. They are rather all aspects of a continuum of Energy and Consciousness, infinite in nature, existing multi-dimensionally beyond the limitations of space and time. When we speak of a "body" therefore we are actually referring to the point along our continuum of Consciousness in which we are focussed at that stage in our evolution, in accordance with our state of perfection. Each point of focus is characterised by a configuration of Energy with a unique vibration and density, which may be considered in this context to be a "body".

The Etheric body also known as the "Energy body" is the densest of the inner, subtle bodies, and as we have already discussed, it is often the main body inhabited immediately after physical death. The Etheric body is a highly complex bio-energetic system including seven main energetic centres often known as the "chakras".

During physical life, the Etheric body effectively acts as a "transformer" or "interface" between the physical body and the inner Astral and Mental bodies, specifically as a "step-up" or "step down" transformer" to mediate between the low vibration of the physical body and higher vibration of the Astral body.

The Energy body is vital for almost every aspect of the health and well-being of the physical body, most physical illnesses manifesting as physical ailments or diseases originate from imbalances within the Etheric body, in turn caused by the conscious Mind of the afflicted person impressing imbalances upon the Subconscious Mind for example through fears, worry, stress, imagined conditions and obsessive thinking.

As already mentioned, healing methods which focus on the Energy body have often proved to be extremely effective, bringing about cures considered by most to seem "miraculous". There have been many cases of cancers cured in this way even though they were deemed by doctors to be "incurable". Ultimately however the basis of all healing is through the power of the Subconscious Mind of the person being healed, Mind always being Principle.

The Chakras: Within the Energy body is a series energetic centres often known as the "chakras". The word "chakra" is Sanskrit for "wheel" or "disk", signifying any one of the seven main Energy centres located within the Energy body. Each of these Energy centres also corresponds directly to a major physical nerve ganglia, or gland, connected to the spinal column. The chakras also correspond to the many levels of Consciousness, Spiritual connection, developmental stages of life, colours, sounds, body functions, and much more.

The Energy body, the chakras, the aura, and all functions associated with these aspects of the Energy body could be the subject of an entire book. Nevertheless, here is a brief summary of the seven major chakras.

The Crown Chakra: This chakra is located around the crown of the head and relates to Consciousness as pure awareness. The Crown chakra is our Divine connection to the inner realms of reality, to a timeless, space-less place of all-knowing. When well-developed, this chakra brings us knowledge, wisdom, understanding, Spiritual connection, and bliss.

The Brow Chakra: This chakra is located directly between the eyebrows and is often known as the "third eye". It is associated with the ability of "seeing", both psychically and intuitively, and it is closely associated with "Clairvoyance" or "clear seeing". A clairvoyant can perceive within the "Mind's eye" inner realms of reality beyond the physical world, particularly the Astral worlds, and can also perceive things in the physical world beyond the reach of the normal five physical senses.

Thousands of years ago, everyone possessed a highly developed brow chakra which enabled them to maintain full contact with the inner realms of life and reality by means of Clairvoyance. However, as mankind has become increasingly focused upon the material world, the perception of the brow chakra has steadily diminished to the point where it is largely unused today in most people. It is, however, quite possible to re-develop the brow chakra to the level of Clairvoyance and related abilities, as we will discuss later.

The Throat Chakra: This chakra is located in the region of the throat and is related to communication and creativity. By means of the throat chakra, the world is experienced symbolically through vibration, such as sound representing language. It is also, therefore, the chakra involved in "listening" to the inner realms through the more subtle vibration of communications.

The Heart Chakra: This is the middle-most of the major chakras and the lowest part of the upper triangle of the chakras (crown, brow, and heart), which are associated with the inner realms. The heart chakra is related to Love and also integrates opposites within the psyche, such as the Mind and body, male and female, persona and shadow, Ego and unity. A healthy heart chakra allows people to love deeply and unconditionally, feel compassion, and enjoy a deep sense of peace, contentment and centeredness.

The heart has always been a symbol of love in most cultures. The emotions that people associate with the physical heart actually originate from the heart chakra of the Energy body.

The Solar Plexus Chakra: This chakra, often known as the "power chakra", is located in the solar plexus area or navel. It rules personal power, will and autonomy, as well as metabolism. When healthy, the solar plexus chakra brings Energy, effectiveness, spontaneity and non-dominating power. The solar plexus chakra is also directly associated with the Subconscious Mind through which it is connected with the higher bodies and with the Ether, known as the Akasha in far Eastern cultures. Through the Solar Plexus chakra and the Subconscious Mind we receive to our conscious Mind intuition and other communication from the inner Spirit worlds and Higher Self. Many people will recall occasions when they have thought about something and instantly received a strange feeling in the area of the lower stomach. People often refer to such experiences as a "gut feeling" or a "sinking feeling" in the stomach. This is a communication from the inner realms or the Higher Self, and is often a confirmation or warning about a thought within the Mind. It can be a positive "gut feeling" or a negative "gut feeling". It is certainly advisable to heed such feelings and to take any appropriate actions without delay.

The Sacral Chakra: This chakra is located around the region of the groin and is related to the water element, as well as to emotions and sexuality. It connects people to others through feelings, desires and sensations. Ideally, this chakra brings fluidity and grace, depth of feeling, sexual fulfilment and the ability to accept change.

The Root Chakra: This chakra is located at the base of the spine. It represents the Earth element and is related to survival instincts, as well as the connection to the physical world. Ideally, this chakra brings good health, prosperity, security and dynamic presence.

The Aura: This is the Energy field produced by the Energy body and can be observed by people who have the ability of "auric sight" or Clairvoyance.

Auric Energy fields are highly complex and very fluid. They are influenced not only by health and vitality, but also by mood. As moods change, the appearance of the aura changes. The aura is also an indicator of Spiritual attainment. People who are highly spiritually evolved will be recognizable by a vivid, clean, dynamic aura with an intense bright golden yellow area extending from and around the crown of the head. Sometimes, the aura is so intense that it can be viewed by people who do not usually possess auric vision. It is also this intense golden aura around the head of a highly Spiritual person that sometimes gives rise to the depiction of a so-called "halo", as is often depicted around the head of Jesus or a saint.

As discussed previously, after the physical body "dies", the deceased person will usually, but not always, find themselves in focussed within their Etheric body. Later, after the Etheric body has exhausted its supply of Etheric Energy, the primary body will be the much finer Astral body, which also includes the integral Spirit body. Once a person has satiated his or her own desires within the Astral words, the Astral body "fades", giving way to the Mental body, which will continue the journey to the Higher Self, the aspect of the human made in the true image of "God".

Chapter 34
The Astral Body - The Soul

After a person has spent some time, often days or sometimes even hours focussed within their Etheric body, living close to the physical world, they will usually proceed to make the full transition to the Astral planes, often known as the Astral "planes", "spheres" or "realms". To reside in the Astral planes, it is necessary to be focussed within an Astral body of exactly the same level and degree of vibration and density as the corresponding level of the Astral realms. The Astral body is also known as the Soul or the "desire body", due to its interaction with the Astral worlds, often known as the "desire worlds", where, having left Earth after the change known as "death", people continue to pursue their material desires.

When a person first arrives in the Astral planes, they still think and express themselves in exactly the same way as they did while living on Earth. They will, for example, still think in terms of food, houses, cars, physical appearance, recreation, etc. These Earthly, material desires are largely driven by the Ego and materialistic thought and a lack of understanding of true purpose and ultimate destiny. This is also the very reason that the mid-Astral planes are so similar in appearance to the physical world. They are created by the minds of humans based upon physical life experiences, believing the physical work to be reality. Humans in both physical and Astral create the things they believe they need, desire and feel most comfortable with.

This is the main reason why the Astral body is known as the "desire body", the body with which all mundane Earthly desires are fulfilled. It is not possible to progress to the true Spirit worlds or to evolve further along the Path until all material desires have been completely purged and seen as the illusions they truly are. This process of realization might take a very short time as measured in Earth time, or it might take hundreds or even thousands of years depending on the person.

Many people believe that upon passing from the physical world, the Astral world is their true home or even "Heaven". Eventually, however, everyone must realize that, like the physical world, the Astral worlds, created by the minds of people after their perception of reality based upon the physical world, exist at the lowest Energy levels of the Universe and are simply another aspect of the ongoing learning process. As previously mentioned, the "Heaven" of the Astral worlds is based entirely upon the human concept of "Heaven", which is, in turn often based upon material things or religious teachings.

If the physical world is first year kindergarten, the Astral worlds are second year kindergarten, still a very long way from achieving graduation from university with full honours. The true "Heaven worlds" are the Spiritual worlds of the Mental, Celestial and Cosmic planes, not the Astral planes. The Astral planes exist as a transition zone created by the minds of humans and other Beings, between the physical world and the realms of Spirit, and, like the physical world, will eventually no longer be needed at which point will dissipate back in undifferentiated Energy.

Every person has a unique Astral body comprised of Energy. The balance of the elements, a person's character, Ego, temperament, beliefs and many other individual factors will be reflected in the composition of the Astral body and its unique Energy signature. Just as the bonding "fluid" between the Astral body and the physical body is the Astral matrix, the Immortal Spirit is connected to the Astral body by means of the Mental matrix. It is through the Mental matrix that all communication and thoughts are ultimately received from the inner planes of life.

Human Beings are endowed with five physical senses corresponding to the four Universal elements of Fire, Air,

Water, and Earth, as well as the Akasha or the Quintessence of the four elements. These elements are not the same as the fire of flames or air as wind. They are rather the symbolic Universal attributes analogous to the physical elements. These five senses are mediated through the Astral body. While still living in the physical world, the Astral body receives sensory feedback directly from the corporeal senses of the physical body by the mediation of the Astral matrix. Ultimately, the seat of the senses with which we experience reality is the Mental Body, which receives sensory feedback from the Astral body through the Mental matrix.

The unique characteristics of the Astral body are determined by the Energy constitution and vibration of the Electric and Magnetic fluids, as well as the elements within the Energy field constituting the Astral body. Again, the Electric and Magnetic fluids are not fluids in physical terms in the same way as water for example, but rather characteristics of Energy. The character of a person is, therefore, in accordance with the balance of the Electric and Magnetic fluids and the balance of the elements which in turn influences the vibration of that person.

The characteristics attributable to each of the elements comprising the Astral body manifests in the physical body as the corresponding attributes of a personality as follows:

Fire Element: This element is responsible for the choleric temperament, manifesting itself in the positive or active polarity as activity, enthusiasm, eagerness, determination, bravery, courage and creativity. The Fire Element of Energy can also include manifestations of negative characteristics such as voracity, jealousy, passion, irritability, argumentativeness, lack of moderation and many others.

Air Element: This element is responsible for the sanguine temperament. The positive or active aspect of Air gives rise to diligence, joy, kindness, lucidity, freedom from worry, cheerfulness, light heartedness, optimism, liveliness, independence, watchfulness, trustworthiness, etc. The negative aspect of Air includes such characteristics as disdain, gossip, lack of resilience, cunning, dishonesty, and fickleness.

The Water Element: This element gives rise to the melancholic temperament. The positive, active character attributes of Water include respectfulness, mercy, modesty, humility, seriousness, fervour, intimacy, comprehension, meditation, compassion, tranquillity, forgiveness, tenderness, and others. The Water element can also manifest itself within the Soul with negative attributes, including indifference, shyness, lack of interest, idleness and more.

The Earth Element: This element is responsible for the phlegmatic temperament in human Beings. In its positive, active manifestations, Earth gives rise to respect, endurance, circumspection, determination, seriousness, firmness, conscientiousness, thoroughness, punctuality, reserve, sense of responsibility, caution, and sense of purpose. The negative manifestations attributable to the Earth element include shallowness, carelessness, disdain, indifference, lack of responsibility, bashfulness, tardiness, ponderousness, idleness, and lack of reliability.

The basic overall attributes, temperament and character of a person while living in both the physical and Astral planes will be determined by the balance of the elements and the actions of the Electric and Magnetic fluids within the Astral body or Soul, in turn under the complete influence of Mind which is Principle. The Soul is the seat of the character and dominates it while living both in the Astral and physical worlds. This is one reason why the general population has so many varied characters and temperaments until they learn to subjugate the Ego and balance the elements and fluids. This is an ongoing process of the ennoblement of the Soul and is vital for the ongoing evolution of every person.

Chapter 35
The Mental Body - The Immortal Spirit

The Mental Body or Immortal Spirit is that aspect of a human being "made in the image of God". The physical Etheric and Astral bodies are only the transient outer garments for the Spirit body. Like the Astral body, the Mental Body is also directly under the influence of the four elements that descended in the beginning from the Ether, the Akasha.

The element of Fire is the fiery aspect of the Spirit and is responsible for will. The element of Air is responsible for intellect. The Water element manifests in the human being as life and feelings. The Earth element is represented by the unification of Fire, Air and Water and is responsible for the individual "I" Consciousness of the human being.

The highest aspect of the immortal "I", the Ether or "Akasha" Principle, manifests in humans as belief in its highest aspect and the instinct for self-preservation in its lowest aspect. The four Universal elements and the Akasha Principle together constitute the "I", the individuality, the immortal Spirit "made in the true image of God". In terms of the elements, we can also expand their influences within the Immortal Spirit to include the following attributes.

Fire is the Energy responsible for Energy, might and passion. Air is responsible for memory and the power to judge and differentiate. Water is responsible for conscience and intuition. Earth is responsible for Egotism and the instincts for self-preservation and propagation.

Just as the Astral body forms its link, the Astral Matrix, with the physical body through the electromagnetic fluids of the Astral planes (the Astral "Od"), the Mental Body is linked to the Astral body through the Mental matrix formed out of the electromagnetic fluids of the Mental planes (the Mental "Od").

The Mental matrix is the most subtle form of the Ether, which regulates and maintains the activities of the Spirit within the Astral body. It is the electromagnetic properties of the Mental matrix that are responsible for the transmission of thoughts and Consciousness to the Immortal Spirit from the Mental planes.

The Mental planes are the spheres and origins of thoughts and ideas. A thought begins as an idea in the Mental planes and develops into a "Thought Form". This Thought Form is conveyed first through the Mental matrix and then through the Astral matrix, where it is received by the Subconscious Mind and then the conscious Mind as a thought appearing to originate in the Mind of the person as their own "idea". Contrary to the perspective of most sciences, all thoughts and ideas originate in the highest aspects of the Mental planes and not from within the organic brain, which simply serves as an organic interface between the body and true Mind, and is incapable of originating thought processes. Likewise, as previously mentioned, long-term memories are "stored" in the causal Mental body, the aspect of the Immortal Spirit having its existence within the causal sphere of the Universe.

The organic brain is not the seat of Consciousness, but, as previously mentioned, is rather a mediator, interface or filter between the conscious and Subconscious Minds and therefore the inner bodies and the physical body. This is why Astral and Mental projection is possible, as we will discuss later, both being an inwards projection of Consciousness into our own Subconscious Mind. The organic brain of a physical human being is not the originator of thought, and the organic brain is accordingly not the Mind.

Humans can be likened to a "receiving station", and all thoughts coming from the world of ideas of the Mental planes through the Mental matrix, the Astral matrix and, finally, the organic brain. Everything in existence that humans believe to be a result of their own intelligence or ingenuity has actually been taken from the world of ideas of the Mental planes where they already exist, have always existed and will always exist beyond space and time within the infinite "Eternal Now", and are received first by the Subconscious Mind in response to the conscious Mind.

The ability and likelihood of receiving any particular thought from the world of ideas of the Mental planes will always be in accordance with the circumstances in which a person exists within the physical world. For example, a scientist, due to conscious thought, will attract scientific types of thoughts and ideas, a technologist will receive technical thoughts and ideas, an artist will receive artistic thoughts and ideas, and so on.

These examples all illustrate one of the most fundamental laws in the Universe, The Law of Attraction, with similar vibrations, in the form of thought, will be attracted. So a particular thought originating from the Subconscious Mind of a person will attract a corresponding idea of a similar vibration, just as a Thought Form for a specific wish, need or desire will always result in a corresponding manifestation along the same frequency of vibration into the experience of the person consciously originating the thought. Everything in the Universe is Mind, which is Principle, of which thought, imagination, vibration and attraction, with Energy being the Universal medium in which everything "lives and moves and has its being".

Each abstract thought is composed of a particular pure element—fiery thoughts, airy thoughts, watery thoughts and Earthy thoughts. A thought can also contain a combination of one or more elements, and such thoughts can be predominantly electric, magnetic or electromagnetic.

All thoughts, like everything else in the Universe in all spheres, are ultimately pure Energy. It is this Energy that gives each thought its own unique characteristics. Within the inner realms of life, where Energy vibrates at a much higher rate and the density of the Akasha is much finer and more subtle, thoughts can be seen to take shape as they are created by the Mind.

It is the Immortal Spirit alone, in the form of the Higher Self, after having freed itself from the cycle of incarnation and therefore the materialism and Egotism of the physical world and the desires of the Astral worlds, that continues the onward ascent, the inner journey, along the sacred path back to our Divine Creator, The Source, God.

Having transcended the cycles of reincarnation, the Immortal Spirit that was represented by the Higher Self continues the journey ever inwards towards The Source, The First Cause, God, through the outer and then mid and inner Mental planes, through the Celestial planes and on to the Cosmic planes, where the ultimate and most sacred opportunity can be finally realized—unity with our Creator, God in state of perfection.

Chapter 36
The Higher Self

The Higher Self is who we truly Are beyond our individual incarnations on Earth, and can be thought of as an aspect of the immortal “I”. The Higher Self is sublime, and as the sum of all of our physical lives and experiences, past present and future (relative to the Earth concept of time), it is therefore infinitely wise. Full access to the Higher Self by individual physical incarnations of the Higher Self is most sought after by those consciously on the path. It is the Higher Self that progresses on to “greater” things once all physical lives have been completed.

It should be noted from the outset that the term “Higher Self” should more correctly be “Inner Self”. However, as the term “Higher Self” has been so widely used and understood, we will continue with its use in this book. It is very important to keep in mind that the physical world and our physical bodies are the outermost aspect of the Universe existing at the lowest rate of Energy vibration, and the highest density, and God, The Source, The First Cause is at the very centre of all creation, existing at the very highest Energy vibration, encompassing the highest vibration of all, that of Unconditional Love. After the cycle of physical incarnation has been completed, we continue the journey inward towards God as our “Higher Self”, as an individual Spiritual Being, the sum of all physical lives, and onward experiences gathered on the quest and journey of perfection and ultimate destiny of the potential to reunite with The Source, God, The First Cause, from Whence we first came.

The Higher Self can provide intuition towards assisting in circumstances where clarification or guidance are needed. The Higher Self provides the highest level of connectedness with The Source and influence within the Universe in all spheres and learning how to consciously communicate with the Higher Self through the Subconscious Mind is a very valuable ability.

Chapter 37
The Physical Universe of Matter

When most people think about “the Universe”, they often think in terms of the observable physical Universe of planets, stars, solar systems, galaxies and other celestial bodies as studied by astronomers, astrophysicists, cosmologists and others. This is the Universe that can be perceived by the five physical senses, and through observational equipment such as telescopes, and other scientific equipment. Science even today tends to make the assumption that if something is not physically measurable by scientific equipment or the five physical senses, it simply does not exist at all, and therefore “out of sight and out of mind”.

In fact, the physical Universe of matter represents only a very small percentage of the entire, greater Universe as a whole. The majority of the Universe exists at levels of Energy and vibration far, far, far beyond the measurement capability of current scientific instruments.

An excellent metaphor for the Universe is an apple. If we cut an apple in half we see the skin, which represents the physical Universe of matter, the flesh, which is the greater Universe of Energy including the Etheric, Astral and Mental realms, and finally the core, The Source, The First Cause, God. We are focused within the skin of the apple at the level of vibration in which we are currently focused.

Upon passing on from the physical world at the time of the transition known as “death”, a person is in reality transitioning from the high density, low vibration environment of the physical word, the skin of the apple, to a much finer level of existence at a much higher vibration and lower density than the physical world of matter within the flesh of the apple.

Upon arrival within the Astral planes subsequent to the transition from the physical world, people find vast, dynamic worlds populated by billions of Souls, worlds which not only seem at least as "solid" and "real" as the physical world, but actually much more so. Matter, by comparison with Energy that has not differentiated into matter, is very crude due to its much higher density and much lower vibration. Throughout the Universe, everything is perceived and experienced relative to Energy and vibration. We perceive, experience and progress relative to the Energy level or "plane" of the Universe of Energy at which we are focused and at which our Astral or Mental Body vibrates.

The level of the Astral worlds to which a person will transition after death will always vibrate at the same level of Energy as that of the Astral body. In fact, as previously mentioned, due to the much finer levels of Energy of the Astral worlds and without the physical, dense characteristics of matter, everything seems so "solid" and so "real" that many people initially do not at first, even realize they have left the physical world of matter. This is particularly true when the transition to the Astral has been particularly sudden or has taken place during sleep, where, upon awakening, everything still at first seems "normal". So, everything in the entire Universe is experienced in absolute harmony with the relative level of Energy and vibration at which it exists in accordance with the perfect and immutable order within the Universal Mind of God.

The Universe in its entirety may be considered to be spherical like a planet, with God, The First Cause, The Source at the center, existing at the highest vibration and lowest density, progressing outward though progressively higher density and lower levels of Energy and vibration until finally reaching the physical world of matter forming the "skin" of the Universe.

Another metaphor that may be applied to the Universe is that of a balloon. Consider a balloon consisting of a rubber skin filled with air, the rubber skin representing the physical world of matter. Scientists have recently noticed that the physical Universe is still expanding very rapidly, but are at a loss to understand why. The reason is fundamental to all life and the existence of the Universe. In the beginning God, The Source, The First Cause sent forth from the Logos powerful Thought Forms, thus creating the Universe and everything in it as recognize it today. Through these living, Spiritual creations, for example human Beings, God, The Source experiences, and thereby expands. This expansion is therefore from within. As the Universe and everything in creation is in a constant state of experiencing, the Universe is in a constant state of expanding from within, but in an outwards direction. We can simulate this by blowing up the balloon. If we draw circles on the surface of the balloon with a black marker pen, the circles representing galaxies, and then inflate the balloon further, representing the expansion of The Source through experience, we will note that the black circles representing the galaxies will move away from each other, which in fact is precisely what science is observing. So the Universe is expanding from within by experience, thereby causing the outer physical skin of the Universe, to expand.

It should also be mentioned that the so called "big bang" of science did not originate from a point on the physical Universe, it in fact originated at The Source, the core, the very center, at the very highest vibration, starting, as all creation starts as a Thought Form, and progresses outwards, the vibration of Energy slowing as it progresses until finally it "freezes", forms subatomic, atomic and molecular building blocks, finally differentiating into matter to create the physical Universe of matter as observed and measured by science. Energy can be considered to be "light"—not physically observable light in the form of photons, but the Divine Light of The Source, Energy, also known simply as "Spirit".

Scientists cannot understand why, if the "big bang" originated from a point in the physical Universe, temperatures throughout the Universe are very similar. In reality of course the "big bang" originated from within, originating from the highest Energy level of The Source and expanded outwards, creating the entire physical Universe uniformly in the same moment, and not from any single physical point in the Universe.

The physical Universe is spherical and, therefore, has no beginning or end. It would be entirely erroneous to think in terms of "the end of the Universe". As with travel on Earth, if we were able to travel in a straight line within the physical Universe, we would eventually arrive back at exactly the same point at which we started. So, notions of "traveling to the ends of the Universe" are as erroneous as seeking a specific, physical place in the physical Universe where all creation started with the "big bang", or of the "flat Earth" of the scientists of a few hundred years ago.

Due to the holographic nature of the Universe as a whole, the physically observable Universe is only one of a potentially infinite number of "parallel" Universes, both physical and non-physical, all existing concurrently. This is possible due to the fact that everything in the Universe is ultimately pure vibrating Energy, and such concepts as "dimensions" do not really exist except to the limited perception of the human senses, while restricted to the three dimensional physical Universe of matter.

Parallel Universes exist at all levels of the Energy spectrum, not just the lowest aspect where Energy differentiates into physical matter. Science even now is beginning to realize the possibility of these parallel physical and non-physical Universes when such "phenomena" as "black holes" were discovered, with "worm holes" being thought of as portals to these alternative physical Universes, and balancing points between physical matter and "anti-matter".

The entire Universe, including the physical Universe, is maintained in a state of perfect harmony by The First Cause,

The Source, God. In the context of the physical Universe, the same balance needs to exist in order to maintain perpetual harmony. Physical Universes are balanced by the opposite characteristics of matter and antimatter which are configurations of Energy at similar levels of vibration and density but with opposite sub-atomic characteristics, for example whereas an atom in this alternative physical Universe contains anti-electrons, or positrons, and antiprotons. Ultimately, as with all aspects of the infinitely perfect Universe, these opposing characteristics conform to the Universal Principle of polarity, one of the Principles that ensures perpetual harmony on a Universal scale.

"Wormholes", are conceptual gateways between the physical Universes of matter and anti-matter. Traveling through a wormhole would result in the arrival within a parallel Universe of anti-matter, and traveling through a further wormhole would result in arriving at a further parallel Universe of matter.

The word "dimension" is also erroneous, only having meaning relative to the concepts of "space" and "time", which we know are illusions perpetuated only by the five physical senses. Ultimately, everything in the Universe without exception is pure Energy differing only in rate of vibration, and infinite manifestations of that Energy in the form of Quanta which have quantum potential, influenced by Mind which as we know is Principle cause. Ultimately, everything within the Universe from The Source, The First Cause, God to the physical world of matter is an inseparable aspect of everything else, all being conscious, intelligent, vibrating Energy within the Universal Mind of The First Cause, The Source, God.

Governments of the world are currently spending vast amounts of money on exploration of a tiny fraction of the physical Universe at a time when millions of people in the world are suffering from disease, famine, war and other situations. In fact, the destiny of every human being is not to travel within the restrictions of the three-dimensional Universe of matter, but to travel inwards through the glories of the greater Universe on the sacred path back to God. It is the ultimate destiny of everything in the Universe, without exception, including every human being, to evolve back to The First Cause, The Source, God in a state of perfection—this is the true meaning of life.

True exploration is not about the temporal, observable, physical Universe of matter, but rather about the magnificence, splendors and glories, far beyond the current comprehension of mortal, Earthly human Beings, of the Infinite Universe of Energy, Mind and Consciousness. Beyond the restrictions of the physical body, the entire physical Universe can be explored at will, instantly, traveling quite literally at the speed of thought. People who Astral project or engage in Out of Body Experiences can and do travel anywhere on Earth in an instant, or to the moon, including the far side of the moon, other planets, solar systems and even galaxies. Most importantly, they can travel inwards to the inner Energy levels and vibrations of the Astral worlds. Those who learn the ability of Mental projection, can travel even further inwards to the great Mental planes of life and reality, even meeting some of the powerful Intelligences residing there, Beings who watch over the evolution of human Beings and life on Earth, as well as Gaia Herself. Beyond the physical constraints of the physical body, a person is a true explorer of the Universe, and it does not cost a penny or require any external vehicle of travel.

While mankind continues to focus exclusively upon the physical Universe as the only reality, no true progress can be made. Only when mankind understands the true nature of the physical Universe, and its role in the grand scheme of things can long-term progress be made towards our true destiny, a destiny that will leave the material Universe, far behind, once it has served its intended purpose as the first year kindergarten of this great Universe of conscious, intelligent, vibrating Energy, of which everything and everyone is an equal aspect.

Chapter 38
The Planes of the Non-Human Mind

The great planes of life include all levels of existence from the outer physical world of matter to God, The Source, The First Cause at the centre. Although science might well refer to these planes as “dimensions”, and others might collectively refer to them as “the beyond” or even “Heaven”, they are more usually referred to in the broadest terms as the physical plane, the Astral planes and the Mental planes. The Mental planes also extend to include the inner planes, mystically referred to as the Celestial and Cosmic planes before the very centre of all creation is reached, The Source, The First Cause, God.

A “plane” is also often referred to as a “realm”, a “sphere” or a “world”. It should always be remembered however that although this terminology is used in order to describe the various levels of life characterized by these planes, the entire Universe is actually a continuum of Energy and vibration. There are no distinct points at which one plane ends and the next one begins. The All truly does include “All”, everything that “is” in the entire Universe—a Universe that is God.

Before discussing the planes of the non-human Mind, we should first take a look at the various level of planes specifically associated with the physical world of matter.

The plane of the physical world of matter can be divided into seven sub-planes—three planes of matter, a plane of “Ethereal substance” and three planes of Energy, all of which are respectively sub-divided into seven further sub-planes of life.

The first of the main physical planes of matter includes all forms of solids, liquids and gases, which are familiar to us.

Moving up, the second plane of matter includes much more subtle forms of matter, which are also recognized by science. These include Radium and other radioactive substances.

The third plane of matter consists of a much more tenuous form of Energy, the existence of which is not formally recognized by science. This is the plane of the "Ether" pervading the entire Universe, the medium in which waves of Energy such as electricity, magnetism, heat, light and radio waves propagate.

Above the plane of the Ether is the first plane of Energy. This is the fourth of the physical planes. This plane comprises all ordinary forms of Energy well-known to everyone, including heat, light, magnetism, attraction, cohesion, gravity and chemical affinity, as well as other forms of Energy not yet formally accepted or named by science.

The next inner plane of Energy includes forms of Energy that have, for the most part, not yet been identified by science. It is within this plane that various forms of mental and psychic phenomena propagate.

The highest plane comprises Energy so highly organized that it can include many of the characteristics of life. These finer Energies are far in advance of anything currently recognized by science.

There are six planes of the non-human Mind, the seventh being the plane of the human Mind itself. The first and lowest of these planes is the first plane of the mineral Mind. Before progressing, we should remind ourselves once again that everything in the entire Universe is a continuum, an integral aspect of The Source, The First Cause, of God. Although minerals are not usually regarded as "intelligent" in comparison with man and other forms of organic life, they are still life forms in the context of Spirit. They also possess an individual aura just as any other aspect of Spirit. It is important to know therefore that it is not necessary for something to possess a "brain" in order to be considered to be "life" or to possess "intelligence" or Consciousness. All manifestations of, and within, the Universal Mind possess, life, Consciousness and intelligence, which may also be known as "Spirit".

The first plane of the mineral Mind contains all entities widely recognized as minerals, chemicals, rocks and so on. We must be mindful of the fact we are talking about the "Mind" of minerals here and not merely the molecules, atoms and sub-atomic particles of which they are materially constituted. We mean the aspect of these minerals that is their Soul.

Although most people will not have considered the possibility of minerals possessing a Soul or being capable of thought, they do exhibit their own likes and dislikes, attractions and repulsions and many other such individual characteristics. In the context of the Universe, it can also be said that the emotions and feelings of minerals and the inner forms of life within all of these planes only differ by degrees relative to each other. All manifestations of minerals are ultimately in the form of vibrations of Energy.

The next plane moving up is the first and lower plane of the elemental Mind. Elementals are invisible to the five physical senses, but occultists and others can and do actively interact with these elemental Beings. This lowest class of elemental Mind exhibits a level of intelligence between that of the mineral Mind on the one side, and the plant Mind on the other.

Moving up the scale to the third level, we reach the plane of the plant Mind. These planes and all of their associated sub-planes contain all those Beings forming the kingdoms of the plant worlds. The fact that plants respond favourably to music is evidence that they possess a Soul. Of course, the vibrations of music influence the Energy of human Beings as well.

A series of experiments carried out in 1966 demonstrated conclusively that plants are capable of intelligent thought processes. The researcher, Cleve Backster, an expert with lie detector equipment, connected a lie detector to a Dracaena plant, also known as a "Dragon tree". He wanted to see how long it would take for the leaves to react when he poured water on the plant's roots. In theory, a plant will increase its conductivity and decrease its resistance after it absorbs water, and the curve recorded on graph paper should have gone upward. But in actuality, the line curved downward. When a lie detector is connected to a human body, the pen reacts differently, tracing a different plot, in accordance with the changes in the person's mood. The reaction of the dragon tree was just like the undulation of human mood swings. It seemed that it was happy when it "drank" water.

Cleve Backster also wanted to see if the plant would display any other reactions. Backster then focussed on the thought of burning the leaves that were connected to the lie detector. With this thought held in his Mind, and even before he went to fetch a match, a strong curve rapidly appeared on the graph paper.

When he arrived back with a match, he saw that yet another peak had appeared on the curve. The plant had perceived that there was a good chance that it could be burned and exhibited the emotion of fright. If he showed less inclination to burn the plant, the reactions of the plant were not so strong. If he merely pretended to take action to burn the leaves, the plant had almost no reactions whatsoever. The plant was fully capable of distinguishing his true intentions from the false ones.

In a further experiment, Backster decided to test how well a plant could recognize objects and people. He selected six students, blindfolded them and asked them to draw lots. One of the choices was to uproot one of the two plants present for the experiment and destroy it by treading upon it. This person was to carry out this task alone, and none of the other students knew who had drawn the task. By proceeding in this manner, only the remaining plant would know the true identity of the "murderer" of the other plant.

The remaining plant was then connected to a lie detector, and each of the students was asked to walk by it. The plant showed no reactions to the five students who had not been involved with the destruction of the other plant, but when the student who had murdered the other plant walked by, the remaining plant showed an extreme reaction on the lie detector recording. The plant was clearly able to identify the exact person responsible for the destruction of the other fellow plant.

This demonstrates extremely well that plant life, like all life in the Universe, is an inseparable aspect of the same infinite Universal Mind of God. Still steeped in the material world and personal Ego, human Beings assume that just because plants do not appear to have a physical brain or animal like characteristics that they are unintelligent or "inanimate". In fact nothing could be further from the truth. The brain is not the Mind. The brain is simply an organic supercomputer under the direct control of the Subconscious Mind, necessary only due to complexity of the human organism. Simpler forms of life such as minerals, plants, and single celled organisms such as the amoeba, have no need for a brain, but they most certainly do have a Mind, and that Mind is an inseparable aspect of the Universal Mind and of us and all life in the Universe.

Moving more inward still to the fourth level, we find the next plane of the elemental Mind. These are a more advanced class of elementals with a level of Mind situated in between those of plants and animals. Entities existing at these levels can exhibit the characteristics of both.

The next plane with its associated sub-divisions is the plane of the animal Mind and comprises the Minds of all members of the animal world. These sub-planes contain all levels of life from the most basic of animal life, such as single-celled organisms at the lowest aspect, to the most advanced animal life at the very highest aspect. The highest level of these planes would include levels of Mind just below that of the human Mind and might, for example, include primates.

The next and sixth level is the highest plane of the elemental Mind. The intelligence of these Beings is between that of the animal Mind and the human Mind. The highest levels of Beings existing in these planes can exhibit semi-human or even human intelligence and might include the Cetaceans such as Dolphins, Porpoises and Whales.

Chapter 39
The Planes of the Human Mind

Moving beyond the planes of the non-human Minds, we reach the final and highest plane—the plane of the human Mind. Like all planes, this plane also has seven sub-planes corresponding with the level of Spiritual evolution achieved by individual human Beings on the path back to The Source, God. Again, these planes are levels of Energy corresponding to the levels of vibration of the human Mind. Remember that by "Mind", we do not mean "brain", but true "Mind" in the Spiritual sense. Awe should also keep in mind once again that although we are conceptually talking about "planes", we do so only to differentiate between different levels of vibration—ultimately everything is part of the great Universal continuum of Energy.

The average human being today has reached the fourth level within the planes of the human Mind. Only the most advanced of humans in terms of Spiritual evolution have transcended this level to reach the fifth level. It should be noted that it has taken mankind millions of years to achieve these levels, and, even though overall rate of evolution is increasing, it will take most humans many more years to attain the sixth and seventh level planes and onward still to the even greater planes of life. This is a major reason why no person should delay their progress.

We are advised, however, that there are races in other parts of the Universe who have transcended these levels before us and have progressed onwards to the inner spheres of life. We are also advised that some races have already evolved back to the First Cause and achieved the potential of unity with God—the true meaning of life.

Within all of these levels or planes of life, each individual life-form can also exist within its own unique "group Mind". We can observe the behaviour of many classes of creatures in nature belonging to the same "group Mind". For example, vast shoals of fish or flocks of birds can be observed to behave as a single, unified Mind, instantly changing direction in the same moment completely as one. Although they might appear to be individual entities as observed at the physical level, these creatures are effectively behaving as a single collective Mind at the level of the mental plane of the animal Mind of which they are members.

Because humans have greater abilities of the Mind and are at a higher level in the great planes of life, we do not overtly behave in exactly the same way. We have been endowed with more individuality and powers of individual thought and freewill through a conscious Mind and Ego. Nevertheless, the group human Mind certainly exists, and humans can and frequently do influence each other upon the plane of the collective human Mind. It is at the level of the group human Mind that some psychic abilities occur, including telepathy.

A very graphic and observable illustration of the group Mind in “higher” level animals can be observed by the “hundredth monkey effect” as reported by biologist Lyall Watson in his book, “Lifetide”. This experiment took place on a Japanese island where researchers fed sweet potatoes to Macaque monkeys, which was a completely new food for them.

The monkeys enjoyed the taste of the sweet potatoes but did not like the sand covering the potatoes from the beach. Soon one monkey started to wash the potatoes in the sea to remove the sand and to add a salty taste. In due course, more and more monkeys on the island started to the potato washing habit. Very soon, the same action was practiced spontaneously by the entire Macaque monkey community.

Before long, whole communities of Macaque monkeys on other totally unconnected islands began the practice of washing their sweet potatoes in the sea, even though there was no apparent communication between the Islands and their respective monkey populations. This is a more dramatic and conclusively observable example of the "group-entity Mind", taking place upon the Mental Plane of that species.

The group Mind makes many so-called "phenomena" possible. Like all "planes" in the Universe, the plane of the Human Mind is a level of Energy and vibration shared by all human Beings having attained that level. Although humans and other entities remain as individuals throughout the multi-dimensional continuum of the Universe they also share a common plane of Mind, or Consciousness.

This Principle also applies to all levels of all of the classes of "entities" from the very lowest to the very highest. Only The Source has a complete "view" of all classes and hierarchies of entities below, or specifically further out from The Source.

The "group entity" has been referenced throughout the ages. Plato referred to transcendent invisible "forms" which cause manifestation in the physical world. The eminent Swiss psychologist, Carl Jung, concluded that humans share one "collective unconscious" which lies deeper than the unconscious of each individual. This "collective unconscious", or "group entity", was further supported by Jung when he also noted that the same symbols, myths, fairy tales and similar traditions could be found in geographically diverse cultures, even though no physical communication could have ever occurred between them.

Each class of entity exists outside of space and time. The humankind entity already includes all humans existing now, as well as all humans who have ever existed and ever will exist. This is also the solution to the very commonly asked question, "how are new Souls created out of nothing?" In fact these Souls have always existed as aspects of Higher Selves of Spirit in the "Eternal Now" and are not therefore "new" Souls at all. Observation of the number of people physically incarnated on the planet is based purely upon the human concept of "space" and "time" which, as we know, is an illusion.

Here in the physical world, humans can only perceive a three-dimensional existence in accordancc with the five physical senses. However, from a multi-dimensional perspective, the Higher Self of an individual can perceive all possible inter-relationships, possibilities and potentials completely beyond the comprehension of human beings living exclusively from the perspective of the physical world. The Higher Self of each individual has full access to the multi-dimensional continuum of reality and Universal Mind, and can provide extremely valuable guidance based upon what The Higher Self can perceive beyond the limited confines of temporal space and time.

Although everyone is a member of the "humankind entity" on the plane of the "collective human Consciousness", everyone is also equally and ultimately a member of "The All Entity". We are all immortal Sons and Daughters of God, Spiritually "made" in the true image of God.

Chapter 40
The Astral Planes

We will now take a more detailed look at the Astral planes, also known as the "Astral worlds", "Astral realms", "Astral spheres", all corresponding expressions to be found in this book, and also "the beyond", "the afterlife" or the "fourth dimension". "Dimension" is a however human scientific concept based upon the perceptions of the five physical senses.

As with all realms in the multi-dimensional continuum of the Universe, the Astral realms are density degrees of The Source, The First Cause, Universal Mind. They are, therefore, fundamental to the creation of everything that exists, has ever existed and ever will exist in the physical world of matter in accordance with the Principle of correspondence—"as above so below". Everything existing in the material world must first within the inner worlds. As we will see later, this is the basis for all manifestation and creation in the material world.

As we will discuss later, learning the ability of Astral Projection and Out of Body Experiences will remove the fear of "death" completely, providing first-hand evidence of the reality of the Astral planes and of the continuity of life beyond the confines of the temporal physical body.

Most people are completely unaware of their own immortal, Divine nature, living life as if it was the only chance they will ever have to "exist". As a direct result, they become steeped in the material illusion of the five physical senses. When mankind finally rediscovers these truths, people will waste no opportunity in doing everything necessary in order to progress on o the glories of the "Heavenly" spheres of life.

The Astral realms are home to a very wide variety of inhabitants besides humans. There are many Beings and intelligences that have never incarnated on Earth, and whose task it is to assist in the evolution of mankind on Earth. There are also the Beings of the single elements, many of which form the basis of Earthly "fairy stories". Also living in the Astral realms are the simpler Beings of the elements known as "elementaries", which still exhibit a degree of intelligence and have their role in the grand Universal order of life.

The Astral realms are also home to a wide variety of Beings of all levels and intelligences, most of which are beyond the comprehension of Earthly man, including Beings originating from other planets in the Universe.

Within the mid-Astral planes, at the level of vibration where most decent people currently find themselves after physical death, life is one of peace, harmony and tranquillity, often in stark contrast to the previous physical existence. These Astral worlds also seem much lighter, solid and "real" to the residents living there, than the physical world, which seems to be a very dull, murky, oppressive place by comparison.

As previously mentioned, there are many levels of vibration and comparative density of the Astral planes, all of which exhibit their own unique Energy. A human being will automatically transition to the most appropriate sphere of the Astral most closely matching his or her own particular vibration, Ego, temperament, character, beliefs and attitudes. If a person is open-Minded and fully understands the true process of "death", they will effortlessly transition to the light, peace and harmony of the mid-Astral planes. More Spiritually advanced people will transition to the inner Astral realms where conditions are even more blissful, and those who are advanced to the stage where they know the illusion of the Astral planes for what it is will transition directly to the world of Spirit, leaving the transient illusion of the physical and Astral worlds far behind.

As we take a closer look at the various density levels of the Astral planes, it is important to again stress that there are no actual definitive borders or boundaries between the various "planes". The entire Universe is a continuum of conscious, intelligent, vibrating Energy from the very highest level of The Source, The First Cause, God, out to the outermost levels of the physical world of matter. All Astral planes form an integral aspect of this vast and infinite Energy continuum.

As human Beings are Spiritually made in the "true image of God", and therefore of the Universe, each finer, subtle body of a human being, the Microcosm, are also "inner bodies". The physical human body, as with the Macrocosm or Universe as a whole, is the outer shell, and each successive body (the Etheric, Astral, and Mental bodies) are all progressively finer, more subtle inner bodies, existing at progressively inner levels of vibration and lower density. This is why meditation and similar disciplines are considered to be forms of "inner exploration".

The Astral planes are a necessary aspect of the greater continuum of Energy comprising the Universe as a whole, and one that many people will become familiar with after the change known as "death". Words alone cannot fully describe the vastness and diversity of the Astral realms and the Beings living there, which is why Astral Projection is an ability well worth learning and practicing that you may visit the Astral realms in person, after which the concept of "death" will disappear forever, the next phase of life becoming something to anticipate and even look forward to, but only when your mission on Earth is complete.

Chapter 41
The Outer Astral Planes

The "lower" or more correctly outer Astral planes are what might well be considered to be the "hells" in accordance with the "Heaven" and "hell" concepts of religion. The lower Astral planes are not actually "down below", as in "beneath the Earth", but are rather the lowest vibrational levels of the Astral planes. These levels are still "inward" relative to the Earth. There is no such entity as "satan", "lucifer", or the "devil" ruling these lower levels of the Astral worlds in a place called "hell", and neither have the people who currently exist at these lower levels of the Astral worlds been sentenced to any form of "eternal damnation". These are simply doctrines of religion that seek to control their congregations by instilling fear of the unknown and of an eternity of "torment", all completely false.

The lowest levels of the Astral planes are inhabited by people who led a particularly dark, or what would be regarded according to human concepts "evil" existence when living in the physical world. Such people might for example include murderers, rapists, criminals, terrorists, some dictators, and all those who otherwise lived a violent, hate-oriented life on Earth. After death, as previously discussed, a person will automatically migrate to the plane where, as with all forms of vibration, "like attracts like", corresponding with the vibrations, beliefs and other characteristics of the Astral body of the individual. Murderers for example might therefore find themselves in a dark, dank, oppressive, misty, hate and fear-filled world that is a precise reflection of their own vibration.

In this "murder world", the residents will engage in the pursuit of murdering other people, who will, in turn, be striving to murder them. There might well be hundreds of thousands or even millions of such murderers from Earth's past, present and future in any particular lower Astral "murder world", all engaged in these same dark activities. The same situation exists in a multitude of similar worlds, where people of similar dark characteristics will exist at the same plane of Energy and vibration, all endeavouring to exert their own influence over the other residents as a continuation of their dark lives on Earth. In the Astral planes, it is impossible to physically harm anyone in the absence of a physical, material body, and the futility of their own thoughts and actions is one of the first lessons the residents of these dark, outer worlds will learn.

There will be many such "murder worlds" in the outer Astral planes, including every type of murderous, dark, low vibration groups that ever existed. These people will always find themselves in exactly those conditions that most closely matched their previous dark lives on Earth. As mentioned before, these conditions facilitate the lessons that will raise the vibrations of their Astral body and allow them to progress to inner Astral planes where more peace and harmony can be found. Such is the immutable perfection of the Universe where balance and evolution are always primary principles.

In appearance, these lower Astral "hell-like" worlds completely reflect the character of the residents and therefore might be experienced by the people living there as dark, damp, cold, misty and oppressive environments, with swamps, waste lands devoid of beauty, dark shadows, trees without leaves, and many other such characteristics. These dark worlds would most certainly seem like "purgatory" to these people, but are, in fact, "hells" they have created for themselves as a reflection of their own dark lives previously lived on Earth.

Contrary to religious dogma, however, none of these people are "stuck" in or condemned to these dark Astral "hell" worlds for all eternity. There is no "purgatory" or "satan" imprisoning people amid the "flames" for all eternity. The residents will rather remain at that level of vibration, regardless of how long it takes, (as measured in Earth time), until they can finally come to understand the negative effects of their past lives upon themselves and other people. They must first fully understand and directly experience the true and precise degree of fear, hate and suffering which their previous physical lives inflicted on other people. Then and only then can they understand and then reconcile their current situation and continue onwards, finally reuniting with their Higher Self with a unique package of experience to contribute the Whole Self.

Again, contrary to the belief of some religions, no human being, regardless of how "evil" they might have been perceived to be during Earth life, is ever condemned to these lower Astral worlds forever. Everyone has the fundamental ability by means of the very freewill possessed by every human, to progress to the inner spheres of life and onwards back to the Higher Self of the person. No matter how very dimly the Divine spark flickers in people inhabiting these lowest, dark Astral worlds, the spark is still part of the brightly burning flame of the Whole, and can and eventually will glow brighter as progress is made, even if such progress takes aeons as measured in physical time.

Chapter 42
The Belief System Territories

As previously discussed, the level of the Astral planes in which a person will find themselves after the transition from physical life depends very much on the overall character and level of Spiritual attainment of the person, especially during the years just prior to passing on. Factors involving the character include the Ego, general attitude towards other people, attitude towards material things, degree of selfishness or selflessness, etc. All these factors influence the equilibrium of the Astral body, including its level of vibration, density and balance.

Upon passing, after the change known as "death", most people will arrive at a density level of the mid-Astral worlds, which are remarkably similar to the Earth life they recently departed. They will be attracted to a community of people of the type of environment, culture and attitudes with which they are most familiar, and with whose vibrations they are most in harmony. Some people settle into their new home quickly, others take longer, often requiring support, but almost all settle in sooner or later once the necessary adjustments have been made.

There are various levels of the Astral planes, located between the lowest Astral planes and the mid-Astral planes. These intermediate planes include what is known as the "belief system territories". Although the belief system territories do not have the same "hell-like" qualities of the very lowest Astral planes, they can seem like a "hell" to people who transition to these territories after physical death and become trapped in the Energy of those particular levels of vibration.

Many people still maintain strongly held beliefs at the time of physical death, and these beliefs become a part of their experience after they "die". These people often find themselves in a lower level of the Astral planes in an environment that is a complete reproduction of the religion or belief "belief" they practiced and were so influenced by on Earth. As we will discover later in this book, "belief" is a very powerful vibration, and one which attracts to us those things in which we strongly believe, and of course "belief systems", including religions, are no exception, especially as many people are so passionate about their religion. "Beliefs" do not necessarily imply religions, but rather can be any strongly held belief about anything at all.

The people in these belief system territories have created entire worlds in which everything revolves around the absolute devotion to a particular belief. Although life in these worlds can be pleasant or at least tolerable, it in no way compares to the serenity of the mid-Astral levels and inner Astral planes, where everyone has the complete freedom of choice to do as they please in an environment of complete peace and harmony.

The main focus of the inhabitants of the religious belief system territories are their churches and an absolute unconditional devotion to the religion prevailing in these worlds. There are levels of vibration for every type of religion, belief and cult from the past, present and future relative to the Earth concept of "time". People who live in these belief system territories very often initially believe they are in "Heaven", experience precisely what they expected to experience, and are often quite content to continue to live within a devoted religious existence within these environments, usually completely oblivious to the freedom and splendours of the inner Astral worlds.

As in the physical world, the leaders of some of these "religious worlds", as with religion in the physical world, maintain a very close control over their "congregations", often using the emotion of fear by threatening to have them "cast out into the darkness", and even "cast down to purgatory" if they do not live by their rules. Again, these threats are similar to the threats of being cast into "hell and damnation" of a religion in the physical world.

Sooner or later, as with the lower "hell" worlds, the residents of the belief system territories begin to see the reality and illusion of their situation and eventually desire to escape these outer planes and progress inwards and onwards. People living within the inner levels of the Astral planes remain vigilant and ready to guide such Souls to the inner levels of more peace and harmony, corresponding to their own level of vibration.

It should also be mentioned that there are large bands of people in the mid to high levels of the Astral planes who are actively involved with assisting those trapped in the lower levels of the Astral planes and close to the physical world whenever such assistance is appropriate and not contrary to the freewill of the people involved. Such is the way of life in the Universe, Beings of the inner levels always assisting those in the outer levels on the great ascent back to our Creator.

Due to freewill, a helper from an inner level of the Astral worlds cannot assist someone in an outer level unless they specifically request that assistance directly or indirectly. Like all communications in the worlds beyond Earth, such a request or plea for help will be sent in the form of a focused telepathic thought that will be received in the inner worlds. Once this thought request is received, helpers from the inner Astral planes can then descend to the lower vibration/higher density of the outer belief system territory and lead the person to their new home in the peace and harmony of the mid-Astral planes.

There are many such belief system territories in the lower Astral planes corresponding to the many diverse beliefs and religions. Beliefs do not necessarily need to be strictly religious in order for a person to become trapped in one of these lower Astral belief system territories. Any sort of strongly held belief or concept, particularly relating to what a person believes will happen to them after physical death, will be sufficient to attract the person to a plane or world which matches their particular belief. As with all of the lower Astral planes, however, people will sooner or later progress to the world of their rightful abode where they will no longer be trapped by their belief.

Obviously, it is of tremendous importance to understand before physical death the true nature of the inner realities and what truly happens after physical death. In physical life, the objective should always be one of Spiritual awareness, remaining completely open to and ready to embrace the inner spheres of life and reality waiting after the death of the physical body. It is never too late in physical life to make the effort to discover and understand these greater realities and to reconcile and dissolve any strongly held belief, religious or otherwise before "passing on" to the next phase of life. Failure to do so might well result in being "trapped in a belief", at which point it becomes increasingly difficult to transcend that belief while living in an environment surrounded by people who are also trapped and living within the same belief, all believing that theirs is the one and only true life.

Those who know the peace and harmony of the inner Astral worlds and beyond would never allow themselves to become trapped in a belief system of the lower Astral planes. Again this is one of the major benefits of Astral Projection. Those who travel to the Astral planes can see and experience these environments for themselves and with that knowledge live an open-minded and sincere quest for Spiritual evolution.

Chapter 43
Outer Astral Entities

There are a wide variety of Beings inhabiting the Astral planes in addition to humans and other more advanced forms of Universal life. These Beings exhibit intelligence, characteristics and purpose in accordance with their position in the grand Universal scheme of things, often existing as members of a single element of Fire, Air, Water or Earth.

One of the most basic Astral Beings of the single Universal elements is known as an "elementary". An elementary can be consciously created upon the Astral planes by a person living in the physical world who is experienced in these matters. Such an elementary can then be endowed with intelligence and abilities to carry out specific tasks upon the Astral planes on behalf of its creator. An elementary thus created and "programmed" is sometimes known as a "servitor".

Of course, the laws of karma still apply in these cases. If a person creates an elementary for negative purposes, or is negligent in the programming of the elementary such that negative effects result, there will be a karmic price to pay. Nevertheless, elementaries can be and often are created for positive use in the Astral planes for a wide range of purposes such as for protection from other Astral Beings and forces.

Elementaries can maintain themselves from human vibrations, but usually have a finite lifespan, the extent of which can be predetermined by its creator who will have "programmed" the elementary to "dissolve" itself under certain circumstances or by means of a telepathic command.

People often create an elementary without knowing they have done so. This can occur, for example, when a person thinks or obsesses about something or someone over an extended period of time. Such thoughts can result in a resilient Thought Form, larvae or the more advanced elementary at the level of that specific thought upon the Astral planes.

Another form of basic Astral being is known as a "phantom". A phantom is created when one or more people think intensively about another person, often a recently deceased person. These phantoms are usually semi-intelligent and can take on the same appearance and characteristics as the deceased person, based upon the thoughts of the people thinking about the deceased person.

Very often, psychic mediums make contact with these phantoms believing them to be the actual Soul of the deceased person. The medium then convinces bereaved relatives that they are in communication with the Soul of their deceased loved one, and all manner of deception can consequently occur, albeit unintentionally. This is one important reason why a psychic medium should never be relied upon without impeccable credentials and proven psychic ability. This is also another reason why Astral Projection is so useful, enabling the ability to visit deceased people directly within the Astral planes, thus leaving no doubts as to the authenticity of the experience and identity of the Being. Once someone ceases mourning and therefore intensively thinking about the deceased person, the phantom will lose its source of emotional Energy and eventually dissolve back into the elements of the Ether.

A further class of basic Astral being is known as "larvae". These Beings are also brought into existence on the lowest levels of the Astral planes by the intensive and often repetitive emotional thoughts of humans. Larvae will endeavour to maintain themselves from the emotional vibrations of people, and will usually seek people who are generating high levels of such intense emotions or passions upon which to feed. Larvae can, therefore, be considered a sort of "Astral parasite".

While they have a very low level of intelligence, larvae have a survival instinct that is satisfied by feeding from strong human emotions originating in the physical world. The survival instincts of larvae can be so strong that they will seek a person upon which to "psychically feed". They typically do this by locating a human who is susceptible to the particular type of emotions they require in order to sustain themselves and then proceed to invoke these emotions in their victims.

In order to grow stronger, the larvae invoke increasingly higher levels of emotions within the host. The more intense the emotions evoked in the human host, the stronger the larvae will become, and it is even possible that whole swarms of larvae will be attracted to the same person. This can then lead to more severe emotional or psychological problems for the victim.

Astral larvae attacks like this are certainly not uncommon. In the physical world, the victim will often be diagnosed with a "psychological illness" which will typically be treated by drugs and behavioural therapies. Of course, none of these can or will heal the root cause of the issue, any more than conventional "drugs" can heal a physical illness. The only way a person can free themselves from such a situation resulting from larvae attachment in the long term is to consciously cease vibrating the emotions upon which the larvae are feeding.

There is yet another broad class of lower Astral life known as "schemata" that can be considered to be higher than an elementary. Among the classes of schemata are particularly well-known varieties often known as "incubus" and "succubus", sometimes wrongly identified as "demons". Incubus and succubus thrive on the vibration of sexual Energy and the passions, emotions and vibrations associated with such Energy. These entities will endeavour to arouse strong sexual sensations within the host. The more the host enjoys and encourages these sexual sensations, the stronger the incubus or succubus will become in its attachment to the human being.

Many people become so involved with the pleasures derived from these entities, not knowing what they actually are, that the situation often progresses to an unshakable addiction. The only way a victim can remove a schemata is to summon sufficient self-control and willpower, as with any addiction, to overcome the addiction and thus the vibrations the schemata is attracted to. Only then will the schemata leave and seek another victim.

There are a wide range of entities and Beings in the lowest Astral realms, some of which can be harmful, from the perspective of humans, and many of which are not. Everyone should be aware of the presence of such Beings however, the role they play in the Universal and in our lives both on Earth, and beyond.

Chapter 44
The Mid-Astral Planes

The mid-Astral planes or "worlds", "spheres" or "realms" are, by comparison to Earth life clean, well-organized, and harmonious. These levels of the Astral are the ideal place for rest after the trials and tribulations of a physical life on Earth.

The mid-Astral planes are very similar in many respects to the most pleasant aspects of the physical world, without any if the less desirable aspects. This is because they were created by humans based on their own perception of an ideal physical world. The people of the Astral worlds have recreated the physical world within the Energy levels of the mid-Astral planes by imagining what they believe it should look like, and in turn based upon their experiences during physical life.

People at this stage of development still tend to be very much focused on materialism, and accordingly perceive an "ideal world" consisting of the material things they previously desired but never realised in the physical world. In the Astral worlds, everyone can have anything they desire simply by focussing on it, which is why this level is often known as the "desire worlds". It should be noted that the same Universal Principles also apply to the physical world, but due to the much lower vibration and higher density Thought Forms take longer to manifest, depending on the nature of the Thought Form.

This Astral planes at these levels of vibration meet the expectations of the people arriving there, therefore enabling them feel "at home".

The Principles of Correspondence, Causation and Attraction are highly evident within the Astral planes with "like attracting like" and an immediate effect resulting from every action. Everything created as a thought in the Mind can manifest instantly, including negative and positive thoughts. New Astral residents soon learn to think only in a positive and constructive manner.

Residents will be attracted to like-Minded people of very similar characters, desires, and aspirations. People who were honest, sincere and friendly on Earth will find themselves in the presence of people of like nature in the Astral planes in stark contrast to Earth where people of vastly differing and contrasting natures co-exist, and hence the value of Earth as an intensive learning experience.

Within the mid-levels of the Astral planes are numerous realms consisting of all cultures from the past, present and future of Earth relative to the human concept of "time". No matter what country, culture or tradition a person experienced on Earth, there will always be a corresponding environment waiting in the Astral planes once their phase of life on Earth is complete.

The usual trappings of the material world such as the need for "money" and "work" simply do not exist in these mid-Astral planes. There is simply no need for them. These are "Mind worlds" in every sense where everything desired can become an instant reality simply by using the powers of the Mind. There are no limits to these powers of instant manifestation. If a person desires a new home in the Astral, whether it is a castle, a mansion, a fortress, a hut or even a tent, it can be experienced instantly. If a different style, interior or furnishings are later desired, it is simply a case of imagining the new design, projecting it, and willing it to become a reality.

Due to their similarity to the material world, there are people who erroneously believe the Astral planes are "home" or even "Heaven". The new residents are often so happy with their new "home" that they accept it as reality, often out of relief that there is after all a "life after death", oblivious to their greater destiny of ascent to the inner, non-materialistic realms, where the great journey back to their Higher Self continues.

Although newly arrived Astral residents usually find themselves in very familiar surroundings, they are still free to explore the vast and limitless realms at these levels. They cannot exceed their own vibrational plane of existence and density of the Astral body, however. A person living in the Astral planes can travel outwards as far as a vibration close the physical world, and frequently do to visit loved ones, relatives, friends and others still living on Earth.

Initially, the sheer vastness and limitless array of realms, environments and variety of Beings encountered can be absolutely overwhelming for new arrivals. There are creations, environments, and ranges of colours and sounds existing far beyond the comprehension of the physical conscious Mind. To the new arrival, the mid-Astral planes can indeed seem like "Heaven" where everything desired can become an instant reality and where peace and harmony prevails in what seem like idyllic worlds of beauty far beyond the comprehension of those living on Earth.

The content and constitution of the Astral worlds have not only been created by Beings and intelligences who have originated on Earth including human beings, but also from every other planet in the physical Universe containing life at that level. Everything imaginable is available to the residents of the Astral worlds and more—theatres, music halls, restaurants, huge libraries, technology, gardens, and everything that exists, has ever existed or ever will exist on Earth, and more. Everything a person could possibly wish for, need or desire is available, subject only to the ability of the person to comprehend it, and no Soul is ever alone unless they desire to be.

As previously mentioned, Beings existing within the inner Energy levels of the Universe, the inner Astral and the Mental planes can consciously lower their vibration to visit any level of the Universe with a lower vibration, but cannot raise vibration to travel inwards due to the fact they cannot tolerate the higher vibration. Advanced Beings, therefore, often "descend" to the level of the Astral and even physical worlds in order to assist mankind with its evolution to inner levels of reality. Many such advanced Beings can be encountered in the Astral worlds, including advanced human Beings such as what many know as "Ascended Masters" and non-human Beings that humans know as "Angels". It should be mentioned that these great non-human Beings are often extremely powerful Spiritual intelligences, all of whom have a Divine purpose in the grand Universal order, and many of whom have the task of assisting mankind.

As the great journey inward continues, the inner realms of life and reality are ever more glorious than the outer. In the absence of a physical body, Earthly needs such as eating, drinking, washing, breathing, sex and any other bodily functions are simply not required. However, to maintain the absolute stability, harmony and balance of these Astral worlds, all of these Earthly functions and activities can still be experienced according to the needs and desires of each individual, especially upon arrival where stability is desired.

Everything available and possible in the physical world is also possible in the Astral worlds and much, much more but without Earthly physical limitations. Although clothing isn't necessary due to the lack of physical weather, most people still adorn themselves with clothing for perceived comfort and as a matter of habit. Needless to say, like everything in the Astral worlds, clothing can be "changed" in an instant. Although temperature does not exist, the "climate" is nevertheless always optimum.

As mentioned previously, the Astral worlds are the "desire worlds" where residents still think and express themselves in physical, material terms as they did on Earth. It is not until all perceived material needs are seen as the illusions they really are can true progress be made to the inner, more glorious spheres of life and reality. Some people are so materialistic in their thinking that this process can take hundreds or even thousands of years as measured in Earth time. Those who are more Spiritually advanced already recognize the illusory nature of the Astral worlds and might simply take a short, welcome rest in the Astral planes before moving straight on to the inner Spiritual realms of life, and onwards back to the Higher Self.

As material desires are satiated and realized for the illusions they truly are, the desire to progress to the increasing glories of the inner spheres of reality, beyond the concept of "form" becomes ever stronger. As this happens, the Astral body becomes increasingly less dense with a corresponding increasing vibrational rate as the density of materialism is shed, and increasing perfection is realised. Achieving this stage, a person will joyously and naturally depart the Astral worlds to make the transition to the next realm of reality, and to continue to the most sacred journey back to God.

Chapter 45
The Inner Astral Planes

Not much need be said about the inner Astral planes, "worlds", "spheres" or "realms" which to a greater extent transcend the materialism of the lower planes. It should be mentioned that many people still regard the inner Astral planes as the "higher" Astral planes. Where this might be true from the point of view of Energy vibration levels, it is important to note that travelling to "higher" Energy vibration is actually to travel inward relative to the physical world and not "upwards" or "higher" as is frequently supposed.

Within these inner Astral worlds, people have finally satiated their Earthly material desires and are resting in a place of peace, light, harmony, splendour and bliss, although the experience is still created by the Minds of people and Beings living there. These inner planes are much more natural, an environment that can often be likened to the most idyllic summer's day imaginable, with mountains, rivers, woodland and other areas of great peace and beauty, as well as intoxicating flowers and peaceful sounds. These inner levels of the Astral planes have been called many things over the millennia, including "Heaven" and the "Summerland".

The inner Astral planes are the last stop on the way to the true Spirit worlds, beyond "form", which are even more glorious, and onwards and inwards on the return to the Higher Self. Once experienced, there will be no desire to again return to the materialistic mid-Astral or physical worlds. Every Spirit aspires to the inner and more glorious levels of life. No person should ever fear "death". The next phase of immortal life is one to be looked forward to with great joy, happiness and anticipation as an opportunity to progress nearer to God, our Divine Creator, from Whence we came in the beginning.

Chapter 46
Fairy Tale Beings

There are a very wide variety of Beings inhabiting the Astral planes at all levels in addition to humans and other forms of Universal life. These Beings exhibit numerous characteristics in the grand scheme of the Universe, often existing as members of a single element of Fire, Air, Water or Earth.

There are particular classes of these inner Beings of the single elements that are extremely well-known to everyone from the "fairytales" of childhood. The Beings featured in these "fairytales" are actually very real indeed but live in the Astral planes rather than in the physical world as is usually supposed. Some of the most well-known of these Beings are:

Salamanders: Beings of the pure element of Fire.

Sylphs: Beings of the pure element of Air.

Undines: also known as mermaids, Beings of the pure element of Water.

Gnomes: Beings of the pure element of Earth.

In addition, other Beings instantly recognizable to most people include fairies (also known as faeries or fay folk), satyrs, wood nymphs, and water sprites, among others. All of these creatures have their own place in the Universe, often being involved with aspects of nature in the physical world.

Although usually invisible to the five physical Earthly senses, those with Astral or clairvoyant vision can often see these Beings at will. People living within the Astral worlds or who travel to the Astral worlds by Astral Projection can easily see and interact with these delightful Astral Beings of the elements.

Fairy stories originally often came about because people with no natural psychic ability experienced a spontaneous "vision" where the psychic senses of the person became temporarily activated. This can happen more often than most people realize. Everyone has this same psychic potential, but in most people, due to a materialistic focus, these inner senses remain in a latent state. Often however, if a person is "mesmerized" by a captivating and beautiful scene such as a beautiful meadow, for example, it becomes possible to "see" these wonderful Astral Beings. This happens when the physical senses become temporarily "paralyzed" while focusing intently on the scene, causing an altered state of Consciousness often known as a "trance", which slows down the brainwave frequencies. When this situation occurs, a person can then "see" beyond the "veil" separating the material world from the Astral planes and into the realms inhabited by these "fairytale Beings".

For example, a person standing on the deck of a cruise liner might be staring intently out to sea at the seemingly endless expanse of shimmering water and all of a sudden see a mermaid. This person might well later doubt what they saw and would probably be afraid to tell other people about the experience for fear of what the others might think.

Undines or mermaids are Beings of the Universal element of Water and tend to be "seen" in the regions of the Earthly counterpart in accordance with the Universal Principle of Correspondence. The same might happen in a woodland setting, where, in an altered state of consciousness, fairies may be seen flitting around a winding stream. In a forest, wood nymphs might be seen. Around hillsides and other such "Earthy" areas, gnomes might be seen going about their busy lives.

Although all of this might seem like something from one of the great fairy story books with which we are all familiar as children, these stories have a very real origin. These creatures abound in folklore all over the world, and what is known to some people as a "fairy", "mermaid" or a "gnome" in one part of the world is known by a completely different name elsewhere. Nevertheless, these creatures most certainly do exist and have been very widely "seen" throughout the ages, with many stories told and folklore written and passed down through the generations as a direct result. The fact that these Beings have been seen and formed the basis of stories, legends and fables among races that had no communication with each other at the time proves that these Beings were viewed independently, and not the result stories being passed on in person.

As with all Astral Beings, these are "Etheric" creatures which, like everything else in the Astral planes, have no material or solid form and are "seen" in accordance with the psychic perceptions or expectations of the observer. These Beings can in fact take on any size and shape they desire at any time. Over the ages, people have formed very detailed perceptions as to how these Beings appear, probably based on the first written accounts, and the many sightings related by word of mouth. Undines or mermaids will often be seen as human type Beings with fins and flippers instead of legs. Fairies will be seen as small, human type creatures with small wings with which they flit around and hover over flowers, water and other features in nature. Gnomes are usually seen as small men and women busily going about their work, sometimes carrying a lantern or other working implements. Male gnomes will often be perceived with a long beard and wearing a familiar tunic as is often pictured in fairytales.

Until the age of five years or so, children are often still highly tuned into the Astral and Spirit worlds and have a much higher degree of natural clairvoyant and psychic ability than older children and adults. From the moment of birth, children are indoctrinated constantly by parents, relatives and others to make full use of their five physical senses and discouraged from playing with "imaginary friends". The fact of the matter is that these friends are often very real to the children who can "see" and interact with them, because they are indeed very "real" indeed. This is another reason why children enjoy hearing "fairytales" about their little friends so much.

It can be considered a great pity that children are often told to stop "imagining things" and thus eventually lose contact with the greater reality of the Astral planes and the wonderful Beings residing there. It is indeed the "adults" giving children this "advice" who have become blind to the wonders of the inner realities of Universal life.

In this new era of expanding consciousness, we can hope that children will be encouraged from the earliest possible age to continue to use all of their inner senses in addition to the lower Earthly physical senses in order to maintain connections with the inner realms of reality and the Beings living there.

Chapter 47
The Mental Planes

As with the Astral planes and the physical world of matter, the Mental or Spiritual planes first came into being when the four Universal elements of Fire, Air, Water and Earth descended from The Source, The First Cause, God in the beginning. Like the Astral and physical planes, the Mental planes are also density degrees of Universal Mind and Spirit, the Akasha, the Ether, the Quintessence of the elements. These planes include the highest and most exalted realms of Spirit, the Celestial and Cosmic planes. It should be pointed out that "Celestial" and "Cosmic" are symbolic and are used to conveniently describe these inner planes of reality, but are not separate from the continuum of Energy and vibration of the Universe as a whole.

The Mental planes are the home of human beings who, having satiated their material desires, have transitioned to the level of the Mental realms beyond form. The Mental realms are the true Spirit worlds. As in the Astral worlds, everyone residing within the Mental worlds is on exactly the same level of Spiritual development for any level of Energy and vibration, the Mental planes simply being an inner extension of the Astral planes and an outer extension of the Cosmic and Celestial planes.

In addition to human Beings, the Mental worlds are inhabited by Thought Forms and Beings known as "elementals". Elementals are very similar to the elementaries of the Astral planes and are brought, or more specifically thought into existence by the process of intensive, focussed and often repetitive thinking. It is through this process of intensive thinking that the elemental receives a degree of intelligence from the psyche of the person who created it, as well as an instinct for self-preservation. The main difference between a Thought Form and an elemental is that a Thought Form usually has one or more ideas as its basis, while an elemental is the result of a single intensive repetitive thought.

Along with the Spirits of human Beings and other advanced Beings and intelligences of the Universe, elementals are the main residents of the Mental planes.

Over the ages intelligences of thc inner realms of life have told people on Earth though many different methods of communications of the beauties, glories and splendours of the Mental planes, far beyond the comprehension of Earthly humans. If only humans knew of these glories while living in the Astral planes, people would not wish to linger there, further perpetuating the illusion of form and materialism, when a far greater and truer life is within reach.

Chapter 48
The Celestial and Cosmic Planes

The Celestial and Cosmic planes include the most exalted spheres of life, the highest levels of the Mental planes, inhabited by human and other Beings who have transcended all of the levels of the Astral and lower Mental Planes as their Higher Self. The Beings residing at these levels include the as yet very few Higher Selves of the human beings who have achieved this level of evolution, and also include other powerful Beings who have never been human. As previously mentioned, the names "Celestial" and "Cosmic" are symbolic names used to differentiate these levels of Energy and vibration from the outer Mental, Astral and physical planes, and are in reality inner extensions of the very same continuum of Energy.

It is a difficult matter to describe the greatness of the exalted Beings residing in these planes. We are advised, however, that their powers are far beyond the comprehension of human Beings still existing at the Earthly level of development. It is also said these levels of life are the abode of Beings who are as high above mankind now as mankind is above the very simplest levels of life on Earth such as single celled organisms like the amoeba. To the exalted Beings of these high Spiritual planes, mankind might appear to be hardly capable of thought processes. The great Minds of these advanced Beings transcend human Beings by degrees totally incomprehensible to Earthly man. However, due to the advanced nature of these advanced Beings, whereas humans often treat simpler, less evolved forms of life with indifference or sometimes much worse, these advanced Beings of the inner spheres view humans as equals but simply further down the path, with Unconditional Love, doing everything they can to assist their Earthly brothers and sisters with their own journey on the sacred path to perfection.

These levels of advancement are the very same destiny for each and every human being without exception. One day, everyone will indeed aspire to and attain these levels of greatness and then go on to journey ever inwards towards The Source. Such is the destiny of all mankind and the very reason each and every person should know and fully understand these vitally important realities, so fundamental to the true meaning of life. Every single moment is yet another valuable opportunity to make true individual progress on the great path and to assist with the progress of others on their path. No such opportunity should ever be passed by to assist others on their own journey.

The seven minor planes of the Great Spiritual Planes include Beings often referred to as Angels, Archangels and demi-Gods. On the lower Spiritual Planes are Beings recognized as Masters and Adepts. Above them are the Spiritual Beings known as "Angels" and "Archangels". Above them still are Beings so highly advanced on the scale of Universal life that they might well be regarded as "Gods" by many. Such exalted Beings are far beyond the comprehension of the Earthly human Mind. Again, everyone should know, beyond all doubt that it is also the destiny of all mankind to ultimately attain these levels of greatness over the course of aeons of time, and even greater. These Beings have, from time to time, intervened in the history of Earth affairs, leading to numerous legends, beliefs and traditions. Many ancient cultures have described "Gods" descending from the "Heavens" bringing great knowledge, wisdom and teachings. These "Gods" have been depicted in all shapes, sizes and abilities, in accordance with the perceptions and beliefs of the cultures describing them.

During the course of the great ascent back to our Creator, the Higher Self will send many incarnations to the physical world, each living a new physical life, before evolving back to the Higher Self with a new package of experiences, eventually, after the cycle of incarnations are complete, continuing as the Higher Self the glorious journey within the worlds of Spirit.

Chapter 49
Angels

Having discussed mankind and the lower forms of life of the Astral and Mental planes, we should now take a look at the Divine Beings of the inner realms often known as "Angelic Beings" or simply "Angels".

Almost everyone will have heard of Angels in one form or another, often depicted with wings and known by such names as Raphael, Michael, Gabriel and Auriel. "El" quite literally means "of the Divine" as for example in "Elohim".

Angelic Beings dwell in the inner realms of Universal life. They have never incarnated into human form in the physical world and have evolved along a completely different evolutionary path to human Beings. Although these Beings are often referred to as "Angels", they are actually very powerful Spiritual intelligences that do not appear human in appearance at all, in fact their realm and state of existence is beyond the human concept of "form". The depiction of Angels by humans, much as with the human depiction of God, is based very much on fables and legends over many centuries and accordance with human ideas, perceptions and symbolism.

Both Angels and humans, like all forms of life and everything else in creation, are equal aspects of our Divine Creator. Although never having incarnated into matter and occupying an inner place in the great planes of life, Angels are still very much involved with the well-being and progress of all mankind and have their own Divine roles in the grand Universal plan.

Angels have followed a different but parallel line of evolution to human Beings and all other life in the multi-dimensional Universe. Although Angels only dwell in the Celestial spheres and beyond, they can and frequently do descend to the lower spheres of life whenever the need arises in order to carry out specific missions within the Mental or Astral worlds and even within the physical world of matter should the circumstances arise. It should be mentioned however that Angels cannot influence the freewill or lives of humans in any way. Angels are not usually able to draw very close to people in the physical world, however, unless the person has absolute control over all their emotions, Ego, and other aspects of character, due to the need to harmonise the vibrations between both, Angels originating from Energy planes of very high vibration.

The Angelic hierarchy plays an extremely important role in evolution, not the least of which is assisting the progress of all human beings, not only on Earth but on all planets in the Universe. It is the ultimate destiny of every single human being to evolve to such levels of greatness as to be "God-people", working alongside the Angelic hierarchy in assisting life evolving on other planets on the path of return to our Creator.

Angels have no fixed form or appearance and are always "seen" in accordance with the perceptions of the person "perceiving" them, which in turn is usually in accordance with the teachings of a religion, belief system or other tradition. For many centuries, artists have depicted Angels as humanoid type Beings, very often with wings, and glowing radiantly from head to foot adorned in long flowing white robes. One person might see an Angel as possessing wings, and another might see the same Angel adorned in a white robe with no wings, surrounded by radiant white light, often carrying a musical instrument. Regardless of how Angels are perceived by the inner senses, there can be no mistaking the strength of presence and high level of Consciousness of these exalted Beings.

Angels, contrary to popular belief, have no fixed formal hierarchies or names, all being an integral and equal aspect of the Universal. Over the centuries, however, Angels have been given names and formal hierarchies by human Beings for convenience and better understanding. These organizations of

Angels are variously described as the "Angelic Hierarchy", "Angelic Hosts", and "Choirs of Angels", often being depicted in terms of the traditional human concept of a musical choir.

I will not describe a typical hierarchy of Angels as depicted by humans lest I influence the reader into thinking such a hierarchy is the "correct" one when in fact such a notion in and of itself would not be correct. Suffice it to say that what humans call "Angels" do exist, are extremely powerful and positive Beings of Light, and whose mission includes assisting humans and other life on the great path back to The Source, The First Cause, God. As such you may feel free to name and perceive Angels in any way that assists your perception of, and to relate to and empathise with these Divine Beings of God.

Chapter 50
Holy Guardian Angel

Much has been said about the presence of our "Holy Guardian Angel", a Being who remains with us from the moment of our very first physical incarnation of our Higher Self on Earth, constantly watching over and guiding us over many physical lives. While this is conceptually absolutely true, the Holy Guardian Angel is in fact the very same Entity as our Higher Self and is therefore not a separate Being or member of an Angelic hierarchy as is commonly supposed.

The Higher Self watches over and guides each individual incarnation communicating with us at a very subtle level, often by means of impressions, intuition or the "voice within" whenever necessary. Such communication can be in the form of warnings, advice, or knowledge from the inner spheres, often arriving in the form of intuition. If we stray from the sacred path, our Higher Self may endeavour to warn or guide us by the subtle but effective means, such communications often being associated with the "Holy Guardian Angel". However, our Higher Self, or Holy Guardian Angel if preferred, cannot directly intervene or interfere with our own individual freewill except in the most exceptional of circumstances.

As our Higher Self, the Holy Guardian Angel has full access to the inner levels of reality and knows and understands everything about us, including past, present and future Higher Self physical incarnations. Those who listen for and are receptive to the promptings of their Higher Self or Holy Guardian Angel should always take heed of such guidance, because it always has the potential to make a massive difference in our lives. Learning the ability of listening to, or even communication with our Higher Self, or Holy Guardian Angel is one of the most valuable abilities that can be attained.

Chapter 51
Spirit Guides

Spirit guides represent a very wide range of Spiritual Beings from discarnate human beings who have previously incarnated on Earth to Beings who have never before physically incarnated. In fact, spirit guides may, and often do originate from a planet in the physical Universe other than Earth. Planetary origin is of no real importance within the inner spheres. All life is ultimately Spirit and an equal aspect of God.

The concept of “appearance” and “speech” is also completely meaningless beyond the physical world of matter. Spirit guides originating from other planets are often much more advanced than Spirit guides originating from Earth, and all communication takes place through such abilities of the Mind such as telepathy, imagery and intuition.

Some people believe that everyone is “allocated” a Spirit guide from birth, while others believe that specific requests need to be made in order to enlist the services of a Spirit guide. Such requests could be made while meditating from a deeper, expanded state of Consciousness, or when the Mind is completely quiet and focused. Just before drifting off to sleep or just after waking in the morning are always good times for communication with Beings of the inner realms as well as for communicating with the Subconscious Mind through which all inner communications takes place.

Genuine Spirit guides have chosen, of their own freewill, to assist a person during the course of a physical life, and often even after the person has made the transition to the Astral worlds. During the course of a physical lifetime, a person might well enjoy the services of a range of different Spirit guides according to life circumstances and ongoing progress along the Divine path. Spirit guides also very often specialize in a specific type of assistance, and when a person no longer requires that particular type of assistance, the guide might leave and be replaced by a more appropriate guide to facilitate further advancement. Again, this is entirely in accordance with the freewill of the Spirit guide, there is never any obligation.

It is also quite possible to request a Spirit guide to leave and be request a replacement at one's discretion as life circumstances change, assuming a person is aware of the presence of Spirit guides. It is also possible to make it clear that no Spirit guide is required, all being completely at the discretion of both sides. A Spirit guide can never interfere with the freewill of the person they are guiding, and the wishes of the person must always be completely respected as a fundamental Universal Principle where freewill is of the utmost importance.

Before proceeding further, a word of caution. There are numerous discarnate entities existing in the lower, darkest Astral worlds who are extremely anxious to establish direct communication with human Beings still living in the physical world, very often for highly dubious and often dangerous purposes. These are the very same types of Beings that are often contacted through using a Ouija board for example. These entities will often claim to be almost anything or anyone you would like them to be in order to gain your confidence, always playing on the Ego of the person for maximum effect. Some of these entities make the outrageous claims that they are Divine Beings such as Archangels or even God. Often they claim that they need help, and that only the person using the Ouija board can help, again manipulating the person by playing on their Ego. Entities dwelling in the lowest levels of the Astral worlds sometimes have the intention to control or possess a human being for their own purposes, often to gain control of situations in the physical world such as revenge or other selfish reasons.

There are, of course, many genuine Spirit guides dwelling within the inner levels of the Astral worlds who are truly concerned with the well-being and Spiritual progress of the person they are guiding. It is not always easy to determine which Spirits are genuine in their intentions and which are not. Should you make contact with a potential Spirit guide in meditation, in dreams or any other way, you should always follow your inner guidance and the voice or intuition of your Higher Self, who will know the true nature of the Spirit you are in contact with. If your inner voice or intuition says "leave well lone", you should always heed this advice without question.

Genuine Spirit guides will never, ever compel you to do anything, especially against your own freewill. They are there to help you according to your needs and evolution, only assisting or answering questions if specifically asked to do so. Your Higher Self (Holy Guardian Angel) can be completely trusted at all times.

The main mission of a Spirit guide, as the name suggests, is to literally guide people through life by offering and providing assistance as Universal laws allow. This assistance includes help in resolving life problems, help with healing, communication with deceased relatives, and much more. Again, however, a Spirit guide can only assist if such help is pro-actively requested, either consciously or Subconsciously, in order to avoid compromising freewill.

It is quite possible to communicate intentionally and directly with Spirit guides by telepathy, although this usually takes a great deal of practice. For those who have not yet established direct conscious contact with their Spirit guide, assistance from the guide can arrive in many and varied forms, including "voices" appearing as thoughts, impressions, intuition, within dreams and by way of synchronistic events. These are events which might seem like a pure coincidence at the time, but which actually have a deeper meaning. People who practice meditation often find themselves communicating with a Spirit guide sooner or later, and once such communication has been established, it will often be ongoing.

Synchronicity is a particular common way for Spirit guides to assist and make their presence felt. If they really want to make a point, they will create a synchronicity in the person's life, immediately causing the person to take notice. Synchronicities are experiences created by the Soul or Higher Self in order to bring greater awareness. A person, either alone or with the assistance of their Spirit guide, creates the synchronistic event in an inner realm through the mediation of the Soul, subsequently manifesting it into the physical world. If, for example, you happen to be walking along one day and meet someone by "accident" that you had previously been thinking about, it is usually because your Soul and the Soul of the person you have just met have made the decision within the inner realms such as the Astral, to meet each other. There is absolutely no such thing in the Universe as "chance". The laws of Cause and Effect are ever present within our lives.

In conclusion, although we do not need a Spirit guide or guides in order to progress through any particular incarnation, they do mean well and by helping others they help themselves in their own evolution, in accordance with "service to others before service to self". Unlike the physical world which presents numerous challenges to be overcome in the learning process, within the Astral worlds, such physical challenges simply do not exist, making progress much more difficult. Residents of the Astral therefore welcome the opportunity to assist their own advancement by assisting humans on Earth. That said Spirit guides should be kept in perspective and treated with respect, but recognised for their true role in our lives. Spirit guides, however well meaning, do not circumvent the truth that we all create our own reality at all levels by means of the freewill provided by our Creator, and are therefore entirely responsible for our own actions and own Spiritual evolution.

Chapter 52
Communications From the Inner Spheres

As mankind has accelerated its descent into gross materialism, away from The Sources of Universal reality and knowledge and the true path, bands of Spirits in the inner spheres have increasingly endeavoured to communicate with people on Earth in an attempt to turn mankind back towards the Light. Throughout all levels of Energy and vibration of the Universe, the Beings of the inner spheres always assist the Beings of the outer spheres on the path of return to The Source from whence we came in the beginning, knowing that we are ultimately all One and therefore all equal aspects of the same Divine Creator.

The Spirits of the inner realms know that if the truth of the physical process known as "death" could be conclusively proven to mankind, the present course of the humanity could be turned back from the brink of where it is currently heading. The main focus of the inner spheres, therefore, especially during the last two hundred years or so, has been to encourage contact with the inner spheres through people usually known as "mediums" who are receptive to such contact.

In more recent years, the term "medium" has been replaced or used interchangeably with "channel", and the act of a medium communicating with inner spheres is usually known as "channeling". There are varied types and degrees of channeling, ranging from transient psychic contact from a state of full waking awareness, to trance channeling, materialization and the direct voice.

Later in this book we will discuss all of these many and varied methods of communicating with the inner spheres in detail

Chapter 53
Psychics

A search on the Internet today will reveal numerous "psychic services", frequently advertised as "psychic hotlines", usually offered through "premium rate" telephone services charging several dollars per minute to the telephone account of the "client". These services are offered in various forms, including psychic, rune, and tarot card readings.

There are certainly genuinely gifted psychics offering services today, but there are also numerous indiscriminate people claiming to be genuine psychics who seem to do nothing more than play on the emotions, desperation and vulnerability of people, many of whom are recently bereaved, with the sole purpose of obtaining their money at all costs.

Psychic readings are not a definitive telling of the future or of a specific direction in life, and any psychic claiming the contrary should be avoided. There is no such concept of the "future", what humans perceiving to be the "future" being in fact Quantum probabilities from which any situation can manifest in accordance with influences in the moment of Now. Genuine psychics can therefore only suggest possibilities based upon their own interpretation of the "psychic Energy" associated with the person receiving the reading. It is then for the recipient of the reading to alter the course of their life, which they often do unconsciously as a result of the influence of the reading, in the direction of the future probable outcome in order to be more "in tune" with that probability in which case it becomes self-fulfilling. There is, however, no guarantee.

Since everyone creates their own reality, it is important to proceed on the sacred path accordingly while not relying on the word of others. Someone believing that a psychic can provide an accurate "reading" may be so influenced as to change their lives in the direction of the reading, with potentially adverse results, because their freewill has been compromised. If you choose to seek the services of a psychic, it is very important to determine the absolute honesty, integrity and level of abilities of the psychic before parting with any money, and definitely before spending any time on a “psychic hotline”. A bad or fraudulent psychic readings can and do leave a person in a much worse state than before the reading took place.

It is certainly not my intention to suggest that all psychics are charlatans, or that genuine psychics cannot provide a worthwhile service. But at the same time, due to the very large and increasing numbers of “psychics” on the end of “psychic hotlines”, extreme caution should be exercised, otherwise there is a serious risk of making a costly mistake in more ways than one. Later we will discuss how avoid these pitfalls in detail.

We will also discuss in a later section of this book how each and every person can assume the fullest control over their own reality without the need for the services of a psychic, medium or any other such service. This is not accomplished by the need for a psychic “predicting” the future, but rather by proactively deciding what your own future should be and consciously creating that future for yourself. Always remember that there is absolutely nothing that we cannot be, do or have, and no psychic reading will ever alter that absolute fact—a truth due to the perfect, immutable workings of the Universe, The Source, of God, of Whom we are all equal and inseparable aspects.

Chapter 54
Psychic Mediums

The most basic form of channeling is that used by “psychics” who “hear” the voices of Spirits “in their heads”. These include the “television psychics” or “psychic mediums”, as they often call themselves. This type of psychic will often work with a large group of people or sometimes on a private one-on-one basis or at longer distance by telephone, email or Internet instant messenger service.

It is often very difficult for the average person to differentiate between a good and genuine psychic medium and a charlatan who uses a technique designed to deceive people called “cold reading”. Any genuine psychic medium should be prepared to do one-on-one personal “sittings”, and should be able to provide a list of verifiable testimonials from satisfied clients.

The importance of such precautions cannot be emphasized enough, as the consequences for failing to do so can be very adverse. The following chapter of this book will provide you with guidelines about psychics and genuine psychic services.

Always listen to your inner guidance and never, ever agree to the services of a psychic of any kind if your intuition of your Higher Self advises against it. Your Higher Self knows everything about you at all levels, and will always serve as your very best and most trusted guidance. Again, there is absolutely no benefit whatsoever to be gained by obtaining the services of anyone purporting to “tell your future”. Not only is it absolutely impossible because the “future” does not exist except as a human concept, most importantly everyone creates their own “future”, their own reality in the present moment of Now, a “future” which can be seriously compromised by listening to the opinions of someone who is not in a position to either predict the “future”, or influence your own reality.

Chapter 55
Genuine Psychic Services

How does a genuine psychic offer their services and how can you tell the difference between a genuinely talented and experience psychic practitioner from a charlatan opportunist cashing in on the expanding Internet "psychic hotline" craze?

First of all, we should recognize the fact that every single human being, as well as many animals, has inherent, usually latent psychic abilities. With most people these abilities are below the surface of the conscious Mind in a dormant state, never having been fully exercised. Genuine psychics, clairvoyants and mediums are often born with conscious psychic abilities to some extent, and then, with that realization, further develop their psychic abilities over the course of many years. It has been discovered for example that many people with these abilities have physical differences in anatomy of their brain, often from birth but sometimes as a result of a brain injury. It should be noted however that abilities such as these are in no way related to how Spiritually advanced a person might be.

Sometimes such people benefit from some high level of training by other experienced psychics. Some psychics are fortunate enough to have high level psychic abilities from birth, but these are relatively scarce.

Other genuine psychics possess clairvoyant abilities and can actually "see" images in their "Mind's eye". The "Mind's eye" is actually an Etheric Energy centre—one of the seven "chakras" often known as the "third eye", "brow centre" or "brow chakra".

Some genuine psychics are "clairaudient", which means that they "hear" answers in their minds, usually from other Spiritual Beings. In this case, the psychic is actually a medium.

There are also genuine psychics who work with the “intuition”, “feelings” or “impressions” they receive in response to the various questions asked. This works in a similar way to remote viewing. Some psychics concurrently possess all of these abilities and can use them in combination.

Few people, however, have psychic powers that can be usefully engaged on behalf of others, i.e. to provide an accurate, meaningful “psychic reading” of the “future”, regardless of what a psychic might claim. Any psychic claiming the ability to provide an accurate psychic reading of this sort should be avoided. Where psychic abilities can be of value are in locating or expanding information on things that already exist, as in finding missing persons for example. Remote viewing works in a similar way, on the basis that space and time do not exist and therefore represent no true barriers.

Other forms of psychic readings make use a method often known as “scrying” or “divination”. These methods use instruments such as Tarot, the I Ching, runes, crystal balls or even tea leaves in order to purportedly view the future. Numerology is a more complex form of scrying. As impressive and even glamorous as these might sound, it is highly doubtful that these abilities are genuinely available to more than a very small number of talented people, and even then, as previously mentioned, it is not possible to accurately tell the “future” which simply does not exist.

Another well-known form of scrying is Astrology. By Astrology, we do not mean “reading the stars” or the “horoscope” in the newspaper, which is not really Astrology and should never be relied upon in any way except as a form of entertainment. True Astrology is a highly sophisticated form of scrying and one which requires considerable experience over many years on the part of the practitioner to be at all accurate.

Again, it must be stressed that no psychic, regardless of any claims to the contrary or whatever instruments they use, can ever foretell the absolute future for anyone. The “future”, as it relates to the “present” relative to the Earth perception and concept of “time”, depends entirely on a range of quantum probabilities—of potential, possible or probable future events existing within the inner multi-dimensional realities beyond the confines of the physical world where space and time do not exist. At any particular time, as it is measured in physical terms, there can be any one of an infinite number of possible quantum probabilities or outcomes for any particular event.

Consulting a psychic can cause people to Subconsciously move their lives in the direction of one of these multi-dimensional quantum probabilities, thereby increasing the chances of that probability becoming a quantum reality in the physical world—in other words it becomes self-fulfilling. Also, if a person believes in their own Mind that the “prediction” is true, then that belief will be impressed upon the Subconscious Mind of the person, which will then manifest it into their reality, so again it becomes self-fulfilling. This is often erroneously misinterpreted as an accurate “psychic reading”.

Assuming all diligence has been heeded and a high quality and genuine “reader” has been located, such services can be of tangible benefit for mental comfort, as a form counselling providing expectations are not too high and the entire situation is kept in a proper perspective by the client.

Be extremely wary of psychics who ask leading questions, seeking too much information from you, or who provide broad, generic type answers that could easily apply to almost anyone. A very large number of charlatans purporting to be psychics, particularly on an a premium rate ”psychic hotline” use a well practiced and proven method of deception known as “cold reading” which fundamentally involves talking to the client and asking certain questions designed to obtain personal information from the client without them realising why the questions have been asked. The cold reading psychic will then later in the sitting use this information, re-arranging and introducing it in such a way as to seem to the client that the psychic has obtained the information by "psychic means".

Such a cold reading question and answer session might proceed as follows:

Psychic: *I am getting someone coming through who says his name is John. Do you know someone by the name of John?*

Client: *I have actually known quite a few people called John.*

Psychic: *I am also getting someone coming through who says they are a grandparent who has quite recently passed over. Do you have a grandparent who has recently passed over?*

Client: *Well my grandmother passed on about 5 years ago.*

Psychic: *Yes, the connection is becoming stronger now. It is definitely your grandmother coming through. I sense that your grandmother would like you to sort out your relationships.*

Client: *Relationships? Relationships with who?*

Psychic: *Your relationships generally, especially with other family members.*

Client: *Oh, I see what you mean.*

And so the session continues with the psychic asking ever more searching questions in order to build a framework of the life and circumstances of the client, in this case around the "deceased grandmother" as the reference. This information is then used to give a convincing psychic reading by introducing the same information into the reading as the opportunity arises. Such a reading, of course, is totally fake and at best worthless.

Another common ploy used by charlatan psychics is to state that something very important (often something the client is longing for) will happen by a specific date. Of course, when that event inevitably fails to transpire on the date stated by the psychic, the anxious person who received that prediction will call back on the premium rate telephone service in a distressed state, wanting to know why the event did not happen and when it will happen. In this way, the psychic can lock the client into a series of very expensive readings for as long as the client is desperate enough to go along with it. This is just one of many such ploys used by charlatans using psychic hotlines. Again I would mention that I in no way mean to imply that all psychic hotlines are fake, but there is no practical way for a person to determine any genuine ones from the fake before making the premium rate phone call.

So the question is this. If you wish to seek the services of a genuine psychic, what should you do?

First of all, it is not at all unreasonable for a psychic to charge for their services, although many of the very best and most genuine psychics actually do not. One characteristic of a genuine psychic is the desire to be of selfless service to other people without any thought whatsoever of reward. This also applies to genuine healers and other Spiritual people whose main objective is to be of service to humanity.

Those psychics that do charge a nominal amount for their services will charge by the “sitting” and never by the minute. Again, charges will vary, but a typical charge might be $50 for a telephone “sitting” of long enough duration to be of tangible value to the client. In most cases, the charge will be a lot less or even free depending on the circumstances of the client. If a psychic does provide their services for free, you should offer a donation in an amount that you feel is appropriate. The most important consideration is not if or what they charge for the services, but whether they are actually genuine or not.

Never be taken in by the clothing in which a psychic dresses, particularly as pictured on an Internet site. Many psychics are often seen to be wearing all manner of mystical looking clothing as "props", often including such theatrical props as a head scarf of the sort worn by "fortune tellers", and sitting in front of a crystal ball or pack of tarot cards spread out on a table. Genuine psychics never feel the need to impress or mislead in this way, always preferring to dress naturally, always with the best atmosphere for communications with the inner spheres.

Also do not be taken in by fancy sounding names or titles beginning with the word "psychic" followed by a mystical sounding name such as "Psychic Sue", "Clairvoyant Kate" or "Tarot Tom".

Another indication of a genuine psychic is their temperament and overall personality. Genuine psychics are usually very sensitive people and would never, ever seem to be rushed, frustrated, or annoyed by your questions. Never be afraid to challenge a psychic directly on any information received. If their character or attitude changes as a result of this challenge, end the session right away.

If you must consult a psychic without obtaining testimonials and recommendations, which is extremely ill advised, the first few questions should be used to establish the psychic's credibility. Ask the following as an absolute minimum:

1. Where did you receive your formal training as a psychic?

2. How many years have you been providing psychic services?

3. In what environment have most of your readings been carried out?

4. Are you prepared to offer at least 30 minutes without charge in order that I can establish the accuracy of your readings by asking you a few simple questions?

5. Can you provide the names and full contact details for at least 10 clients who are willing to be contacted?

These are all totally reasonable questions and ones that should be asked first. Now, let us look at the sort of answers you should receive:

1. Even naturally gifted psychics require training from other experienced psychics in order to maximize their own potential, as well as for the benefit of the client. This can be a long and ongoing process. If a psychic says they have not received such training, leave.

2. As with all things, a psychic requires time and experience in order to develop their abilities to a high degree. There are no fixed timescales but a minimum length of experience of ten years would be reasonable.

3. Most genuine psychics will be familiar with and utilize traditional psychic "sittings". These will typically take place in the home of a psychic or client or in another recognized environment such as a Spiritualist church. If a psychic has only Internet, telephone, email or other long distance experience, this is not sufficient experience. First-hand psychic sitting experience with the client present is crucial.

4. Most genuine psychics should be prepared to provide 30 minutes of their time free of charge in order for you to fully satisfy yourself they really are genuine. Despite what any psychic might claim to the contrary, 10 minutes, 15 minutes, or even 20 minutes is not sufficient time to determine the authenticity of a psychic providing you are asking the right questions.

5. Obtaining genuine, reachable and verifiable references from satisfied clients is an absolute must before accepting any consultation with a psychic. Obtain at least half a dozen such references and always follow up by contacting each reference personally, asking them for the basis of their testimonials for the psychic. Only if all of the references prove to be totally authentic and their answers are satisfactory should you proceed with the consultation.

I should mention that you should not be influenced by "ratings" and comments on the web pages of psychic hotlines. Those comments have often been made immediately after a reading, before the client has had the opportunity to "cool off", and to calmly consider the reading and its true value.

Once you have found your psychic, and you believe them to be genuine, it is extremely important for you to know how to interact with the psychic for your own maximum benefit while allowing the psychic to be able to function efficiently.

Never get involved in chatty conversations with the psychic. If you do this, you will unwittingly provide the psychic with plenty of information they can use to make the reading appear impressive. Always be polite but remain detached.

Never volunteer any information of any sort. Answer any questions as briefly as possible without elaborating on them and without disclosing fundamental information that the psychic could make use of later in the reading. Always keep in mind that if the "psychic" really is psychic, and are communicating with someone in the non-physical world, they should be easily able to obtain this information for themselves.
If this is a one-on-one local reading, observe the body language of the psychic to see if they seem comfortable with the session. If they do not seem comfortable, the psychic connections are probably not there, and the sitting will serve no useful purpose.

Observing body language is also a very good indication as to whether the psychic is genuine. The psychic should appear to be relaxed, friendly and focused at all times.

There is much more that could be said about the “psychic hotline” industry which is now becoming a billion dollar business. However, it is important to know that we all create our own reality, and nothing any psychic can ever say or do can detract from that truth. So, rather than take a large risk by consulting a psychic, it is far more preferable to know exactly what you wish for and set about bringing that wish into reality yourself, by means of your own God-given natural powers.

Chapter 56
The Ouija Board

The Ouija board has long been a popular method of attempting to contact "the other side" and is probably the only product sold on a large scale for this specific purpose. The name "Ouija" is derived from the French and German words for "yes", "oiu" and "ja". The Ouija consists of a flat board upon which is printed the letters of the alphabet, some numbers, punctuation marks and the words "*yes*" and "*no*". The participants proceed by placing their fingers lightly on a pointer, known as a "planchette", which then supposedly moves to spell out a series of messages from purported spirits.

Many users of the Ouija board regard this activity simply as a novelty for parties and other group experiences without fully realizing the very real dangers involved. The Ouija board can and often does work at times, and many "communications" received can be from "the other side". Many of these contacts however are with entities residing in the lowest levels of the Astral whose intentions are often much less than honorable.

As discussed previously, humans and other Beings living in the lowest Astral worlds are there not out of choice but rather because of the dark, negative and sometimes very "evil", low vibrational lives they previously led on Earth, now existing at these correspondingly low levels of vibration. The danger with this is that the lower in the Astral plane an entity exists, the easier it is for them to make contact with the physical world through the Ouija board, due to the fact that vibrations between the two spheres of existence are relatively close together.

Always remember that these low Astral planes are a perfect reflection of the character of the entities existing there. The more "inner" the Being relative to the physical world, the more evolved and trustworthy the Being is. At the same time it is more difficult for people living in the physical world to contact such evolved Beings due to the much wider difference in vibration. This simple guideline should always be kept in mind in these situations.

The entities of the lower Astral worlds will frequently revel in claiming to be Angels, Archangels, famous people or even God, while others will have no hesitation at all in claiming to be deceased people known to the Ouija board sitters, in fact these entities will claim to be anything the Ouija board sitters wish them to be in order to gain their confidence and by playing on the Ego. On other occasions, these lower Astral entities might even use obscenities. Why do these lower Astral entities behave in this way? Aside from the fact this is very often inherent the character of these entities at this stage of their evolution, and a reason why they inhabit the lower Astral worlds in the first place, their despair is often pushed to the extreme because they can no longer physically experience the material things they once enjoyed and very often abused. If they had any sort of reasonable capacity for true Love, they would not be in the situation they are in at that level of vibration. If they even had the capacity to ask for help to relieve them of their state of misery, such help would soon be forthcoming from more highly evolved Beings of the inner realms.

Mediums who have contacted entities at these lower Astral levels often report extremely hostile, abusive and sinister voices. These are the voices of the very same entities often contacted through Ouija boards. Because users of the Ouija board are usually hoping for genuine and useful contacts with inner level Spirits, they will almost always be deceived by these lower Astral entities.

Sometimes, this can be quite harmless, and although the Ouija board users are misled, there is no permanent harm done. There is a very real danger, however, of making contact with lower Astral entities with much darker and sinister motives. Such dangers include a lower Astral entity posing as a deceased relative. Once the lower Astral entity has been able to convince the Ouija board sitters of its identity as a deceased relative, it will often be very manipulative, proceeding to request or even demand certain things to be done for them, often flattering the Ouija board users and appealing to their Ego by saying that "I need help, and only you have the capability to provide it". Such requests are often carried out by the Ouija board sitters without question, both because they have been led to believe that they have "special powers", and not wanting to risk upsetting or offending what they genuinely believe to be a deceased relative, friend or inner Spiritual Being in need of help.

Lower Astral residents do not like dwelling in their dark worlds and will seize any opportunity to take control of a physical body in the material world. This could very easily lead to a full possession resulting in all sorts of potentially adverse consequences, including but not limited to severe psychological illnesses. The personality of the possessed person might change dramatically for the worse as the lower Astral entity exerts more control.

The Ouija board should always be regarded as a potentially dangerous instrument and avoided altogether. Those insisting on ignoring these dangers should at least be aware of the type of entity they are likely to meet and what their real motives are. Any entity claiming to be a deceased relative should be thoroughly tested by asking questions to which only such a genuine relative would know the answers. The same principle also applies to all entities purporting to be Angels, Archangels, "Ascended Masters", famous people or even God.

Stoker Hunt, a person who carried out research into the effects arising from the use the Ouija board, summarized a common pattern of communication that can often develop when people make contact with entities within the low levels of the Astral worlds. He said:

"The invader focuses on the victim's character weaknesses, if one is vain, appeals to vanity are made. 'I need your help' the seducer will say, 'and only you can help me'. The entity is malicious and does not hesitate to lie, misrepresent itself (usually as a deceased loved one) and flatter. It's better for the invader of course if the victim is alone, isolated and ill. If needs be the invader will terrify its victim, materializing in ghastly form, inducing grotesque visions, inciting poltergeist activity, causing objects to appear out of the blue, delivering false or tragic news, levitating objects, perhaps levitating the victim. All these things and more might be done, not as ends among themselves, but as a means to an eventual complete possession".

Dr. Carl Wickland, an American psychiatrist, wrote his classic work on mental illness, "Thirty Years Among the Dead", in 1924. He warns:

"The serious problem of alienation and mental derangement attending ignorant psychic experiments was first bought to my attention by cases of several persons whose seemingly harmless activities with automatic writing and the Ouija board resulted in such wild insanity that commitment to asylums was necessitated. Many other disastrous results which followed the use of the supposedly innocent Ouija board came to my notice, and my observations led me into research in psychic phenomena for a possible explanation of these strange occurrences".

Not all Ouija board contacts are malevolent, of course, and there have also been many positive, long-term communications made with friendly inner level Astral Beings. One particularly noteworthy case was that of Pearl Curran who used a Ouija board with her neighbor on July 12, 1912. After a year of experimenting, she began to receive messages from Patience Worth, a Spirit entity who claimed she was born in 1649 in Dorsetshire, England. Between 1912 and 1919, she dictated five million words through the board, including epigrams, poems, full-length novels, allegories and short stories. Her collective works filled 29 bound volumes, and 4,375 single-spaced pages. These works included five full length novels, the most successful being "A Sorry Tale", a 300,000 word story of the Earthly life of Jesus which was reviewed by the New York Times on July 8, 1917: *"This long and intricate tale of Jewish and Roman life during the time of Christ is constructed with the precision and accuracy of a master hand. It is a wonderful, a beautiful and noble book".* Patience Worth won many more accolades and awards over the years for a wide variety of literary work.

Another famous Spiritual entity who first appeared by means of the Ouija board called himself "Seth", and he first made an appearance when Jane Roberts and her husband began using a Ouija board in 1963. The entity eventually introduced itself as Frank Withers, an English teacher, who died in 1942. He preferred to be known as "Seth" and stated his mission as helping people to understand themselves and reality better.

Through Jane Roberts, Seth dictated several best-selling books dealing with the nature of reality, reincarnation, Astral travel, dreams and the nature of God. Seth also provided step-by-step teachings on meditation techniques and extrasensory perception. He was able to diagnose illnesses, correctly describe the contents of buildings and rooms many miles away, and also materialized as an apparition.

There have been many other such successful uses of the Ouija board that proved to be of great value to the people concerned, and in some cases, such as Seth, to humanity as a whole. This should not be taken as reason in and of itself to justify the inherent risks involved in using the Ouija board. James Merrill, a Pulitzer Prize winner, describes his Ouija board experiences when he wrote "The Changing Light at Sandover" in 1982. His frightening experiences including visions, body transformation, and the feeling of powerful presences, as well as more memorable and joyous ones recorded in the poem. After thirty years, however, he no longer recommends people use the Ouija board because "one can never tell how susceptible a given person will be".

On balance, the use of a Ouija board and similar mechanical instruments such as automatic writing should be strongly discouraged. Due to the nature of the way these instruments function, it is much more likely to attract low-level Astral entities than well-meaning or even helpful inner-level Beings. Those who do attract lower level entities ultimately stand a very high chance of possession and/or serious mental illness, both of which would be nearly impossible to overcome by modern medical means.

The most sensible solution is to resist any such temptations completely, leaving the Ouija board and similar, alone for your own safety and for the safety of those around you.

Chapter 57
Trance Mediums

Trance mediums place themselves in an altered state of Consciousness known as a “trance” with the objective of “channeling” information directly from Beings of the inner realms. Although trance mediums can and often do make contact with deceased humans, they have also been successful in making contact with inner level Spirits, many of whom can provide valuable and accurate information on Spiritual matters.

Over the years, genuine trance mediums with high level channeling abilities have channeled a considerable amount of valuable information from Spirits of the inner spheres. These inner-level, “higher” Beings have sometimes channeled information through the same medium for many years, the information received being the subject of many and varied books. The following are just three of the most notable cases of channeling from such advanced Spiritual Beings.

White Eagle: A high level Spirit who for many years during the first part of the twentieth century channeled a very large quantity of advanced information and teachings through the mediumship of Grace Cook.

Silver Birch: Through the mediumship of Maurice Barbanell around the middle of the twentieth century, Silver Birch was present at numerous “sittings” during which he patiently answered questions for the “sitters”. A “sitting” is a group of people attending what is often known as a “séance”, where the medium invokes a trance. The Spirit will then “talk” through the body of the medium directly.

Over the course of many years, such sittings were frequently held at the home of Maurice Barbanell, during which time

Silver Birch answered literally thousands of questions for hundreds of visitors from all over the world.

Both "White Eagle" and "Silver Birch" are pseudonyms for the purposes of communicating with people on Earth who expect these Beings to have names. These great Spirits actually represent entire groups of very high level Beings all working together as one within the inner Spiritual realms for the direct benefit of mankind through these individual identities.

In the case of Silver Birch, in order to achieve contact with his medium Maurice Barbanell from the inner realms of the Mental plane, it was necessary to make use of the vacated Astral body of an American Indian as an "interface", effectively functioning in the same way as a "step down transformer", in order to mediate the differences between the very high Energy vibrations of the inner Spiritual worlds where Silver Birch resides, and the much lower Energy vibrations and density of the physical world of the medium.

Maurice Barbanell was also the editor of a publication called "Psychic News", in which he published full transcripts of the question and answer sessions that had previously taken place between Silver Birch and the sitters. In addition, there were many books published detailing the Silver Birch question and answer sessions, all providing considerable information on a wide range of important Spiritual matters. These valuable books are still available today.

Seth: As previously discussed, through the mediumship of Jane Roberts, a Spirit referring to himself simply as "Seth" channeled a large volume of Spiritual information over a number of years. These channeled sessions resulted in a series of books still available today.

There are several other groups of advanced Beings channeling valuable information to Earth through mediums, the teachings of many of which have been made into books and other media.

Chapter 58
Materialization Mediums

Materialization mediums are a less well-known type of medium, who are able to allow the Spirits with whom they are communicating to draw large quantities of ectoplasm from the body of the medium (and to a lesser extent from the sitters present for the channeling), allowing the Spirits to materialise and actually become visible either completely or in part.

Unlike Spirits channeled by the trance mediums mentioned in the previous chapter, these Spirits tend to be mid-Astral level Souls who are not able to impart much high level Spiritual information, but do provide valuable evidence for the continuation of life after the "death" of the physical body, and of the conditions and their own experiences encountered after passing. Usually, only low to mid-level Beings can lower their vibration enough to interact with ectoplasm and thereby materialize. Entities known as "ghosts" have a low level of vibration and correspondingly higher density, a reason they are so often "seen" as apparitions. Materialized Spirits, like channeled Spirits, nevertheless provide compelling evidence for the continuity of life after the death of the physical body, thereby providing a valuable service to humanity.

One of the most famous of all materialization mediums was Helen Duncan, who carried out numerous successful séances where Spirits of the deceased would materialize completely in ectoplasmic form and were able to communicate with all present at the séance on a one-on-one basis using exactly the same voice they were recognised by while living on Earth. Many of the séances of Helen Duncan took place in the 1930's and 1940's during the time of World War II. Not surprisingly therefore, many of the Spirits who materialized were people who had been killed during the fighting. The services of Helen Duncan often provided great comfort to bereaved relatives, many of whom were actually able to see and hold conversations directly with their "deceased" loved ones.

Throughout the war years, Helen Duncan reunited many grieving relatives with servicemen who had lost their physical lives in action. At one particular séance in Portsmouth, a sailor materialized and was reunited with his mother. The sailor said that his ship, HMS Bahrnam, had very recently sunk. Maurice Barbanell, the editor of "Psychic News" and the medium for Silver Birch, heard about this and made inquiries at the admiralty as to whether this sinking was true and if so why the relatives of the deceased crew members had not been officially informed. The admiralty was furious because the sinking of the HMS Bahrnam was still considered to be classified information. The military authorities became very concerned that a medium of the capabilities of Helen Duncan could obtain further classified information from deceased army personnel, especially sensitive information regarding the forthcoming D-Day landings. Of course, this was not her intention at all.

The authorities subsequently arrested Helen Duncan, who was by that time a frail lady, with six children and a disabled husband to support, and sent her to jail for nine months, causing her husband and children to be evicted from their family home as Helen was no longer in a position to support them. The authorities needed to find a suitable law under which to charge her, finally deciding to make use of the extremely primitive, archaic and barbaric witchcraft laws that were still in force in Britain at the time. Helen Duncan was later visited in jail by Winston Churchill, who was absolutely appalled by the situation. As a direct result, Churchill promised to repeal all such archaic and barbaric laws at the very first opportunity.

During her subsequent trial, forty one highly credible witnesses swore under oath that they had been present when their loved ones had materialized and communicated with them during Duncan's séances. One such witness was a high-ranking wing commander who stated that he had met his dead mother, father and brother at these séances. Not a single one of these highly credible witnesses was broken under cross-examination.

The court also contrived a case that all of these materializations must have been the work of accomplices wearing false beards, wigs, white cloaks and other such items, but no such evidence, of course, was ever found. Helen Duncan did not charge money for her services, so such an elaborate deceit would not have made any sense whatsoever.

Some years later, a team of stage magicians headed by William Goldston, the founder of the magicians club, carried out an experimental sitting with Helen Duncan. He and his colleagues were completely astounded when a deceased famous stage magician, "The Great Lafayette", materialized and spoke to the group in his own voice. Goldston later reported in "Psychic News" that Duncan must be genuine, and that no magician could possibly duplicate the phenomena he and his colleagues had witnessed that day.

In 1956, police in Nottingham raided a séance held by Helen Duncan. Despite the police knowing very well that materialization séances need to take place in semi-darkness due to sensitivity to light of ectoplasm, they apparently made a grab for the medium and took flash photographs of the surroundings. Needless to say, nothing was ever found, and the photographs revealed no evidence of any sort of malpractice. However, the shock incurred by the sudden withdrawal of ectoplasm due to exposure to the bright lights of the camera flashes was sufficient to very seriously injure Helen Duncan, and most sadly, she passed on within five weeks of the raid.

Helen Duncan was certainly one of the world's most gifted materialization mediums, and it is a sad reflection that the life of this frail, well-meaning lady should have been terminated in such a brutal way for no other reason than the continued ignorance of the "authorities". Her legacy continues to this day.

The Noah's Ark Society for Physical Mediumship was formed in England in 1990 and now has a membership of 1700 people and 150 member circles worldwide. It was established to provide a safe haven for mediums and to protect them from what the President of the society describes as: "the harsh treatment meted out to early pioneer physical mediums from so-called researchers who insisted on trussing up the medium, demanding endless tests, and inflicting grave harm physically through violating the laws governing physical phenomena".

Chapter 59
The Direct Voice

The direct voice is one of the most compelling forms of mediumship, in which the people present at a sitting are able to clearly hear Spirits speak aloud in their normal voices—exactly the same voices as they were known by in physical life. This was particularly reassuring for the relatives of the deceased ones as they then knew beyond any doubt from the accent, style of speaking, phraseology, words used and information received that they were indeed in direct communication with their loved ones speaking to them from the "beyond".

As with materialization, direct voice involves the use of ectoplasm. Spirits draw ectoplasm from the throat chakra and other parts of the medium (and from the sitters to a lesser extent), to form the ectoplasm into an "Etheric voice box" through which they are able to speak from the Spirit side of the channel, manifesting in the physical world as a Spirit voice. This Etheric voice box functioned by making use of the ectoplasm to reduce the higher thought vibrations of the Spirits communicating through the "voice box" to a much lower rate of vibration that could translate to physically audible sound, working in much the same way as an electrical speaker converts electrical impulses into audible sound.

These Spirit voices were very often so clear and loud that it was exactly as if speaking to a physical person in the same room. Although direct voice sittings needed to take place in darkness, as with materialization sittings, due to the sensitivity to light of ectoplasm, the sitters could sometimes easily observe the whitish coloured ectoplasm exuding from the throat chakra and other areas of the medium. The ectoplasm could also be very clearly observed and photographed by means of infrared viewing equipment that did not affect it.

From the Spirit side of the channel, the ectoplasmic "voice portal" could be seen as a large glowing disk of Energy into which they would "speak". It should be noted that Spirits do not actually physically "speak" in the same way as physical people due to the absence of a physical body, but rather communicate by means of a projection by the Mind of thought toward the voice portal, which then in turn translates the thought vibrations into a clearly audible voice, again, just as an electronic audio speaker converts electromagnetic vibrations into audible sound. This process can also be likened to the hearing system of the physical body where vibrations of the eardrum are interpreted by the brain as "sound" that we can differentiate due to the wide range of vibrations received.

One of the most notable direct voice mediums was Leslie Flint. From 1911 to 1994, thousands of voices of discarnate Spirits were recorded through his mediumship. When these discarnate Spirit voices first began appearing to Leslie Flint, he was expelled from cinemas and theatres due to the disturbances caused by the Spirit voices, and, of course, people had no idea where the voices were actually coming from.

The voices channeled by Leslie Flint during his numerous sittings ranged from the Souls of the deceased relatives of the sitters to people who were once famous on Earth who came to deliver important messages, usually involving evidence for the continuity of life after physical death.

Of course, there were the usual groups of sceptics who believed Flint was a fraud. Flint often agreed, in order to dispel the claims of the sceptics, to conduct sittings in the presence of "researchers" who had carte blanche to carry out whatever experiments they deemed necessary in order to prove or disprove that the voices were indeed genuine. In one particular experiment, as reported in the "Psychic News" edition of 14 February 1948, Leslie Flint was physically tied to a chair with sticking plaster stuck over his lips to seal them together completely, and with bandages placed over his mouth over the sticking plaster. The researchers observed the Spirit voices still arrived with their usual volume and clarity. There were twelve people present during that particular sitting and all agreed the voices were most definitely not those of Leslie Flint but were rather of the Spirits who had arrived in order to communicate with the sitters. At the end of the sitting, everything previously applied by the researchers remained intact and undisturbed.

The information received directly from Spirits by means of the direct voice mediumship of Leslie Flint was not simple vague information of the type that could easily apply to anyone, but was rather extremely specific and accurate. A typical example involved an airman who was killed in action during World War II. This airman originally appeared at a sitting attended by Lord Dowding, giving his name as Peter William Handford Kite. The Spirit asked if his parents could be contacted at an address he supplied and be invited to attend a sitting where he would be present for them. The parents duly accepted the invitation and for nearly forty minutes, the airman communicated with them in his own clearly recognizable voice. His parents were able to confirm everything he said. Among the things he spoke of was a joke about buying an Alsatian dog, that his mother had put photographs of his grave in Norway in her bag that very morning, that he liked the cherry tree in the memorial garden they had planted for him, that his bedroom had not been changed in the six years since he had "died", that he had not liked the wallpaper in his bedroom, and that his father was still driving his car although it was too small for him.

Sceptics tried everything possible to discredit Leslie Flint, just as they had previously tried to discredit many other genuine mediums. In 1971, Leslie Flint had this to say:

"When I first began to allow myself to be tested, I was naive enough to believe that if the tests were successful the scientists and researchers who had carried them out under their own conditions would proclaim to all the world the truth of life after

death. All too soon I learned the hard way that many of those who call themselves researchers have immutable values of their own which preclude belief of a meaning or purpose in man's existence or the possibility of a life after death. Their concern was to disprove the reality of my voices and they would postulate any alternative, however far-fetched or absurd, sooner than admit the implication of their own successful experiment".

Some of the more ludicrous explanations put forward by some of these "researchers" included suggestions the voices were the result of some "hypnotic power" accompanied by "mass hallucinations". This was later disproved when a microphone was attached to the throat of Leslie Flint during a sitting such that even the slightest sound made through his larynx would be enormously magnified, while the researchers continuously observed him through an infrared telescope. When Flint proved them wrong, the best suggestion the researchers could claim was that he must "have the ability to talk through his stomach".

One impartial, open-Minded expert who did investigate Leslie Flint very thoroughly was Professor William R. Bennett, professor of electrical engineering at Columbia University in New York City. Engineers are usually regarded as highly practical and level-headed people, so his evidence was widely regarded to be of particular value. Professor Bennett said this:

"My experience with Mr. Flint is first hand; I have heard the independent voices. Furthermore, modern investigation techniques, not available in earlier tests corroborate previous conclusions by indicating the voices are not his. But to be thorough, one should consider the possibility of live accomplices. This suggestion became untenable to me during his visit to New York in September 1970, when, in an impromptu séance at my apartment, the same voices not only appeared, but took part in conversations with the guests".

Chapter 60
Electronic Voice Phenomena

As time has progressed since the days of materialization and direct voice mediums, science has played an increasingly important role in communicating with Spirits of the inner spheres. Many voices from the "beyond" have been captured on magnetic media and audiotape, often unintentionally while recording other sounds. There have been numerous cases, especially in recent years where the voices of deceased people now living in the Astral worlds, have appeared to the amazement of relatives and others who have heard these voices, by suddenly being heard on an ordinary magnetic audiotape. This often took place when something quite normal was being recorded, and these voices "from beyond" were not heard until the tape was played back. These voices are often very clear, carrying a short but simple message—enough to provide ample evidence of the presence of the deceased person.

It is this sort of experience that has prompted further extensive and controlled investigation into obtaining the voices of "deceased" Souls now living in the Astral realms by recording them on tape and similar electromagnetic recording devices. These experiments are often carried out in a similar way to conventional sittings or séances. The sitters simply sit around the recording device providing the necessary focus and Energy.

These messages cannot actually be heard while they are recorded due to the vast differences and vibrations between the Ether of the Astral and physical worlds, the vibration frequencies of the communicators being far higher than those of the capabilities of the human ear.

How does this situation occur? The entire Universe consists of Electric and Magnetic "fluids". These "fluids" are not actually liquids as recognized in the physical world, but are the electric and magnetic characteristics of the Universal Fire and Water elements. It is the electromagnetic propagation properties of the Ether and Electric and Magnetic fluids that facilitate communications of the Spirit voices—which are thought waves in the form of very high frequency Energy—to pass through the electromagnetic continuum of the Ether and be recorded.

During one particular set of experiments carried out under strictly controlled conditions in a soundproof studio, two researchers left a tape recorder running for 27 minutes, during which time 200 Spirit voices were recorded. As with all of these "phenomena", there were several sceptical scientists who endeavoured to find a "logical" explanation for these voices recorded on the tape, but they were completely unable to do so.

This area of research became known as "Electronic Voice Phenomena" or EVP. Many famous people considered pioneers in their fields, such as Marconi, Edison, Sir Oliver Lodge, Sir William Crookes and John Logie Baird, were totally convinced of the reality of Spirit communication by EVP and were using their professional skills and reputations to prove it. Even the Christian churches were open-Minded to EVP, including Catholics, Protestants and Fundamentalists.

The Catholic Church has in the past actively encouraged research into EVP. Two of the earliest religious investigators were Father Ernetti and Father Gemelli, who stumbled upon the Electronic Voice Phenomena while recording Gregorian chants in 1952. Father Gemelli apparently heard the voice of his own deceased father on the tape saying, "Zucchini, it is clear, don't you know it is I". "Zucchini" was the childhood name of Father Gemelli. Pope Pius, the cousin of the Rev. Professor Dr. Gebhard Frei was co-founder of the Jung Institute and an internationally recognized and respected parapsychologist who worked very closely with Dr Konstantin Raudive, a pioneer of EVP in Germany. Of these phenomena Dr. Frei stated:

"All that I have read and heard forces me to believe that the voices come from transcendental, individual entities. Whether it suits me or not, I have no right to doubt the reality of the voices".

Rev. Professor Dr Gebhard Frei passed on in October 27, 1967. In November 1967 at numerous EVP tape recording sessions, a voice claiming to be Gebhard Frei was recorded. The voice was positively confirmed and identified by Professor Peter Hohenwarter of the University of Vienna as unquestionably the voice belonging to Dr Frei.

The Catholic religion became increasingly supportive of EVP research with several Vatican-approved researchers producing compelling evidence for EVP. Father Leo Schmid, a Swiss theologist, collected more than ten thousand recorded voices in his book, "When the Dead Speak", in 1976, published shortly after his death.

In England in 1972, four senior members of the Catholic Church became involved in the famous Pye Recording Studio tests conducted by Peter Bander. Father Pistone, Superior of the Society of St. Paul in England, said this after the tests:

"I do not see anything against the teaching of the Catholic Church in the voices; they are something extra-ordinary, but there is no reason to fear them, nor can I see any danger".

A series of high and respected officials of the Catholic Church subsequently lent support to EVP in what has now become a firm Vatican position of acceptance for these "voices from beyond". The following definitive statement was issued by Father Gino Concetti at the Vatican:

"According to the modern catechism, God allows our dear departed persons who live in an ultra-terrestrial dimension, to send messages to guide us in certain difficult moments of our

lives. The Church has decided not to forbid any more the dialogue with the deceased with the condition that these contacts are carried out with a serious religious and scientific purpose".

Printed in the Vatican newspaper, *Osservatore Romano,* and cited in Sarah Estep's American Association Electronic Voice Phenomena, Inc Newsletter, Vol 16 No, 2 1997.

The "ultra-terrestrial dimension" to which Father Concetti refers is, of course, the Astral worlds, often referred to as the "beyond" or the "afterlife". The church itself does not as yet officially support the reality of the true multi-dimensional nature of the Universe or the reality of the true purpose and destiny of mankind. It is a positive thing, however, that it does at least officially support the reality of the continuity of life in an inner dimension after the "death" of the physical body.

Chapter 61
Instrumental Transcommunication

Instrumental Transcommunication or "ITC" is a particularly fascinating extension to the work of EVP. World ITC, an organization specializing in this field has this to say in introducing their cause:

"For thousands of years mediums and shamans have been in contact with a type of communicator that we don't see and we cannot touch. These types of communicators can't be perceived through our five senses. And the so called "normal" people (who are not aware that they might have mediumistic capabilities), often say that they feel that they are in contact with something/somebody in a way that other people cannot understand or believe. We define: Transcommunication takes place with partners we cannot perceive by use of our five senses. That is, partners inhabiting realms beyond our perception"

Note: Again, the "realms beyond our perception" is a reference to the Astral worlds.

ITC is a range of technologies and means by which communications arriving from people within the Astral worlds can be received and stored by technical equipment. Unlike Electronic Voice Phenomena, which largely focuses on audiotape recordings, ITC greatly extends the range and sophistication of equipment used to record these communications to include TVs, radios, computers, telephones, mini-disk recorders, video recorders, the psychophone, microphones, video cameras, amplifiers for microphones, noise generators, mixing desks, lasers, and ultrasonic's.

The big advantage of ITC is the possibility to prove to others that something out of the ordinary or "paranormal" is taking place. People generally have more faith in scientific evidence that they believe to be more "physically tangible".

The entire field of ITC has been evolving for a number of years. In the 1920's, Thomas Alva Edison, inventor, among many other things of the electric light, the motion picture camera and phonograph, was busy at work in his laboratory building a machine to achieve Spirit communication "with the dead". His assistant, Dr Miller Hutchinson, wrote:

"Edison and I are convinced that in the fields of psychic research will yet be discovered facts that will prove of greater significance to the thinking of the human race than all the inventions we have ever made in the field of electricity".

This was a most profound and important observation relating to the work of one of the greatest innovators that has ever lived.

Edison himself wrote:

"If our personality survives then it is strictly logical or scientific to assume that it retains memory, intellect and other facilities and knowledge we acquire on Earth. Therefore, if we can evolve an instrument so delicate as to be affected by our personality as it survived in the next life, such an instrument, when made available, should record something".

Around 1925, Oscar d'Argonell wrote a book entitled, "Voices from Beyond by Telephone", in which he detailed long conversations with his friends from the Spirit world. His book also gave details of how the calls were actually accomplished from the Spirit worlds.

In 1936, Atila von Szalay started experimenting with record cutting equipment and achieved success in recording Spirit voices on phonograph records.

In 1949, Marcello Bacci began recording voices using an old vacuum tube radio. A team of Spirits subsequently developed around his work speaking to him through radio sounds. It should be noted there are large bands of Souls within the Astral worlds who appoint themselves with the task of making and maintaining contact with people on Earth. The primary reason for this is to conclusively establish the truth, reality and importance of the continuity of life after the death of the physical body, thus assisting the advancement of mankind. People would visit Marcello Bacci at his home, and deceased relatives would often speak with them through the equipment.

In 1959, a Swedish film producer, Friedrich Juergenson, captured voices on audiotape while recording bird song. Listening more intently to his tapes, he heard his mother's voice say in German; *"Friedrich, you are being watched. Friedel, my little Friedel, can you hear me?"* During the next few years, he continued to record hundreds of voices from the Astral worlds. Friedrich Juergenson went on to publish two books on his work called "Voices from the Universe" and "Contact with the Dead".

In 1967, a researcher named Franz Seldel developed an instrument known as the "psychophone" for recording voices from the Astral worlds.

In 1971, a very important series of experiments took place involving the chief engineers of Pye Records Limited when they invited EVP pioneer, Konstantin Raudive, to their sound laboratory to install special filtering equipment to block out noise from radio waves. Raudive spoke into the microphone for eighteen minutes, during which time no other voices were heard in the studio. When the tape was played back, the researchers heard over 200 different Spirit voices from the Astral worlds. This well-known experiment led to a large number of independent people using home tape recording equipment to record and collect Spirit voices.

During the late 1970's, considerable progress was made when USA-based Spiritual researchers, George and Jeanette Meek, met a gifted psychic by the name of William O' Neil. The Meeks provided the resources for an advanced project in direct Spirit communication and invited the Spirit friends of William O' Neil to participate. One of his Spirit friends was Dr. George Jeffries Mueller, a deceased university professor and NASA scientist, who simply appeared in O'Neil's living room one day as a semi-materialized Spirit and announced he was there to assist in the project of Meek and O'Neil.

This became a remarkable collaboration between the Astral and physical worlds with Dr. Mueller assisting O'Neil to design a new piece of equipment that could convert Spirit voices into audible language. The device became known as the "Spiricom" and was comprised of a series of tone and frequency generators emitting 13 tones spanning the range of the adult male voice.

By late 1980, the Spiricom had evolved to the point where the Spirit voice of Dr. Mueller was loud and easily understandable. The pioneering work of the Meeks with their friends, William O' Neil and Dr. Mueller in the Astral world, became the catalyst for many similar experiments and research carried out all over the world.

Between 1982 and 1988, Hans Otto Koenig developed a new type of Spirit communication device utilizing extremely low frequency oscillators as well as ultraviolet and infrared lights. In 1983, he appeared on the popular Radio Luxembourg, where his equipment was set up under the close scrutiny of the radio station engineers. One of the engineers asked if a voice could come through in direct reply to a question, and a voice quickly replied, *"We hear your voice. Otto Koenig makes wireless contact with the dead"*. Stunned, the radio show presenter, Rainer Holbe, addressed the millions of listeners across Europe saying, *"I tell you, dear Listeners of Radio Luxembourg, and I swear by the life of my children, that nothing has been manipulated. There are no tricks. It is a voice, and we do not know from where it comes".*

Between 1984 and 1985, Ken Webster received some 250 messages on his computer from a Spirit named Thomas Harden who had passed on in the 16th century. The Spirit claimed he had owned the same property four centuries earlier. Thomas Harden appeared to have remained in the Etheric region of the Astral planes closest to the physical world and was, therefore, what is commonly known as a "ghost". Thomas Harden referred to the computer as a "light box" and sent information accusing Ken Webster of "stealing his house". The many messages that followed in an old English dialect contained much information about the life of Spirit and of that era, all facts that were later confirmed.

ITC has progressed over the years with many seemingly amazing "phenomena" involving Spirit communication from the "beyond". In 1985, Klaus Shreiber, began to receive the images of Spirits on his television set, including Albert Einstein and deceased Austrian actress, Romy Schneider, as well as various deceased family members.

In 1985, the science of ITC entered a new phase when Mark Macy of the World ITC organization and website (where many of the above examples of Spirit communications can be found) began to work closely with scientists and researchers on both sides of the Atlantic. Mark Macy said:

"Sixteen of us met in England to discuss this modern day miracle, its tremendous possibilities for our world, and the obstacles that stood in the way. We formed new friendships, and by the end of a long weekend we also formed INIT; The International Network for Instrumental Transcommunication. In the coming months ethereal Beings told us that they were observing our efforts closely and would provide guidance and support. We began to observe unprecedented miracles in our

research. Many of us received phone calls, from Spirit friend Konstantin Raudive, and the Harch-Fischbachs; (radio based ITC equipment of Maggy Harsch-Fischbach and her husband Jules Harsch of Luxembourg) *received astounding pictures and messages through their computer, all as a result of resonance among INIT members. It was clear that a new phase of ITC research on Earth had begun. Our Ethereal friends told us that the greatest strides would be made by individuals from different countries who committed to work together in harmony with pure intentions".*

As these aging researchers in turn passed on to the Astral worlds themselves, they very soon began to communicate with their colleagues still remaining on Earth. These researchers turned Spirit communicators from the Astral worlds included Konstantin Raudive, Friedrich Juergenson, Klaus Schreiber, William O' Neil and George Meek, all of whom wished to continue their research from their new side of the veil in the Astral worlds.

The World ITC website sums up this remarkable research with an equally remarkable conclusion: Ethereal Beings told INIT on more than one occasion that simply opening the door to the Spirit worlds can be dangerous, but researchers who work together and dedicate their efforts to inner human principles will receive ethereal guidance and protection.

As years passed, the Ethereal friends of Mark Macy, along with a team of more than one thousand Spirit Beings who had once lived on Earth, shared vast and astonishing information with INIT members through computers, telephones, radios and other technical media. Advanced ethereal Beings said they had accompanied our world for many thousands of years and had come close six times before when Earth had reached a crossroads, leading either to a dark age or a period of enlightenment. This was the seventh time, they said, and they wished to establish a lasting bridge with their formless realm of wise, loving Consciousness.

ITC research would be the means by which to establish that bridge. Through the work of INIT, it became evident that the more miraculous forms of ITC contact were made possible by such ethereal Beings who also provided protection and guidance for ITC researchers and their Spirit friends. Mark Macy has been a leading researcher in ITC for many years. In 2001, he experienced "miracles" in his laboratory, including color images of Spirits on a regular basis and the steady improvement of radio contacts toward a loud and clear dialogue.

It is clear that the field of Instrumental Transcommunications has proved to be very important in verifying the continuity of life after the death of the physical body. As the years progress, the work of people like Mark Macy and his World ITC, together with the numerous other scientists and researchers working together from both within the physical and Astral worlds, will become progressively more important as one of the main routes for inner level Spirit communications.

Chapter 62
Channeling Conclusion

There are numerous means by which to establish and maintain contact with a wide range of Beings from the inner spheres of reality, especially human Beings. While some methods of communications can be considered to be relatively safe for the genuine and experienced channeler, medium or researcher, others are potentially very dangerous, especially to those not understanding the consequences of their actions, as we have already seen while looking at the Ouija board.

Any form of channeling by inexperienced people should be regarded as potentially dangerous, and even ultimately fatal, and should therefore never be attempted. Genuine channelers, mediums and EVP experts have been practicing their particular disciplines for many years and fully understand any dangers involved and how to deal with them should they arise. Many of these people also have entire bands of Beings in the Astral and inner spheres assisting, watching over and protecting them.

Although many forms of channeling are highly effective when practiced by genuine channelers, mediums and researchers, including those mentioned earlier in this section, there have been many incompetent practitioners, as well as large numbers of outright charlatans. Such charlatans are particularly dark as they are more than happy to prey upon recently bereaved people and others suffering in various ways. The general public tends to take the cynical and skeptical view by focusing on the charlatans, claiming them to be representative of all mediums, channelers and communicators which is far from the truth.

In other cases, researchers who are totally rooted in the Newtonian three-dimensional world of physical matter have tended to commit much of their time and Energy to disproving the ability to contact Beings of the inner realms. Many people have become understandably disillusioned after one or more experiences with fraudulent mediums or those purporting to be "psychics".

It is not at all surprising therefore that genuine channeling, mediumship and instrumental research has never achieved the level of acceptance necessary for mankind to take it seriously.

As mentioned earlier, there is a whole hierarchy of more advanced Beings, often very advanced, of the inner spheres of life and reality who are concerned with the progression of the entire human race. These hierarchies extend ever inwards, the inner always assisting the outer in the most sacred objective and destiny of all life, during the great ascent back to The Source, The First Cause, God. As humanity has strayed further and further from its true path and ultimate destiny in favor of a path of illusion, built around creed, dogma, indoctrination, gross materialism and the demands of the Ego, Beings of the inner spheres of life and reality are involved with many strategies with the objective of bringing awareness back to humanity of the inner truths and realities.

These advanced Beings realize that channeling and most other forms of mediumship have largely failed due to mass skepticism, and therefore alternative, more direct and convincing approaches are required. The new focus over the last few decades has been to encourage people to verify these important Spiritual matters for themselves first hand, rather than relying on mediums, psychics and channeling. This strategy has resulted in numerous seemingly miraculous experiences, as mentioned at the beginning of this book, such as lucid dreams, near death experiences, Out of Body Experiences and many other psychic and inner experiences.

This is the new paradigm moving forward during this pivotally important era for mankind as we experience a transition from one great age to the next. Once a sufficient number of people on Earth have expanded awareness and Consciousness to fully realize, encompass and accept the inner realities and Universal truths, and to structure their lives accordingly, this will result in a much wider and accelerating expansion of Consciousness encompassing the entire group Mind. Then, the same Universal truths will become an integral component of the Consciousness and life of every human being on Earth and beyond.

It is no coincidence that these seemingly "miraculous" events are occurring more frequently during this period. Channelling, mediumship and other indirect methods of contact and research all have their own place and are no less effective or important to those who practice them or to the people who genuinely benefit from them. However, the emphasis has now shifted.

The remainder of this section is dedicated to this new and vitally important approach to the inner realities. We will discuss how you can consciously visit the inner worlds, verifying at first-hand the truth and nature of our own immortal existence. We will talk about how to visit the Astral worlds to communicate with deceased human Beings, including family and friends, gathering a multitude of extremely valuable experiences and information.

Chapter 63
Contact With the Inner Spheres

There are numerous ways in which the inner spheres of life and reality, ranging from the Astral planes to the much more inward Mental or Spiritual planes, can be contacted and visited. Many of these methods, in particular those required to safely communicate with the inner spheres of life beyond the Astral worlds, are advanced and require the necessary degree of dedication, discipline, practice, balance, and personal evolution. That having been said, almost anyone can potentially achieve these with commitment and dedication, and by diligently applying individual self-development methods, including those discussed in depth in the next section of this book. For those who are willing, the rewards can be very profound and almost always life-changing.

The methods to be revealed in the following chapters will not only result in a much higher quality and more reliable level of experience and communication with the inner spheres and the Beings residing there as compared to channeling and other indirect methods, but they are also completely safe. Having successfully accomplished any of these methods, any temptations to interact with the inner worlds by less direct and less safe or even dangerous methods, such as channeling, Ouija board, automatic writing and other such approaches will be set aside forever, and recognised for what they are.

Chapter 64
Clairvoyance

Clairvoyance quite literally means "clear seeing", which may be defined as the ability to view within and beyond the confines of space and time without the need for the use of physical eyesight. There are many levels of Clairvoyance, those with clairvoyant abilities experiencing anything from the entire range to simply one or two.

In general terms, Clairvoyance includes the ability to view things at any distance beyond the scope of the eyesight and other physical senses, as well as to "see" beyond the confines and limitations of temporal space and time, thereby enabling the viewer to "see" the Astral worlds and the people and Beings living there. The images "seen" by a clairvoyant might range from a still image similar to a photograph or even an impression, to full motion pictures in vibrant colours appearing every bit as real and lifelike if not more so than the physical world as seen through the physical eyes. The Astral worlds and beyond exhibit colours, sounds and vibrations way beyond anything perceivable or comprehensible by the physical senses, but a clairvoyant can often view these in all of their splendour.

Clairvoyance is often known as the "sixth sense" and is associated with the area of the forehead often known as the "third eye" or in Eastern mysticism the "brow chakra". At the location of the third eye, there is a corresponding physical gland known as the "pineal gland" located slightly above and between the physical eyes, approximately midway between the eyebrows.

The physical pineal gland itself has steadily atrophied during the course of the evolution of mankind, particularly in recent millennia, progressively shrinking from its original size of a ping pong ball to the current size of a pea. This atrophying of the pineal gland is mainly due to its lack of use, not only from a physical point of view, but from a Spiritual point of view, as humanity has focussed away from our inner abilities and towards the temptations of the outer material world.

The pineal gland has also shrunken as a result of breathing habits that became progressively less centred on Vital Energy and more centred on the inhalation of atmospheric air through the mouth and nose. Of course, humans need to physically breathe oxygen in order to survive, but the breathing of Vital Energy throughout the entire body is also necessary for the existence of life in all spheres of the multi-dimensional Universe including organic life in the physical world. In many respects, the pineal gland resembles an eyeball, and it still has many of the same characteristics as an eyeball except, of course it is restricted to limitations of physical sight.

The biological pineal gland functions in conjunction with the brow chakra of the Energy body in order to bring Spiritual or inner visions to the Mind. As previously mentioned, however, due to the progressive lack of use of the Spiritual vision over the course of thousands of years as mankind has become increasingly obsessed with materialism and the physical senses, the brow chakra has succumbed to disuse, and the associated pineal gland has accordingly atrophied over the millennia.

This has resulted in mankind seeing things in a very limited three dimensional way, only in accordance with the perception of the five physical senses, a major contributing factor in mankind's loss of contact with the inner spheres of reality and own Spiritual nature, true purpose and ultimate destiny.

Children up to the age of five years or so have very strong clairvoyant and other inner connections to the Astral worlds and can still "see" beyond space and time. Young children are still very much a part of the world of Fairies, Gnomes, Mermaids and other delightful and very real Beings of the Astral worlds. Clairvoyance, as naturally enjoyed by young children brings the ability see distant places, view things happening in those places in both the physical and Astral worlds, and even to see into the past, present and future. There really are no limits. Young children also have the ability to see the aura of humans, animals and other life, as well as other Spiritual characteristics that reveal more about a person than any physical observation can, allowing them to sense the nature of another person easily. Many animals including cats and dogs share the same abilities for much the same reasons, as do tribal cultures living in remote places away from the materialistic world of "modern society".

Anyone can however work towards reactivating the brow chakra, the third eye to develop clairvoyant abilities. First and foremost, however, there must be the true determination and commitment, without which level of commitment and sincerity, no true progress can or will be made.

As with all inner and Spiritual exercises, an adequate state of relaxation is required in a location where you know you will not be disturbed. A comfortable chair or recliner is ideal, provided you will not be prone to falling asleep. For this reason, lying in or on a bed is not advisable unless you are supported in a semi-upright position.

When firmly settled and completely comfortable, spend a few minutes becoming as deeply relaxed as possible. The next section of this book provides full details on achieving a state of deep physical relaxation.

Next, in order to increase your state of relaxation, perform rhythmic breathing for a few minutes. Breathe in slowly through your nose to a count of five, hold your breath for a slow count of five, and then breathe out slowly through your mouth for a further count of five while imagining all tension leaving with your breath. These procedures will slow down your brainwaves to a more receptive level, deepening your state of relaxation.

Next, close your eyes and focus on the area of your third eye which is located between your eyebrows. To do this effectively, you will need to focus your physical eyes upward and inward as if going slightly cross-eyed. At first, this might feel uncomfortable and might even cause tension or a slight ache, but these sensations will pass with continued practice. Maintain your full attention at the position of your third eye, and do not to allow any thoughts to enter your Mind. Your entire attention should be entirely focused on the area of your third eye and viewed behind your closed eyelids.

Continue to concentrate as much as you possibly can, and watch for anything appearing within your field of focus. You might, for example, begin to see colours, shapes, symbols, or even images. Continue with this exercise for at least ten minutes and preferably, thirty minutes (the longer the better). When you wish to conclude the session, slowly bring yourself back to your normal waking awareness. Once you are fully aware, immediately write down everything you saw while focusing on your third eye, no matter how insignificant it might seem at the time. Keeping a notebook or journal specifically for these exercises is very important.

Make these exercises a daily habit. The more often you practice, the sooner results can arrive. Should you not see or perceive anything at all for the first few sessions, do not be concerned. It might well take some people many weeks or even months to penetrate the veil between the physical and Astral worlds—a veil that has become ever thicker and less accessible due to the exclusive use of the physical senses.

Consider these exercises to be a peeling away of the dense physical layers that have been added over the years, until the Astral worlds are finally revealed. Patience and perseverance are extremely important. This third eye activation exercise may also be done at the end of a meditation session where you will still be very relaxed and your Mind quiet and highly focused.

Having gained Clairvoyance, constant use of this ability will be further enhanced over time by continued daily practice.

In addition to Clairvoyance, there are the related abilities of "clairsentience" and "clairaudience". Clairsentience is a more general ability involving the inner equivalent of the senses of smell or touch. Like all inner abilities, clairsentience might appear spontaneously as a result of Spiritual progress or as a result of the practice of other abilities, such as Clairvoyance. For example, you may suddenly sense a perfume or floral scent, even though there are no flowers anywhere near you. Or you might suddenly feel something brush past you or feel a tickling sensation on your face when there is apparently no one else present. These are all examples of clairsentience.

Clairaudience is the ability to perceive sounds originating from the inner spheres, sounds not detectable by the physical ears. These sounds can vary dramatically, ranging from random noises such as pops, whistles and knocking sounds, to the full reception of other Beings and events within the inner worlds. Beings residing in the inner worlds will often attempt to communicate directly with humans in this way, and this might therefore be considered a form of channelling. However, as with all communications from a completely unknown source, these should be approached with extreme caution.

Clairvoyance is a rightful ability of all human Beings. Like all such abilities, however, it should always be used for good and honourable purposes, particularly in service to others. Never be tempted to use any inner ability against others in any way.

Chapter 65
The Akashic Record

Every single thought, action and event happening now, has ever happened and will ever happen anywhere in the entire Universe in all dimensions of reality are instantly "recorded" in the causal sphere of the Universe, often known in Eastern mysticism as the "Akasha". This is another name for the Ether or The All, Universal Mind, an aspect of the Universal multi-dimensional continuum that is The Source, God. This repository of Universal information is also often mystically known as the "Akashic Record" or sometimes even conceptualized as the "Akashic Library".

On an individual level, the Akashic record holds every minute detail of every physical life of each and every person, and later, after transcending the cycle of incarnation, as their Higher Self. When a person has progressed far enough along the path, this information will be made available to reveal the full details of all lives in perfect context.

Although the Akashic record is frequently conceptualized as a vast, library with shelves upon shelves of books, it exists in reality, as with everything else in the entire Universe, as a pure Energy form within the Ether, and is still an aspect of ourselves and Higher Selves and all that Is. The Akashic record can however be accessed by humans having the necessary psychic abilities. Very often, prophets predicting the future are doing so by accessing the Akashic record and "viewing" details of probable future events existing as Quantum probabilities. One such famous person was Edgar Cayce, sometimes known as the "sleeping prophet". Over the course of many years, he channeled a considerable amount of information, much of which was recorded. It is quite probable that other famous prophets such as Nostradamus also obtained predictions of future events by directly accessing the Akashic record.

It is quite possible that many cases of afterlife regression, Clairvoyance, remote viewing and other forms of psychic access are also achieved by access to the Akashic record. There are people with advanced abilities who can pro-actively access the Akashic record with such a high level of accuracy that the information they make available has the potential to alter the course of humanity. These people are however usually very secretive, fearing ridicule and cynicism. The time is arriving, however, when access to the Akashic record will become fully accepted, and those with the abilities to do so will be respected for the service they provide for the benefit of mankind.

Chapter 66
Astral Projection

No longer is it adequate, necessary or even desirable to rely on psychics or channeled information for evidence of Spiritual realities, and in particular the truth of the continuity of life after the "death" of the physical body. Over the last few decades, Astral Projection and Out of Body Experiences have become increasingly more important in reconnecting mankind with the inner and greater realities. Astral Projection is, together with the closely related Out of Body Experience the best possible preparation for physical death. Those who can Astral project or have Out of Body Experiences never fear "death", knowing, beyond any doubt that the finality of so-called "death" does not really exist. This also applies to "near death experiences". "Death" becomes something to be embraced with excitement and anticipation, once a person knows, beyond all doubt of the peace, tranquillity and harmony waiting beyond the confines of the physical world, and in particular first-hand proof of the continuity of life and therefore the illusion of "death".

Those experiencing Astral Projection, Out of Body and near death Experiences see and know the physical world for what it really is—a temporal learning experience—and have a much more profound understanding of the true meaning of life, usually resulting in a complete revaluation of earthly priorities.

There is nothing at all new about Astral Projection. Even the most ancient cultures, such as the "stone age" people, made maximum use of this natural ability. Many cultures, such as Native American shamans, use Astral Projection extensively today for many purposes that benefit their people.

There are many references, in symbolic form, to Astral Projection in the books and bibles of the popular world religions. Highly advanced, no longer visible ancient civilizations of thousands of years ago used Astral Projection extensively to manifest things on Earth. Even the very earliest humans of hundreds of thousands of years ago at the very dawn of civilization were capable of Astral Projection, very often practiced by the tribe shaman or “medicine man”. The entire tribe would often participate in the Astral Projection process by performing drumming and other repetitive actions designed to invoke the required altered state by lowering the brainwave frequency of the shaman. It is now thought that paintings found on the walls of caves around the world, many of which are very similar, notwithstanding the vast distances separating them across continents, depict experiences of Astral travel and relate important information bought back from the Astral worlds by the shaman for the benefit of the tribe. However, as with so many inner abilities such as Clairvoyance, mankind has largely lost the instinctive ability to Astral project.

So what exactly is Astral Projection? First of all, it is important to keep in Mind that Astral Projection is a perfectly normal and natural ability of all human Beings. Every night upon attaining a certain state of sleep, the Energy and Astral bodies as well as the Mental Body are automatically projected out of phase with the physical body, often associated with rapid eye movement (“REM”), signifying the onset of Astral Projection. Most people who are untrained in remembering dreams and sleep activities will have no recollection of this process. Many people however have experienced a “falling” feeling followed immediately by a sharp jolt as if landing hard on the bed. This experience is the Energy, Astral and Mental bodies suddenly reuniting with the physical body.

The projection of the Astral body during sleep and the various modes of dreaming will be discussed in detail later in this book, but the main difference between Astral Projection during sleep and Astral Projection in the usual meaning of the term is that that latter includes full conscious awareness and control over the process. Rather than both Mind and body being in the sleep state, the body is in a sleep state, but the Mind is fully awake, aware and in conscious control. This also applies to Out of Body Experiences, the characteristics of which will be fully described later in this book.

As discussed earlier, humans fundamentally comprise three distinct bodies: the physical body, the Astral body, and the Mental or Spirit body. There is also an intermediate body effectively acting as an "interface" or "transformer" between the physical and Astral bodies, usually known as the Etheric or Energy body. Under normal circumstances, most people are only aware of the existence of their physical body, being entirely focused on the feedback and perceptions of the five physical senses. The inner, much more subtle bodies are always present, only the Mental or Spiritual body being immortal, made in the true image of The Source, God.

Astral Projection is the inner projection of Consciousness beyond the limitations of the five physical senses in order to assume awareness and control of the Astral body with its own Astral senses within the Astral planes. Astral Projection is not actually projecting "to" the Astral plane in the way we think of it physically. Where we perceive ourselves to "be" at any time is determined by the level of vibration of Energy our conscious awareness is focusing within. Astral Projection is, therefore, a projection within our own Mind, into the realms of the collective Subconscious Mind, where the experiences is shared with others focussed within the same level of vibration relative to the Astral worlds.

The Astral worlds are very real and seem to be more solid and real than the physical world. The physical world is merely a pale projection of these inner realities. As previously noted, Eastern traditions often refer to the physical world of matter as "maya", which means "illusion". Although the Astral worlds appear to be much more solid, "real" and vibrant than the physical world, the Astral worlds are still created by the Minds of human Beings in accordance with recent experiences within the physical world and based upon what these people believe to be reality. The Astral worlds are, therefore, not true reality, they are rather the creations of and within the Minds of humans. Our true reality is our true home as immortal Spiritual Beings within the inner realms of Spirit, beyond all concept of physical "form".

Astral projectors, like people who have passed on, do not find themselves in some intangible "dream world". They experience a very solid, vibrant, intense environment where all senses seem greatly magnified. The senses involved, of course, are the inner Astral senses which perceive and "decode" Energy configurations and Thought Forms. Within the Astral worlds, thoughts can be seen to take shape instantly, and anything desired can be instantly manifested by the power of the Mind.

In the peace and harmony of the mid to inner Astral worlds, there is no money, no factories or offices, no formal "work", no "bosses" and no formal "leaders". Everyone works together harmoniously for common causes. People living within the Astral worlds still nevertheless retain their materialistic perspective and Earthly desires, which is the main reason they are still living there. It is not until these desires have been completely satiated, with material things seen as illusions and barriers to progress, that further progress can be made to the more blissful conditions of the inner realms of life and reality.

It is these human characteristics of the mid-Astral residents that cause the mid-Astral worlds—where many Astral projectors find themselves—to be very similar in appearance to Earth, created by the desires of the human Mind and represented within the Astral worlds as Energy forms. The Astral worlds were therefore not created for humans, but by humans as a reflection of what they believe and expect life at that level to represent. This applies to all Energy levels and realms of life of the Astral worlds. The Astral worlds of other Beings, including those from other planets are similarly created according to their own particular, experiences, expectations and perceptions.

Upon passing over to the Astral worlds after physical death, everyone will be focussed in the precise degree of vibration and density that corresponds precisely to that of their own Astral body. Everything in the Universe perpetually seeks harmony, doing so by precisely matching equivalent vibrations of Energy—this is a fundamental Universal Principle. It is very important therefore to remember, that all of these worlds exist concurrently within the continuum of the Universe. Unlike Earth, the Astral worlds contain everything from the past, present and probable future as relates to the Earth concept of time. In addition to a familiar Earth-like environment and people, the Astral worlds are inhabited by numerous entities and Beings who have never physically existed on Earth.

Within the Astral worlds, a cause in the form of a thought, often known as a "Thought Form", will immediately result in a corresponding effect whether it is positive, neutral or negative. New residents of, and visitors to the Astral very quickly learn this important Principle. The Astral projector should always know and understand these laws before projecting, otherwise, it is very easy to become caught up in undesirable situations that are no more than the manifestation of his or her own Mind. If the Astral projector is afraid of meeting an "evil being", he or she will come into contact with that very same "evil being". The "evil being" will, however, be merely a projection of the person's imagination and not at all real, but it will seem very real and terrifying for those unprepared for such situations.

It is most important for the projector to maintain a passive state of Mind at all times, but with an air of mild curiosity. In this way everything will seem normal, and opportunities to explore and learn will rapidly present themselves, including the meeting of Astral residents who are happy to serve as guides. The guide might be a personal "Spirit guide" or one of numerous Astral guides who are willing to help Astral projectors. The best way to learn about the Astral planes and the Universal laws is to actually go there and gain first-hand experience.

There are many aspects of Astral Projection and the Astral worlds that the projector will need to get used to very quickly. Travel is instantaneous—it is simply a matter of thinking where you wish to go or who you wish to be with, and you will instantly find yourself there. Of course, a projector needs to know where they wish to go in the first place, and this is where an Astral guide can be most useful. Meeting deceased relatives, friends and others is very straightforward, assuming they are still dwelling at the same or lower level of the Astral worlds. A person within a lower Astral world cannot project to visit a person within an inner Astral world due to the higher vibrations existing there. By simply thinking about the person, and creating the intent to be with them as if you are already there, you will instantly find yourself in the presence of that person.

All communication within the Astral worlds takes place by thought transfer and is, therefore, instantaneous. Such thought transfer can be in the form of basic telepathic communication or the exchange of entire packages of information in symbolic form. New arrivals within the Astral might instinctively talk with their "mouth", but actual communication is carried out telepathically by words, images or symbols over any distance. Although telepathic communication can be performed by a single word or symbol at a time, it is much more efficient, as the people of the Astral worlds soon discover, to send entire "packages" of thoughts which the recipient can absorb at will.

Is Astral Projection safe? Yes, absolutely. No actual harm can come to an Astral projector. A question often asked is whether another being can enter and "takeover" the physical body of a projector while the projector is still "away" from the physical body in the Astral worlds. This cannot occur any more than it can happen while experiencing normal nightly sleep projections. The projector is never "away" from the physical body, but rather focussed at a different level of Consciousness within their own Mind.

Another question often asked is whether it is possible to get "stuck" in the Astral planes and not be able to return to the physical body. Again, there is no danger whatsoever of this occurring. While still possessing a physical body, a fine silver cord ("the Astral matrix") maintains a permanent connection between the physical and Astral bodies, and this connection is only finally severed at the point of physical death. In order to return to the physical body, it is only necessary to think about it, and the return will instantly take place. And as mentioned before, there is no projection "away" from the physical body in absolute terms. Projection is in fact a projection of Consciousness into our own Mind, which then becomes focussed in an area of the Astral planes corresponding with the relative vibration of Mind and Astral planes.

There are numerous methods for achieving Astral projection, many of which are taught in modern books. Almost all of these methods require considerable practice, discipline, willpower, patience, concentration, and very often even a high degree of natural ability. Many of these methods are therefore beyond the scope of most people, who, as a result, either never even practicing, or start and then give up soon afterwards.

Many of the methods are designed to initially result in what is commonly known as an "Out of Body Experience" or "OBE". The terms Astral Projection and Out of Body Experience are often confused or used interchangeably. In fact, Astral Projection and OBE properly describe distinctly different experiences. Astral Projection may be defined as a projection of Consciousness beyond the confines of the five physical senses to assume control of the Astral body, which then becomes the Principle centre of conscious awareness and the vehicle of travel while interacting with the Astral worlds. OBE can best be defined as an "Etheric projection", where the centre of Consciousness is projected away from the physical body to the Etheric body, also known as the Energy body. The Etheric or Energy body is comparatively much denser than the Astral body with correspondingly lower vibrations. An OBE, therefore, takes place closer to the physical world. Although an OBE appears to be taking place in the physical world itself, the environment experienced during an OBE is actually a dense reflection of the physical world within the Etheric plane, and accordingly has many characteristics of the Astral plane of which it is a lower vibration, including sensitivity to thoughts.

Thoughts can quickly cause what are often known as "reality fluctuations" where familiar surroundings and objects can suddenly appear, alter in appearance or position, or even disappear completely. It is quite possible and common to convert an initial OBE to a full Astral Projection simply by consciously raising the vibrations of Consciousness and therefore of the Etheric body. This can be accomplished by using the power of the Mind to form the definite intent to transition to the Astral, achieved by focusing on a particular Astral locale or a particular person residing within the Astral worlds. Intent is thus formed and projected to be at that locale or with the person, or by issuing a definite statement in the form of a command in the present tense, such as, "I am now in the presence of my grandfather".

Astral Projection and OBE, as with all inner abilities, usually requires commitment and practice in order to impress the Subconscious Mind, which ultimately controls these experiences, with the objectives. Success will not be realised by approaching these abilities as some sort of novelty. Everyone can succeed with Astral Projection or OBE, but the Mindset for success must be absolute, regardless of how long it takes. Likewise, the desire for Spiritual exploration must be absolute and for all the right reasons. Your Mind, and in particular Subconscious Mind, should be so programmed to succeed with Astral Projection and OBE that it becomes an integral part of your Consciousness and therefore a natural ability that the Subconscious Mind will carry out fully automatically. The more you desire to experience these abilities, the more likely you are to succeed, and the sooner you are likely to succeed. The profound benefits for those who do so will more than justify the commitment, and the experiences will become increasingly more frequent and profound as time progresses.

Chapter 67
Three Astral Projection Methods

The following methods and their variations for achieving Astral Projection contain the major requirements for success.

The first three methods are oriented towards Astral Projection as opposed to Out of Body Experiences or "OBE". These particular methods are sometimes also known as "phasing", as conscious awareness is "phased" or "projected" away from the sphere of the five physical senses of the Earthly physical body in order to assume conscious awareness and control over the inner Astral senses of the Astral body within the Astral planes. Again though, the "Astral body" is simply symbolic. What is actually happening is a raising and projection of Consciousness into the realms of our own Subconscious Mind, and therefore the realms of the collective Mind of everyone living at the same level of vibration and therefore shared experience.

All successful methods of Astral Projection require the projection of Consciousness away from the physical body and senses. One of the most fundamental aspects of achieving this is to first attain a state often known as "Mind awake, body asleep". In this state, the physical body is fully asleep just as it would be during your usual night-time sleep, but the Mind remains fully conscious and aware just as it would during daytime waking hours.

The Mind awake, body asleep state involves focusing your attention fully away from the five senses of your physical body until your physical body goes to sleep by itself while the conscious Mind appears to remains fully awake although in reality the conscious Mind is simply expanding its sphere of awareness to encompass the realms of the Subconscious Mind. The Mind awake, body asleep state can be accomplished at any time with sufficient abilities of concentration and relaxation.

Such abilities, as with all inner abilities do require time, practice and commitment, however.

There are quicker and easier ways of achieving the Mind awake, body asleep state without the need to formally practice to the same extent. This is achieved by making use of this state as it naturally occurs during sleep cycles, such as might be experienced immediately before sleep or just after awakening from your normal night's sleep a couple of hours earlier than usual. When you first awaken from the sleep state, including even after a daytime nap, your body is normally in an extremely relaxed state while your Mind starts to awaken to a state of daytime conscious. The basis of this Astral Projection method is to maintain and deepen this already physically relaxed state until your body goes back to sleep to continue its normal sleep cycle while you focus your Mind to keep it fully alert and conscious and focussed or "projected" into the realms of the collective Subconscious Mind.

It is quite possible to achieve the required Mind awake, body asleep state just after going to bed at night and just before sleep by allowing your body to fully relax and drift off to sleep while maintaining full conscious awareness of your Mind. If you can allow your body to fully relax into sleep while maintaining your Mind in a fully conscious state of awareness, you will become aware of the projection process that automatically occurs during normal sleep and can then assume full control. Again, this occurs because the conscious aspect of our Mind is no longer required to be concerned with the sphere of activities of the physical body, and can therefore expand into the realms of the Subconscious Mind which, during a waking state, most people remain unaware of. This transition is characterised by what are known as "hypnagogic" imagery, which might manifest as "swirling" shapes, colours, images and many other possibilities. This occurs when the sphere of activity of the conscious Mind encroaches upon the sphere of activity of the Subconscious Mind.

Method 1: The Third Eye Focus

For this first method, set your alarm clock to awaken you at least two hours before your normal waking time. This method involves allowing your physical body to go back to sleep while your conscious Mind remains fully awake. By awaking early in the morning, before you usual waking time, your body will want to naturally return to the sleep state. The objective of this method is to allow it to do so while maintaining full conscious awareness.

As soon as you awaken, start the procedure immediately. Do not be tempted to roll over and go back to sleep. Lie flat on your back, and maintain the extremely relaxed feeling you enjoyed immediately upon waking. Next, immediately focus your full attention on the area directly between your eyebrows. This area corresponds with a major centre of the subtle Energy body known as the "brow chakra" or "third eye", as discussed previously. To accomplish this, you will need to force your focus upward and then move your eyes inward in order to focus exactly on the area between your eyebrows as if you are going slightly cross-eyed. Some people might find this to be very straightforward, while others might find it somewhat of a strain at first. The strain will however soon settle down with practice, so do not be discouraged if you experience this.

Next, while maintaining your focus between your eyes, become fully aware of the entire area of the top of your head. This is known as the "crown chakra". Finally, while keeping your attention firmly fixed upon your third eye, also become aware of the region of your upper chest, which is the "heart chakra". It is not necessary to firmly focus on your crown and heart chakras, but rather only to maintain awareness of them. Your point of focus should remain on your brow chakra, your third eye, located between your eyebrows. Do not worry if you have trouble maintaining awareness on your crown and heart chakras at first. It is most important to maintain focus on your third eye and brow chakra.

While focusing on your third eye, remain fully relaxed, and empty your Mind completely of all thoughts. It is most important to maintain your physical body in a state of complete stillness and total relaxation throughout. It is also important to remain flat on your back. Do not roll over onto your side or any other position. This might seem like a difficult process at first, but if you remember to do this from the outset, as soon as you awaken, you will soon be able to prevent your normal mundane waking thought processes from starting, and will be able to resist the temptation to roll over and go back to sleep. If a thought does enter your head, simply acknowledge its presence and allow it to drift through your Mind without giving it any further consideration. Do not fight your thoughts or become upset by them, otherwise, your concentration and naturally relaxed state will be broken, and you will have to either start the process again or leave it until another day. Again, the benefit of waking two hours early in the morning is to achieve and maintain the necessary state of deep physical relaxation while not allowing thoughts to enter your Consciousness.

While maintaining your attention firmly on your third eye and with your conscious awareness on your crown and heart chakras, all while keeping your Mind totally clear of thoughts, begin to breathe rhythmically through your nose. Slowly and deeply breathe in through your nose to a slow count of five, hold your breath for a further slow count of five, exhale through your nose for a further slow count of five, and then relax your breathing for a final slow count of five. Repeat this breathing process five times.

Next, imagine with as much feeling as possible that you are a feather falling very gently from a great height. Feel yourself drifting very slowly and peacefully downward while enjoying the floating feeling immensely. Should your attention drift away from being the floating feather, repeat the breathing exercises, and start drifting as a feather once again. This might all seem like a lot to remember at first, but it is really a fully integrated process, and very soon, you will not even have to think about it at all. As you become more proficient with this stage of the process, you can modify it to suit the best method for you. The main objective is to achieve that all important Mind awake, body asleep state, after which the projection will come naturally.

As this procedure progresses, you should feel your body maintain a state of deep physical relaxation and soon start to feel progressively heavier as if sinking right into your bed. You might also feel a very pleasant wave of warmth sweeping through your body representing the onset of a trance state.

Soon, you should completely lose all sensations in your physical body to the extent you forget about it altogether. You should never be tempted to ask yourself whether you can still feel your body, as this will break your concentration. This Mind awake, body asleep state is absolutely fundamental in order to achieve success with almost any method of Astral Projection or Out of Body Experience. It can take anywhere from between five minutes to an hour or more to reach this state, so please do not hurry this process and above all remain patient and completely focussed. The time taken to achieve this fundamental Astral Projection state will reduce with practice. You must proceed in a calm and controlled way, always knowing beyond any doubt that you have already succeeded.

If after one hour, you have still not been able to achieve the required Mind awake, body asleep state, it is best to simply accept the time as valuable practice and continue again another day before discouragement sets in. As previously mentioned, in comparison to most Astral Projection methods, this procedure is more straightforward and easier to accomplish because it is an extension of the normal sleep process. Be absolutely honest with yourself at all times. If you are still aware of your physical body or cannot maintain the focus on your third eye area, or if you cannot prevent thoughts from entering your

Consciousness, do not continue with that particular session. There is always another day, and practice makes perfect.

Having successfully achieved the Mind awake, body asleep state, it is very important to maintain it. Then, it will not be long before the Astral Projection process naturally commences. Do not allow any thoughts to linger in your Mind, and do not ask questions of yourself, such as, "Have I achieved the Mind awake, body asleep state yet?" When you have reached this state, you will know it. You will have no feeling of your physical body and will probably start to see swirling colours like clouds drifting across your field of inner vision of the hypnagogic imagery which is an extremely good indication that you have achieved the important first state in readiness for the next stage of this method. It is now very important to maintain this state without breaking your concentration. Do not lose patience with yourself if it proves difficult at first, however. Some people have achieved success at the very first attempt, but others might take weeks to accomplish it, know however that anyone can accomplish this sooner or later with practice.

The hypnagogic imagery will soon become more and more intense and might begin to form more recognizable scenes or symbols. These are actually visions of the Astral worlds, and you should welcome them in the knowledge that you are very close to fully projecting. You might also start to hear noises such as hissing or popping, but these are only the audible equivalent of the imagery originating in the Astral worlds. Another very common experience is "seeing" your surroundings through your closed eyelids. If you experience this state, it is a very good sign that the projection process has commenced. Your physical body will be asleep, and your centre of conscious awareness will be focussed more with your Subconscious Mind. You will then be viewing your surroundings with your Etheric centred sight rather than your physical eyesight. In fact, what you are viewing is not your actual physical surroundings, but an Etheric reflection.

One of several possibilities might present themselves at this pivotal stage. You might suddenly find yourself travelling toward the imagery at great speed, after which you will quickly find yourself within the Astral worlds. Another possibility is that the imagery might suddenly take on the appearance of a "television screen" where you can plainly view a part of the Astral planes. If this happens, imagine as intensely and realistically as possible that you are moving toward the screen, and as it gets larger and larger, the scenery becomes more vivid. Once you reach the screen, imagine yourself passing right through it into the scenery. You should then find yourself fully in the part of the Astral plane you were viewing within the Astral screen.

Yet another possibility is that you see "tunnel" type structures appearing in your Mind's eye. If this happens, simply imagine yourself moving into one of the tunnels, and you should then be transported to the Astral planes, often at high speed and after an exhilarating ride.

These are the most common situations encountered during this stage of the Astral Projection process just before projecting to the Astral planes. You might find that an alternative scenario presents itself. Is this is the case, simply relax and go along with whatever you experience it without questioning it. No two experiences are exactly the same.

There is another possibility that you might encounter while practicing Astral Projection—the sudden onset of what appears to be rapid and dramatic vibrations. These vibrations might feel localized, often around the top of your head, or they might spread throughout your entire body. It is also quite possible for some or all of your Etheric body to suddenly start "floating" out and separating from your physical body. If this happens, you have the possibility of converting to an "Out of Body Experience" or "OBE", which is dealt with in much more detail later.

If you wish to continue with your Astral Projection experience rather than converting it to an OBE, you must remain totally calm, relaxed and passive as the vibrations progress. This might seem easier said than done as the vibrations may feel alarming, but simply allow the vibrations to "wash" over you as if you were bathing in them. Soon, the vibrations should dissipate, at which point you might find yourself focussed within the Astral world, at which point you will have succeeded with your Astral Projection. The vibrations could also become a full OBE situation where you simply float right out of your body. If this occurs, remain calm and proceed with the procedure as for an OBE, as detailed later.

While practicing this Astral Projection procedure, there is also another state you might encounter—that of "three-dimensional blackness". This will appear in your Mind's eye as an area of deep blackness encompassing your entire field of inner vision. However, unlike seeing blackness with your physical eyes behind your eyelids, which might seem flat and two-dimensional, this blackness will appear to have three dimensions and will feel much more solid and real. This three-dimensional blackness is still located within the area of Energy associated with the Astral planes, but it is, in fact, an intermediate state usually experienced before fully transitioning to the Astral planes.

One approach to this situation is to use your imagination as intensively as possible in order to create a large, brightly coloured door in the blackness with the wording "To the Astral Planes" written on the door in large letters. This symbolizes a portal into the Astral planes through which you will travel. It is very important that the door is made as solid and real in your imagination as possible before passing through it. The best way to determine if the door is ready to open is to imagine yourself knocking on it or imagine yourself throwing pebbles at it. If the sound seems muffled when you knock on the door with your imaginary hand or when the pebbles hit the door, continue until the sound of knocking or pebbles becomes very real, meaning the door or portal itself has become real enough to enter. When this happens, imagine yourself opening the door and walking right through it. Don't see yourself in your Mind's eyes in the third person, however, as if observing yourself walking through the door. Instead, actually imagine yourself in the first person within your Astral body walking through the door. Then, you should find yourself in the Astral world.

It is most important to maintain total concentration, relaxation and focus throughout all of these scenarios. If you allow your Mind to wander or think of physical, mundane things, you will immediately return to the world of your physical senses. If this happens, it is best to resume the practice another day.

If the Astral door method does not help you to move beyond the area of three-dimensional blackness, there is another method of progressing to the Astral planes which requires more concentration. This involves the "placing of intent". While in the three-dimensional blackness, form a strong intent to travel to the Astral worlds with as much concentration as possible. Similarly, if you wish to visit a certain place or person within the Astral worlds, you must place a strong intent, imagining yourself with as much clarity as possible that you are already in that place or in the presence of that person. Having formed your intent, you should either find yourself suddenly travelling at great speed, soon finding yourself at your Astral destination.

Sometimes, a "portal" might appear in the form of a tunnel, area of colour or other symbol through which you should imagine yourself passing.

If none of these procedures succeed, it is highly advisable to terminate the session, knowing that you have at least made excellent progress towards success next time. It is important to never feel discouraged. Each time you practice will bring you a stage nearer to your objectives, and every practice session is extremely well worth the time and effort committed.

Do not forget to record everything—successes or otherwise—in your journal immediately after your experience has ended. If you delay in doing this, even for a few minutes, you might forget valuable details.

When arriving in the Astral, you should again remind yourself that this is a "Mind world" where everything you think or imagine can and almost certainly will become an instant reality. Always maintain an air of passive curiosity and never overreact to your surroundings. It is useful to remember that everyone on the level of the Astral to which you have projected has a similar personality and level of evolution as yourself. If anything happens that scares you or makes you feel uncomfortable, it will always be a product of your own Mind and not of any circumstances "external" to you.

If you are presented with a situation you feel you cannot handle, it is best to conclude that particular Astral journey by willing yourself back into your physical body. If this happens, resolve that you will remain in complete mental control the next time. It is also possible once in the Astral to mentally request the presence of a guide. At least one guide should appear who will not only show you around or take you wherever you wish to go within the Astral Planes. The presence of a guide will also help you to keep your emotions under control. If you wish to meet with a "deceased" person such as a relative, simply form an image of the person in your Mind, mentally imagining yourself to be already in their presence. You can also include the thought, "I am now in the presence of…". and then state the name of the person. Again, this statement must be in the present tense. In the Astral and inner worlds, there is no "space" or "time". Everything is happening in the Eternal Now. The person should very soon appear before you, or alternatively, you will find yourself instantly in their presence.

After several visits to the Astral, some people become involved in an extremely worthwhile activity known as "Soul retrieval". There are many guides in the Astral worlds who specialize in the retrieval of Souls who have become "trapped" for some reason in a lower part of the Astral, such as a belief system territory, or very close to the physical world where they are perceived as a "ghost". Trapped Souls seem to respond much more favourably to people who are still physically alive on Earth but travelling within the Astral body. For this reason, people in the Astral planes involved in the process of Soul retrievals welcome the assistance of an Astral traveller.

Each Soul retrieval is different, but equally important. It should be noted that some Souls become "stuck" close to the physical world due to circumstances surrounding their physical death. A ghost is simply repeating a series of actions within the Eternal Now without any concept of "space" or "time". You should be prepared for this eventuality and allow your guide to take the lead. Soul retrieval broadly consists of gently convincing the trapped Soul that they are in the wrong place, that they do not belong there, and that you are there to help them to their rightful home. While communicating this mentally, project thoughts of reassurance, Unconditional Love and other positive thoughts and emotions. When the trapped person agrees to leave their current circumstances, they can then be guided to the level of the Astral worlds to which they rightfully belong.

When you wish to conclude a journey to the Astral, all you need to do is intend to be back in your physical body, and you will arrive there almost instantly. Once you return, always immediately add detailed records in your Astral notebook, recording everything you remember about your journey.

While this method is best performed after awakening early in the morning, it is also quite possible to Astral project using this phasing method at other times of the day. Just after retiring to bed at night is a particularly good time, but there is a much higher likelihood of the Mind falling asleep with the physical body before the process is complete, and therefore more practice is sometimes required. Some people however have a natural tendency for their body to drift off to sleep before their Mind, and such people have an excellent opportunity to succeed at Astral projection at night after retiring to bed.

Performing this procedure during the daytime from a fully waking state requires the development of high-level deep physical relaxation and concentration abilities (which will be discussed later). After learning such abilities, however, you will be able to achieve the Mind awake, body asleep state at almost any time without having to rely on the sleep cycle.

This method can also be utilised after a daytime nap, where your body will already be in a naturally relaxed state. In this situation, start the method as soon as you awaken after your nap, and ensure you remain totally relaxed in the "just awakened" state of deep physical relaxation before proceeding with the rest of the method, just as you would do in the early morning waking period.

Method 2: Creative Visualisation

This is a very effective variation of the "Third Eye" method, and one which can often result in a much more rapid transition to the Astral planes. This method might work if you have not succeeded with the first method. It can also be used if you feel unable to maintain the necessary focus on your third eye while keeping your Mind clear of thoughts.

Although this method is based upon the use of the imagination, it also involves the use of all of the inner senses for maximum effectiveness. Imagination should never be confused with mere "fantasy", however, or simply a "figment of the imagination". In this case, imagination is your door key to the Astral worlds.

As with the first method, this method should ideally be commenced immediately after awakening a couple of hours earlier than usual, or at night-time just before sleep. If night time is chosen, the same caution applies as with the first method due to the possibility of drifting off to sleep before Astral Projection has been accomplished. This method can also be performed immediately after awakening from a daytime nap or after invoking the required state of deep physical relaxation at any other time during the day.

To proceed, begin by focusing your attention on your third eye/brow chakra keeping your Mind totally void of all thoughts as with the first method and then proceed as follows. Use all of your powers of imagination to realistically and vividly create a pleasant scene of your choice, such as a park, a beach, your garden or anything else attractive or memorable to you, and which will best engage your interest. The more engaging the scene, the more effective this method will be. The scene can also be one created entirely by your imagination. Whatever location or scenario you choose it must hold your attention and generate the same excitement, relaxation and anticipation as actually being there in person.

Imagine yourself becoming an integral part of this scene with complete realism, knowing, beyond any doubt that you are actually there already. Again, this must be performed in the first person so that you are actually placing yourself into the scene, and not just "seeing" yourself in your mind's eye in the scene in the third person. This means that you actually vividly experience the environment with your senses just as you would with your physical senses if you were actually there in the physical world. Make your scene as real and vivid as you possibly can, engaging all the senses. Smell the freshness of the air and the fragrance of the nearby flowers. Feel the warmth of the sun on your face and the firmness of the ground beneath your feet. Hear the birds singing cheerfully, taste that cooling drink you are casually sipping, and feel the welcome breeze playing against your face as you hear the breeze rustling the leaves on the trees.

Maintain this scenario in your Mind with all of your powers of concentration while maintaining your deeply relaxed state. Soon, you will find that your scene assumes a life of its own and you will know that you are really part of it. Continue this involvement with your scene, following its course and allowing it to unfold while maintaining an air of passive anticipation.

When you reach this stage, you will have successfully made the transition to the Astral world. Everything occurring will no longer be purely a creation of your imagination but will be a very real Astral locale in which you are focussed in your Mind. Remember to stay completely calm as a passive but curious observer while waiting to see what transpires next. It is important not to think about anything in particular, or have any preconceived ideas, because these will then become real, but a product of your own Mind. You can at this stage also assume full control over your situation. You might desire to meet a deceased person. If so, simply visualize the person as in the previous method. If you wish to visit another part of the Astral world that you are already familiar with, simply imagine that you are already there, and you instantly find yourself there.

The use of imagery and the imagination as a route to Astral Projection can be a very powerful catalyst, and even imagining a static object such as a flickering candle flame or a fruit can help to focus the Mind away from the five physical senses and towards the Astral plane, while invoking the all-important Mind awake, body asleep state. Any image or scene you personally find absorbing for any reason whatsoever can be very effectively used for this technique.

Astral Projection is all about projecting your conscious awareness away from the five physical senses, a process also known as “phasing”. You are quite literally limited only by your imagination, which in itself has no limits because it is the basis of all creation. When you Astral project, you will soon discover that your Mind shapes your reality in the inner worlds, as well as the physical world, but in the Astral world the process is instantaneous.

Method 3: Communication with the "Deceased"

Unlike the first two, this method is not defined as Astral Projection per se, but nevertheless shares many characteristics with it. This technique has proven to be extremely effective in enabling many people from all walks of life to communicate directly with deceased relatives and friends and to gather irrefutable proof of the continuity of life after physical death without the need to commit to a full Astral Projection method. This method is more akin to psychic communication as with a medium or channeling than Astral Projection in the purest sense, but can nevertheless be very effective indeed.

People using this procedure have been able to communicate with deceased relatives now residing in the Astral worlds and return with information only those people could have known. This method might appeal to those who do not feel ready for full Astral exploration or who are unable to commit the necessary time and effort.

Other people might simply wish to reunite with deceased loved ones or friends and be assured that they are fine and happy in their Astral home. One of the biggest advantages of this method is the possibility of communicating directly with "deceased" people without having to rely upon the services of a psychic of unknown abilities. Making contact with a loved one who has passed on to the Astral through a psychic medium will always leave room for doubt, but communicating with a deceased relative person to person within the Astral worlds will provide first hand, provable evidence beyond any doubt.

This method might not initially result in as vivid an interaction with the Astral worlds as with full Astral Projection, and most certainly is not intended to do so. Nevertheless, the quality of the Astral experiences will steadily increase with practice, and even from the very first success, the experience should be unquestionably real. Those who commence with this method might wish to later progress to a full Astral Projection method.

This method also relies principally on the powers of imagination. Many people might question their ability to visualize effectively or even at all, but everyone can visualize, at least to some extent. As with most abilities, the more visualisation is practiced, the more success will be experienced. For example, close your eyes for a moment and relax as much as possible. Next visualize in your Mind's eye your own home, your car, a pet, relative or anything or anyone else well-known to you. The image should come to Mind very quickly and easily, and then do the same thing again, but this time, add the feelings and emotions you associate with these people, animals and scenes with as much depth as you possibly can. Depth of feeling and emotion support imagination in an extremely powerful and important way. You will very soon realize that you can visualize and add emotion to any situation at will.

To commence with this procedure, the first requirement is to sit or lie down comfortably in a place where you will not be disturbed and relax as much as you possibly can. If you already have a method by which to achieve deep physical relaxation, please use it. For those who do not formally practice deep physical relaxation, the next section of this book will deal fully with this subject. It is most important not to attain such a relaxed state that you fall asleep, however. You merely need to be as relaxed and focused as possible on your objectives while remaining awake.

Stage 1: While sitting or lying down in as comfortable position as possible, but without the possibility of drifting off to sleep, gently breathe in through your nose to a slow count of five, hold your breath for a further slow count of five, and then gently exhale to a final slow count of five. Repeat this procedure at least five times or until you feel deeply relaxed. This relaxation process is the first stage in shifting your focus away from your physical environment and is very important for success, so do take your time over it.

Stage 2: In your now relaxed state, visualize, by means of your most intense imagination, a pool of sparkling, clean white Energy, located a small distance beneath your feet. Start to gently inhale and "feel" this pure, sparkling white Energy first enter your feet and then steadily travel up through your entire body, eventually reaching the top of your head. As this vibrant Energy travels up through your body, notice how exhilarating, refreshing and relaxing it feels.

Now feel this vibrant Energy passing through the top of your head before drifting down as if it were a beautiful sparkling white waterfall flowing from the crown of your head, gracefully drifting down in a glittering fall of Energy before rejoining the pool of Energy just below your feet. Repeat this process at least three times as vividly and with as much feeling as possible, each time with the Energy rising steadily up through your body and through the top of your head before gently falling back to the Energy pool beneath you, in a beautiful sparkling shower of pure, white sparkling Energy in a continuous process.

Stage 3: Next, feel a large pool of the same pure, white, vibrant sparkling Energy located just above your head. As with Stage 2, start to gently inhale and "feel" this exhilarating, refreshing, relaxing Energy start to drift gently downward, passing first through the top of your head and slowly down through your body until it reaches your feet. Then, visualize and feel the Energy leave both feet and gently curve back upwards to rejoin the vibrant, while pool of Energy that is located just above your head.

Again, as with stage 2, repeat this at least three times until you feel completely energized, calm and relaxed. You will soon discover how many times you need to repeat this process before progressing to the next stage. It is most important to "feel" this glowing Energy as intensively as you possibly can.

Stage 4: This stage involves the placing of intent to visit someone within the Astral worlds, for example a "deceased" relative. At this stage, intent should be conveyed to your Subconscious Mind to travel to the Astral worlds in order to meet someone residing there by imagining yourself as already being in the presence of the person. This stage alone will not in and of itself usually result in a direct shift to the Astral world, but it rather primes your Subconscious Mind so that it does not place any barriers before the process, as well as providing the intent required to proceed to the final stage in the process.

Note: the next stage in this process is absolutely fundamental to success, and might well take some practice before success is achieved. Whatever happens, do not be discouraged—this stage requires summoning your very highest possible level of imagination and concentration. Eventually, you should be able to simply form the firm intent to explore the "afterlife", meet deceased relatives, guides and anyone else you wish. For your first journey, however, the Astral worlds will not be familiar to you, and you will not usually be able to place the intent to visit a specific locale. You can also request the services of a guide who will be familiar with a very wide variety of locations.

Stage 5: Having formed the intent to visit a deceased relative, then proceed as follows: With all powers of imagination you can summon, visualize a location that you would associate with the person you wish to visit. The garden of the home where the person used to live is ideal, for example. If you do not have such a clear memory, you can create your own ideal scene such as a garden or a park.

When the location is as clear in your Mind as possible, start to create your entire scenario for the meeting, involving all of your senses as deeply, vividly, and with as much emotion as you can possibly manage. By emotion, we mean positive emotions such as. It is extremely important to know in your own Mind and beyond all possible doubt that this is the means by which the gateway to the Astral world is created and the meeting with the "deceased" relative accomplished. This will start out as a scenario created entirely by the powers of your own imagination, but will gradually, or perhaps even suddenly, switch to a dynamic scenario where everything assumes a life of its own. The scene will simply unfold before you like a movie. An example might progress something like this:

You are sitting on a bench in your favourite park where your grandparents used to accompany your family when you were very young. It is a very beautiful, idyllic, warm summer's day. The sun is shining brightly, and the birds are flitting in the skies and sitting in the trees while singing cheerfully. A gentle, cooling breeze makes ripples over the park pond where the water lilies are blooming and bobbing up and down on the shimmering water. The sweet scent of rose's drifts across on the gentle breeze from the nearby rose garden, and the trees just behind you look beautiful and green with leaves rustling in the gentle breeze. In the distance, you can see and hear children playing joyfully with their own friends and families.

Suddenly, you see a figure walking toward you. It is your dear grandfather who passed away some years before. He ambles up to you, and with a joyful look on his face, he says, "Hello, it is lovely to see you again, how are you doing?" "I'm fine", you reply. "Why not take a seat and we can have a nice chat like old times". Imagine your grandfather just as you remembered him when you were younger, and continue your conversation with him as if it is completely natural which of course it is.

"Do you remember the fine times we all used to enjoy here?" your grandfather asks. "Yes", you respond, "we used to come here every week in the summer, and on really hot days I used to look forward to a nice cold ice cream". Maintain this two-way conversation in a completely natural way, never for a moment doubting its reality, and you will find the answers from your grandfather becoming increasingly more spontaneous. When this happens, you will know that you have established a connection with the Astral presence of your grandfather, and your own conscious awareness has crossed from the physical world to the Astral world within the realms of the collective Subconscious Mind. The scene is very real because you have created it in the Astral through your imagination based upon a scene in the physical world. This is a creative process whereby you are creating an Astral environment and inviting your grandfather to meet you within that shared environment within the realms of Mind. Although this experience is taking place within the collective realms of Mind, you are both focussed within your Astral bodies, in his case permanent, for now at least, and in your case as an Astral Projection. If you question the reality of the situation, you will almost certainly lose the Astral connection within your Subconscious Mind causing you to return to your physical conscious level of awareness.

Your grandfather then goes on to say, "Your grandmother and I used to come here before you were born, when your parents were about your age". "What did you talk about?" you ask. "Your grandmother was always talking about her jewellery collection" says your grandfather. At this stage, you should focus entirely on asking the questions and maintaining the dialogue as well as remembering the answers and information provided by your grandfather.

"What was in this jewellery collection?" you ask. "There were many beautiful pieces in the collection" says your grandfather. "Your grandmother's favourite piece was a large brooch made from 22-carat gold set with a ring of diamonds and it had a large red ruby set in the middle. As a matter of fact, your own mother has that same piece of jewellery now". At the end of your conversation you remember to thank your grandfather and tell him how much you have enjoyed your meeting before you both say cheery goodbye.

You can then imagine walking home before gradually bringing your conscious awareness back to your physical surroundings. Taking a few deep breaths, relax and reflect for just a moment on your meeting with your "deceased" relative. The next thing to do, most importantly, is to immediately write down the entire experience in as much detail as possible in a notebook designated for the purpose that you keep by your bed.

The large gold and diamond brooch with the ruby set in the middle has aroused your curiosity, and when you next see your mother, you ask her about it. Your mother seems absolutely amazed and asks you how you could possibly know about the brooch which is now a treasured family heirloom and safely stored away. Your mother then goes upstairs and brings down her jewellery box, lifts up the lid and takes out a brooch that is absolutely identical to the one described by your grandfather. The brooch is very "real" because your meeting was very real.

By going through all of the stages of this procedure, you first created an Energy location in the Astral realm by means of your imagination where you could meet with your grandfather at the same level of vibration and therefore Conscious level awareness. This was a meeting between the Mind of your Grandfather and your own Mind, within the Astral realms of the collective Subconscious Mind. The initial scenario created a connection with the Soul of your grandfather, who responded to your projected invitation to join you in your created scenario within the realms of collective Mind known as the Astral.

Once the initial contact has been established within the Astral locale you created, the entire scenario becomes very real and progresses without any effort, just as such a meeting would in the physical world. It is important not to concern yourself too much with the details but rather focus on the connection, and on maintaining the conversation with your grandfather or whoever else you choose to meet. Know the connection is absolutely real, and so it will be as will be clear from the unique and provable information and you will bring back from the experience, evidence that will convince you, beyond all doubt, and encourage you to continue this process, before moving on to full Astral Projection or Out of Body Experiences.

Consciousness, like the Universe itself, is a continuum, there is no separation of Consciousness, and any evidence by the five physical senses to the contrary is simply an illusion. This method works by focusing, projecting and raising your Consciousness to the inner Astral levels within a range of collective Consciousness of which you are an aspect within the realms of your Subconscious Mind, which is analogous to tuning your television set to a different channel. In the physical world, there are literally thousands of radio and TV programs, as well as other types of transmissions being broadcast concurrently over a very wide range of radio frequencies. However, you can only tune your TV into one of these frequencies at a time. In changing a TV channel, you might be tuning into a wavelength higher in the radio wave frequency spectrum, thereby bringing the next channel into view on your TV screen. The process just described is identical to this. Each individual living in the Astral or indeed any level of Energy in the Universal continuum has a unique vibration or frequency, and, like a TV tuner, we can tune into any frequency in order to resolve a clear picture and thereby participate on the same frequency.

Your physical senses exist at a relatively low frequency through which you normally “tune in” the physical world at the same frequency and decoding the corresponding vibration of Energy. By using this method based upon the immense powers of imagination, you are, as previously mentioned, like a TV receiver, tuning your conscious awareness into the much higher frequency of the vibration of the Astral worlds, where direct contact can be made with relatives, friends and others already living there at those corresponding levels of Energy. This same process applies to many different forms of inner communication, including, but not limited to Remote Viewing, Clairvoyance and Channelling.

As mentioned previously, this method of Astral Projection might not in the beginning produce the quality, intensity or vividness of a full Astral Projection, but nevertheless, after time and practice, the experience will become increasingly more vivid until sooner or later it will become a full Astral Projection, and every bit as effective as any other method. Most importantly it provided the necessary faith in the process of contacting the Astral worlds to impress upon your Subconscious Mind, which in turn will facilitate Astral Projection much more readily.

From your first "afterlife" exploration success, you will never doubt the reality of the experience or the truth that life truly continues after the "death" of the physical body of matter.

Chapter 68
The Out of Body Experience

While practicing Astral Projection, there is another experience that can occur spontaneously and which you should be fully prepared for. Having achieved the Mind awake, body asleep state, you might suddenly feel as if some or all of your body begins to "vibrate" very rapidly. These vibrations can steadily increase in intensity to the point where they can seem very dramatic and alarming. In addition to these vibrations, there is the possibility that your physical body will become completely "paralyzed" to the extent you simply cannot seem to move any part of your body at all—a state known as "catalepsy". Do not be alarmed if this experience occurs—you are in absolutely no danger whatsoever.

A further possibility during this process is for some or all of your Etheric body to start to "float" out of, or above your physical body. These are all very common characteristics of the early stages of what is usually referred to as an "Out of Body Experience" or "OBE".

Should you find yourself in an OBE situation while practicing Astral Projection, the first thing to remember is to remain totally calm and relaxed. The vibrations will often increase to the point where your conscious awareness will leave your physical body and become centred within your Etheric body. At this point, you will be completely free to travel in the Etheric plane beyond the confines of your physical body.

The actual separation process between your physical and Etheric bodies during the vibrational stage can happen automatically, or you might have to encourage the process of separation. There are various ways to achieve this. A particularly effective method of leaving your physical body with your Etheric body is to imagine that you have already floated some distance above your physical body. As with all creative processes involving visualisation, you must imagine this situation in the present tense as if it is already an absolute reality. If this succeeds, you should find yourself floating above your physical body.

If separation using your imagination does not work, a more direct approach will be required. Move your Etheric body "out" of your physical body by rolling it to one side. It is most important not to actually attempt to move your physical body while doing this if your physical body has become paralyzed.

You can also gradually sit up with your Etheric body, and if successful, slowly stand up and move some distance away from your physical body. Once again, it should be noted that it is very important during this process not to tense or move your physical body in any way. All movements should be with the Etheric body only, otherwise, you could suddenly terminate the OBE process and suddenly return to your physical body.

Separation from your physical body while the vibrations are in full flow is not as difficult as it might seem. At this stage of the OBE process, your centre of conscious awareness will be within your Etheric body, which will feel very real and solid, even while your physical body is unable to move. Again, it is most important to absolutely remain calm at all times, ensuring you are in full conscious control of the separation process.

It sometimes happens that immediately after the initial exit from your physical body, your Astral "vision" might seem somewhat dim or even non-existent. Should this happen, will yourself to move further away from your physical body by imagining you have already done so, and then with as much emotion as possible, firmly and meaningfully state the command in your Mind, "full clarity now". Repeat this command with absolute authority as often as is necessary until you have achieved full perception of your surroundings.

Remember that your Mind is in full control, and whatever you desire must become your reality.

It is highly advisable to understand the characteristics of your Etheric body and how to maintain full control over it during an OBE. Although the Etheric plane is not on the same level of vibration as the Astral planes at a much higher vibration, it is still an outer extension of it and very similar in characteristics to the main Astral planes.

The Etheric plane is much closer to the density of the Astral planes than the physical plane, and like the inner planes, the Etheric plane is also a "Mind world" highly responsive to thought Energy. Accordingly, one of the first characteristics you will notice is that any thought will instantly become a cause with a correspondingly instantaneous effect. If you do not achieve control over your emotions and thoughts, you have the potential to "scare" yourself back into your physical body.

Another characteristic you will notice once you are out of your physical body is that you will experience full vision, which is now better than 360 degrees, experienced spherically. This might seem alarming or confusing at first. You might, for example, see a cupboard behind you that would normally be in front of you. This "illusion" is caused by the fact you are used to your normal narrow physical field of vision while confined within your physical body, and your Mind simply cannot at first comprehend the characteristics of full, unrestricted spherical vision. It should not take long to get used to this situation, however, particularly if you are prepared for it and fully understand what is happening. Your quality of vision might initially vary between non-existent to crystal clear.

The next challenge to confront you once out of body will be that of moving around. In the Etheric plane, you are not confined by gravity or movement on two legs. You can move in any direction at all at will, including up through the roof and down through the floor. Objects appearing to be solid will now present no barrier. In your Etheric body, you are identical to what people commonly refer to as a “ghost”. The only tangible difference between a ghost and a person in the OBE state is that the latter can return to their physical body at will while the ghost cannot.

A person in the OBE state can materialize as an apparition before other people, especially in places with a particularly high concentration of ectoplasm. Similarly, with sufficient Etheric Energy and density, both a ghost and a person in the OBE state can also influence objects in the material world by making them move or make sounds. Such a person is often known as a “poltergeist”. A person in the OBE state can also meet and communicate with “deceased” humans. Deceased humans can either be people from the Astral worlds “visiting” the lower Etheric plane or sometimes can be “ghosts” still residing within the lower Etheric planes.

The newcomer to OBE will often, particularly at first, find moving around to be an awkward process with a tendency to unintentionally float through doors and walls. Although you will initially tend to move around by instinctively moving your legs as you would in the physical world in your physical body, all movement will ultimately be controlled by the focused powers of your Mind. You are not in any way restricted by the physical constraints of the physical world, and can travel anywhere in the world or even within the physical Universe at the speed of thought. Once again, however, it is important to understand that your travels will take place within an Etheric reflection of the physical world rather than within the density of the actual physical world itself. It is also important to understand that you are not actually “travelling” anywhere as well all already exist everywhere, and travelling therefore is a projection of Consciousness and awareness.

While travelling during an OBE, you are not actually “seeing” the physical world itself or passing through physical objects.

What you perceive is an Etheric “reflection” of the physical world. So, when you travel through a door or a wall or visit anywhere in the physical Universe, you are actually in a very close “copy” of that environment. That is why the Etheric environment is so susceptible to the Mind where you can create objects, situations and even complete alternative realities.

Some people in the OBE state visit the Moon, a nearby planet such as Mars or even distant star systems. If you wish to move forward, simply imagine you have already done so. If you wish to visit someone in the physical world, simply intend to do so.

Of course, the people you visit within the physical world will not usually be aware of your presence. If the person you are visiting possesses psychic abilities, however, they might be able to perceive your presence and even be able to communicate with you. A pet such as a dog or cat is often acutely aware of people in the OBE state.

The next thing you will need to learn while in the OBE state is how to control acceleration, speed and momentum, all of which have no limits in the inner planes of life and reality, but in fact are still an illusion, with your Mind using physical speed as a reference point. “Speed” is normally a function of “time” and “space”, neither of which exist beyond the physical world. You can seem to accelerate to the speed of a car, a plane, or even beyond the speed of light. Full control of what is perceived as “movement” simply takes practice. Remember to do everything smoothly and with full focus and presence of Mind. You will soon get used to moving around. Even if you do find yourself in outer space or some other unfamiliar location, do not panic. You can always return to your physical body at will at any time simply by imagining that you have already returned to it.

You might also want to experience flying, which is perfectly possible in the OBE state with no physical gravity to contend with, although it is still an illusion brought about by Mind using physical travel as a reference. As with basic movement, flying is an ability that needs to be learned and controlled. It is much easier to blast off into outer space than to soar gracefully over the treetops like a bird. To fly, simply form the will and intent to do so and imagine having already launched into the air like a bird. As always, these thoughts should be in the present tense. If you wish, you may even imagine yourself with your arms outstretched like Superman, or you can flap your imaginary wings. Again, although in absolute terms, in the absence of time and space this is an illusion, the experience still feels very real indeed, and many find it great fun.

At first, you might find yourself drifting back down to the "ground". This is due to your own concept and expectation of the force of gravity as experienced within the physical world. You initially expect not to be able defy the physical laws of gravity and drift back down just as you would expect to happen in the physical plane. Always remember that your thoughts and imagination are your reality. You need to lodge the reality that there is no gravity within the Etheric planes firmly in your Mind when flying, and then you will remain airborne at will.

After plenty of practice, flying during an OBE will become second nature, but anticipate many amusing situations in the meantime, such as drifting through the roofs of strange homes or blasting off to the moon.

Passing through solid objects might also present problems, mainly due to the belief, like flying, that it is impossible to do. After the first time of passing through a wall or door, you will be left in no doubt whatsoever and will happily travel through any seemingly solid objects with complete confidence. It is advisable to avoid passing through reflective surfaces such as mirrors or windows, however. These can often cause an anomaly or confusion by projecting you into a mirror image of your Etheric surroundings, which are, in fact, a mirror image of the physical world.

Leaving your home by passing through a wall, a door or even through the ceiling will prevent such situations arising. Once outside, you can travel at any speed you desire, from a casual walking speed to flying at the speed of an aircraft, thus covering good distances in a relatively short time while still being able to view the scenery as it passes beneath you. You can travel around the world by using normal navigation techniques, following roads, rivers and landmarks. But for travelling great distances, it is better to travel to your destination simply by forming intent to do so and imagining yourself to already be there. It is quite possible to travel at the speed of thought, which is much, much faster than the speed of light, and again, it is your point of conscious awareness that is actually travelling, not your "body" as such, even though it seems that way due to your perceptions of "travel" as relates to the physical world of matter.

You can, as previously mentioned in the context of OBE, even travel to other planets and galaxies. The problem with travelling instantly in outer space, however, is that you will not be able to easily imagine a destination much beyond the moon, Mars, or other better known inner planet, simply because there is not sufficient data to form a proper image within your Mind. Many people in an OBE state do travel to the Moon. It is certainly worthwhile visiting the moon at least once just for the experience, especially the far side of the moon that faces away from Earth, which cannot be viewed by physical means.

If you do wish to explore the physical Universe, the best way to proceed is to fly at the highest possible speed you can summon, launching yourself into outer space, heading for whichever star system strikes your fancy.

If you do find yourself in an OBE situation rather than the originally intended Astral Projection, it is still quite possible to transition from the Etheric to the Astral planes. In theory, this is achieved by simply raising the vibrations of your Etheric body until you match the vibrations and density of the appropriate level of the Astral planes. Your Etheric body should then simply fade, giving way to your Astral body as you find yourself within the Astral planes. This is exactly the same process occurring naturally with recently deceased people when transitioning to their next home in the Astral worlds after their supply of Etheric Energy expires. To raise your vibrations to the Astral planes, as with all inner travel, it is simply a case of forming the will and intent to do so while using your imagination to visualize yourself as already being at your desired Astral destination or in the presence of the desired person. You can also use a mental command such as "now I travel inwards".

Sometimes, tunnel or tube-like structures might also appear while in the Etheric plane. These are conceptualised as "portals" to the Astral planes, where entering such a tunnel will often result in travelling at a very high speed before soon arriving within the Astral planes. This is a very similar experience to the "tunnels of light" reported by people during "near death experiences" or "NDE", and also the same tunnels encountered by recently deceased people when transitioning to the Astral worlds. There is no risk in entering tunnels of light, as you can always return to your physical body at will.

In addition to experiencing a spontaneous OBE situation while practicing Astral Projection, it is also quite possible to induce an OBE by design. As with Astral Projection, there are numerous methods for inducing an OBE. Many, if not most, such methods are difficult to achieve however. Many people become discouraged with persistent failure, simply believing OBE's to be beyond their capability.

The main reason for failing to accomplish an OBE is the failure to achieve an adequate state of deep physical relaxation. There are several natural methods which, as with Astral Projection, make use of the naturally occurring sleep state in order to accomplish the necessary relaxation.

Excellent powers of concentration are required to achieve an adequate state of trance if endeavouring to perform an OBE from a fully awake state. Methods with which to invoke OBE from the natural sleep state are much easier to achieve. It is simply not necessary to attempt an OBE from a fully waking state unless there is a particular reason for doing so. If the desire is to OBE during the daytime, it can be achieved by taking a daytime nap. It is also more convenient to OBE during the night or very early morning, as most people are otherwise occupied during daytime hours. Another excellent benefit of performing OBE at night is that your physical body will still be asleep and receiving all the rest and recuperation it naturally requires while your Etheric or Astral body is travelling.

There are three different methods for achieving an OBE from the natural sleep state, all of which have proved to be highly successful for a wide range of people. The three times when these OBE methods can be used to the greatest effect are:

- Just before sleep, after retiring to bed.
- After awakening a couple of hours earlier than usual.
- Immediately before or after a daytime nap.

The second of these possibilities—immediately after awakening a couple of hours earlier than usual—also relies on drifting back to sleep. This particular time of the morning, after two or three normal sleep cycles, seems to be particularly effective in invoking OBE and Astral Projection, as well as Lucid Dreaming. This is due to the fact the body is in a particularly advanced state of deep physical relaxation, and the Consciousness is clear of the mundane thoughts usually present in the Mind after a full waking day. At this time, the Consciousness is much more tuned into the inner realms where it will have been normally focused during sleep.

As previously mentioned, everyone naturally projects during the physical sleep process, and therefore the object of the OBE and the previously discussed Astral Projection procedures is to achieve a fully conscious and controllable experience.

All of the following three Out of Body Experience methods involve programming your Mind before sleep in order to invoke a conscious OBE at some stage during the sleep cycle. Using these methods, OBE occurs shortly after falling asleep. As with Astral Projection, the more these methods are practiced, the more they will be impressed upon the Subconscious Mind, and the more reliable and successful they will become.

Chapter 69
Three Out of Body Experience Methods

OBE Method 1: Affirmations

The use of affirmations is an extremely powerful and proven way of invoking an OBE. While the conscious Mind sleeps, the Subconscious Mind remains active, never sleeping. The affirmation method works by impressing your Subconscious Mind with the appropriate instructions to bring about a fully conscious OBE, and at the same time, alerts you that the process has started in the form of typical pre-OBE characteristics such as vibrations and catalepsy.

One of the greatest benefits of this method is that it requires no formal training in deep physical relaxation, concentration, trance or any of the other arduous OBE training methods. Instead, it relies completely upon the immense powers of the Subconscious Mind and the normal functions of the body in order to bring about these inner states in a completely natural way. It might take anywhere from a couple of days to a month or so to achieve an OBE by this method, but once the Subconscious Mind is programmed to invoke a conscious OBE state, it should become a regular occurrence achievable at will.

An affirmation is a short phrase repeated in the present tense with as much emotion as possible, as if it already an absolute reality. The consistent use of such an affirmation will impress upon your Subconscious Mind to accept and follow your instructions.

At your chosen pre-sleep time, minutes before you feel yourself drifting off to sleep, start to repeat your affirmation over and over again as you drift off to sleep. When you feel yourself close to sleep, continue to repeat the affirmations with as much emotion and focus as possible, while knowing beyond any doubt whatsoever that your instruction has already become an absolute reality. Your affirmation can be repeated aloud or silently within your Mind.

Another approach is to write down your affirmations until you become sleepy or until you completely fall asleep. If you feel you cannot go to sleep while writing, then write down as many affirmations as you can until you feel tired. Then, relax and continue to repeat your affirmation in your Mind until you drift off to sleep. Writing down an affirmation is a particularly powerful way of impressing your wishes on your Subconscious Mind through an action in the direction of your intentions, particularly immediately before and after sleep.

There is yet another possibility for impressing your affirmation on your Subconscious Mind. Obtain a length of fine string, or other fibre, and tie it into a series of fifty knots equally along its entire length. Just before your chosen sleep time, repeat your affirmation, and as you repeat it each time, move your fingers to the next knot along the string. The physical action of sliding your fingers from knot to knot helps to impress the affirmation upon your Subconscious Mind.

Another potentially powerful enhancement to this process is to record your affirmations and set them to replay as you drift off to sleep. You can either record or play the affirmations a specific number of times or set the playback to loop through the affirmations continuously. An affirmation relayed to your Subconscious Mind in your own voice while you sleep has a very powerful, which will then accept and act upon that affirmation. The Subconscious Mind never, ever "questions" your intent; it will always accept your instructions expressed and impressed in the present tense without question, and work with your conscious Mind and Higher Self to bring your instructions into reality.

The affirmation chosen should be short, concise, and always spoken in the present tense as if it were already an absolute reality. Here are some examples:

"I am now out of body".

"I now travel out of body".

"I now leave my physical body".

"I now travel out of body with full awareness".

"I now enjoy an out of body experience".

If you continue to repeat your affirmation as you drift off to sleep, as well as listening to a recorded affirmation, the next thing you will be aware of is awakening to the pre-OBE characteristics of vibrations, catalepsy or floating out of your physical body. This often happens very shortly after falling asleep or might happen at any time during the night. When this happens, you are well on your way to an OBE and all you need to do is simply follow the procedures as previously discussed in order to complete the exit from your body.

Again, never, ever be discouraged after only a few days of practicing this or any other OBE or Astral Projection method. Keep practicing until you succeed—which you surely will.

OBE Method 2: Visualisation

The use of visualisation is an extremely effective method of achieving an OBE, particularly when used in conjunction with an affirmation as discussed in method 1.

This method works by projecting your conscious awareness away from the confines of your physical body while you drift off to sleep, focusing on the visualisation of a particular scenario or object and becoming completely involved with it. A scenario is more effective than an object, however, because you can become more involved with it, thereby engaging your inner senses, and projecting your conscious awareness away from the physical world. Whatever you choose, it can be something you are already familiar with or something you create. Any scenario will potentially work fine, but the more detail and involvement you create, using as many senses as possible, the more effective it will be.

Whatever scenario or object you select for this purpose needs to be sufficiently captivating to hold your complete attention for at least ten minutes and preferably much longer—ideally for thirty minutes or more. An ideal choice might for example be a favourite holiday location. You can also use your imagination to create an ideal scenario that does not physically exist.

Another possibility is to use a scenario based upon your own home. In this case, walk around your home a few times and take particular note of several familiar objects. Ideally, each object should appeal to a different sense. For example, a ticking clock for sound, a fragrant potted plant or air freshener for smell, and a plastic or rough surface for touch. Note the characteristics of each of these objects and how they stimulate your senses, committing these sensations to memory in as much detail as possible.

Commence this technique at your chosen pre-sleep time. Start by imagining your scenario or objects by using all of your powers of visualisation and senses. In the case of the tour of your home, imagine yourself walking around your home, pausing at each of your chosen objects in order to fully appreciate them. Completely immerse yourself in the process as much as you possibly can.

Continue to engage your imagination in this way until you drift off to sleep. As you feel yourself falling asleep, deepen the sensations and emotions associated with your scenario. By projecting your conscious awareness away from your physical body, you have primed yourself for an OBE experience. As with the affirmations method, you might well find yourself suddenly awakening with the typical pre-OBE characteristics either very shortly after drifting off to sleep or at any time during your sleep period. Again, this method might take anywhere between a couple of days to a few weeks to be successful, so do persevere. You can achieve an OBE.

OBE Method 3: The Floating Balloon

During normal waking hours, the Etheric body is usually firmly integrated with the physical and inner bodies. During sleep time, however, the inner bodies automatically move out of phase with the physical body during what is actually a projection to an inner level.

The floating balloon method works by using the imagination in order to consciously invoke a feeling of floating upwards just prior to sleep. When you drift into sleep, your Subconscious Mind will continue to consciously invoke the upwards floating feeling associated with your Etheric body, which can then become a full OBE. This method is particularly effective when used in conjunction with affirmations as with the previous method. Like the other methods, this can be used prior to any sleep time.

Commence this method as you begin to drift off to sleep by imagining with as much realism as possible that you are a balloon filled with helium. Feel with all of your imagination how extremely light you are. As you drift nearer to sleep, feel yourself floating gradually higher and higher, ever upward toward the glorious blue sky. Feel warmer and warmer as you continue to float up toward the sun shining brightly above you. As you drift higher, visualize your home, street and town becoming smaller and smaller. Maintain this feeling of extreme lightness and of floating ever higher with the scenery below you becoming smaller until you drift off to sleep.

Continue this awareness of drifting upward with as much intensity and realism as you can, while enjoying every minute of it as you continue your gradual ascent, with the landmarks beneath becoming specks against the planet Earth. Soon, the Earth itself will become smaller and smaller as you continue to rise upwards.

When successful, you will suddenly be awakened by vibrations or state of catalepsy. You may awaken to find yourself already floating above your body, at which point you can assume full control over your out of body state, as previously discussed.

These three simple methods have the additional advantage of producing results before any frustration sets in, which often causes people to give up before OBE success is achieved.

It is advisable to discover as soon as possible which method is best for you, and keep practicing it every day. Above all, enjoy the experience of learning and succeeding. Both Astral Projection and OBE are great inner adventures which will certainly bring profound benefits and truths into your life, not the least of which being proof of the continuity of life after the "death" of the physical body, enabling you to face both your current life on Earth and your inner destiny on your path in the knowledge that you are, without question, an immortal Spiritual being of the Universe, a true Son or Daughter of God.

Chapter 70
The Near Death Experience

Throughout recorded history, people have returned from what humans call "death" to tell of their experiences during the time they were "out of their physical body". The situations leading to such experiences are many and varied, including accidents, war, heart failure and extreme medical conditions.

These near death experiences or "NDE's" share common characteristics, including the perception of floating above or near the physical body, observing it from an unusual situation, such as from the corner of a room, or from the corner of an operating theatre during surgery. If doctors are present, the person experiencing the NDE will usually see them endeavouring to revive their physical body, after which, if unsuccessful, a doctor will often pronounce them as "dead", going on to record the time of death.

Some people later choose to relate their NDE experiences to doctors, relatives and friends. Many do not, however, because sometimes they simply do not trust their own experience or fear others will think they are deranged, or mentally affected by the near death experience in some way, even "brain damaged".

To most people experiencing an NDE, relating the experience to others seems pointless anyway because the experience itself is so profound and personal. Research has proven, however, that literally millions of people have experienced an NDE, most of which are described as profound and life-changing experiences. One of the most significant effects of an NDE for people who are deeply religious is that they immediately know, beyond doubt, the creed and dogma of religion for what it really is.

There have been many famous people, especially in the last century or so, who have experienced an NDE and spoken of their experiences publicly. Due to their standing, the NDE experiences are usually taken seriously and form the basis of some of the most compelling evidence existing today as to the truth of NDE and of what happens to the physical body immediately after physical "death".

There are many similar experiences reported by people who have experienced an NDE. These include "seeing" and experiencing their entire life "pass before their eyes" seemingly in an instant. Although this "life review" seems to happen in just a brief moment in time, it only appears so because the Etheric plane is beyond the confines of space and time. Another common feature of the typical NDE is intense radiant white light, which is the Divine light of God. With it comes an overwhelming and all-encompassing feeling of absolute Unconditional Love—an experience that is beyond the scope of communicating with the written word.

Frequently, people experiencing an NDE perceive the presence of deceased loved ones, friends and other "Beings of Light" who are there to guide them at the moment of transition from the physical to the Astral worlds. The person experiencing the NDE will often be told by one of these people to "go back", or "it isn't your time yet". This is often all the motivation needed to return to the physical body, serene in the certain knowledge of the glories waiting one day upon the final passing. Some however enjoy the experience so much that they do not wish to return to their physical body, feeling sad at the prospect. Regardless of the precise experience, as with those practicing Astral Projection and OBE, those experiencing an NDE will never again fear the state of transition from the physical to the non-physical worlds, still erroneously known as "death".

An NDE is very similar to an OBE or Astral Projection. As with final physical death, it is possible to initially transition either to the Etheric plane closest to the physical world, the same process as an OBE, or to transition directly to the Astral world as occurs with Astral Projection. The Etheric NDE is the situation where the circumstances associated with the NDE are witnessed from outside the confines of the physical body. Tunnels and Beings of light are all characteristics of an NDE sharing similar characteristics to an Astral Projection.

People experiencing an NDE only experience the greater realities for a short time, while those experienced with OBE and Astral Projection can experience them at will for extended periods of time, as "time" relates to the physical Universe.

NDE, OBE and Astral Projection are all experiences reproducing what will happen to each and every person at the point of physical death, resulting in a profound knowing of the truth of the higher realities and the continuation of life after the death of the physical body. Anyone enjoying these experiences will profoundly know beyond any doubt that the state known as "death" is not final but is instead the continuation of a much greater adventure—the next stage in life as an immortal Spiritual being of the multi-faceted Universe on the glorious path of perfection back to our Source, Supreme Creator, God.

Part 3

Realizing Your Destiny

Chapter 71
Progression Through Life

Most people progress through each life on Earth without any true sense of purpose, understanding or control over their own true meaning or destiny. To many, "life" still seems to be something that simply "happens" or to be tolerated, or to simple "survive", doing little more than merely existing from day to day, endeavoring to exist in what is often perceived as a harsh, unfriendly, unforgiving world, providing for themselves and their families as best they can, often wondering whatever will "happen" next, attributing everything that "befalls" them to such superstitious notions as "luck", "chance" or "fortune".

Many people resign themselves to accepting their "lot" in life, often from birth, while feeling envious of those whose lives seem to be much better than their own. Of course, they give little thought to the vast numbers of people who are much worse off than themselves. And so it is with life—people carried along like corks on the ocean, controlled by the tides of their Egos, striving to gather as many material possessions as possible during what is perceived to be an only "life". Most people are still completely oblivious to the higher realities of the infinite Universe and of their true purpose for living on Earth, a purpose which was actually chosen by their own Higher Self before their current life. What most people fail to appreciate is that whatever their life's circumstances, it was initially chosen by their own Higher Self as presenting the best opportunity for lessons that need to be learned for Spiritual evolution, with their precise experiences being a result of their own Mind..

The human race of planet Earth has a very long way to progress in the grand Universal scheme of things, and each Higher Self lifetime on Earth should be spent wisely with personal evolution at the forefront, but while still experiencing health, happiness and abundance. Those who or fail to recognize these important facts will find themselves lagging behind their brothers and sisters who will progress through the inner spheres of life beyond the physical and Astral worlds to greater realms of life and reality, beyond the kindergarten of Earth where eventually the illusion of form is no longer required. Those who fail to structure each life accordingly will cause their Higher Self to continue sending "representatives" to Earth time and again until all necessary lessons are learned and the Higher Self, now as complete as is necessary for this stage of evolution, can move onwards and inwards to far greater things as a co-creator within the great and infinite realms of the Universe in which we live and move and have our Being.

Every single human being, without exception, has God-given abilities to manage each and every life to the fullest. Just as God is the Prime Creator in the Macrocosm, human Beings are creators in their own Mind world the Microcosm. We create every single success, every failure, every illness, relationship, problem, trauma, incidence of "good fortune", incidence of "bad luck", abundance or lack of money and every single need.

In accordance with the immutable Universal law of Cause and Effect, nothing in the Universe ever happens by "chance". Everyone is responsible for who they are and what they have in life. Negative emotions invoked by adverse circumstances attract further unhappiness, and so it goes on ad infinitum—a whole series of negative effects resulting from a corresponding series of negative causes. The opposite also applies of course. Those who are happy with their lives will focus on that happiness and attract and experience even more happiness, and so it goes on. Such is the way of the Universe—the power of attraction, of Cause and Effect, and all other Universal laws unfailingly operating with total immutability by virtue of the only fundamental Principle in the Universe – Mind, which humans beings in physical incarnation experience in three spheres of activity—conscious, Subconscious and Universal.

There is no such concept as favoritism in the Universe. Everyone is completely equal and has an absolute God-given right to have all genuine needs fulfilled, to be happy and content at all times, and to live in absolute peace and harmony with the Universe and all life within the Universe. Everyone, without exception, has equal opportunities to progress as an Immortal Spirit on the path or perfection back to The Source, The First Cause, God—such is the true meaning of life.

In this section of this book, we will discuss how you can take full control over every aspect of your life and your own ultimate reality regardless of your current circumstances. We will discuss the importance and methods of true concentration, focus and relaxation, all fundamentally important in everyday life. We will discuss how you can manifest anything you could possibly wish for, need or desire into your experiential reality. Finally, we will discuss the many abilities and disciplines required for personal progression and Spiritual evolution, not only for the benefit of your own current life, but for the benefit of all mankind, and of The Source, The First Cause, God, of Whom we are all individuated channels of experience.

The more people who begin to live their lives in harmony with Universal Principles and God, the more the collective Consciousness of mankind will be expanded until all of mankind will be liberated from the shackles of creed, dogma and materialism, to express of God to the full.

These things are crucially important, not only at an individual level, but also as we approach the end of this great age, a great cycle which will bring profound changes at all levels. How we experience this great transition of the ages depends entirely on our own individual Consciousness, wisdom, expectations, state of perfection at all levels and Spiritual progression. The following chapters of this book will guide you towards fulfilling all of these and thereby towards your own true destiny as an inseparable aspect of our Divine Creator.

Chapter 72
Deep Physical Relaxation

By relaxation, we do not necessarily mean reclining in a comfortable chair in front of a television, relaxing in the garden or taking a holiday or vacation, pleasant and welcome though these activities might be. We are rather referring to deep physical relaxation. Deep physical relaxation is an ability that is important to integrate into your daily lifestyle in order to combat stress and negative feelings, and is also important in the development of many other abilities required to manage your own life and destiny by achieving the necessary state of Mind.

The benefits of learning and regularly practicing deep physical relaxation cannot be underestimated. You might feel that you are already relaxed, but if you check all of your muscle groups and your current state of Mind, you will soon discover that the reality is often very different and you are far from relaxed.

Before commencing these relaxation exercises, it is important that you are not too tired, otherwise, the effectiveness will be reduced, or you might fall asleep. It is also best to not have eaten a large or heavy meal beforehand. Loose, comfortable clothing will facilitate a better experience. Taking a warm bath can also be very beneficial before commencing these exercises.

First of all, make yourself as comfortable as you can in an armchair or similar place where you can relax in an upright or semi-upright position. Good posture is very important. If you allow yourself to slump in your chair or bed it will be counterproductive to the relaxation process. If your armchair does not allow your head and neck to be completely comfortable, place a pillow behind your head, adjusting it until your head is comfortably supported.

The objectives before commencing deep physical relaxation exercises are for your body to be as balanced and free of strain as possible from the outset. One of the best conditions for relaxation is to sit completely upright in a straight-backed chair while not leaning against the backrest of the chair. This will enable you to achieve the necessary balance between deep relaxation and alertness.

The practice of deep physical relaxation:

Breathe in deeply but slowly to a slow count of five, and imagine with as much realism as possible that the air you are inhaling is a very bright, radiant, sparkling white light. As you progressively inhale, feel the positive Energy of this white light enter your body and spread throughout from head to foot.

Hold the breath for a slow count of five while enjoying the light as it bathes your entire body. Then, slowly exhale to a further slow count of five. As you exhale, imagine that your breath is a dark grey color containing all negativity and tension that you have been holding. As this negativity and tension leaves your body, you feel progressively more relaxed.

Now, continue to relax for a further slow count of five, and repeat the process of inhaling pure, radiant, white sparkling light, again feeling its Energy entering and permeating your entire body from head to foot before finally exhaling the dark grey light. All inhalations, pauses and exhalations should be to the same slow count of five for each part of this process.

Repeat each breathing cycle at least five times, ideally continuing until you are feeling generally relaxed, refreshed and positive. Please note that while doing these breathing exercises, you should inhale by using your entire diaphragm and not just your upper chest. You can accomplish this by drawing in each breath by using the entire area from your lower stomach to your upper chest.

The next stage in deep physical relaxation involves progressive active relaxation, starting at your feet and finishing at the crown of your head.

Imagine, as vividly as possible, a large sphere of bright, glowing, radiant white light positioned just beneath your feet. Make this sphere of light as intense as possible—even brighter than the sun on a clear summer's day.

Feel the warmth of this energizing light around the entire area of your feet, toes and ankles. Feel all remaining tension drain quickly away as your feet become free of all tension. Maintain this visualisation as vividly as possible until all remaining tension completely dissipates from your feet and ankles.

Next, imagine the bright sphere of radiant light moving slowly up your legs to your calves. Feel this area completely bathed in the soothing white light until both of your calves are completely free of all tension.

Next, the light moves slowly up your legs until it reaches your thighs. The sphere of light can expand as much as necessary to fully encompass any area of your body. As before, allow the sphere of light to remain in this position until you know beyond any doubt that all tension has fully dissipated from your legs and they are feeling completely relaxed.

Repeat this process as the glowing sphere of Energy travels slowly up your body, reaching your hips and buttocks, followed by your stomach and lower back, your chest and upper back, arms and shoulders. Your arms should ideally remain totally straight by your sides, allowing the sphere to encompass the entire trunk of your body and arms as it progressively makes its way up through your body, encompassing everything as it leaves each area totally relaxed.

When the sphere of radiant white light reaches your neck, allow it to remain there as long as necessary for you to release all tension. Your neck can collect a considerable amount of tension, and sufficient time must therefore be allowed for it to completely dissipate.

Finally, the glowing, radiant sphere of light reaches your head. Allow it to remain around your head while all tension leaves your face and head muscles. After all of the muscles feel totally relaxed, imagine the radiant, glowing white sphere of light traveling to the top of your head, where it pauses for a while before moving onwards into the infinite Universe.

Take time to bathe in this pleasant feeling of deep, full body relaxation. Feel how blissful it is to have removed all of that stored tension and stress from your entire body. You can remain in this position of deep physical and mental relaxation for as long as you wish while you fully appreciate it.

As has been previously mentioned, this deep physical relaxation exercise is a valuable precursor to Astral Projection, OBE, concentration, manifestation, healing and many other important abilities to be discussed later in this book. In this stressful world, it is very useful, however, to learn the art of deep physical relaxation for the benefits it brings.

After sufficient practice, deep physical relaxation can be performed anywhere at will and without the need for a formal comfortable location or visualisations. Ultimately, you should reach the stage where you can sit completely upright, spine erect on a non-padded chair, and totally relax by simply focusing and willing your body to so. When you can achieve such a state of deep physical relaxation at will, you will find that many more latent abilities will open themselves to you.

Chapter 73
Concentration

The ability to totally concentrate at will is not, as with deep physical relaxation not only extremely beneficial but is one of the most important of all abilities, and one upon which most other abilities rest. Without adequate powers of concentration, nothing worthwhile can be achieved. On the other hand, with advanced powers of concentration, anything is possible.

The benefits of developing your ability to concentrate include peace of Mind, self-confidence, inner strength, willpower, focus, improved memory, better ability to make and carry out decisions, more control over your daily life, the ability to learn more quickly, freedom from obsessive or upsetting thoughts, freedom from habits, advanced powers of the imagination, and the ability to meditate effectively. These abilities will also greatly enhance your use of The Law of Attraction, powers of healing and every condition requiring the Power of the Mind.

Many people have considerable difficulty concentrating for more than a few seconds at a time. The Mind constantly jumps around from thought to thought without any conscious control or structure. People are heard to complain, “I cannot possibly think of a hundred things at once”. Ironically, that is actually the issue. They are thinking of a hundred things at once instead of just one single focused thought—the immediate task at hand.

Another expression for this inability to concentrate on a single thought is “monkey mind”. The Mind is constantly chattering away with endless noise that dims its true power and effectiveness. In some parts of the world, people who are unable to maintain any single thought for more than a few moments are known as “quinhentos pensamentos”, which literally means, “five hundred thoughts”. This applies equally however to people of all cultures throughout the world.

Diluting the Mind with thoughts is like diluting anything. The totality of its effectiveness will be reduced in proportion to the amount of dilution. A single focused thought is extremely powerful. As previously discussed, thought is Energy, and focused thought is focused Energy. The vibrations of this Energy can have a profound effect on the object of the thought, and the power of the Thought Form, with results that might appear to the casual observer as "miraculous".

A graphic example of such immense power of concentration has often been observed and related by those who have traveled in India. They tell of how they have personally witnessed a seed being planted in the Earth, which immediately sprouted and grew before their very eyes. Very soon thereafter, the plant produced fruit that could be immediately plucked and tasted. All of this occurred in just a few moments. This "phenomena" was accomplished by the most intense powers of concentration and use of the imagination by the "fakirs" of India.

Controlling your thoughts involves exercising a much higher level of control over every aspect of your life. Lack of concentration and control over thoughts generally can be likened to piercing a sheet of thin paper with a blunt pencil. The paper will simply tear. If the pencil is sharp, however, the point will pierce the sheet of paper very easily, leaving a small neat hole.

The same situation can be applied to concentration. If concentration is blunt and undisciplined, and the Mind is crowded by hundreds of different thoughts, the Mind will be equally blunt and ineffective. Accomplishing any single objective will then be very difficult. If the concentration of the Mind is sharp with the entire Energy of the point of focus in one place towards one single intended objective, the results will be far more effective and experienced much sooner.

The ultimate objective of concentration is to attain a state of "single-pointedness" of Mind. Such single-pointedness is the unwavering focus on one single thought or on no specific thoughts at all (total emptiness of Mind).

Although almost anyone can develop high levels of concentration and willpower, there are certain barriers to success that should be taken into account. Any inherent physical or mental weaknesses brought about by an ongoing illness, for example, can affect concentration. At the same time, such conditions can be healed, as we will discuss later. A lifestyle too filled with a wide range of activities can make it difficult to achieve any degree of worthwhile concentration. The Mind of such a person will always be preoccupied with thoughts of their ongoing activities, to focus effectively on a single objective.

Chapter 74
The Practice of Concentration

Initially, concentration can be practiced from any sufficiently relaxed position. You should ideally start by devoting at least ten minutes each day to these exercises, later increasing to at least thirty minutes or as much time as you can find.

There are several progressive stages involved in achieving a high level of concentration. First of all, you need to ensure that you are completely relaxed by performing the deep physical relaxation exercises described in chapter 72.

The following concentration exercises are progressive, so there is nothing to be gained by moving on to the next exercise until the previous exercise has been successfully accomplished.

Concentration exercises should ideally be practiced while sitting upright, with spine absolutely straight in a hard chair, such as a dining chair, without leaning against the backrest.

Commence by sitting up straight with your spine absolutely vertical, not leaning against the back of the chair, with knees together and hands face down on your knees or thighs.

Exercise 1: Close your eyes, and count backwards in your Mind from 100 to 0. If you miss any numbers, start again at 100. You should be able to do this exercise 10 times in a row before proceeding to the next exercise.

Exercise 2: Close your eyes, and count backwards from 100 in increments of two: 100, 98, 96, 94, 92, 90 and so on down to 0. If you miss any numbers, again, start again from 100. You should be able to succeed with this exercise 10 times in a row before proceeding to the next exercise.

Exercise 3: Repeat exercise 2, but this time counting backwards in increments of three: 100, 97, 94, 91 and so on. As before, start over if you miss any of the numbers. You should be able to succeed with this exercise 10 times in a row before proceeding to the next exercise.

Exercise 4: Select any word of your choice, one that you find interesting is better, and repeat the word over and over in your Mind. If another word enters your Mind, start over. When you can repeat the same word in your Mind for at least 10 minutes without interruption, this exercise is complete.

Exercise 5: Select a convenient object such as a fruit, and spend at least 10 minutes examining it from all sides. You must apply your entire unwavering attention to this exercise, the objective being to memorize the object as completely and in as much detail as possible from every perspective. Do not allow any other thoughts to intrude during this exercise. Your entire focus should be on memorizing your chosen object. Only when you have completely memorized this object from every perspective should you move on to the next exercise.

Exercise 6: Close your eyes, concentrate, and visualize your chosen object from Exercise 5 as realistically as possible. Visualize the object from every perspective, exactly as it appeared when you were previously examining it, making it appear so lifelike that you believe you can reach out and touch it. Should you have difficulty with this, return to exercise 5. This is also an extremely valuable exercise for visualisation and other abilities that we will discuss later in this book. Once you have successfully completed this exercise with the original object, repeat the same exercise again with a range of objects of various shapes, sizes and colors.

Exercise 7: Obtain a fruit of your choice, and divide it into sections. Examine your fruit thoroughly, not only with your visual senses, but with your senses of smell, touch and taste.

Commit all of these received impressions to memory in as much vivid detail as possible.

Exercise 8: Close your eyes, and imagine exactly how the fruit appeared while you examined it, utilizing all of your senses, sight, smell, taste, sound, and touch. Imagine you can smell, taste and feel the texture of the fruit, completely recreating it in your Mind in every detail.

The fruit should appear to be so solid and lifelike that you desire to actually reach out and eat it. As with the previous exercises, should you not be able to achieve this task, return to Exercise 7 and try it again before progressing with Exercise 9.

Exercise 9: Close your eyes, and imagine you can hear the sound of a clock ticking loudly. The ticking must seem completely real as if there is actually a clock in your room. Once you have established the sound of the clock ticking in your imagination, maintain the ticking for a full 10 minutes without interruption. If your concentration is broken and you miss a few ticks of the clock, you should either start over again or leave the exercise for another day until you can imagine the ticking with total reality for a full 10 minutes.

Exercise 10: The objective of this final exercise is to achieve a state of total emptiness of Mind. This is an extremely valuable state and is the basis for achieving many inner abilities including meditation. Close your eyes, relax, and vigorously reject any thoughts attempting to enter your Mind. At first, this might seem difficult as thought after thought tries to encroach upon your imposed silence. Simply passively observe the thoughts, and allow them to drift through your Consciousness without giving them any focus or emotion. If you do latch onto a thought and start to give it any importance, it will occupy your Mind and become more difficult to remove.

The objective of this exercise is to hold your Consciousness completely clear of all thoughts for at least ten minutes. This exercise might well take several weeks of practice before fully achieved. Eventually, it will become possible to maintain this state of Mind for as long as you wish, and certainly for many hours at a time, during which profound experiences can occur.

After you have successfully completed all of these exercises, your concentration and willpower will have increased considerably and will prove to be an excellent asset in the future. It is important to practice these exercises regularly—ideally every day, otherwise, you could very easily start to diminish your powers of concentration. If you find this happening, repeat the necessary exercises to bring your concentration levels back to those of exercise 10 once again.

It is also highly beneficial to be able to control all of your thought processes throughout the day. This involves focusing your thoughts exclusively on what you are doing and never allowing your Mind to wander to any other activities. Thought control will further enhance your concentration abilities and sharpen your levels of Consciousness and powers of memory.

We will conclude this section with three high-level concentration exercises that are a challenge but very rewarding to accomplish. These are truly tests of absolute concentration and willpower. These exercises are by no means absolutely necessary for developing inner abilities, but for those who wish to develop powers of concentration to a very high level, they are very worthwhile. These exercises involve the ability known as Telekinesis or sometimes known as Psychokinesis, and while they might seem impossible to some people, you may be assured that they are both absolutely possible and achievable.

The candle flame:

Before commencing this first exercise, it is important to ensure that you are fully relaxed and focused both physically and mentally, with no distractions or potential distractions whatsoever. (The previous concentration exercises must have been fully accomplished before moving on to these exercises).

Place an ordinary candle on a table safely secured in its holder. While remaining as relaxed and focused as possible, and while keeping your Mind completely clear of all thoughts, sit in your chair with your elbows resting firmly on the table and with your chin cupped in your hands.

Now focus exclusively on the candle flame with complete, unwavering concentration. Take some time to completely relax, focusing entirely on the candle flame while seeing and thinking about nothing else whatsoever. Your thoughts should be totally focused upon the flame flickering before you. When you have achieved the required state of Mind, use all of your concentration and willpower to move the candle flame. It is very important while you are doing this to imagine, as realistically as possible and without any doubts whatsoever in your Mind that the flame has already moved in the desired direction. Never imagine that it will move—you must know that it has already moved beyond any doubt.

By using your willpower and concentration to move the flame while imagining that it has already moved in the required direction, you will influence Energy, beyond the physical limitations of space and time, to comply with your Mind.

Remember that thought is Energy, and the Energy of your thoughts will influence other Energy in order in the direction determined by the focus of your Mind. This applies to everything in the Universe in all spheres of life and reality. You must also know, beyond any possible doubt that not only can you achieve this, but that you have already achieved it. At first, the flame might appear to move only a small, almost imperceptible distance. Never have any doubts that you have moved the flame, however, and continue to move it more.

You might succeed at the very first attempt with this exercise, or it might take longer. With practice however, moving the candle flame with your Mind through "Telekinesis" will become progressively easier until it becomes a natural ability.

This is an excellent exercise for increasing concentration and willpower, as well as for understanding the importance and effects of the inner Energy and forces involved. When doing any of these exercises, it is extremely important to remember there is no such concept as "try". "Try" is a word of total weakness, and one which implies failure from the beginning, and should therefore be completely eliminated from your thoughts, actions and vocabulary. "Try" does not exist.

Once you have succeeded in moving the candle flame from side to side, next it up and down. When you have succeeded with that, extinguish the candle flame using your powers of concentration and willpower alone, always remembering to imagine the flame is already extinguished beyond any possible doubt in your Mind. When you have succeeded in extinguishing the candle flame, re-light it again with your Mind, again, knowing, beyond any doubt the candle is already lit. You will soon find with regular practice that you can exercise total control over the candle flame using the focused powers of your Mind and concentration alone.

The Psi wheel:

This is another Telekinesis exercise which is also achieved by exercising complete control over the powers of powers of your Mind with focused concentration. As with the candle exercise, it is highly advisable to ensure that you are totally relaxed and completely focused before proceeding.

You will need a needle, a base to stick the needle in vertically, such as a cork, Blu-Tack, also known as Sticky Tack etc, and a sheet of thick, white paper.

Next, cut out a square from the sheet of white paper of approximately 3 inches x 3 inches or 7.5cm by 7.5cm. Next fold the square of paper in half, both ways so the edges touch and you now have a small square of paper. Next unfold the paper and fold it again along the diagonals this time. Now unfold the square of paper again, turn it over, and then push the opposite ends together until it resembles an umbrella.

Now place the needle in its base so it sticks up vertically, and place your psi wheel with the edges pointing downwards on top of the needle tack so it balances perfectly.

This then is your basic psi wheel. There are more elaborate psi wheels that can be made, but this will provide the necessary means to practice your telekinetic powers, and know that it is not caused by some external influence such as air movement or thermal currents.

Again, you need to ensure that you are totally relaxed for these exercises with no extraneous thoughts in your Mind. Place your elbows lightly on the table, and sit with your chin cupped in your hands a short distance from your psi wheel. Now, cause the psi wheel to turn around by using your powers of Mind and concentration alone. This can be achieved by focusing deeply on one corner of the psi wheel while imagining that it has already moved in the desired direction. You can also imagine a hand or a white beam of light originating between your eyebrows, your third eye or brow chakra reaching out and pushing the psi wheel around.

As with the candle flame exercise, it is very important to imagine and know beyond any doubt that the psi wheel is already actually moving in the desired direction. When you succeed, the psi wheel will start to physically move on its axis (the tip of the needle). It might move very slowly at first, but with practice, the psi wheel can be made to spin faster and faster until it is spinning like a fan.

When you achieve this, you will feel a great sense of satisfaction and accomplishment. In order to be totally convinced of your powers of Telekinesis, you can also place the psi wheel in a transparent, clear box or other container and place a lid on the top of the container to seal the psi wheel from external influences. When you do your telekinetic psi wheel exercises with the psi wheel sealed in the clear box, you will notice that the psi wheel still turns even though there can be no possible external physical influences. Physical matter of any sort represents no barrier whatsoever to the powers of the Mind and the Energy of the Universe.

The floating needle:

For this third exercise, you will require a wide glass or bowl of water, an average sized needle, and some heavy grease with which to coat the needle. Place the glass or bowl on a table, and fill it with water very near to the rim. Allow the surface of the water to settle completely. Next, grease the needle, ensuring it is fully coated, and very gently place the needle upon the surface of the water so it floats upon the surface tension. Allow the needle to settle until it is completely still and floating in the center of the container.

As with the first two exercises, you must ensure that you are totally relaxed and focused on the task at hand before proceeding. Sit with your elbows resting on the surface of the table and with your chin cupped in your hands, and using all of your willpower and powers of concentration, cause the needle to move across the surface of the water. As with the previous exercises, you can imagine a beam of light or hand projecting from between your eyes, your brow chakra, reaching out to the needle and pushing it across the surface of the water. Again, it is very important to imagine to the extent that there is no possible doubt in your Mind that the needle has already moved across the surface of the water and reached the other side.

As with the first two exercises, total unwavering focus and concentration are required in order to accomplish this successfully. You might find that you succeed with this exercise at your first attempt, or you might need several weeks of practice. Do not be discouraged whatever happens. The satisfaction of gaining this telekinetic ability is very well worth the effort, and your powers of concentration will have advanced further, powers that will serve you well for many other abilities utilizing the powers of the Mind.

After you have succeeded in causing the needle to move across the surface of the water, cause it to spin around on its axis.

Pursuing these abilities should always be solely for the benefit of your own individual development. Never seek to impress others with public demonstrations of your abilities, otherwise, your focus and progress will be adversely affected. Your own development is very individually focused, while always being willing to assist others with any aspect of their lives or personal development when requested to do so. There are those with powers of the Mind that most people cannot even begin to comprehend, but these never speak of their abilities or perform in public, and for good reason that everyone should follow.

Chapter 75
Meditation

Meditation is, without question, one of the most worthwhile and valuable practices anyone can undertake on a regular basis. Many people however still associate meditation with a Far Eastern mystical practice involving a person sitting on the floor in a seemingly impossible looking position, surrounded by candles and burning incense, while chanting a mystical sounding mantra. For the vast majority of practitioners, meditation is actually nothing like this at all and neither does it need to be. Meditation is a daily habit for millions of people the world over within all cultures and walks of life, and more people join them every day as they discover the considerable benefits of this ancient and powerful practice.

So, what exactly are the benefits of meditation? Meditation to start with calms the Mind and dissolves tension from the body. In the longer term, the Mind begins to experience much higher levels of peace, tranquility and serenity, not only during the meditation itself, but during daily life. There is a progressive and profound increase in happiness, tolerance, love, understanding, fearlessness, and of inner abilities.

With meditation, powers of concentration increase, and the Mind becomes progressively sharper and under control, including freedom from unwanted thoughts, emotions and influences. Meditation greatly strengthens the body, Soul and Spirit, resulting in a much higher and more positive life.

While in a state of deep meditation, we are more open to the inner realms of reality and Energy, making it possible to contact and communicate with Beings of the inner realms, including Spirit guides, people residing in the Astral words who have passed on from Earth, and even your Higher Self These communications can be filled with valuable information, intuition, insights, advice, encouragement and much more, all assisting in your daily life and Spiritual evolution.

During deep meditation, you can ask questions and receive answers on issues of importance to you. Remember that space and time do not exist within the inner realms of life and reality.

Most meditation techniques have one ultimate objective: to achieve absolute silence of the Mind and to reach the real "I" level of pure awareness, resulting in a more direct channel of communication with your Inner Self and a greater, more profound connection with The Source, The First Cause, God.

When meditating, we are focusing inwards towards our Soul and Spirit, as well as to the inner realms of life and reality. Keep in Mind that the inner realms are identical to what are often erroneously referred to as the "higher" realms although the inner realms can certainly be considered to be a higher state of Consciousness. It is in meditation that we reach far beyond the illusions of the physical and Astral worlds to focus inward towards the true Source of All that Is.

When involved in meditation, Astral Projection or any other journey of the Mind beyond the physical world, we are really embarking on an inner journey towards higher states of Energy, vibration, Consciousness, Being and above all Unconditional Love, the most powerful and Divine force in the Universe.

Chapter 76
The Practice of Meditation

In order to meditate effectively, a sufficient degree of concentration is required, without which it is difficult to silence the Mind and achieve anything worthwhile.

As previously mentioned, it is very important to meditate while sitting in an upright position with your spine completely straight as in the concentration exercises. Meditation cannot be effectively accomplished while lying on a bed, reclining or even leaning back in a comfortable chair. It is best to sit with the spine absolutely vertical on a hard backed chair with your legs and knees firmly together and your hands palms down on your thighs. Alternatively, you may sit cross-legged on the floor with your spine totally straight. It is not necessary to use a formal Yoga type position such as the full or half Lotus, but you may do so if you wish. Gaining proficiency with the concentration exercises as practiced in chapter 74 of this book will help considerably with the practice of meditation, and I would highly recommend accomplishing this before commencing the practice of meditation.

It is fine in the early stages to sit on a pillow to make yourself more comfortable, but never sit with your back against the backrest of a chair or against any other support. Your back must be straight and unsupported. Should you suffer from a disability that prevents you from achieving this posture, you can lie down on a bed, flat on your back, if possible, but with no pillows. You will need to make a particular conscious effort however not to drift off to sleep.

It is a good idea to meditate at the same place and time of day when you will not be disturbed. Although candles, incense and other materials are not required, you might find them to be useful in setting the meditative mood and focusing your Mind. Certain scented candles or incense will become associated with your meditation time and can assist you in reaching the required level of Consciousness and relaxation more quickly. But this is a matter of personal choice.

Next, perform some deep breathing exercises such as those discussed earlier in this section to help you achieve the required level of relaxation and focus your Mind away from mundane matters. Breathing in for a slow count of five, hold your breath for a slow count of five, and breathe out for a further slow count of five. Repeat this five times or more if you feel it is beneficial until you have achieved deep relaxation.

While performing the breathing exercises, you can also imagine inhaling pure, glowing or sparkling white light, and exhaling grey light through your nose to release any tension or negativity stored in your body. When you are totally relaxed, use all of your powers of concentration to empty your Mind of all thoughts. Only a complete vacancy of Mind should prevail. Should you have difficulty in achieving this at first, you can progress in stages over several sessions. It does not matter how many sessions it takes to achieve the total vacancy of Mind state, but you must nevertheless achieve the total vacancy of Mind state before proceeding to meditate effectively. Again, the concentration exercises as set out in chapter 74 are an excellent way of achieving complete vacancy of Mind, and I therefore strongly recommended that you fully complete the concentration exercises before commencing the practice of meditation. I have arranged the exercises in this book as a progression, each leading to, and a pre-requisite of the next.

To commence with your meditation, assume your chosen meditation position, known as an “asana” in far eastern terminology, asana being Sanskrit for “seat”, and attain the necessary degree of deep physical relaxation. Next empty your Mind of all thoughts, and maintain that emptiness of Mind.

Should thoughts appear or linger in your Consciousness, simply passively observe the thought, allowing it to drift through your awareness without becoming involved with it. Continue this exercise for as long as you can, but ideally for at least ten minutes, with least thirty minutes as your objective, during which time no thoughts should be allowed to linger in your Mind. When you first do this exercise, you may be besieged by thoughts, particularly if you have not practiced the concentration exercises of chapter 74 first. The number of thoughts will gradually diminish, however, until they finally become few and far between, and finally you will reach the stage where you can maintain complete emptiness of Mind.

Reaching this stage might take some time to accomplish, but you can reinforce the process throughout the day by utilizing concentration exercises, only thinking about and focusing on what you are doing at any particular moment in time, but not allowing any unrelated thoughts into your Mind. For example, if you are driving your car, think only about driving the car, and do not allow your Mind to wander on to other matters however important or mundane you perceive them to be. The same applies for any other activity. This process will assist greatly in thought control and strengthen your ongoing powers of concentration.

The next stage in the process of learning to meditate is to select a single thought or object of your choice and hold that thought or image in your Mind for as long as possible. This might be a memory of a place you enjoy visiting, a memorable holiday or any other happy memory. It might be easier at first to visualize a familiar object such as a favorite picture, an item of household furniture, or the image of a loved one. It does not need to be something you are actively involved with or interested in. Any object will do, such as a fruit, candle, or cup. After deciding on your object, assume your meditation posture by sitting in your chair or on the floor with your back totally straight. After relaxation and breathing exercises, bring the thought or image firmly into your Mind with as much presence as possible. Ideally, your thought or image should fill your entire Mind. It is very important to immediately reject any intruding thought the very moment it tries to join your chosen thought or image. You will find this exercise will become progressively easier over time, with your thought or image becoming stronger, and with less and less intruding thoughts.

When you can hold your thought or image solidly in your Mind for ten minutes without wavering, at the end of the session you can move on to the final stage of this process which is to dismiss the object you were holding in your Mind, resulting in a complete vacancy of Mind. Hold your Mind completely empty for a few moments before gently raising your Consciousness back to the physical level. After this has been successfully accomplished, you can proceed to the full meditation stage—full vacancy of Mind.

This next step involves assuming your meditation posture and holding your Mind totally void of all thoughts for at least ten minutes. When you can achieve this stage, you are now ready to meditate effectively.

Remember that you are focusing inwards towards The Source and not to some "higher" level relative to The Source. With dedicated daily practice, meditation will become progressively deeper and with more profound levels of inner awareness, soon becoming a very blissful and valuable experience. Ideally, you should reach a stage where you completely lose the feeling of your physical senses, body and surroundings, becoming totally focused within the inner states of Consciousness.

During the process of deep meditation, there are some situations that might occur and which you need to be aware of. These situations often involve imagery to varying degrees and intensity. One of these is known as the "TV screen" or "cinema screen" effect. This is exactly the same effect as frequently occurs during Astral Projection. This "screen" is actually a "window" into the Astral planes. If this occurs, you have two choices, you can either observe the screen and simply learn from these visions or convert the meditation into a full Astral Projection by imagining yourself moving toward the screen as it becomes larger and larger, eventually passing straight through the image in the screen into the Astral worlds. If you choose to do this, proceed as for an Astral Projection as discussed in chapter 67 where we looked at Astral Projection.

You may also have a full Out of Body Experience. The first signs of this are usually the ability to "see" through your closed eyelids. This means that your point of Consciousness has already shifted to your Etheric body and out of phase with your physical body as happens naturally during a normal sleep cycle. You are then actually viewing your surroundings with your inner senses rather than your physical eyes. If this occurs, maintain absolute concentration and remain in your meditative state, or, if you prefer, decide to leave your body to enjoy the Out of Body Experience. If you decide to remain concentrating on your meditation, your Etheric vision might remain, it might fade, or as your vibrations rise, it may give way to the "viewing" of the Astral worlds.

As this is a meditation session, it is preferable to choose the "viewing" option rather than converting to a full Astral Projection or an OBE, but the choice is always yours. It is always best to follow your inner guidance.

While meditating, your Mind is tuned to the inner worlds of the Astral and Spiritual planes. This can be at any level depending on your level of vibration. This focus can frequently result in communications with Beings such as Spirit guides, deceased relatives or even your Higher Self. These possibilities are one of the most valuable aspects of meditation. If you establish contact with these Beings, you will clearly "hear" their voices in your head, often just as clearly as if they were speaking to you in the physical world. Of course these are not physical voices, the communication is telepathic, between Minds.

As you progressively absorb yourself in your meditations, your brainwave frequencies will slow down. This also happens naturally from time to time during the day depending upon the type of activity you are engaged in, but usually occurs just before going to sleep at night when the brain passes through decreasing frequencies before the full sleep state occurs. The highest brainwave frequencies occur in the normal waking state. This is known as the "beta" brainwave state, characterized by very fast frequencies of between 13Hz and 40Hz. If brainwaves slow down somewhat, as often happens while daydreaming during the day or during meditation, the "alpha" brainwave state is reached, characterized by brainwave frequencies in the order of between 7Hz and 13Hz.

During meditation or trance work, brainwaves can slow down even further to the "theta" state, which is characterized by brainwaves of a frequency of 3.5Hz to 7Hz. Theta level is the most profoundly clear and focused state. Many people experience profound inspiration, intuition, and ideas while in the theta state, originating both from Beings of the inner spheres and from the Higher Self. Theta is also the state of vivid imagery where the powers of imagination and visualisation are particularly enhanced.

Throughout history, famous scientists have placed themselves into the theta state for maximum inspiration and creativity. This has resulted in many important inventions and theories, such as the "special theory of relativity" which was postulated by Albert Einstein while in a deep thinking theta state of Mind.

As previously stated, meditation is an excellent means through which to receive answers from your Higher Self, Who is primarily concerned with your Spiritual evolution. Any inspiration, intuition or message from the Higher Self must always be acted upon without question.

These are just a few of the numerous possibilities and benefits resulting from deep meditation. For many people, particularly of the Far Eastern cultures, the ultimate objective of meditation is to achieve such a profound level of inner Consciousness as to become One with the very highest of the Spiritual planes—a state mystically known as "Samadhi". Those who achieve this state of extreme bliss, approaching the innermost levels of Energy and vibration, know, beyond any doubt, that everything in the Universe is One and that everything and everyone is an integral part of "All that Is", The Source, The First Cause, Universal Mind—God.

Chapter 77
Twin Hearts Meditation

Twin Hearts is a specially constructed meditation. Although not exactly the same as meditation in the normally accepted terms, Twin Hearts is nevertheless a valuable exercise.

This meditation is based upon the Energy centers of the Etheric body—the chakras—being gateways to expanded levels of Consciousness. For the purposes of the Twin Hearts meditation, the principal chakras are the crown and heart chakras.

The objective of this special meditation is to bless the Earth with loving kindness through the crown and heart chakras, which then become channels for Spiritual Energy. Many practitioners of the Twin Hearts meditation have reported heightened levels of intuition, increased healing powers, sharper and more organized mental faculties, inner peace, loving kindness, compassion, enhanced Spiritual service, a brighter and more balanced aura, larger chakras, enhanced communication with the inner spheres and Higher Self, the development of Clairvoyance and other psychic abilities, a healthier physical body, more success in life with less stress, and a more balanced personality.

The practice of Twin Hearts Meditation:

It is useful to first perform some physical exercises of your choice for about five minutes in order to cleanse and energize your Energy body.

Then, sit in your usual asana, your meditation posture, either on the floor or sitting on a chair with your legs and knees together, back and spine absolutely straight, and your hands turned down and resting on your thighs.

Next, mentally request with sincerity Divine blessings for guidance, help, protection and illumination.

Activate your heart chakra simply by becoming aware of it. You should feel your heart chakra activate with a feeling of warmth and Unconditional Love emanating from your entire chest area.

Send sincere blessings from your heart to the entire planet Earth, including all life, every person and every Being, with loving kindness, great joy, happiness, Divine peace, understanding, harmony and good will.

Activate your crown chakra located across the top of your head, again simply by becoming aware of it. As with the heart chakra, you should feel a pleasant, warm glow or similar sensations emanating across the crown of your head. Send blessings to planet Earth through your crown chakra just as you did from your heart chakra.

Allow yourself to become a channel of Divine love and kindness, great joy, happiness, understanding, harmony and Divine peace, sharing these with the whole planet. When projecting your blessings, it is important to feel and appreciate the implications of each and every thought, feeling and word.

Next, meditate and bless the Earth with loving-kindness through both the heart and crown chakras simultaneously. This will align both chakras and make the blessing much more powerful.

Gently imagine a brilliant white or golden light at the crown of your head. Remain aware of this light and the inner stillness for a few minutes, and then gently and silently chant the mantra “Om” or “Amen”.

When meditating on the interval between the "Om" or "Amen", simultaneously be aware of the light, the stillness, and the bliss while you let go completely.

Continue this meditation for about ten minutes before slowly bringing back your awareness to your physical body. Raise your hands to your chest level facing them outward. Release excess Energy by blessing the planet Earth with light, loving kindness, peace and abundance for several minutes until you feel your body is normalized. You may bless specific persons or your family and friends after releasing the excess Energy.

After the meditation is complete, always give thanks to God, your Higher Self and to your guides for their Divine blessings. It is advisable to ground yourself afterward by gently performing some physical exercises for a few minutes.

Chapter 78
The Human Paradox

The vast majority of people in the world today still fail to achieve their full potential due to a complete lack of understanding of the immutable perfection of the Universe, or of the relationship between themselves and the Universe.

When we, as our Higher Self, chooses to incarnate into the physical world, we do so in the full knowledge of who our parents will be, where we will live, what circumstances we will encounter and potential challenges we will face, as well as the determination to meet those challenges, in the knowledge that it is only in accepting and prevailing in these and other important objectives that we can progress further towards The Source in the Divine process of Spiritual evolution and perfection.

We are all equal aspects of The Source, The First Cause, God, expressing in all spheres of existence with Unconditional Love, and the natural, instinctive, powerful desire to evolve back to The Source as a perfected aspect of God. Over the years, however, mankind has steadily and increasingly turned its back on God towards an alternative, darker existence of gross materialism, dogma and indoctrination, often driven by the Ego and the desire for power and control. Most people are influenced by such erroneous factors as what other people think of them, the desire to conform to the expectations of family, friends, neighbours, society, others, and only to live in strict accordance with "the way things are done".

It is only when an individual has the courage, strength and determination to face the truth that he or she can become truly free to fulfil his or her own true destiny with joy, meaning and real purpose, and to consciously attract anything and everything that they can possibly desire into their lives.

In order to achieve this Divine state of awareness, it is necessary to consciously become an open channel through which God can express and experience in the physical world, a process that we, as humans, control ourselves as individuated aspects of The Source. We determine our own experiences and God provides for all our wishes, needs and desires necessary for those experiences, and thereby, through us, God experiences and expands, and thus the entire Universe expands.

Most people however are doing exactly the opposite by striving to conform to the expectations of others, pursuing material gain as a first priority, and forcing things in a perceived direction by physical means, instead of being an open channel of expression of The Source, The First Cause, God, and are therefore often contrary to the perfect flow of the Universe. Quite simply, such people are failing to "let go and let God", the inevitable result of which is suffering and lack of Spiritual evolution, ultimately resulting in the Higher self of the person sending yet another incarnation to Earth for the opportunity to learn the lessons once more that were not learned in the previous incarnation.

Even in the 21st century, "society" is still operating by a system through which people are trapped from a very young age into a system that often prevents happiness, fulfilment and evolution. From the very first day a child is born into what should be a glorious, joyful and fulfilling life on Earth, the child is immediately and continuously indoctrinated into the trappings of the material world. A child is taught to focus exclusively upon the five physical senses, to behave in a certain way that precludes maintaining their strong connections with the inner worlds, and taught to treasure material things, such as toys, as a prelude to coveting bigger material possessions later in physical life, often as a first priority over everything else.

Later, young children are expected to go to school in order to get the "qualifications" required to obtain a "job" that they may "work" for the next 40 or 50 years before "retiring" on a meagre “pension”, after which they may live out what remains of this life in the hope of simply surviving in a generally non-caring world where very often service to self comes before genuine service to others.

From the moment of birth, the Minds of most children are shaped by parents based upon their own perceptions of what life “is all about”, usually based in turn upon their own current circumstances, and the lifestyle, traditions and “values” of their own parents before them. Many children are taught that it is wrong to aspire to anything outside of their “station in life” and should instead focus on the lifestyle that their parents have always accepted and found to be quite “adequate”. The Mind of a child at both conscious and in particular Subconscious levels is highly impressionable, and it does not take many years of such indoctrination for the Subconscious Mind of a child to accept what their parents have thrust upon them as “reality”.

Once the transition to the Astral worlds has taken place during the change erroneously known as “death”, the Soul will have every opportunity to reflect on what might have been, what was not accomplished and why, eventually returning to their Higher Self with an incomplete package of experience, resulting in the Higher self sending forth another representative to Earth in order to complete the mission on the next visit.

Humans have been trapped in this paradox, a cycle that often results in misery as a result of living a false reality that is inconsistent with their true mission. It is not until this cycle is broken, and people recognise, understand and exercise true freedom based upon their own reason for being here, can they finally realise true joy, fulfilment and happiness, and the means by which to complete their mission on Earth this time around.

The current systems of society originated three hundred or more years ago. It might well have worked back then to the extent it was consistent with the people living at that time, but with society still enforcing these very archaic systems, mankind has failed to progress at many fundamental levels.

People might say that money is necessary to acquire the basics of survival, such as food, clothing and shelter. While this might appear to be superficially the case, but the truth is that we are here to attract and enjoy unlimited abundance, health and happiness if desired through our Divine connection with The Source, God, and not simply the basics for mere survival. There is a very big difference between true "abundance" and "money", and it is this distinction that has led so many people astray. "Money" is a human concept that largely does not even exist, except as notional data created and stored on computers, whereas true abundance is a fundamental Universal Principle.

The Universe has unlimited abundance waiting to be delivered to each and every person simply for the asking. "Ask, and you shall receive", every time, no exceptions. There is nothing that we cannot be, do or have. The Universe does not recognize favouritism, "luck", "chance" or any other such superstitions. Most people simply do not know how to ask or to receive, and they therefore fail to achieve abundance, joy and happiness.

The vast majority of people in the world today are not taught how to attract abundance, but rather how to "make money". It is in the "making of money" that so much misery has been, and still is wrought upon humanity, being the catalyst for gross materialism driven by the Ego and self-interest and often urge for power and control. Few people achieve true financial freedom, and even those who do are often not at all happy, fulfilled or joyous about their situation, simply because they felt compelled to "make" their money at a very physical level, often attracting much misery in the process to both themselves and others. "Making money" is not the same as "attracting wealth" and abundance for the right reasons, and the resultant true emotional freedom, joy and fulfilment that these bring.

Only those who can fully understand how The Universe expresses abundance through human beings can realise as much abundance as they can possibly desire, along with the true joy, happiness and emotional freedom associated with it. This means throwing off the shackles imposed by society in order to become a true channel of abundance for The Source of all abundance. Those who can do accomplish this will answer those who may be critical of their defiance of "societal norms" by virtue of an extremely abundant, joyous, fulfilling life on Earth, and one in which all desires are realized at will.

It has often been noted that those who physically seem to "work" the hardest for all of their lives seem to have the least money, possessions and true happiness, while those who "work" the least often seem to enjoy unlimited abundance, joy and true freedom. Many people will jealously view such happy, joyous and fulfilled people with envy, often accusing them of achieving their riches through some sort of illicit means, or ascribing their success to such superstitions notions as "luck", "chance" or "fortune".

Many people cast blame on others and even revel in the failure of others instead of celebrating success. The simple and powerful truth is that those who have achieved such levels of true fulfilment have done so by casting off the shackles of society and the expectations and pressures to conform, instead becoming open channels through which God can express and thereby experience fully in the physical world, thus being blessed with unlimited abundance, joy and happiness.

So, how can anyone escape from the chains of modern society thereby gaining the opportunity to realize their true potential? These questions and others will be fully dealt with in the next chapters of this book. But suffice it to say, the truth is that every single person on the planet has the equal ability to attract unlimited abundance, health and happiness.

One of the most powerful and truest expressions of all is quite simply "let go and let God. In China, a philosopher known as Lao-tsu said:

"In the practice of the Way every day something is dropped. Less and less do you need to force things until you finally arrive at non-action. When nothing is done nothing is left undone".

These are very powerful words, and once they are fully grasped and assimilated into your life, they will place you in a much better position to attract anything desired, without the need for physical action. If a person desires something, they automatically assume that some sort of physical action is required to obtain it, thereby "forcing" things in their own perceived direction. Such force might well bring about the intended result, but Universal Principles are immutable, and the force of that cause will always have a corresponding effect which will not always be positive. Whatever the person was forcing is not actually a "physical thing". It is ultimately Energy, the very same Energy from which all things are made, and in forcing that Energy in a certain direction which might be unnatural, a disharmony has resulted which the Universe will always balance in order to maintain harmony, a fundamental Universal Principle. As we will see from the coming chapters of this book, the entire Universe is conscious, intelligent, vibrating Energy, influenced only by Mind, and existing within the infinite Mind of The Source, The First Cause, of God. Mind therefore is the true and only power behind all creation including within the physical world, not physical "doing".

People are generally still focused on "doing" instead of "Being". In order to achieve anything, it is first necessary to "Be" rather than to "do". "Being" always precedes "doing".

This is not to say that we should never "do" things, of course. Action is often necessary in the physical world, arising from

Being, but such action must always be aligned completely with the flow of the Universe. It is only by being an open channel of the Universe, always receptive to intuition and inspiration from inner sources that the necessary Energy arrives, sometimes requiring an action that is in alignment with that Energy flow.

You might for example have projected a desire for something in accordance with the Law of Attraction, and the realization of that desire may have required a physical action in order to align with the Energy and allow the object of your desire to manifest into your physical reality. But it is important to note nevertheless that in this case, we first experienced the "Being" before the "doing". There was no forcing involved whatsoever.

There is always a process that must be followed in order to attract true, lasting, abundance, joy, health, happiness and fulfilment, which will be discussed further in the coming chapters of this book.

So, herein is the true human paradox. Mankind still remains largely trapped within a "no pain, no gain" society, often driven by materialism, vanity, the desire to conform to the expectations of others and the uncontrolled demands of the Ego, usually brought about by a materialistic focus, largely as a direct result of programming, conditioning and indoctrination from a very early age, by a society which, at all levels, for the most part lost its way millennia before.

It is only when this human paradox can be recognised for what it is and thus reconciled, can mankind as a race once again fully align with The Source, The First Cause, God to finally become open and free flowing true channels of expression and experience of God, with abundance, freedom and joy, the birth right of every single person as a true Child of God.

Chapter 79
The Eternal Now

What people perceive and experience as “time” is, like “space”, quite simply an illusion, albeit a very persistent illusion, a construct of mankind, contrived for convenience and in order to measure a perceived “past”, “present” and “future” as well as a point of reference. The illusion of “time” on Earth is maintained by the scientific measurement of the relative positions of the Earth and the Sun in order to observe the “seasons”, and the time for Earth to complete a full rotation relative to the Sun, thereby ultimately arriving at a calendrical system measured in days, weeks, months and years.

Beyond the perceptions of those living in the physical world, “time” simply does not exist. There is only the Eternal Now where everything that has happened, is happening and ever will happen relative to the Earth concept of time already exists, always has existed and always will exist. Beyond Earth, the concepts of “past”, “present” and “future” simply do not exist.

Before I continue I would like to note that one of the possible outcomes of the transition of the ages that we are currently experiencing, and of which the date 21 December, 2012 is associated as a potentially pivotal date, is the dissipation of the illusions of “time” and “space”, leaving humanity in a state of “timelessness” and “spacelessness” in which everything is experienced in the present moment of Now. This has numerous implications for humanity, and the way life is experienced, not the least of which would be that there will no longer be a perceived delay between a thought and its corresponding Thought Form manifesting as an objective experiential reality. The transition of the ages and implications for humanity and all life on Earth is discussed in depth later in this book.

As discussed previously, the entire Universe is conscious, intelligent, Energy vibrating at a frequency relative to The Source, The Source being the very centre of the entire Universe of Energy and the physical world being the outermost shell.

All Energy is influenced by the causation of thought before manifesting as a Thought Form under the influence of that thought, eventually manifesting as an observable effect in the plane at which the thought originated. Everything that happens, has ever happened and ever will happen in the entire Universe, including the physical world, first originates as a conscious thought and resultant Thought Form originating from the Mind of a Being capable of originating thought.

The ultimate act of creation by The First Cause of the entire Universe, in all its glorious spheres, planes and dimensions, originated in the very beginning as a thought in the Mind of God, The Source. It can truly be said that we as human beings as with everything in creation exists as "expressions", "ideas" or "Thought Forms" within the infinite Mind of God, truly made in the Spiritual image of God.

The tendency of humans to force everything to happen in compliance with a notional concept of "time" has a very profound effect on the lives of people. When a person thinks in the future tense and says, "I will", "I want", "I could", the Energy influenced by those thoughts will be influenced only in the Eternal Now, with the perceived "future" never actually arriving. So if someone thinks, says or behaves in a manner that implies "I want", that person is placing themselves into a perpetual state of "wanting" but of never actually receiving. The vast majority of the human race today exists to some extent in a state of such wanting, while never being in a state of Mind, Energy and vibration to receive what they really "want".

The importance of the Eternal Now must be fully grasped and fully understood as a continuous aspect of enjoying total fulfilment, joy and Spiritual evolution. How we think has the most profound effect over what occurs in our lives. In fact, nothing has a more profound effect.

It is not sufficient to only recognize and express these fundamental Universal Principles when it suits us, when we desire something or when there is a situation that demands it. It is absolutely necessary to live life completely in accordance with these immutable Universal Principles, in the knowledge that as aspects of God, we are also channels of experience and expressions of God, with the same God-given powers as God. Those who do live their lives, either consciously or Subconsciously according to these Universal Principles will always seem to others to live a “charmed”, “lucky”, “fortunate” existence. In fact, they are actually living a “magical life”, always in total control over their life, consciously shaping their own reality with the powers of their own Mind, as a channel of experience for The Source, Universal Mind, God, and always in a higher degree of harmony, with the Universe.

In order to begin the process of living the life of your dreams, with total control over your own destiny, you must first of all develop that level of awareness. Rather than thinking random thoughts, often reacting to what you see or hear, start to become fully aware of your thoughts and their corresponding effect on your reality, knowing that every thought is a cause that must result in a corresponding effect. This is where powers of concentration as practiced in the previous exercises within this book are so valuable. Presence of Mind, conscious awareness and concentration are very powerful in creating your own reality and living that truly magical life.

Always think as you wish things to Be, Now. Two of the most powerful words that you can possibly think or say are “I Am”. As you live your life, therefore, the first stage of awareness is to always stop your thoughts short of a statement that implies the future tense and to transmute them into the present tense. So “I will” becomes “I am”, “I want” becomes “I have”, and “I might" becomes "I do". Also keep in Mind that there is absolutely no such concept as "try". We either "do" something or we do nothing, we never, ever "try". To "try" simply does not exist except as a concept of a person wishing to achieve something, but not having the knowledge or confidence in their own God-given abilities, or the inner power to achieve it. Starting now, eliminate the word "try" from your vocabulary.

If you have a bill that needs paying, and you decide that you do not have the money to pay the bill, never think in terms of "I want the money to pay this bill", always think in terms of "I have the money to pay this bill effortlessly". Bringing this statement into the present tense, rather than as a future statement of lack will, supported by belief and faith in your own powers cause the means by which the bill can be paid to manifest into your reality, and the bill will duly be paid in full.

The Universe always delivers in absolute accordance with your thoughts. There are no exceptions to these Principles. Again, the statement or though "I might succeed at this objective" implies never "actually" succeeding. The "might" places success and experience of that wish into the indefinite and infinite range of possibilities and never as an actuality. So, "I might succeed with this objective" should become "I am enjoying complete success with this objective", which will then become your Thought Form, stated in the Now, manifesting into your experiential reality where you can enjoy it.

Those who understand and consciously apply these immutable Universal Principles to their lives in the Now, will be never experience lack, always precisely experiencing that which is desired in accordance with their thoughts, faith and gratitude.

Chapter 80
The Law of Attraction

Quantum physics describes the energetic characteristics of the Universe and therefore the fundamentals of the Law of Attraction. It should be mentioned that "Principle" is a more appropriate word than "Law", as we are indeed discussing characteristics of the Universe that are natural Principles. "Law" is an authoritarian word implying something contrived and that must be followed for fear of penalty. "The Law of Attraction" is however a widely recognised phrase, so in the interests of understanding we will continue to apply it, even though the "Principle of Attraction" may be more appropriate.

We know, from even the most fundamental basis of quantum physics that everything in the entire Universe consists of pure Energy, differing only in characteristics such as rate of vibration. Every "thing" or "Being" in the Universe exists as a Thought Form, a unique configuration of Energy created by Mind. Quantum physics also acknowledges the fact that Energy is influenced by Energy, and like Energy attracts like Energy in accordance with its unique characteristics of vibration. This is the very basis of how the Law of Attraction works throughout the Universe, with vibrating Energy always seeking harmony with like vibrating Energy, thereby maintaining the overall vibrational harmony of the Universe.

This fundamental truth can easily and unambiguously be demonstrated by means of a pair of tuning forks. If the second tuning fork is placed a distance from the first fork, and the first tuning fork is struck, causing it to emit a sound at a certain pitch or frequency (vibration), the second tuning fork located some distance away will immediately start to vibrate at exactly the same frequency, and are therefore observed to be vibrating in harmony with each other. This demonstrates one of the most fundamental of all Universal Principles—like vibrations attract.

This is not only true of, for example, The Law of Attraction, but also during Spiritual evolution. As we evolve, through the process of perfection, the frequency of vibration of our Spiritual body increases. As this process occurs, we naturally transition to the inner level of the Universe corresponding precisely to our unique frequency of vibration. This applies to all levels or "planes" of the Universe except for the outermost physical Universe, where the physical body of everyone lives on the same level of vibration. Even on Earth however, at the level of Mind, which is not the same as our body or physical brain, everyone "lives" or experiences a different vibration in accordance with their level of Spiritual evolution, character and other individual traits—it is only the physical body through which we experience the physical world that is bound to the "Earth vibration", not our Mind.

Similarly, when a person "passes on" from the physical world, they will transition to the Astral realm that most precisely corresponds to the vibration of their Astral body, in turn depending on their characteristics, thought processes and state of perfection relative to the Source. It can easily be recognised just how perfect this Universal Principle of Attraction truly is.

It is also very important to fully understand that, contrary to the belief of some branches of the sciences, Energy does not simply stop or cease to exist when it becomes no longer measurable by physical scientific instruments. The extent of the Energy spectrum that can be measured by scientific instruments is in fact extremely small by comparison with the entire spectrum of Energy representing the entire Universe to The Source. Energy and its corresponding vibration exist all the way from the physical world to The Source of all Energy, Who exists at the very highest frequency. All is Energy, including thought, and all Energy vibrates in accordance with its unique characteristics and therefore state of perfection.

Another very important aspect of quantum physics is "quantum potential", which describes how everything that "exists" already "potentially" exists in the Universe as a "quantum probability" until observed at which point it becomes a "quantum reality". Everything that exists now, has ever existed and ever will exist already exists, at the quantum potential level. It is by the process of observation, subsequent to the manifestation of a Thought Form in turn created by Mind that causes the quantum potential of the quanta of Energy involved to shift into quantum reality where it can be experienced.

Just as our senses and Mind interpret the Energy around us, we similarly influence that Energy with our thoughts, whether conscious of it or not. This is the same influence that determines "reality" as experienced by each and every individual, whether that experienced reality is positive, negative or neutral. The importance of quantum physics is discussed more in chapter 16 of this book, and is well worth reading again in the context of this chapter.

Like everything in the Universe, we are all Beings of pure Energy, extensions of Source Energy, always attracting into our own individual experiential realities corresponding Energy vibrations in accordance with the vibration of the Thoughts Forms we create through the infinite power of our Subconscious Mind, as directed by our Conscious Mind.

Another fundamental truth is "ask and it is given". The moment you make a request to the Universe in the form of a thought, whether spoken or not, it is instantly granted. We are all here to ultimately evolve back to the First Cause by utilizing the freewill provided by our Creator. In order to evolve, all of our perceived needs that we believe to be necessary for our own evolution and well-being must be forthcoming, otherwise our ability to experience, express and thereby evolve would be subject to factors beyond our control, and this clearly is not and cannot be the case. So, for example, if we believe we need to live in a castle, then The Source, Universal Mind will always provide it. Nothing is ever too large or too small. God never judges whether we truly need something or otherwise, whether we are "worthy" of it or not, or whether it will facilitate Spiritual evolution—those are factors human Beings are entrusted to take into consideration on an individual level, The Source will unconditionally deliver all requests in accordance with the freewill we enjoy. This must be true because we are channels of the Source, God, through which The Source experiences. If The Source were to make our individual needs and therefore experiences conditional in any way, those experiences would be influenced by the Mind of God, Who would accordingly not gain the benefit of unbiased experiences. In order for The Source to freely experience and thereby expand therefore, all channels of experience must have freewill, and the all wishes, needs and desires freely provided.

As you begin to fully understand these realities and integrate them into your own Consciousness and experience, seemingly amazing things will start to happen in your life. You will begin to attract everything you desire, people will begin to appear in your life and circumstances will manifest, all in tune with your unique vibration.

As your entire existence changes in accordance with your own unique vibration, you will know, within every part of your Being, that you are a co-creator of and within the Universe and in that knowledge will approach life with unbounded joy, enthusiasm and empowerment. "Enthusiasm" is indeed a highly appropriate word, being a derivative of the Ancient Greek word "entheos", literally meaning "to experience God within". To live "in God" or "in Spirit", "entheos", is to be in complete harmony with God.

To live in Spirit is to "let go and let God" in the full realization, knowledge and joy that as immortal Sons and Daughters of God, no harm can ever come to us. We create our own realities by the thoughts, ideas and images that we hold in our Mind. Beyond the thoughts we hold in our Mind, we should all know that God is Pure Unconditional Love, and nothing negative can possibly happen to us unless we attract it by the thoughts we ourselves originate by virtue of our own freewill.

As you practice "entheos", your "realisation of God within" grows, and you will become increasingly in vibrational harmony with that which you wish to attract. This is a self-perpetuating process that will very soon be noticed by those around you, who will often dismiss your apparent "good fortune" as "luck". If appropriate, always strive to share your knowledge with those people. If they are not ready to understand, never force anything upon them. Their own day of realization, their glorious awakening will arrive in due course.

The fundamental basis of making use of The Law of Attraction is to impress our Subconscious Mind with our needs, wishes and desires, upon which our Subconscious Mind will proceed to do whatever is necessary in order to bring the specific wish, need or desire into experiential reality where it can be enjoyed.

In accordance with The Law of Attraction, when a desire is impressed upon the Subconscious Mind for something that we wish to be brought into our experience, our Subconscious Mind in turn impresses that desire upon the Universal Mind which is also the realm of the collective Subconscious Mind.

The Subconscious Mind of people who share a similar desire will cause both to vibrate that similar desire at a similar frequency and Energy "signature" of that desire, and accordingly the same people or group of people vibrating this same desire will be attracted to each other by the Law of Attraction. The Subconscious Minds of these people then communicate with their respective conscious Minds, causing the person to desire to take physical action. An example of this process in practice is where one person is vibrating "sold my house" including the characteristics of the house, number of bedrooms, bathrooms, size of kitchen etc., and another is vibrating "bought my house" with the same or very similar characteristics. The Subconscious Minds of these people brought them together within the realms of the collective Subconscious Mind of the Universal Mind, which in turn brought it to the attention of their respective conscious Minds to take the necessary physical action.

In attracting our desires, the stronger, more focussed and more precise the vibration is, supported by faith in the outcome, the more successful we will be. Taking the example of the house seller and buyer, if the seller only vibrates his desire to have sold the house very weakly, lacking focus and faith in the house being sold, they might not attract many, if any potential buyers, and likely none that would pay his price. If on the other hand the seller was vibrating his intent very strongly, with focus and faith, he would attract many potential buyers, and could choose the one offering the best price. Likewise with the house buyer—the stronger, more focused and with more faith they vibrate "found the perfect house" the more potential houses will arrive in their experience and the wider would be the choice.

This also applies to business. A business person with a strong vibration, focus and "entheos", enthusiasm for what they are selling, with the faith and belief in their own abilities to attract customers, will indeed attract many customers and the business will be extremely successful in accordance with the law of Attraction. This is why we frequently see to shops, in the same street, selling the same type of products, and one is always busy with customers while the other empty. The only difference is the Mind of the respective shop owners—one attracts many customers and the other does not.

All desires, except for personal health or healing, which the Subconscious Mind manages directly, are fulfilled in this way, in perfect harmony, where all involved benefit equally, through the spheres of activity and vibration of individual conscious Minds and corresponding Subconscious Minds, through the Divine Providence of the Universal Mind, The Source, God.

It is important to note at this point that The Law of Attraction is only one aspect, albeit an important aspect of the manifestation process through which we attract our wishes, needs and desires, an example of which is the harmonisation process which will be discussed in greater detail later in this book. The Law of Attraction is therefore part of a much wider range of processes that are applied during the full manifestation process, and is not the entire process in and of itself.

All imagination is creative. When we imagine something, it is very real, not some sort of dream or fantasy or "figment of the imagination" implying an illusion. This is one of the reasons why creative visualisation is so powerful. By visualizing and mentally becoming a part of that which we are attracting, we begin to harmonise with those vibrations which will in turn, supported by faith in the process and belief in the outcome in cause the object of the visualisation to manifest into our individual, physical, experiential reality.

A further important aspect of realizing wishes is "desire". Unless you are in harmony with whatever your wishes, they will not manifest into your existence, or at least will take longer. Desire for whatever we wish for is a very important component of this process. If you do not genuinely desire something, you cannot be in vibrational harmony with it, and it will therefore not appear within your reality. Your wishes must always be fuelled by desire and expectation as well as faith, belief and gratitude, while never, even for a single moment, doubting the outcome as already true in the moment of Now.

The Law of Attraction applies equally to attracting or repelling people. Everyone without exception is a "transmitter" and "receiver" of vibrations which are picked up by those around you or sometimes even at great distance. People who feel attracted to you or you to them are those who are most in vibrational harmony with your own specific vibrations. Everyone, usually at a Subconscious level, detects and assimilates the vibrations of others to some extent. This is the reason why people in close proximity often take an instant like or dislike to someone else. They are "picking up" on the vibrations of the other person. Many species of animals in particular are much more tuned into the vibrations of people and can instinctively determine the character of someone, and whether they present a threat or not.

The future chapters of this book will describe the various factors, processes and methods that will enable you to realize your own true powers as a creator of your individual reality within the Universe, but before we move on to those chapters we should also discuss other emotions that are very important in the realization of your wishes—joy, gratitude and faith.

The more joyful, happy and "light-hearted" you are, the higher will be your corresponding overall rate of vibration. The higher your inherent rate of vibration, the more powerful your attractive powers will be. Joy is a very high level emotion. The more joyful you are, the more aligned you will be to The Source. This will enable you to manifest your desires more freely. Therefore, it is important to maintain a high state of joy. And why not maintain a blissful state of joy? You are a Divine, immortal, Spiritual Being, an expression of God made in the true Spiritual image of God, and the creator of your own reality—what is there not to be joyful about?

Those who are not joyful are in a state corresponding with a focus on the physical, material world, and when physical things do not conform to their own wants or hopes, they become angry, sad or in a state of despair. These emotions will always perpetuate more of the same in accordance with the Law of Attraction. It is vital to never embrace negative, angry or depressive thoughts because once this process starts, it can become self-perpetuating, and the person can very easily become trapped in a vortex of destructive, negative Energy.

Once you realize that you are immortal, Divine and the creator of your own reality, you will always be joyful, which will further accentuate the process of creating your own reality. When you reach that high state of Energy, aligned and realised with The Source, you will know beyond doubt that there is absolutely nothing that you cannot be, do or have, and you will continue to exist in a perpetual state of joy, seeing the material world for what it really is. You know beyond any possible doubt that you have the potential to constantly create your own existence every single moment as a natural aspect of your life.

Another very important state of Being is “faith”. By “faith”, we do not mean faith in the religious sense or faith based merely upon hope. We mean absolute faith in the immutable workings of The Universe, and the fact that you are a much loved Son or Daughter of God with the same unlimited powers and potential as God. To have true faith means to know, beyond any possible doubt, that all of your wishes, needs and desires are always provided without exception, and that all you need to do for your part is to be in vibrational harmony with them. If you do not have faith, it will considerably impact your ability to create.

Another extremely important emotion is “gratitude”. Although the Universe will always provide our wishes, needs and desires, gratitude is very important to the vibrations that you send back to the Universe. The vibration of gratitude maintains our connections with The Source at the highest levels.

It is most important not to think of gratitude in the religious sense. A personified God according to religion “hears” worship, praise, and thanks in return for which grants future requests by way of some form of repayment for being worshipped. This concept is a purely human construct. The truth is we are God, and to worship ourselves makes no sense in that context, and The Source, of which we are an integral aspect, and is omniscient, omnipotent and omnipresent has no need of “praise”, “worship”, flattery or other human concept.

Gratitude can more correctly be considered as a specific type of powerful vibration that influences the Universe in accordance with the Universal Principles of Attraction and Correspondence. To ask, receive and then to be grateful for what you have received transmits the right vibration to the Universe, which will enable you to attract much more of what you desire.

Those who demand things or who ask and expect to receive and are not grateful for what they have received will send out the corresponding vibrations of Energy into the Universe that will make it much more difficult to receive subsequent wishes.

Gratitude is also related to faith. Those who are always deeply, emotionally and sincerely grateful for what they have received from the Universe will also have faith that they will continue to receive. So, gratitude reinforces faith and the entire process of creation. The Universe is always in a state of harmony, and gratitude helps to accentuate our personal harmony with the Universe. Ask in the certain knowledge and in complete faith that we will receive, always maintaining absolute, sincere and emotional gratitude for what the Universe has provided.

Chapter 81
The Truth about Money

One of the most detrimental issues with humanity today, particularly in terms of Spiritual evolution, is the obsession with money and material possessions.

The Universe is pure Energy and simply does not recognize the concept of "money", which is an entirely human construct. Our distant ancestors were manifesting everything they required relative to their specific needs at their stage of evolution, long before "money" was even conceived by more recent humanity.

The only reason people are so dependent on money is because they believe that money is an absolute necessity, required in order to realize their wishes, needs and desires. If everyone in the world ceased focusing on money, the illusion of money could not be sustained and would accordingly cease to exist as a concept along with the misery it causes. While people hold this belief about money it will always be a self-perpetuating aspect of their experience, and such people will remain a slave to money for the duration of their entire physical life. From a human perspective, money somehow is supposed to represent value. The question being what precisely is "value"? Value is a purely notional concept relative to the perception of each individual. The notion of value fluctuates dramatically as the "economy", "rate of inflation", "foreign exchange rates" and many other such human constructs, change. The irony is that even these factors, in and of themselves are simply human constructs, which can and are often manipulated by world governments, institutions and in particular "central banks" for their own ends. No one really understands how or on what basis the "central banks" print money. In the USA for example the amount of money in circulation is supposed to be "backed" by the equivalent in reserves of gold, but of course there is no way for most people to verify this is actually the case.

In any case, only a very small percentage of the money in the world tangibly exists in the form of physical coins and notes. Most money is in the form of electronic data, bits and bytes held on a network of computer systems that can simply move money around at the touch of a computer key. So, even "money" itself is a notional concept—an illusion existing only to perpetuate the human concept of "value", but which for many people, businesses and governments has long been an obsession at the expense of everything else including compassion, service, Love and the needs of the majority.

It is not, never has been and never will be within the sphere of human Beings to decide how things should be manifested into physical reality where they can be experienced. It is this erroneous belief that is one of the greatest sources of all misery, with people making money the centre of their priorities. Again, "money" is at one level simply a human construct, a notional method of exchange, and at the most basic level most money does not really exist in a tangible form except for the few percent that remains in circulation in the form of notes and coins that people can "spend" in exchange for products and services.

In reality money has never been necessary to obtain our every wish, need and desire. Our ancient ancestors lived quite happily without money, because they understood the true source of supply. People may say "well they did not have the luxuries that we do today", but that again I is materialistic thinking. True abundance is not, never has been and never will be measured in terms of money and material possessions—it is always relative to each individual. The realisation of our needs is, always has been and always will be a natural function of the Universe and of the Mind by, The Source providing our every need unconditionally, if only humanity knew how to realise this powerful truth instead of relying on an illusion.

Money is the fuel of materialism and the basis for the enforcement of human power over what is perceived as "others—one of the main reasons that humanity has been heading away from its own true purpose and destiny and towards potential disaster. While so many people focus on money as an object of power, control and means of obtaining goods and services, it will be associated with the Energy that perpetuates that same power, and so the association of money with power and control will be perpetuated. While we all create our own realities at an individual level, the same is also true at a consensual level of the human Mind. While the consensus Consciousness of the majority of human Beings is that money is important and necessary, then this will remain a consensus reality. Again—money is in fact nothing more than a large-scale illusion perpetuated on a massive scale. While people place so much emphasis on money, and while money can be used as an instrument of control and power, this situation will continue until mankind wakes up and recognises the illusion of money for what it truly is.

Universal Principles work with absolute, immutable perfection, have always worked with absolute, immutable perfection, and always will work with absolute, immutable perfection. So, all humanity needs to do is to cease to focus on the Energy of money and start to focus on these immutable Universal Principles. When this happens the world will become a vastly happier place, and the adverse consequences of money, such as poverty and oppression will become a thing of the past.

Like health, wealth and abundance is a state of Mind. Everyone was born wealthy, and all anyone needs to do is to realise that health, wealth and abundance by aligning with the Universe and coming into vibrational harmony that it may be received.

Money is intangible and unreal, while abundance is your birthright as a Divine aspect of The Universe. To be dependent on money is to be out of harmony with the Universe.

Chapter 82
The Power of Positive Thinking

The power of positive thinking is an important aspect of the Law of Attraction. The way in which we think has a profound effect on our lives in almost every way. To many people, a thought is something intangible because it cannot be seen or even measured by scientific instruments. Nevertheless, thought, like everything else in the Universe, is Energy, and Energy influences other Energy resulting in a cause which will immutably result in a corresponding effect.

In the first section of this book, we looked at the structure of the Universe and how we can all influence our own lives, the lives of others and the Universe as a whole by the way we think in conjunction with other attributed of the Mind such as imagination, feelings and emotions. The laws of Attraction and Correspondence are always operating whenever we project our thoughts, ideas, emotions, feelings and imagination. In all spheres of life, including the physical world, like always resonates with and thereby attracts like. If we focus on something negative, it will result in the resonation of the corresponding negative Energy, thus attracting more of the same negative Energy—in other words, negative causes will give rise to the corresponding negative effects. Of course, the same Principle also applies to positive thinking, with causes in the form of positive thoughts attracting correspondingly positive effects.

Many people become trapped within a vortex of negativity due to perceived negative circumstances in their lives which, due to Universal Principles have become self-fulfilling. For example, someone might have lost their employment or feel trapped in an unhappy relationship, spending their days worrying, thinking about and dwelling on their perceived "situation". What this person does not realize is that by dwelling on the situation, constantly thinking about them and always imagining the worst, they will always attract more of the same into their experience. Constantly thinking about lack or debt will always result in more lack or debt, while thinking in terms of abundance always results in more abundance. It is for these very reasons that wealthy who only think in terms of wealth almost always become wealthier, and the "poor" who always think in terms of poverty always become poorer—these must happen by Principle. Most people simply react to their circumstances as evidenced through the mediation of the five physical senses, thereby attracting more of the same, without ever realising that a simple change of focus, perspective and thought to a positive nature, focussing on what they actually do want instead of on what they believe their senses are telling them, they can turn their situation around completely.

Most people have heard of the sceptics and cynics phrase "seeing is believing". In fact the exact opposite is true in accordance with immutable Universal Principles – Believing is Seeing.

It is particularly important therefore, no matter how difficult circumstances might seem to be according to your physical perceptions, to think positively at all times. For example, if you were to attend a job interview feeling negatively about your "chances", you will almost certainly not receive the position. If on the other hand you go to the job interview knowing beyond any doubt that you will be offered the position, you will almost certainly be awarded the position. Your positive thought Energy will, through the level of the plane of the group human Mind, influence the Mind of the interviewer in your favour. This is why many successful business people almost always succeed in consistently winning large business deals, knowing, in their Mind, beyond any doubt, that the deal is already theirs.

Only by thinking the most positive thoughts, while excluding all negative thoughts, and by imagining the most positive things happening in your life with as much emotion, knowing and positive Energy as possible, will you attract only those most positive things that you truly desire for your well-being.

On a more conscious level, if you really need something in particular to happen in your life, endow that situation with as much positive emotional Energy as you can.

Someone might genuinely be currently experiencing severe financial issues and another with an unhappy relationship. Difficult though these situations seem to be, the more a person dwells negatively on the situation, the worse it will become by attracting more of the same.

The solution to these situations is to break out of the self-perpetuating vortex of negative thinking and to start thinking only in the most positive terms at all times. It is particularly important to go to bed at night thinking only the most positive thoughts, never, ever dwelling even for a single moment on any situation in negative terms. Just before sleep, the link to the Subconscious Mind is particularly powerful, the being the aspect of our Mind that brings our thoughts into experience.

Of course, these manifestations will not usually happen immediately, but the more positive Energy behind a thought or desire, the sooner the desire will manifest as an observable and experiential effect within the material world. It is most important therefore to maintain this positive Energy at all times, charging it with as much positive emotion as possible.

If a negative thought ever enters your Mind, it is very important to be aware of it and replace it immediately with a corresponding positive thought, preferably a thought that is consistent with your desires. If you do not immediately have a positive thought with which to cancel the negative thought, it is still crucial to cancel the negative thought and not allow it to take root in your Mind. An excellent way of achieving this is to say to yourself, either aloud or in your Mind "cancel, cancel,

cancel", and keep repeating "cancel" until the negative thought has dissipated and no longer poses a threat to your well-being.

Another powerful way of reinforcing positive thoughts is through the use of positive affirmations, the power of which we have already seen in the context of OBE methods. Affirmations will also be discussed in greater depth further later in this book.

Positive thinking should become a Mindset and way of life and not something that you force yourself to do in accordance with perceived situations. Recreate the feelings of great joy and happiness felt during such previous events in your life and project them onto whatever you wish to manifest into your life.

The more Conscious we are the more powerful we become. By this, we do not mean being conscious of your physical body and experiences, but Conscious of being a Divine channel of expression of The Source, The First Cause of God of which we are all inseparable and Unconditionally Loved aspects, immortal and infinite with true abundance as our heritage.

Chapter 83
Affirmations

The power of positive thinking can be enhanced and reinforced by the use of affirmations. As we have already discussed, an affirmation is a short statement repeated frequently in the present tense, that impresses your desire upon your Subconscious Mind. The Subconscious Mind in turn either acts directly upon the physical body in the case of a personal healing, or interacts with the Universal Mind if something is to manifest into your experience through The Law of Attraction.

Often however people unknowingly convey negative affirmations in reacting to a perceived negative situation by repeating or thinking such statements as:

"I will never get a promotion in this job".

"I will always be short of money".

"This relationship will never improve".

Even though the person is not aware of the consequences of what they are saying or thinking, these are nevertheless all examples of negative affirmations which, if continued, will result in corresponding negative experiences. The person who is constantly repeating these negative affirmations, either consciously or Subconsciously, will be much less likely to receive that promotion in their job, will have progressively less money, and might well become even more trapped in their unhappy relationship resulting in further unwanted misery.

Many people tend to use a wide range of negative affirmations on an ongoing basis without ever realizing it. For example, someone might say to themselves or even aloud; "I simply cannot complete this task", or "this is much too difficult", or "I do not feel at all well today". These are all examples of negative affirmations that will impress on the Subconscious Mind, and if repeated for any length of time become negative correspondingly realities. In these cases the tasks will never be completed, will be always too hard, and the person will continue to feel unwell.

Positive thinking and conscious positive affirmations on the other hand will not only bring correspondingly positive experiences, but will also transmute existing "bad" things into the opposite good things. Beyond the confines of the three-dimensional world of matter, time and space simply do not exist, so it is never too "late" to transmute a negative situation to a positive situation through the use of affirmations.

In the examples above, this person should immediately suppress any negative affirmations they find themselves repeating and replace them with the equivalent positive affirmations. For example, instead of complaining to themselves and others in the form of what amounts to negative affirmations, they should be saying:

"I am so pleased with my excellent job promotion".

"I have all the money I could ever need".

"My relationship has never been better or happier".

It is very important to remain alert at all times to these negative thoughts and affirmations, immediately transmuting them into their positive opposites as they arise and before they have their effect. For example: "I have easily accomplished this task", "that was all very easy", and "I feel really fit and well today".

It is very important to not only make use of affirmations in order to consciously manifest desired changes into your life, but also to be alert to Subconscious, negative affirmations that must be immediately transmuted to their positive polar opposites. The more often an affirmation is repeated, consciously or otherwise, the more quickly and effectively it will impress on the Subconscious Mind, and subsequently manifest into observable experiential reality.

An excellent time to repeat affirmations, with as much sincerity and emotion as possible, is just before drifting off to sleep at night, and just after awakening in the morning. At these times, your conscious Mind is most closely in communication with your Subconscious Mind which in turn interacts with the Universal Mind. Repeat your affirmation throughout the day, write it down, place copies around your home, and repeat it frequently. If you make use of a personal computer for long periods of time, it is a very good and effective idea to have a copy of your affirmation placed on your PC desktop utilizing some appropriate software for the purpose. You might not always notice the affirmation, but it will still nevertheless sink into your Subconscious Mind where it will have its effect.

The ideal affirmation must be as short as possible and totally unambiguous. It is important to note that the Subconscious Mind cannot easily assimilate long or ambiguous statements. The Subconscious Mind, immense and powerful though it surely is, is actually very "childlike" in the way it perceives, and is more easily influenced by short, unambiguous, appropriately worded statements. The Subconscious Mind never questions any statement. It accepts the affirmation as an absolute statement of fact, and sets about bringing the object of the statement into reality though whatever means is necessary.

Affirmations should never be performed in a stressed situation where you cannot adequately relax or concentrate or be repeated in a positive, meaningful, joyous way. For maximum effect, affirmations should be repeated several times each day, ideally while in as relaxed a state as possible, and continued until the affirmation has become an absolute physical reality in accordance with you desires. Ideally the affirmation should evoke the corresponding positive feelings associated with the affirmation, feelings impressing the Subconscious Mind in a very powerful way.

Affirmations can often become a physical reality very quickly, but at other times, it might take longer. Note that we use the words “physical reality”, because as soon as you start stating the affirmations, the object of the statement will instantly be accepted and acted upon by the Subconscious Mind. The Universe will answer your affirmation through the Subconscious Mind making it a reality within the inner Energy levels immediately. Frequent repetition of affirmations, with emotion, feeling and absolute knowing, beyond all doubt that it is true Now, will harmonise the Energies involved, allowing the object of your affirmation to manifest as a tangible reality in the physical world where it can be experienced and enjoyed.

The speed at which an affirmation becomes a reality depends on numerous factors, some of which are within our control, and some of which are not, including, but not limited to the complexity of the desired outcome, the number of people involved, the frequency of repeating the affirmation, and most importantly, the extent to which we place emotion, focus, feeling, faith and gratitude behind it. Never become anxious for the results of the affirmation to be realized or wonder why they have not yet manifested. These emotions will cause vibrations of negative Energy, thereby slowing the process down.

Developing and maintaining faith in your affirmations will result in belief, and it is the belief that will bring you into energetic, vibrational harmony with the object of your affirmations allowing them to manifest into your physical experience. Make maximum use of controlled, conscious, positive affirmations whenever you need to convert a negative situation into a positive situation or when you wish to bring something into your life that you need, wish for or desire.

Chapter 84
Powers of the Imagination

Imagination is one of the most powerful forces in the Universe. Imagination must never however be confused with mere fantasy or simply a "figment of the imagination". The power of imagination is, in reality, an extremely powerful, natural, God-given ability that every human being possesses. Many people associate imagination with "visualisation", the process of picturing something in our Mind. While it is true that visualisation is an important attribute of the imagination, other attributes of imagination include feelings, impressions and other senses equivalent to the physical senses such as sound, touch, smell and taste, all of which can be used aspects of the imagination.

Within the inner spheres of reality, as everyone will discover very soon after the transition from the physical world at the change known as "death", everything desired is brought into instant manifestation by the use of the Mind, by will, intent and the power of imagination. In the Astral worlds, due to the much higher state of vibration and lower density in comparison to the physical world of matter, and due to the fact that "time" and "space" do not exist, thoughts take shape instantly, and the more power and emotion projected into those thoughts, the more real they become and the longer they remain. Transient thoughts on the other hand will result in transient manifestations.

Most thoughts projected by people during normal activity are transient in nature, appearing, lingering for a time and then dissipating depending on the Energy behind the thought or act of imagination. To create something more permanent requires use of the imagination with emotional Energy, will, intent and focus, the duration of the resultant manifestation being proportional to these factors, and therefore how long the resultant Thought Form exists before dissipating into native Energy one again.

The more we constantly think about something, the more real it will become, and the longer it will persist. Within the Astral worlds, there are vast areas of Energy comprising just about every type of environment, all of which are consensus creations of numerous people from the past, present and "future" relative to the Earth concept of "time". These creations are the result of vast collective, consensual Energy formations that are continually being influenced by the Mind of those residing there, and which endure under that consensual Mind influence almost ad infinitum. In practice however, in due course, as evolution of the human race progresses, humans will realise the Astral worlds for the illusion they are, and will progress to inner Energy levels beyond the concept of "form", at which pointy, with no Mind to sustain them, they will dissipate back into formless Quanta of Energy, from whence they came.

On an individual level, a person might create his ideal home in the Astral, while large numbers of people at a consensual level will imagine and thereby create larger scale constructions such as entire villages, towns and cities, just as they were accustomed to in physical life on Earth. This scenario applies to all Energy levels of the Astral planes from the darkest outer levels to the most blissful inner levels. This is why, like the physical worlds, the Astral worlds are ephemeral, transient projections, ultimately an illusion created by the Mind of humans based upon their concept of reality at that stage of their evolution, but which will eventually dissipate as humans transcend that illusion, continuing onwards and inwards on the path, to the glories of the Spirit worlds beyond form.

Manifestation takes place in the physical world in accordance with exactly the same Universal Principles, without the need for any preceding direct physical action. The physical world, however, is very dense and existing at a much lower vibration than the inner Mind worlds of the Astral and Mental spheres. Therefore, more Energy, concentration and focus is required in order to bring about a manifestation observable in the physical world. In addition, as previously mentioned, on Earth we are also subject to the effects of "time" and "space" which gives rise to the illusion of a delay between thought and experience.

Many people will have heard of "Magic", but by "Magic" we do not mean the performances of stage illusionists, prestidigitators, conjurors and others from the areas of stage entertainment. Magic is, in reality, a sacred science, the word "Magic" originating from the Magi who fully understood and applied natural Universal laws in order to bring about manifestations that many might consider as "miraculous".

The practitioner of true Magic understands, aligns him or herself with, and makes appropriate use of Universal Principles in order to manifest the desired results. People often erroneously associate Magic with occult practices, sorcery and witchcraft, but even these are not Magic in their truest, highest and most Divine form. This is not to say that sorcery, witchcraft and similar types of "magic" are not effective because they often are, depending on the abilities of the practitioner.

Sorcery and witchcraft are often performed by loosely utilizing some Universal principles in the desired direction, often by means of spells and rituals, which also serve to impress the desired result on the Subconscious Mind of the practitioner is usually not fully aware of what Universal Principles are involved or of the role of the Subconscious or Universal Minds in the process, and accordingly, due to this lack of understanding, the results can be unpredictable or even undesirable.

True Magic is to exert full conscious control over Universal Principles through the infinite powers of the Subconscious Mind. What most refer to as "Magic" in the context of spells, and rituals, and again we are not referring to stage performers in this context, is in actual fact more often properly referred to as “sorcery”, particularly if performed without conscious use of the Universal Principles involved and in particular the role and extreme importance of the Subconscious Mind.

What most people consider to be “Magic” could more properly be referred to these days as “manifestation” as spells, rituals, witchcraft, sorcery and other such practices, are giving way to a more general level of understanding of The Law of Attraction, and how it may be used by anyone at all using only the powers of the Mind, and without the need for special regalia, words and physical actions in the form of rituals.

Manifestation is the conscious cooperation with Universal Principles in using our inner abilities and powers of the Mind, including imagination, to manifest the object of the imagination into physical reality, with the individual Subconscious Mind being the main channel through with these great Universal Principles can be naturally enjoyed.

Chapter 85
Creative Visualisation

Many people have heard of the term "creative visualisation", but what exactly does it mean? Creative visualisation is the process of creating and "seeing" images in your Mind using your powers of imagination.

Your outer, physical reality is always a perfect reflection of within, which in turn is a reflection of what we impress upon our Subconscious Mind. This is not only the basis of all manifestation, but is also the basis of all health and healing. All diseases of the physical body originate from within, due to thought processes, often resulting in stress, before eventually manifesting as a physically experienced disorder of the physical body. Of course, modern medicine seeks to "fix" these ailments somatically within the physical body itself, not realizing that the Thought Form giving rise to the disorder, as a result of wrongful thinking, still exists as an impression within the Subconscious Mind of the ailing person.

As already mentioned, in order to manifest this inner Energy into a form where it can be experienced in our present physical reality, we must first bring ourselves into vibrational harmony with that configuration of Energy. Creative visualisation achieves this by allowing us to experience the object of our visualisation through the powers of your imagination. The more we can experience our desires by utilizing all of our physical senses, and the more we integrate the object of our visualisation into our conscious awareness, the more it will in turn be impressed upon our Subconscious Mind, which will in turn either influence our physical body, in the case of health, or through Universal Mind in the case of anything else, in turn manifesting into our physical experiential reality.

Unlike the immediate, observable manifestations of visualisation in the non-physical realms, the process in the material world is slower due to the much lower vibration, much higher density and the influence of how humans perceive and experience “space” and “time”.

As we already know, all individual human Minds are connected at a level Consciousness upon the Mental plane of the human Mind. When a desire, for a pay raise for example, is impressed upon the Subconscious Mind through creative visualisation and other methods of focussed thought, the Subconscious Mind then acts through Universal Mind, which in turn will influence the Subconscious Mind of the person awarding the pay rise, who will in turn award the pay rise, providing the process is in harmony. You need not and should not seek a reason for your increase in pay. Once the Thought Form has been created, and the person is vibrating in harmony with it, the Thought Form must manifest by the most direct means, which may often be surprising and unforeseen. It should be mentioned once again that in reality all aspects of Mind are One, all individuated conscious Minds being spheres of activity with their corresponding Subconscious Minds, in turn being spheres of activity of Universal Mind.

There is nothing at all wrong with desiring to bring good things into your life and living comfortably with all of your genuine needs fulfilled. The Universe is infinitely abundant, and there is always enough for everyone to share in that abundance. The flow of life from The Source is always in the direction of expansion, abundance and well-being. One of the greatest issues on Earth at this time, however, is that due to the gross materialistic attitudes and demands of the Ego of many people, often with a desire for power and control, together with a total lack of understanding of their own true reality, purpose and destiny, and of the way the Universe works generally, there is a considerable imbalance between those who have great wealth and those who have insufficient for even the most basic needs. Only when mankind fully understands the immutable operation of both conscious and Subconscious aspects of the human

Mind, and of Universal Principles, and to live their lives accordingly, will these imbalances be reconciled, and every human being in every part of the world can live in the peace, harmony, happiness, health and abundance that are our heritage.

In utilizing your own powers of creative visualisation, you should never be tempted to become trapped within a spiral of materialism or the demands of the Ego by manifesting more than your genuine needs. Never seek accumulate material wealth or things simply for the sake of it or to impress others.

Creative visualisation can be applied to manifest anything at all without limits. The larger or more complex the desire, however, the longer it may take to manifest it into physical reality. It might not even be possible to manifest some desires in an acceptable time scale due to the sheer number of other people projecting the same Energy into exactly the same desire. A very good example of this is winning the lottery. When millions of people purchase a lottery ticket each week, each and every one of them is projecting exactly the same desire and intent to win the jackpot. The sheer individual focus required to overcome this collective desire of millions of people would be extremely difficult to produce and project for most people.

There are literally an infinite number of ways through which a desire can manifest into physical reality, most of which are not immediately obvious. For larger manifestation projects, it can be much more effective to manifest in stages. For example, you might wish to manifest a successful computer business. First you might first manifest the new PC to learn the necessary skills. Next, you might manifest a series of training courses in business management, and then further courses in advanced computer skills. Having successfully achieved this, you might then manifest an office from which to launch your new computer business and finally start to manifest your customers. Later, when your business is a success, you might wish to manifest larger offices and some employees. Finally, if you wish, you can manifest a thriving computer business with many employees, providing you and your family with all of your genuine needs.

This is a fairly basic example of manifestation but serves to illustrate a sequential process toward achieving a desire. Of course, it is also possible to use the creative visualisation process to manifest your successful computer business without any interim stages at all, allowing your Subconscious Mind and the Universal Mind to manage the "details". Many people have difficulty at first "believing" this is possible, and lack of belief, in other words doubt, will prevent the desire manifesting. It is often advisable at first therefore to divide the objective into "believable" stages.

Creative visualisation is just one aspect of our powers of imagination, albeit a very important one, that can be used with other powers of the Mind and attributes such as emotion, intent and gratitude to manifest into our experience anything at all that we could possibly wish for need and desire from the infinite abundance of the Universe as we will see later in this book.

Chapter 86
The Practice of Creative Visualisation

Learning to visualize effectively, as with most worthwhile abilities, requires time to be set aside, ideally every day, in order to develop and maintain these abilities. Ten minutes will suffice to start with, but as you progress, thirty minutes each day would be more effective in the long term. Any spare time during the day can easily be used to practice creative visualisation, the only tool required being your Mind.

To begin these creative visualisation exercises, first obtain five household items of your choice, such as a fruit, a cup, a pen, a spoon, a coin. Any items will suffice, but it is preferable if they are all of a distinctly different size, shape and colour.

Commence the exercise by attaining a good state of physical and mental relaxation in a place where you can concentrate and will not be disturbed. It is best to sit upright on a hard kitchen-type chair without leaning against the backrest. This will enable you to achieve the necessary state of relaxation and concentration with your spine completely straight, without falling asleep. For these reasons, lying on a bed or reclining in an armchair are not advisable, and would in any case make these exercises more difficult than they should be unless you have the discipline to remain awake and focussed.

Place your five chosen items in front of you, and fix your eyes on the first of them. Inspect the item closely from all angles, and memorizing it in as much detail as you possibly can, including shape, size, colour, texture, patterns and any other significant attributes that will help you to remember it.

Next, close your eyes, and recall the object in your imagination in as much detail as possible. The objective is to visualize the object in your Mind as clearly or even clearer than it appears to your physical sight. You might well find that at first, the object will frequently fade from your imagination. If this happens, simply use your willpower and concentration to recall the object back into your imagination. After time and practice, the object will disappear and reappear less frequently until finally you can maintain a solid and realistic image of it in your Mind.

Should you become tired of focussing on one object, move on to the next, repeating the visualisation exercises as before. It is very important to remain as relaxed as possible while maintaining the image of each object in detail for as long as you can. There is nothing to be gained by making yourself tired however, so if you feel tired it is best to stop the exercises and commence them again another day. Although these exercises might seem difficult in the beginning, it is extremely important to persevere, and you will find it becomes progressively easier.

The object of these exercises is to maintain an image of your chosen item with total, absolute realism, just as it would appear to your physical sight for at least five continuous minutes without it fading from your Mind. When you have achieved this with the first five chosen, select another five objects, and repeat the exercises until you achieve the same results.

For the next stage of these exercises, rather than starting with five physical objects, recall any object or scene of your choice from memory, and visualize it with as much realism as possible. This might for example be a scene in your house such as a favourite room, a view in your garden, or perhaps a favourite location such as a place in the country, or indeed any favourite object that you can easily bring to Mind. It really does not matter what image you select, provided you can retain it in your Mind and become emotionally involved with it.

Having attained as clear an image as possible in your Mind from memory of your chosen object, person or scene, maintain the image as it would appear to your physical senses for a full five minutes without it fading from your imagination. When you can maintain any image vividly in your Mind with total realism for a full five minutes, this part of the visualisation exercises is complete.

The final stage of these exercises is to visualize objects with your eyes open. It doesn't matter which objects you choose for this purpose, although it is better to start with the objects previously visualized with eyes closed and can recall at will.

With your eyes open, imagine your object suspended in the air standing on a shelf, a table, or anywhere else of your choice. Your object must appear to be every bit as solid and real as the original physical object, so much so that you feel you could actually reach out and touch it. There must be absolutely no doubt whatsoever as to the complete realism of your visualized object as it is suspended in the air or standing on a solid object such as a shelf or table. This exercise is complete when you can maintain in your imagination your visualisation, with complete realism, of any object in any location with your eyes open for a full five minutes.

Once you have successfully completed these visualisation exercises you will have taken a significant step forward to in consciously making use of your natural power of visualisation which will be of great value in controlling your own reality.

Chapter 87
Other Senses of the Imagination

Powers of imagination can be enhanced when used in conjunction with the other inner senses of hearing, sentience, smell and taste. Sentience refers to touch but also includes the ability to sense temperature, lightness or heaviness, hunger, thirst, tiredness, etc.

We will commence these exercises by developing your inner sense of hearing within your imagination.

Begin by assuming your usual relaxed position in a location where you will not be disturbed.

Now imagine, as clearly as possible the ticking of a clock. You must hear this clock ticking as distinctly and realistically as possible to the extent that you have no doubt whatsoever in your Mind that there is really a clock in your room.

When you can maintain this sound in your imagination continuously for a full five minutes, select another familiar sound such as a bell, rain against a window, or the noise of a household appliance.

As previously, imagine, as clearly as possible your chosen sound for a full five minutes before moving on to the next sound. We are only concerned with the auditory aspect of this exercise. Should an image of the item appear in your imagination, use your willpower to dismiss it immediately.

Once you can imagine any sound of your choice with absolute clarity and realism for a full five minutes without interruption, the auditory exercises are complete.

The next exercise involves the development of sentience within the imagination—the senses of touch, temperature, lightness, heaviness, hunger, thirst and other feelings.

As with the previous exercises, in a location where you will not be disturbed, assume your usual relaxed position.

Now close your eyes and select a sentient feeling of your choice—warmth, for example. With complete concentration, imagine this sentient feeling as realistically as possible. In the case of warmth for example, you should feel the warmth all over your body even if the room is cool.

When you can maintain this first sentient feeling, as realistically as possible for a full five minutes without any interruption, including any spurious images appearing in your Mind that must be immediately dismissed, you can move onto the next sentient feeling.

This time, it might be a texture such as a carpet or sandpaper. Again, imagine yourself feeling this texture as if you were actually running your fingers across it. As always, maintain the feeling for a full uninterrupted five minutes, with absolute clarity while knowing beyond any doubt in your Mind that it is real in every respect.

Now, move on to the next object of your sentience exercises. This time, summon a feeling of thirst or hunger. Imagine that you feel very hungry or thirsty as if you really need food or drink. Maintain these feelings with total realism for a full five minutes after which this exercise is complete.

Next is the development of creative olfactory abilities—the sense of smell within the imagination.

Assume your relaxed position in a location where you will not be disturbed, and close your eyes.

Using all of your powers of imagination, imagine you can smell a favourite fragrance. It might be a perfume, a flower, food cooking, or any other smell of your choice. The smell need not be pleasant; it can be anything as long as it is distinctive and can be easily brought to Mind.

As with all of the previous exercises, maintain this smell in your imagination as vividly as possible for at least five minutes without any interruptions and without any visual images intruding. You must be totally focused on your selected smell and be totally convinced of its realism, as if it is actually strongly present in your room. If you are imagining the scent of a favourite flower for example, be absolutely convinced you are in the presence of the flower in question. Again, it is most important to focus exclusively on the olfactory aspect of the object and not to allow any other sense to intrude.

Having maintained an exclusive sense of smell in your imagination for a full five minutes, select another smell with which you are familiar and repeat the exercises. Continue with these olfactory exercises until you have exclusively maintained in your imagination various smells for a full five minutes, after which these exercises are complete.

The final sense to be creatively developed in the imagination is taste. Begin as with the previous exercises with complete relaxation. Now imagine that you can taste a favourite food or drink as if you are actually eating or drinking it. As always, you must be totally convinced as to the reality of this sense, and there must be no interruptions externally or from other senses or thoughts.

When you have succeeded in maintaining the sense of the first taste for five minutes, you can then move on to another taste of your choice.

As with the other exercises, once you have successfully maintained in your imagination a range of tastes with total realism and without interruption for a full five minutes, these exercises are complete.

As the final exercise, you will now put together all of your senses in an imaginary scenario. Select any scene of your choosing, ensuring that all of your senses are fully included and involved within the scene. Ideally choose a scene that is memorable or attractive, and one in which you can become full involved. As an example we will use taking a stroll in the park with your family.

Assume your usual relaxed position, and bring your imagined scenario into your imagination as vividly as possible.

Using our example of the park, first visualize yourself strolling through the park gates with your family. If you do not have a family, simply imagine you are strolling through the park with relations, or a friend or friends with their family. You can adapt this scenario to suit your own situation and preferences, but make it as engaging as possible.

As you begin to stroll along the path, you clearly hear birds singing cheerfully in the trees as you feel the gentle, warm summer wind playing against your face. You can feel one of the children tugging excitedly at your hand as the sounds of other children playing happily drift across the vivid green parkland lawns. As you pass by a rose garden, you can smell the distinctive fragrance of the roses as you observe them blooming in many different beautiful colours.

Soon, you reach the park cafeteria and stop to buy nice cold ice creams. You can taste the ice cream as it melts in your mouth and enjoy the welcome coldness as it slides down your throat, continuing to savour the ice cream as you continue your gentle stroll, taking in the atmosphere of your surroundings. Soon, you reach the children’s play area where you sit down on the soft, lush, green grass, which has the distinctive smell of being freshly mowed which is very distinctive. The children shout happily as they go off to play while you absorb the atmosphere of the gorgeous summer's day, the smell of the flowers and freshly cut grass and enjoy your delicious ice cream.

As you finish your ice cream, you notice the wind rustling through the nearby trees intermingling with the noises of the children happily playing nearby. As time progresses, you can feel the midday sun becoming progressively hotter, and you realize it is time to go home before it becomes too hot. You call the children, and set off together on a slow stroll home, taking in all of the familiar sights, sounds and smells along the way with the children excitedly talking about everything they had just enjoyed doing in the park. When you arrive home, you relax with a nice cool drink while the children go off to safely play in the back garden.

During this scenario you have engaged all of your five physical senses. Practice this sort of scenario using all of these senses of your imagination as often as possible. The resulting abilities will be of profound value in your life and for the path ahead. Imagination is creative, indeed it is a primary creative force in the Universe, and learning how to apply your inner senses in a focussed way will greatly enhance your own natural, God-given powers of creation.

Chapter 88
The Power of Emotions

Emotions are also powers of the Mind, and like all powers of the Mind, they influence Energy. Emotions can, therefore, be thought of as E-motion or "Energy in motion".

Although all thought influences Energy to some extent, emotions exert a particularly powerful influence over the Subconscious Mind and accordingly Universal Energy. Therefore, the speed at which we attract anything into our individual physical reality is largely a function of our emotions.

We should always immediately eliminate negative emotions by use of the will, or by immediately saying, either aloud or in your Mind, "cancel, cancel, cancel" until the negative though dissipates. Alternatively and even better you can transmute negative emotions into their polar opposite positive emotions as soon as we become aware of them. Again, we should always remain fully aware of our feelings, thoughts and emotions at all times in order to create our reality and control our lives.

It should be mentioned that this is a fundamental Principle behind true "alchemy". When most people think of "alchemy", they often think of the transmutation of base metals such as lead into gold. True alchemy, however, in its purest and original form is not about transmuting material things from one physical state to another. It is rather about the evolution of the physical human, Soul and Spirit where the "lead" of negative human attributes is transmuted to the "gold" of corresponding positive attributes—an ongoing process of perfection that continues along the path until finally arriving back to The Source, The First Cause, God from whence we came in the beginning, before embarking on our individual quest for perfection. Transmutation of negative, dense, low vibrations of Energy to the polar opposite positive, fine, high vibrations is a part of the ongoing evolutionary process of all life.

Awareness and control over emotions can be profoundly valuable, especially in terms of manifestation. Because emotions are such a powerful aspect of Mind, they have an equally powerful effect on the Subconscious Mind, and thus the Energy in the form of thoughts, i.e. "Thought Forms" that shape our individual experiential reality.

The scale of emotion ranges from the very highest vibration of all—the emotion of God, the emotion of Unconditional Love—all the way down to the very lowest emotion at the lowest end of the emotional scale of vibration—abject hate.

It should be noted that the base level of emotions will have a profound effect on the level at which people find themselves after the change known as "death". As we already know, The Law of Attraction is always in immutable operation throughout the Universe. In the context of the transition from the physical to the non-physical worlds, everyone will transition to the level of vibration of the Astral worlds that most closely match the overall vibrations of the Astral body or Soul. Therefore, those who have lived a hate-oriented physical life will transition to a lower vibratory level of the Astral worlds. They will find themselves existing within a dark, dank, oppressive environment with perpetual mist, fog and bare trees devoid of leaves—always a perfect reflection of their current state of Mind and vibration. Such a world will be inhabited by other people with similar Energy characteristics.

Even these worlds, however, are places of learning and evolution, and accordingly residents there will eventually learn the meaning of the phrase "do unto others as they would do unto you", learning the errors of their ways, desiring a more harmonious existence. Once learned, they can integrate those experience and more positive, life loving attitude into their being, thus raising their vibrations thereby facilitating the transition to more pleasant vibrations of the inner Astral worlds.

The same Principles apply all the way down the scale of emotion from Unconditional Love at the highest aspect of the vibrational scale, through joy, passion, enthusiasm, positivity, optimism, hope, contentment, satisfaction, boredom, frustration, overwhelm, disappointment, doubt, worry, blame, discouragement, anger, revenge, insecurity, jealousy, fear and abject hate at the lowest aspect of the vibrational scale.

It is well worth noting that "fear" is a level of vibration that is very far down the emotional scale, yet, many people create a powerful fear-driven reality for themselves while on Earth. It has been said that "there is nothing to fear but fear itself" and this is very true indeed. Like worry, fear will always feed upon itself, manifesting even more of the object of that fear, resulting in a spiral of fear driven emotion inevitably manifesting into a state of hopeless and despair.

Our emotions are our inner guidance system as we progress along the Divine path back to the Source, The First Cause, God. By always being consciously aware of our emotions, and by only allowing positive, high vibration emotions, while rejecting low, negative emotions, we can steer our lives in the desired direction instead of being swept along in a river of uncontrolled emotion like flotsam on a river. As we already know, we are open channels of experience and expression of God, and by keeping these channels as open as possible, we allow God to express and create though us. This, in turn, enables us to easily attract and share in the infinite abundance of the Universe.

By paying close attention to our emotions and accentuating the most positive powerful, high vibration emotions, while neutralizing or transmuting negative emotions, we can align ourselves with God. The more positive, focused and emotionally charged Energy we can impress upon our Subconscious Mind, the more of our desires we will attract from the Universe of infinite abundance.

One of the most powerful of all aspects of positive emotion is passion. Charging our manifestation exercises with passion will greatly enhance effectiveness, as well as how soon the object of our manifestation becomes an experiential physical reality. So, in life, following our passions is one of the best things we can do in effortlessly attracting our wishes, needs and desires.

Following passions is particularly powerful in business. Those who start a business with the exclusive idea of "making money" will never be truly wealthy. They may "make money" in the short term, but making money and attracting true abundance are very different things. We are all Sons and Daughters of God, made in the Spiritual image of God, and we must always first and foremost serve our Brothers and Sisters of the Universe before we even think of serving ourselves. Selfless service is extremely important, both in the context of personal evolution and in attracting abundance. By serving others, we also serve ourselves, but this should never be a primary motive.

More importantly, a person following their passions will be rightly filled with pride, fulfillment and joy, often having touched the lives of many people and provided a valuable service. Passion is a very powerful emotional Energy that will influence like-Minded people through the realms of the collective Subconscious Mind within the Universal Mind. When a person is passionate about the products or services being offered, they will vibrate that passion, causing people who are equally passionate about the same products or services it to be attracted to purchase them with as much joy as the seller experiences in selling it to them. This Principle can be likened to two tuning forks separated by a distance. When one tuning fork is struck, the other tuning fork resonates at exactly the same frequency of vibration. If you consider yourself to be one of these tuning forks and your potential customer the other, both resonating at the same frequency of vibration, it is simple to understand how the Law of Attraction operates in these situations, with a completely harmonious outcome for everyone involved. The conscious Mind impresses the desire on the Subconscious Mind within the realms of the collective Subconscious Mind within the Universal Mind, and the Subconscious Mind then vibrates at the same frequency, attracting "like-minded" Subconscious Minds which bring it to the attention of the conscious Mind which can then take action inspired action towards it.

There is plenty of evidence of this on the Internet today where people are following a passion in providing goods and services, often receiving very large sums of money each year for what might seem to be very obscure goods and services.

The Universe often requires physical channels, in the form of people in order to bring physical things into physical reality. The Internet is the ultimate physical medium for those channels in that there are many hundreds of millions, and very soon billions of people already connected to or have access to the Internet, with more connecting each day.

As we will see in the next chapter of this book, emotion is an extremely powerful catalyst to apply in the process of conscious manifestation. The higher and more charged the emotion, the higher and more powerful the vibrations and therefore the attractive power of those vibrations.

One of the most powerful emotions aside from Unconditional Love is joy. Joy is an emotion that is very high on the Energy scale of vibration. The more joy that is projected into manifestation exercises, the more effective will be the result. People with a genuine passion for something almost always follow that passion with great joy and enthusiasm, which is why The Law of Attraction works so powerfully in their favor in attracting an unlimited abundance relating to that passion.

Two further emotions that are very important are appreciation and in particular gratitude. Taking anything for granted results in low vibrations, and your life will reflect that perfectly. Sincere appreciation and gratitude create a vibration that will attract more of the same into your life, reinforcing the object of your desires as an absolute reality Now. It is all part of maintaining an open channel of God, through which God can express in the form of unlimited abundance, evolution and expansion during in the process of creation. Always project sincere gratitude in your Mind for everything you have attracted into your life from the Universe of infinite abundance, and you will continue to attract even more abundance.

Empowering your manifestation exercises and life with vibrations of joy, passion, enthusiasm, gratitude and appreciation will assist greatly with attracting all your desires.

Chapter 89
Creating Your Own Reality

We will now look more deeply at the process of manifestation—the conscious manifestation into your experiential reality of your wishes, needs and desires.

It is highly advisable before embarking on any manifestation project to consider precisely what you desire, and if you believe you already know to consider very deeply whether you really need that particular object of your desire. Many people "desire" a "better life", "better health", "more wealth" etc, without actually knowing what these abstract statements really mean. If you cannot precisely define those things that would give rise to the fulfilment of your desires, your Subconscious Mind cannot manifest them.

It is also very important to think only in terms of genuine needs and in particular being of service to others and never of greed or anything driven by the demands of the Ego pressure to conform, as for example in the desire to impress others or to conform to the expectations of your family in some way. Before you manifest "money", for example, meditate on precisely what this "money" will really add to your own life, as well as in the lives of your loved ones. It is also much better to focus on what that money means to you, for example a new home, rather than on the money by which to buy it.

As we know, the outer physical Universe consists of illusions—a duality conceptually existing as the "observer" and the "observed". In this way, God evolves by experiencing through expressions of Him/Herself, as do all individuations of God, including we as human Beings. The observed is meaningless without an observer, and the observer is meaningless without being observed. It is through the process of individuation that the observer and the observed are perpetuated, and expansion and evolution of the Universe continues.

The illusion of separation is perpetuated through the way in which Mind perceives and decodes vibrations received from the five physical senses. So, “things” only exist because we actually observe them.

Everything in the Universe exists as a quantum probability with “quantum potential” until observed, at which point, the quantum probability becomes a quantum reality until the object is no longer observed, at which point it reverts to being a quantum probability with quantum potential once again. This equally applies to our individual realities and consensus realities such as what we observe on Earth, this being a very basis of manifestation.

When you know, beyond any doubt that you are a co-creator within this magnificent Universe, on that day you will know beyond any doubt that you can experience anything you wish.

As previously discussed, it is desirable to understand the processes through which our wishes, needs and desires are delivered into our experiential reality. Often The Law of Attraction is described as the entire manifestation process, when in fact it is only involved with certain aspects of the manifestation process such as with the very important harmonisation, which will be discussed in the next chapter.

But first let us briefly review once again the process through which we receive our desires.

When a desire is impressed upon the Subconscious Mind for something that we wish to be brought into our experience, the Subconscious Mind will in turn impress the Universal Mind, the Energy field, the medium through which all individual Subconscious Minds have an intimate connection, with that desire. The Universal Mind then operates through individual Subconscious Minds by intuition, inspiration or other forms of communication to take specific action which then emerges as the corresponding impulse in the conscious Mind of the same person receiving it. That person will then take that specific physical action, which in turn will benefit the person who originally invoked the process by impressing their desire on their own Subconscious Mind. All desires, except for personal health or healing, which the Subconscious Mind manages directly, are fulfilled in this way, in perfect harmony, where all involved benefit, as cooperation between individual conscious and Subconscious Minds, through the overall Divine Providence of the Universal Mind, The Source, God.

The process of manifestation is conceptually extremely simple, broadly consisting of the following five steps:

1. Know your desire.
2. Ask for your desire.
3. Harmonise your desire.
4. Action towards your desire.
5. Gratitude for receiving your desire.

These five steps will enable you to manifest absolutely anything into your own physical reality. Once learned, you will apply these steps naturally in your life to become a conscious creator of your reality, shaping your world in precise accordance with your desires. You can enjoy a magical life of unlimited health, wealth, joy, harmony and fulfilment, always knowing that there is absolutely nothing that you cannot be, do or have.

Now let us take a look at these steps more closely.

Step 1: Know your desire:

This might well seem obvious, but the fact is that many people really do not know what they desire. They might think they want this, that or the other, but they have never really considered these things in great depth, perhaps only wanting the thing to impress others, or because someone else has the same thing, or even simply to conform to the expectations of others. Often it is simple an abstract desire "to be rich".

When a friend takes delivery of a new car for example, you may immediately believe that you need an even better car, being driven by the Ego. Very often people simply decide on a whim or an impulse that they need a particular item or event in their lives, without giving any thought whatsoever at what value it will bring into their lives and the lives of family.

Knowing what you really need as opposed to "want" is an extremely important first step in the manifestation process. Before proceeding, take time to contemplate your desire, meditating upon it, asking yourself what tangible benefits it will bring to yourself and family, and in particular whether it will bring genuine happiness and fulfilment. It should be pointed out that very often people receive things that they believed would make them happy, only to experience the opposite later.

Consider in considerable detail how the object of your desire will really benefit you. How will it make you happy? What tangible benefits will it bring? How will it enhance your reality? How will it help you to fulfil your mission on Earth this time around? How will it impact of benefit those around you? And so on.

You need to be brutally honest with yourself about these questions. Wanting something because someone else has it is really not a very good reason at all in any respect. Your desires would then be driven by the demands of the Ego and motivated by such negative emotions as vanity, jealousy or envy.

If you cannot yet achieve that level of certainty, use your imagination to visualize and experience what your life will be like if you had your objective at this very moment. Experience it. Observe the reactions of those around you. Place yourself forwards in time, and ask yourself whether you enjoy or regret having this thing in your life.

If you still have difficulty deciding, ask for inner guidance. Just before sleep and just after awakening are excellent for this. Simply concentrate as deeply as you can, and ask very clearly in your Mind, "Do I really need __________?" Your Subconscious Mind will know whether this desire would add tangible value to your life or not.

Always be alert for the answer in the form of inspiration, intuition or simply a sense of "knowing". Your answer might also arrive during a dream, so it is a good idea to keep a notepad by your bed and write down whatever you remember about your dreams as soon as you awake. When your answer arrives, you will know beyond any doubt. Always follow this inner guidance, even if it is not what you wanted to hear. What seems like a good idea from your very narrow, physical perspective within the confines of space-time, may not be a good idea from the perspective of the grand scheme of things—your Higher Self will always know this beyond question.

Once you know beyond all doubt what you really want, you can proceed to the next step.

Step 2: Ask for your desire:

"Ask, and it shall be given you; seek, and ye shall find; knock, and it shall be opened unto you: For every one that asketh receiveth; and he that seeketh findeth; and to him that knocketh it shall be opened. -- Matthew 7:7-8

So says the Bible. These are indeed ancient and wise words. The Universe never denies anyone anything whatsoever, and there are no exceptions to this truth. Each and every person must experience exactly that which they need to experience in order to learn and evolve back to God using their own freewill.

Every wish is immediately and unconditionally granted by the Universal Mind within the realms of the collective Subconscious Mind

Asking is an important and very precise step in this process. You need to be positive, unambiguous and precise about how you ask for your desire. The asking process can be purely in the Mind, but one of the most powerful methods of asking is to write your request down on paper as if it is true already. The physical action of writing down your desire impresses your wish on your Subconscious Mind, which is in direct communication with The Source, and it focuses your intentions in a positive and unambiguous way.

Always write down your wish in the present tense. We have discussed and emphasized this previously and must do so again because it is one of the primary mistakes many people make. If, for example, you use the words "I want", you will find yourself in a perpetual state of "wanting" but never receiving. "Wanting" is a human concept, but nevertheless, the Universe never argues and will always gladly oblige.

Your written request should be presented in the present tense and be as precise and to the point as possible. There is no need to write an essay on why you must have this desire. Simply state it exactly in the present tense exactly as you wish for it to manifest. The Subconscious Mind, although sublime, is very childlike in the way it perceives instructions. The Subconscious Mind will perceive direct instructions but not the rationale behind those instructions. If you endeavour to explain the reasons for your desire, your Subconscious might become confused, and your results will reflect that confusion.

The correct way to ask in the present tense could be as follows: “I am now enjoying my new car. My new car is blue in colour, has five doors and a CD player. I am really grateful for my new car”. You may also add any other features that you desire, but keep the list as short and unambiguous as you can.

Always remember to avoid restricting the Universe by including too many details, by imposing timescales or in particular stating how it is to be done. The Universe can and will provide you with anything at all, but the more you restrict the Universe by applying conditions, the longer this process will take. What is more, the Universe might well be able to provide you with something even better than you are currently able to imagine.

For example, you might write: “I am enjoying my new home. It is a two storey house with four large bedrooms, three bathrooms, a large well-equipped kitchen and a large integral double garage. My new home is close to my business office and to my children’s schools, and it is perfect for my family in every possible way”. Once you have written down your wish, place the sheet of paper in a drawer or other safe place.

It is very important after this step to start wondering where it is, when it will arrive or become frustrated. These are thoughts of doubt and lack of faith that will have a correspondingly negative impact on your manifestation, either slowing it down or preventing it altogether. You must know beyond any doubt whatsoever and with total faith in your own God-given powers, that your wish has already been granted in full, that it already exists, and that all you need to do now is to experience it in your physical level of Consciousness.

Know, with complete faith that you have asked for your desire, and that it has already been given, and that all you need to do now is to allow your desire to appear within your experience in due course which it surely will if you allow it to do so.

Step 3: Harmonise your desire:

Harmonising with the object of your desire in your Mind is an extremely important step toward receiving it, to such an extent that the next chapter is entirely committed to this important aspect of the process. In order to experience what you have asked for, you must allow it to manifest into your physical reality by bringing your individual vibration into harmony with the object of your desires. This is an extremely fundamental and important step, and one where many people fail without realising it, often blaming other factors or worse losing faith in the process, faith being another extremely important factor.

We often hear the expression, "seeing is believing", but the opposite is actually the case. In accordance with the Law of Attraction, "believing is seeing". You must believe it before you can actually see it and not the other way around. If you believe something is so in your life, it shall be in your life in accordance with The Law of Attraction. Another way of looking at this statement is "believing is experiencing". If you can experience it in your Mind, by means of your imagination, you can experience it in your physical life.

Whenever you have the opportunity to remain undisturbed for a time and your Mind is clear of other thoughts, sit down comfortably, relax as deeply as possible by taking a few deep breaths, and imagine yourself in the presence of the object of your desires. This process is particularly powerful just before sleep at night and just after awakening in the morning. Use all five senses to the maximum extent to experience your desires. Feel it, live it and be an integral part of it. For the time you are involved with this exercise, you must be totally at one with the object of your desires. This process can be likened to playing a movie in your head in vivid Technicolor and surround-sound, while experiencing every aspect of the situation with all of your senses. This is one reason why we practiced creative visualisation in the previous chapter, learning how to engage all of the senses.

While playing this movie in your Mind, feel all of the emotions associated with it. Physically experience your desire as intensely as possible. The movie in your Mind should be totally realistic in every possible sense as if you are really a part of it.

The more you can experience and become excited by the object of your desires, the more powerful the attraction will be, and the more rapidly you will bring yourself into harmony with it. Feel the joy and fulfilment of experiencing your desire as if it is already in your physical possession. There should not be the slightest doubt in your Mind. This is a joyful process.

This process will impress your desire upon your Subconscious Mind which will then, with the Universal Mind, bring your desire into your physical reality through the Law, or Principle of Attraction.

The next chapter will provide a much fuller meditation process for bringing yourself into absolute harmony with your desires.

Step 4: Action towards your desires:

Although The Universe will deliver anything at all that you desire, the process will be empowered considerably if you also take your own steps towards realising your desires. This does not mean however that you should physically go out and do everything yourself. By taking positive steps in the direction of your desire, you invoke another very powerful Energy—the Energy of intent. The Energy of intent will work in conjunction with the knowing, asking and experiencing in a very powerful way by reinforcing your claim on the object of your desire that by now already exists in the Eternal Now of the Universe.

In addition to the Energy of intent, you must also firmly impress upon your Subconscious Mind that you are very serious about manifesting the object of your desire. Your Subconscious Mind is extremely powerful and is in direct communication with the Universal Mind as an integral aspect and sphere of activity of Universal Mind, and the more intent you can impress upon your Subconscious Mind, the more your intent will be correspondingly impressed upon Universal Mind.

If you are asking for one thing and vibrating something completely different, this will influence your Subconscious Mind accordingly, thereby acting as a negative influence on the manifestation of your desire.

Your ability to manifest anything will be directly proportional to the net effect of your influence over your Subconscious Mind in that direction. You require a net influence in the direction of your desire in order for it to manifest into your physical reality. Negative influences will effectively cancel out positive influences projected at both a conscious and Subconscious level, and that is why you need to ensure that the influence in the direction of your desire is as positive as possible. Physical actions in the direction of your desire will increase the positive influence in proportion to your degree of intent.

This is one reason why if you wish to manifest a new home, you should take positive actions to physically go out and look for one. You do not have to worry about whether you can "afford it" or not because that would be a negative emotion resulting in a negative influence on your Subconscious Mind. Simply know that the final realization of your home is not your concern, and that your Subconscious Mind, with Universal Mind will manifest your house for you in Divine order.

In the case of your new home, the very act of physically going out and looking for at houses will not only project the positive Energy of intent, but will also favourably invoke other emotions such as excitement and expectation. The same Principle applies to any material thing or situation. The more steps that you physically take in the direction of your desire, for example looking at other homes that represent your ideal home, the more emotion you will feel as a result, and the more you can impress that emotion on your Subconscious Mind. This in turn more strongly impresses the Universal Mind by adding more power to the Thought Form of your new home. The more powerful your Thought Form, the greater the influence over your Subconscious Mind and therefore in turn, Universal Mind.

The bigger and the more frequent the actions you take the better. Never take the Universe for granted or delay the process by waiting until tomorrow, because when tomorrow arrives you will defer your actions until tomorrow once again, never taking that important positive action in the direction of your desires. Failure to take positive action is a major reason why people do not realise the results they wish for.

Your original Thought Form of your house is like a seed that you have sown in the garden of your Subconscious Mind. Like any seed it needs to be fed and watered and tended to, in order for it to germinate and eventually grow and blossom into the object of your desires in your experiential reality.

In addition, as the seed of your desire begins to sprout and grow, you will be prompted to take certain actions which you must take as part of the receiving process, and it is therefore important to be vigilant for and recognise these inner prompts.

Step 5: Gratitude for your desire:

Gratitude is another extremely important emotional Energy that you should project when manifesting your desires. If something is worth having, it is worth giving thanks for.

Note that gratitude has nothing to do with thanking a personified "God" deity, who, according to the dogma of orthodox religion, enjoys being praised, flattered or "worshipped". These are merely religious ideas and superstitions that have no relation to reality.

The power of gratitude functions at several levels that have more to do with Energy and vibration. To feel sincerely grateful is to be in tune with the Universe. It conveys the Energy that you already know and appreciate that you are an integral aspect of The Source, The First Cause, God, and that you are grateful for existing as a conscious, infinite, immortal Being and co-creator within the Universe, and that you are blessed with the Divine ability to create your own reality and evolve back to The Source of Unconditional Love on the path of Divine perfection.

Gratitude also conveys an acknowledgement for having already received the object of your desire. For example, you might say: "I am grateful for my wonderful new house". Along with those thoughts should be the feeling of the most intense gratitude for what you have already received from The Universe. Gratitude makes the object of your desire a real, tangible, integral aspect of your own reality, and the more real it is to you, the sooner it will manifest into your personal experiential reality.

Gratitude, conveyed with genuine sincerity, brings you more into harmony with the Universe, and with it you become an even more natural creator of your desires. Those people who are completely aligned with the Universe are natural creators who live what to others seems like a "charmed", magical life, instantly manifesting anything at will. Such people are true Magicians, and nothing is impossible to them.

Never take anything at all for granted. Always feel deeply grateful for everything that happens in your reality, regardless of whether you consciously attracted it or whether you perceive it to be positive or negative. In the grand scheme of things, everything that manifests into your physical reality has always been attracted by you at some level, and therefore you should always be grateful for it. Aside from the fact that sincere gratitude should be firmly integrated into the Being of everyone and for everything, a lack of gratitude will greatly weaken your powers of creation.

Being deeply grateful also helps to ensure that you never convey the Energy of dissatisfaction, which is a very negative Energy and therefore destructive emotion. Dissatisfaction sends the wrong Energy into the Universe, which will react with immutable perfection in reciprocating those negative emotions with more of the same, which will eventually manifest in your life as negative experiences.

Conversely, those things that you feel extremely satisfied, grateful and happy about will create a much higher, positive vibration, attracting more of the same into your life in the form of positive experiences. The Universe always naturally moves in the direction of expansion and evolution, and never in the direction of contraction or destruction. So, positive emotions are always much more powerful than negative emotions, even though they are both causes with the corresponding effects.

These are the five powerful steps to attracting anything you could possibly desire into your life. All of these five steps are individually very powerful in their own right, but collectively, they are so powerful that you can manifest almost anything you desire into your personal experiential reality with what might seem like amazing speed.

Create joyfully in the knowledge that you are fulfilling your Divine role as a co-creator in the Universe. The Universe is infinitely abundant and enjoys infinite expression, expansion and growth.

Chapter 90
Harmonising Your Desires

During the previous chapter, we looked at the process of manifestation and discussed importance of bringing yourself into harmony with the vibrations of the object of your desires in order to allow your desires to manifest and be experienced.

This matching of vibration of Energy is not only a very important aspect of the manifestation process, but is also as an ongoing process. The Universe, of which we are all integral, inseparable aspects, always seeks and achieves complete harmony. Through the infinite power of our Subconscious Mind there are no limits to what we may attract into our lives, all desires asked for being immediately answered by the Subconscious and Universal Minds, but nevertheless we still need to provide the right environment into which these desires can become physical experiences.

The Law of Attraction is in constant operation, not only during manifestation processes, but during every thought process. Every thought is Energy and is therefore a cause with a corresponding effect on the Energy of the Universe, so all thoughts should only be in the direction of our wellbeing. Random thoughts will be transient and attract little, while powerful, constantly focused thoughts will exert a correspondingly powerful influence. Likewise, random, unfocussed thoughts will result in weak, ineffective Thought Forms, where as strong, focussed thoughts will give rise to powerful, creative Thought Forms.

In a previous chapter of this book, we practiced single-pointed concentration. Your entire Consciousness should always be one of awareness, focus and concentration in the direction of your desires and in the direction of your immediate intentions. This is to live a magical life where you are the perpetual creator of your own reality. The more you can focus on and experience your desires and intentions on an ongoing basis, while knowing beyond any doubt that everything you desire is already yours, the more you will be an open channel of expression of The Source through Whom infinite abundance is yours for the asking.

The following meditation is very powerful in bringing you into harmony with your desires, especially if performed regularly. This process is so powerful that it can be used for the process of manifestation in its own right, although the process is greatly enhanced by performing it in conjunction with the five-step process for manifestation.

A good state of relaxation is very important for this harmonization process—ideally deep physical relaxation, but certainly in a position that you will not cause you to be susceptible of drifting off to sleep or being disturbed.

An excellent time to harmonize your desires is at night just before or after sleep, when your brainwaves slow down and your conscious Mind becomes much closer to your Subconscious Mind than during day. This exercise can however be performed at any time of the day where you have the opportunity to completely relax. Another great benefit of doing these exercises at night just before sleep is that you will carry the focus of the object of your imagination into the sleep state which will enable your Subconscious Mind to continue to process your thoughts during sleep, without the conscious Mind interfering in any way.

When you are completely relaxed, or, if in bed at night, just as you enter a sleepy state, but without drifting off to sleep completely, commence by closing your eyes. Create an image in your Mind as vividly and realistically as possible of the object or situation that you are manifesting into your life from the exercises of the previous chapters.

Again, it is extremely important to imagine the object of your manifestation in the present tense, knowing that it already exists within your experiential reality now, feeling all of the emotions and gratitude involved. If you are manifesting a new television set, for example, you should actually "see" your ideal TV set already in position in your living room, with yourself and your family happily seated around it. Hear the television, view the pictures, and experience your reactions to what you see, as well as your enjoyment of this new TV. Bring as many of your senses into your scenario as you can. Imagine your family watching your favourite program. See the images on the screen as clearly as possible, and be totally engrossed with what you are watching. If you have a pet, visualize your pet sleeping on a rug in front of the TV. The more detail you can add to this imagination, the more effective it will be.

It is also very important, as previously discussed, to place as much emotion behind your visualisation as possible. Feel and know as intensively as possible that your manifestation is already a complete reality. Feel with as much emotion as possible your feelings of great joy, passion, enthusiasm, appreciation, and gratitude. Add all of the emotions relevant to the objective of your manifestation. Again, emotion is a very powerful force, and the more emotion you can inject into your imagined scenario, the more powerful the effects will be.

An extremely powerful way of charging your visualisations with emotion is to bring into your Mind situations in the past that invoke powerful emotions, and integrate the feeling of those emotions into your current visualisation. Recall your most joyous, passionate and enthusiastic times, experience those emotions as if you were actually experiencing the situation again, and then move the feeling of those emotions into your imagination and visualizing the object of your desire.

This level of emotion has a profoundly positive influence on the Thought Form that your Subconscious Mind receives which will in turn attract your desire into your reality through the

Universal Mind, unless it is personal health in which case the Subconscious Mind acts directly upon your physical body, over which it has absolute dominion. Another very powerful way of raising your vibration is to invoke the senses of hearing and smell by recalling favourite music that has particularly joyous memories and fragrances that evoke positive memories.

You can make use of these senses in two ways. If it is a particular piece of music, you can have that music playing gently in the background, or, better still to avoid external factors, you can recall the music in your Mind.

Throughout history, fragrances have been used to influence emotion. You may have heard of “aromatherapy”, which functions in the same way. You can recall these fragrances in your Mind, but the most powerful way of making use of a fragrance is to actually place it in the area in which you are conducting your harmonization exercises. If for example it is a fragrance associated with cooking, it is possible to use a device known as a “censer” to burn a small quantity of that food, for example a favourite herb, spice or seasoning upon the charcoal block of the censer. A censer can also be used with any sort of burnable incense. Of course, safety is extremely important. If you are going to use a censer, please make absolutely certain that it is not placed where it will be a fire hazard. If you are doing this in bed, just before sleep, it is very unwise to leave a censer burning, in which case you can recall your favourite fragrance within your Mind. If you do wish to make use of a favourite fragrance, and you will be using a censer or any other burning object such as a candle, then burn it for a time before bed so that your room is fully impregnated with the fragrance, and then ensure that it is completely extinguished before getting into bed.

It is also, as discussed previously, extremely important to feel deep gratitude for receiving the object of your desire. Feel the gratitude with total emotion and genuine sincerity, giving thanks to the Universe for bringing it to you. It is also very useful to add affirmations to your creative visualisation. For example, repeat to yourself: "Here I am sitting in my house and watching my wonderful new television set". Always phrase these affirmations in the present tense and be totally, completely convinced in every way of the absolute reality of the situation as if you are experiencing it now.

Maintain in your Mind this complete creative visualisation scenario, together with all other senses and emotions, for at least 10 minutes, after which express your gratitude to the Universe with absolute sincerity for enjoying your desire, Next take a few deep breaths, and if during the day, continue with your daily activities, or, if just before sleep, empty your Mind completely and drift off to sleep, allowing your Subconscious Mind to process your thoughts while you sleep. Whenever the opportunity arises, focus on and experience the object of your desires. This does not need to be a full manifestation session, but by positively imagining the object of your manifestation as often as possible, knowing you are experiencing now and giving thanks for it, you further influence your Subconscious Mind, and the sooner it will manifest into your physical reality.

As previously mentioned, you should move towards a state of experiencing the object of your desire during your normal conscious state until it is integrated into your very being to the point where you are totally convinced that you are experiencing that reality. The object of your desire will then be attracted to you in a very powerful way.

When you are not specifically focusing on the object of your manifestation, it is very important not to crave success, wishing it to manifest into your life too soon. This will send out negative Energy that could slow the process of attraction, and it also affirms that you have not yet received delivery of the object of your desire, which will result in delays.

Always be patient and follow the exercises completely as often as possible with dedication. If you do this, you will surely succeed. These processes will become an integral, joyous and natural part of your life.

Sometimes, you might decide that as a result of experiencing your visualisations, you no longer desire the object or situation, which is fine. Simply let the desire go, and move confidently on to the next object of desire.

The Treasure Map

For those who might initially have problems with creative visualisation and use of the imagination generally, creating a "treasure map" is a highly effective alternative method. All you need for this is a large sheet of paper to draw, paint or paste images representing the object of your desire—again, always depicted in the present tense as if it is already a complete reality Now. If you are not an artist, you can easily create a collage by cutting out the appropriate images representing your desires from magazines, and attaching them to your sheet of paper, thereby building up a complete collage representing your desires.

Your treasure map does not need to be particularly detailed, but does need to convey your desires to your Subconscious Mind in an unambiguous way. It is also very important to place a representation of yourself within the treasure map. A photograph of yourself is ideal, preferably right in the very centre of your map. Somewhere on your treasure map, write a statement, such as: "Here I am watching my new TV set", if a TV set is the object of your desire, or "here I am in my new home" or "here I am washing my new car" etc.

Your completed treasure map should contain all of the elements necessary representing the object of your desire, and most importantly should convey the entire picture as if it is already a complete reality within your life which you are enjoying now.

When your treasure map is completed, proceed as before, but this time, instead of closing your eyes and using your powers of imagination within your Mind, focus on your treasure map with your eyes open and with as much concentration as possible. Do not allow your attention to be distracted. Again, just before sleep at night, and also just after awaking in the morning are excellent times for this process, due to your closeness with your Subconscious Mind.

Gaze at your treasure map with your full attention focussed upon it, not allowing yourself to be distracted, and as before, place as much emotion as possible into your treasure map, placing yourself within it as if it is a complete reality now. Become totally involved with your picture, feeling the joy and other emotions of experiencing it, knowing that it is already yours, and thus feeling the gratitude for it. As before, you can recall other situations where you were extremely joyful and inject those emotions into your picture with yourself. And again you can use favourite music providing it is not intrusive and your favourite fragrances providing you observe the safety precautions as previously detailed.

After focusing on your treasure map for 5 minutes or so, you do not need to count the minutes, whenever it feels right for you, close your eyes and recall your image, again with as much feeling and emotion as possible, placing yourself in the centre and fully involved. Do not worry if you cannot achieve this process straightaway. Simply open your eyes and refocus on your treasure map, allowing the images, and the emotions involved to sink deep into your Subconscious Mind. If at night, after you have achieved these objectives, simply put the picture down and drift off to sleep retaining the images in your Mind in as much detail as possible, and with an absolute knowing that the object of your desire is already yours, feeling the emotions and gratitude as you drift into the sleep state. You will soon find that the more you concentrate on your treasure map, the more you will be able to recall the images when you close your eyes. This is also an excellent exercise for practicing and gaining valuable visualisation abilities generally.

Whenever you have a free moment during the day when you will not be disturbed, relax as completely as you can, take out your treasure map, and completely concentrate on it. The more often you do this, the more your Subconscious Mind will be influenced towards your desire as you bring yourself into harmony with your desires, and your Thought Form becomes increasingly clearer and stronger. After any manifestation exercise, or any time you are working with The Universal Mind, The Source, God through your Subconscious Mind, always remember to convey your gratitude most sincerely for the blessings received, feeling intense gratitude for these blessings.

Remember that you can use these processes to manifest almost anything into your life. It does not need to be a physical object or money. It can be health, happiness, a holiday, job promotion, a pay raise, losing weight, fitness, greater creativity, friendships, relationships, anything at all that you can imagine—nothing is too great for the Universe.

Always keep in Mind that manifestation should also be applied to your own Spiritual evolution and for the benefit of others. We are all here to evolve first and foremost, so it is most important that you also use these exercises for your own personal evolution and not become obsessed with material things which will hold back your own personal evolution. Service to others before service to self is a fundamental Principle that everyone should observe.

Chapter 91
Let Go and Let God

"Let go and let God" are extremely important words that everyone should heed at all times.

People often make demands, usually driven by the Ego or the urge to conform, become impatient, and try to force things in the direction of how they think they should go—you cannot rush the infinite. Everything in the Universe happens in an immutable sequence of causation. However, it is most important to keep in mind at the same time that everything that has ever happened, is happening now or ever will happen in the future already exists within the Eternal Now beyond the illusion of space-time, in the case of the "future", relative to the space-time continuum of the physical Universe, in the form of quantum probabilities. It is only a matter of attracting something into personal awareness from the Eternal Now in order to experience it in a tangible form.

This is an ongoing basis of Taoism as discussed in chapter 4, Taoism, a process known as "going with the Tao", which is to progress with the flow of the Universe. The Universe and everything within is evolving perfectly. All we have to do is to evolve with the flow of the Universe rather than resist it, or force it in the way we think it should go.

The reality is that no one knows, from our physical human perspective, what the "future" will bring. As previously discussed, the "future" only exists within the Eternal Now as infinite quantum probabilities, or "quantum potential" encompassing every possible outcome, until such time as it is brought into existence as a quantum reality by the power of the Mind and by physical observation of the manifested reality. The course of that perceived "future" will continue to unfold regardless of any resistance, any resistance to the immutable flow of the Universe only bringing unhappiness. Everything is a perfect expression of God, The Source, the First Cause, and it is for each and every one of us to express that perfection as it flows from God and through each of us as Divine channels of experience and expression. Always know in the very core of your Being that you are an aspect of the Divine, The Source, of God, and that no harm can ever come to you.

"Let go and let God" is an extremely important part of the manifestation process. Never physically force anything in the direction you wish it to go because it will be counterproductive to creating what you desire, which can only come from the Universe in response to the Mind. Manifest your desires and live this temporal physical life in accordance with the immutable flow of the Universe. The more in harmony you are with that flow, the faster your wishes will manifest into your reality as a free-flowing expression of God.

Should you find yourself in a situation that you perceive as "hopeless", or if you feel "stuck in a rut" and do not know how to progress your life, then "let go and let God". Simply completely open yourself to the Universe and ask for guidance with absolute sincerity and gratitude, and it will be forthcoming. There have been countless cases of people who, when it seemingly hopeless situations, such as being homeless or destitute have submitted themselves completely to the Love of God, to find that very soon their life changes dramatically for the better, often better than it ever was before. God both experiences and expresses through each one of us and all life.

Relax, rejoice and be grateful and know that you are an infinite and immortal son or daughter of God, made in the true Spiritual image of God, and that the entire Universe including you is unfolding perfectly. Let go and let God, with perfect trust and perfect faith, and you will be blessed with infinite joy, abundance and health as you progress on your own path of perfection back to The Source, Our Prime Creator, God.

Chapter 92
The Joy and Power of Giving

The Universe unconditionally provides us with all our wishes, needs and desires in accordance with immutable Universal Principles. There are no exceptions. Receiving must include giving, however—it is in giving that we may also receive.

Giving must never seem like an obligation or be carried out due to pressure from others. Giving should always be from a position of Unconditional Love, Gratitude and the strong desire to serve and put wealth back into the Universe that has unconditionally provided us with our wealth.

A primary Universal Principle that everyone, without exception should know, assimilate into their very being, and practice at all times is this: Service to others before service to self.

The vibration of giving out of Unconditional Love and of being of unconditional service to others is a very high vibration that positively impacts the Universe as a whole. The very act of giving in this way will raise your own vibration, enabling you to receive more readily. Giving and receiving are two aspects of exactly the same thing. The joy with which you give will be reflected within your joy in receiving, which is why giving and service to others should always come from the heart, and not out of a sense of obligation or thought of receiving in return.

The Universe unconditionally gives all creation with Unconditional Love, and it is in that same Spirit that we should give to all in creation, including all mankind, flora and fauna.

Giving need not necessarily be in terms of "money" which is simply a human concept. Giving anything of true value, out of Unconditional Love that benefits others, without expecting anything in return, is true giving in the context of the Universe.

Chapter 93
The Joy and Power of Healing

When most people think of "illness" and medical treatment, they think in terms of the physical body, consultants, surgeons, doctors, medicines and hospitals. This is quite understandable as most illnesses appear to the physical senses to affect the physical body or state of Mind, leading most to believe that the afflictions originate within these areas. While this might well be true in the case of physical acquired injuries such as a broken limb, most spontaneously occurring afflictions including the most serious illnesses such as cancer do not generally have a physical origin at all. All illness originates from within, either due to thoughts in many forms that have been impressed upon the Subconscious Mind, all of which must outwardly manifest sooner or later, or due to imbalances and arising from the inner bodies of Energy, particularly the Energy body, due to stress and other influences.

Due to the holistic nature of the Universe and the human body, all of which are inseparable aspects of each other, anything arising at inner Energy levels will always be correspondingly reflected at the outer levels. The axiom of "as above, so below" again proving to be very true, but should be more accurately stated "as within, so without", with ailments originating in the inner bodies manifesting in turn in the physical body "without" in accordance with immutable Universal Principles. As infinite, multidimensional Beings, we have an infinite number of "bodies" ranging from the very highest aspect of God to the physical body of matter in which most people are focused in the physical world of Earth. Diseases can occur in any of the inner bodies, causing an imbalance that has to manifest in the physical body as an effect in accordance with immutable Universal laws.

It should be pointed out that the term "body" is entirely notional, being only relative to what we know as the physical body, the outer "shell" in which we live for the time being on Earth. In fact all "bodies" are unique configurations of Energy, which in absolute terms have no "shape" or "form", these characteristics being simply perceptions in the Mind of the observer. Within the Astral worlds, due to the fact that the people living there were used to living in a physical body on Earth, they create a "body" of Energy in the Astral that usually appears to the observer as a replica of their Earth body, but usually perceived as being at an age when the person considered themselves to be in the "prime of life", often mid-twenties to mid-thirties, depending on how the person with the Astral body perceives their own body. Ultimately we all "live and move and have our Being" as unique Energy fields, Thought Forms, "ideas" in the infinite Universal Mind of The Source, The First Cause, God, therefore we all exist in the form, extensions and expressions of Source Energy.

It is a fact that our entire physical body is completely renewed every few years, many parts within days or months. The only reason therefore that "ageing" occurs at all is because people believe they must "grow old" with all of the associated symptoms of aging that society expects. These ageing ideas are then impressed upon the Subconscious Mind which is, in turn, more than happy to externalise them into physical aging. The same applies to diseases, illnesses and conditions of all sorts.

Any ailment can healed likewise be healed through the Subconscious Mind. The Subconscious Mind maintains a perfect image of health, the same perfect image held for each and every one of us by our Divine creator. All we need to do is to hold in our Mind only that image of perfection, and that then must be our reality, a reality of perfect health and youth, should that be the desire. Most modern methods of holistic healing however seek to treat the Energy imbalances within the Energy body. Although this can be and often is effective, it is still nevertheless a secondary treatment that seeks to replace processes which properly belong to the Subconscious Mind.

There are various methods of treating the Energy body, many of which you might already be familiar with under the general description of “alternative medicine”. This description is somewhat misleading, however, as it could be much more appropriately described as “primary healing”. Well-known examples of energetic or holistic healing include acupuncture, Pranic Healing and Reiki.

There are also healing methods broadly based on the practice of homeopathy, where the objective is to bring the body into balance, allowing a healing to take place. Homeopathy is not generally considered to be a practice having an effect on the Energy body, although with certain treatments, the Energy body might be influenced favourably. An example of this is healing by the application of various herbs, plant extracts, and crystals which are believed to have a direct affect on the balance of Energy body, or can relieve physical symptoms, thereby bringing about a cure. Herbal-based healing is a separate and extensive discipline in its own right and often a very effective one.

In many cases, the herb or other natural substance become a point of focus resulting in faith in the patient that a healing will result. It is the very focus on this belief within the Mind of the patient with absolute faith that will bring about the expected healing by the Subconscious Mind of the patient. This is how the “placebo” effect works. Although a placebo has no medicinal properties associated with it, the very act of faith in the patient that a healing will occur, results in the actual healing. The patient has in reality been healed by their own Subconscious Mind.

Another method of healing involves the use of naturally occurring crystals such as quartz, which again can have a direct effect on the Energy body due to the natural vibrations of these crystals. Different crystals exhibit different types and levels of vibration, all of which can influence the Energy body in a specific way. It is well-known that Quartz exhibits “piezo electric” properties—the reason quartz crystals are often used in watches, clocks and other precision instruments for maintaining accuracy. Again, however, as with herbs, healing might be well more a function of the Mind of the patient and their faith in the healing power of the crystal, than due to any healing properties inherent in the actual crystals.

Healing by the use of herbs, crystals and other naturally occurring substances can nevertheless be very effective in the hands of practitioners with the appropriate knowledge and experience. The precise healing mechanism is not important in the context of the end result. These skills can be learned and practiced by almost anyone with dedication. Learning about the healing properties and methods of herbs, crystals and other substances is extremely worthwhile and rewarding. In addition, there are less well-known methods of healing involving the use of the Magnetic fluid of the Ether by a practitioner known as a “magnetopath”.

Everyone has the ability to heal any illness, even the most serious, many of which are often considered to be “terminal” by doctors who remain oblivious to the true nature of healing, and who rely exclusively on what their “instruments” tell them. There is ultimately only one source of disease and only one source of healing and that is the Subconscious Mind. All other methods, as with physical medicine, are very much secondary.

In order to heal any ailment, disease or disorder, whether manifesting physically or mentally, all we need to do is to call upon the infinite powers of our Subconscious Mind which has total dominion over all our physical functions and experiences.

Chapter 94
Pranic Healing

The recognized founder of the practice of Pranic Healing is Choa Kok Sui who created a process which heals physical or mental ailments by treating the Energy body with Universal Energy, often known as "Prana", a Sanskrit word meaning "life-force".

Pranic healing is a method of energetic healing that balances the Energy of the Energy body, focussing on the affected corresponding areas of the physical body.

There are several fundamental Principles and stages associated with the practice of Pranic healing. Treatment usually commences with a process of cleansing "diseased" Energy from the Energy centres. Next these centres are revitalized with sufficient Energy to bring about the healing process. It is most important to perform the cleansing process before the healing process. It should be noted that no Energy is actually "diseased". All Energy of God, is inherently perfect. The "disease" is actually a physical manifestation corresponding to the way the Energy of the person has been configured under the influence of their own Mind.

According to Pranic healing practice, it is very important for the Pranic healer to avoid becoming drained of their own Energy or being contaminated with the "diseased" Energy of the patient. An advanced Pranic healer will avoid this situation by channeling Energy directly from the infinite supply of the Universe directly into the Energy body of the patient.

Decontamination is also a very important aspect of the practice of Pranic Healing in the belief by healers that they can become ill themselves by the absorption of "diseased" Energy from the patient, not only on a physical body level but also at the level of the inner bodies. Decontamination involves the energetic purification of the healing space, not only for the safeguard of the healer, but also for future patients. It should be noted however that Energy cannot, in and of itself be "diseased". Energy only differs in the way in which it manifests under the influence of Mind of the person influencing it, and which in turn will be unique to that person. If a person, due to their own thought processes has manifested an Energy imbalance in their own physical reality, that Energy imbalance cannot be "transmitted" to the healer or another person, unless the healer, or another person believes it can, and even then they will simply be reproducing the same imbalance in their own body.

The same principle also applies to positive healing. We are all One in the Universal Mind, and therefore share the same Energy Source. We are also therefore all One at the level of the collective Subconscious Mind. We can therefore heal another person using the power of the Mind alone, with the power of Faith, at that level, because ultimately there is no "separation", and the healer who realises that can heal anyone as they would heal themselves. Again—all healing is of the Subconscious Mind with absolute Faith, Gratitude and the realisation of God within, and in the perfection of God in Whose image we are made.

The process of Pranic healing includes direct treatment of the main chakras. Different ailments are usually associated by the Pranic healer with one or more chakras. More advanced methods of Pranic healing seek to make use of Energy of the appropriate colour, relating to the type of ailment and the area of the Energy body or chakra involved. This colour healing process is performed by the use of creative visualisation in conjunction with the projection of Energy by the Pranic healer.

An example of the use of colour in Pranic healing is red Energy for sufferers of Asthma, which has the corresponding physical effect of dilating the bronchial tubes of the sufferer, thereby relieving the breathing process. More severe ailments such as

AIDS and cancer are often said to be responsive to the more powerful colour frequencies of violet.

In addition to physiological problems, Pranic healing can be used to treat psychological problems. Negative emotions originate on the Mental Plane or are a result of a psychic attack or larvae. Negative thoughts and emotions become attached to the Energy body and specific chakras of the patient. Conventional psychotherapy can often take many months or even years to release this negative Energy by conventional means, if they ever fully succeed. Psychotherapists treat the physically manifesting symptoms of the condition, as if it originated within the physical brain, rather than the true, inner origins of the condition. However, by using advanced Pranic healing techniques the affected chakras, all traumas, phobias, obsessions, compulsions, addictions and most other psychological problems can be healed much more efficiently.

More importantly for the patient, there is no requirement whatsoever to disclose any sort of personal information to the healer. Very often after the first Pranic healing session for a psychological affliction, the patient feels a sense of great peace and serenity, as if a large weight has been lifted from their shoulders. Again however, this however is a result of faith on the part of the patient that they will experience positive results from the process, the Subconscious Mind of the patient duly obliging.

The usual cautions apply when seeking the services of a Pranic healer. Always ensure that the practitioner is genuine by thoroughly checking their experience and credentials and by obtaining and verifying as many testimonials and references as possible.

Chapter 95
Reiki Healing

Like Pranic healing, Reiki healing is said to be the practice of healing by means of the manipulation of Universal Energy. Reiki it is not taught in the usual sense. The ability to practice Reiki is rather said to be "transferred" from a "Reiki Master" to the student by a process known as "attunement" after the necessary preparations, knowledge and other conditions have been attained.

Reiki is considered to be a Spiritually guided form of healing, with "Rei" the Universal Consciousness or "God Consciousness" guiding the "Ki", the Universal Energy. People treated by Reiki often describe a glowing radiance surrounding and within their entire body. In addition to healing, recipients of Reiki treatment sometimes feel peace, security and a sense of well-being after treatment.

During the process of a Reiki healing session, Energy is said to flow through and around the affected part of the Energy body and aura of the patient, charging them with positive Energy, raising the vibrational level of the entire Energy field of the Energy body in and around the physical body where negative thoughts and feelings are attached, causing the negative Energy to "break" and fall away. In this way, Reiki is said to clear, straighten and heal Energy pathways in and around the Energy body, allowing Energy to flow in a healthy and natural way.

As with most healing, the patient is ultimately healing themselves by virtue of their Faith in the process, and Belief they will be healed.

Again—before accepting the services of a Reiki healer, always ask for and verify for yourself as many references and testimonials as possible.

Chapter 96
Healing Yourself and Others

Just as we have the ability to manifest our desires, we have the ability to manifest our own healing through the infinite power of our own Subconscious Mind. It is our Subconscious Mind that originally "built" our body in accordance with the genetic blueprint it was provided by the father and mother through their respective DNA, and it is the Subconscious Mind that maintains all of our vital processes such as eating, assimilation of food, breathing and every other bodily process. The Subconscious Mind keeps our heart beating, regulates our breathing process, and the function of every organ in our body.

Although the Subconscious Mind carries out these functions completely automatically, day and night, throughout our entire life, it will also carry out instructions from our conscious Mind without question, and regardless of whether they "make sense" or not. The Subconscious Mind never analyses or argues with instructions from the conscious Mind, simply executing those instructions perfectly, regardless of the consequences.

As mentioned before, our physical body is completely replaced every few years, many parts much sooner within days or even hours. It should be clear therefore that such human conditions as disease and ageing should not even exist at all. "Ageing" only exists because, from a young age, children are taught by parents, society and later the "vanity" industry through the media such as television that as they get "older" they start to show signs of "ageing". For example people are told that their body loses its shape, their hair turns grey or falls out, their skin wrinkles and so on, which in turn is impressed upon the Subconscious Mind as a fact by the conscious Mind. Later in life the Subconscious Mind manifests these Thought Forms in as the physical experience of ageing which people then come to accept as a "natural part of growing old".

All spontaneously manifesting diseases of the physical body are the result of wrongful thinking including fear, worry and in particular stress. Although "stress" is considered to be a state of Mind, what most people, including the medical profession, fail to understand is that the Subconscious Mind has absolute dominion over the body, and accordingly stress originating as a state of Mind will faithfully translate that stress on to the physical body and its organs, which in turn will eventually manifest as a physically experienced disease such as cancer.

Similarly, if people believe they have an "illness", or if they believe they will contract a disease as a result of being in the presence of someone who already has a disease such as influenza, then the Subconscious Mind will duly oblige and ensure that the disease is contracted and experienced.

Much more can be said about the infinite range of diseases, afflictions and ailments that are contracted as a result of the conscious Mind impressing the Subconscious Mind with the seeds of that disease, but it is much more productive to discuss the positive aspects of healing and perfect health.

Just as the Subconscious Mind can easily manifest a disease under the influence of the conscious Mind, it can equally as easily manifest a total complete healing of any disease, however serious, including cancer, blindness and deafness. The Subconscious Mind can also maintain perfect health and even prevent the effects of physical ageing, which, as previously mentioned, is another result of the influence of the conscious Mind over the Subconscious Mind which believes that "getting old" is inevitable, and accordingly, to that person, so it is.

It is a scientific and medical fact that our physical bodies are completely renewed every few years, some parts in a matter of days, so ask yourself, this being the case, why do people age?

The answer once again is in the Mind, or more specifically the influence of the conscious Mind and its beliefs over the Subconscious Mind.

There are people who manifest a disease in their physical body and who simply do not wish to be healed. It is not possible to heal someone against their own freewill and who have impressed their Subconscious Mind with the intent not to be healed. Such people often believe their mission on Earth is complete, and all they wish to do is complete their current physical life and pass on to wherever they are destined next, often believing it to be the religious concept of "Heaven".

The Subconscious Mind has total dominion over the physical body, just as it has over our entire external physical reality. As with the Law of Attraction therefore, use of the imagination, including creative visualisation and other inner senses is a very powerful means by which to impress the Subconscious Mind with perfect health, which will in turn proceed with the process of manifestation of perfect health within the physical body.

As with applying the Law of Attraction, it is extremely important to imagine in the present tense, knowing only total, unconditional health

A demonstration of how this works in principle is the "placebo" effect as observed by medical researchers. A placebo is an inactive substance such as sugar pill or flavoured water, which, when given to a patient, they believe to be real medicine. In numerous cases, the patient is healed simply by taking the placebo without any supporting medication. This works because the patient sincerely believes, beyond any doubt in the Mind, and with complete faith, that the placebo is the "real" medicine and that it will completely cure them, and the Subconscious Mind manifests this belief as a healing, the result being the same, or very often even more effective than had they taken the actual medication they believed they were taking.

This process works both ways, and there are people who become ill due to the conscious or unconscious use of creative visualisation. This occurs when a normally healthy person strongly believes that they are or should become ill for some reason, perhaps out of guilt, or due to contact with an ill person, believing they have "caught" the disease, or sometimes due to a condition known as "hypochondria", where the person constantly believes themselves to be ill, which later the Subconscious Mind ensures will become self-fulfilling. This is the healing process in reverse, but the Principles are exactly the same. The Subconscious Mind will always, without exception, provide whatever is "asked for"—in other words, what we hold in our conscious Mind, whether it is positive, negative or neutral. The Subconscious Mind does not "decide" whether any particular thought is "good" or "bad" for a person, it simply delivers in precise accordance with the persistent thoughts, supported by belief, held within the conscious Mind and thus impressed upon the Subconscious Mind, especially those thoughts that are focussed on or obsessed about continually, and particularly with emotion.

As previously mentioned, an excellent example of this situation is the person who comes into contact with someone, for example a family member, co-worker, or while standing next to someone in a queue while shopping, who is suffering from a contagious disease. The person creates within their own imagination a strong belief that they will inevitably "catch" the same disease themselves. The disease then duly manifests in accordance with the Principle of the Subconscious Mind.

Millions of people unknowingly do this every year with very common ailments such as colds and influenza. A family member contracts a cold or flu, and immediately creates the belief that they must also inevitably contract the cold or flu, soon imagining themselves, with fear and other emotions that they feel unwell. These feelings are then impressed upon the Subconscious Mind which soon brings them into physical reality. Yes, it is the virus that ultimately gives rise to the symptoms, but it would have been impossible to contract that virus in the first place if a person believes it to be impossible to do so. The virus is simply an instrument of manifestation used by the Subconscious Mind to manifest the disease in accordance with the thoughts, fears and other emotions of the person contracting the disease.

Had the person in all of these cases instead consciously visualized themselves, with absolute faith, to be in full, radiant health, they will remain healthy by the Principle of Mind.

An ailment can also be a "message" from the Higher Self or Subconscious Mind indicating another health issue. Sometimes, the meaning of this message is obvious, as in the case of a heavy smoker who develops chronic bronchitis or pneumonia. In these cases the message is very clear: continue smoking, and health will deteriorate, possibly leading to physical death. A heavy drinker might, for example, develop liver problems. These are all cases of "wake-up calls" to conscious Mind manifesting within the physical body.

In deep meditation, questions can be asked and answers received regarding the origins and reasons for an ailment. With the benefit of this knowledge, the appropriate actions can be taken in order to change the thoughts, or to remedy those aspects of life to which the warning relates. Should you receive an answer during meditation or in the form of inspiration or perhaps in a dream, you should always take heed and act upon it immediately. The Higher Self is sublime, and only has your best interests of progression at heart, and does not wish to see this life and opportunity wasted through careless thought processes or by such abuse of the physical body or wrongful thinking. Ailments that are warnings from the Higher Self are never intended as punishments, but rather as gentle nudges.

When healing self or others it is most important never to focus on the ailment or part of the body afflicted. All healing arises from knowing only total, radiant, perfect health, as humans made in the true image of God, which the Subconscious Mind recognises as Principle, knowing the true meaning of perfect health of the body it created. Therefore, impressing the Subconscious Mind with thoughts of only the most complete health will result in perfect health, and any existing ailment will dissolve completely as if it had never existed. Likewise, if we do not focus on or recognise "ageing", then the Subconscious Mind will maintain our physical body in accordance with our own impression of our ideal appearance.

Again, there is only one Principle for our own individual experience at all levels of life and reality, including all physical health, vitality and healing—The Subconscious Mind as an aspect of The Source, The Prime Creator, The First Cause, Universal Mind, God. We do not need to tell the Subconscious Mind how to achieve these physical states, in fact it is detrimental to do so. Universal Mind, through our individual Subconscious Mind made every single one of us in the perfect Spiritual image of our Creator, who knows only absolute perfection. Each and every one of us was created to be perfect in every way, after our Creator, and all anyone needs to do in order to realise perfect health, is to recognise and thereby realise that perfection, thus impressing only the picture of perfection on our Subconscious Mind. Thus, by immutable Mind Principle only perfection can manifest into our experiential physical reality. The more we can realise the perfection of God, and the truth that we are made in the perfect image of God, with perfect Faith in this truth, and therefore of our God-given powers, the more we can realise perfect health and anything at all we could possibly wish for, need or desire.

Chapter 97
The Principles of Healing

The first Principle of healing then is to express our perfection in the image of God through the infinite powers of our own individual Subconscious Mind, thus manifesting the same absolute perfection in every aspect of our Being including our physical body as ongoing perfect health, regardless of our state of health before this great realisation.

If we were to focus on a diseased aspect of our body, even in the context of wishing it to be healed, we will attract more disease. We must therefore always focus on total perfection of which our Subconscious Mind has a perfect model, and we will then express accordingly. It is absolutely crucial therefore never to acknowledge any form of imperfection, including disease in our physical body.

Here is an example of an effective basic healing session.

First, locate yourself in a place where you can relax completely without being disturbed. It is better to sit upright in a firm chair, but lying on a bed or in a comfortable chair is fine providing you can resist the urge of falling asleep.

Relax, clear your Mind of all thoughts not associated you're your healing, and then imagine with complete concentration and focus that your entire body is glowing with radiant health in every possible way, knowing this to be true beyond doubt.

Use all of your senses with the power of your imagination to visualize, feel and enjoy this total, complete and absolute feeling of glowing, radiant health. Feel how joyful it is to experience such perfect health. It is important, not even for a single moment to focus on the presence of any sort of ailment. Focus only on the absolute feeling and knowing of health throughout your entire body, Mind and Spirit to the exclusion of all other thoughts and feelings. Continue with this exercise for at least ten minutes, deeply enjoying the feelings of radiant health throughout your entire body, and feeling all of the joyful emotions associated with those feelings. Finally, before concluding, always convey your extreme gratitude for your perfect state of health by giving sincere thanks.

As with manifestation, your imagination must always be in the present tense. Any thought of your ailment, however vague, will have an unwanted influence on your Subconscious Mind towards the presence of the ailment and against your healing.

Continue this exercise at least twice each day for at least ten minutes until you are fully healed. As with manifestation exercises generally, just before sleep at night, just before arising in the morning, and just after a daytime nap are all excellent times for this healing process. The more frequently you perform your healing exercises, the sooner you will be fully healed. It is most important however not to become despondent or to focus on any ailment wondering if it is "improving" or whether you are "healed yet"—only think about, know and give joyous thanks for your perfect Divine health in the knowledge that it is already true, and all you have to do is realise it which you surely will.

One reason why people who are not aware of true healing cannot be healed is because they believe in their own Mind that only doctors, surgeons and other members of the medical profession can "cure" an illness, or they may believe that their religious faith will see them through. These very factors will ensure that they continue to experience the same underlying disease, which, in the case of serious disease can eventually result in physical death.

It is sensible to visit a doctor with any ailment, especially if it is potentially life-threatening, and to respect their words and actions, but it is extremely important to know beyond any doubt that the true origin of healing is within the infinite powers of Mind, and to proceed accordingly. Even if you are prescribed a course of medicine, exercises or even a surgical procedure, view these as very much secondary, while always knowing that true, effective and lasting healing is of the Mind.

During your normal daily activities, ensure that you never focus on your ailment, or discuss it with others, or even allow thoughts of your ailment to enter your Mind. Always focus on and know perfect, radiant, health and that will be your reality.

Always remember—we are made in the true image of God, who imaged each and every one of us in the same perfection—all we have to do is to realise this powerful truth, remembering also that there is ultimately only one healing Principle—Mind.

Chapter 98
The Practice of Healing

Now, let us look at a more formal step by step healing process.

Healing Step 1:

Commence by going to your usual place where you will not be disturbed. Sitting upright in a hard chair with your hands placed face down on your thighs is ideal, but you can also lie flat on a bed or supported in a comfortable chair providing you will not drift off to sleep. If using a bed it is best to not use your own bed if possible

Now proceed to do the deep physical relaxation exercises as detailed in chapter 72 of this book. Taking a warm bath prior to commencing your session can also be very beneficial for achieving deeper relaxation. Your objective is for your body to be as deeply relaxed, balanced and free of stress as possible from the very outset, and to maintain this deeply relaxed state throughout the healing session, again without falling asleep.

Healing Step 2:

Breathe in deeply through your nose to a slow count of five, imagining at the same time, with as much realism as possible, that the air you inhale is a radiant white. Note that it is important to breath in deeply using your entire diaphragm, not only your upper chest area. You can accomplish this by using the entire area from your lower stomach to your upper chest.

As you progressively inhale, feel the positive deeply relaxing Energy of this radiant white light enter your body, and as you continue to breath in it gradually spreads down through your body from your neck to your toes and also up to the crown of your head until you are filled with this radiant while Light.

Hold the breath for a slow count of five while feeling and enjoying the radiant white light, circulating around and infusing your entire body, and then slowly exhale through your mouth to a further slow count of five. As you exhale, imagine that your breath is now a dark grey color, and all negativity and tension is expelled through your mouth, never to return.

Continue to relax for a further slow count of five, and repeat the process of inhaling the radiant white light, before exhaling and expelling again the dark grey light knowing that all tension and negativity leaves your body as you do so.

Repeat each breathing cycle for at least five times, continuing until you are feeling relaxed, refreshed and positive.

The next stage in deep physical relaxation involves progressive active deep physical relaxation, starting at your feet and finishing at the crown of your head.

To proceed with this phase of the exercises, while still retaining your relaxed feelings after the initial breathing exercises, imagine, as vividly as possible, a large sphere of radiant white light positioned just beneath your feet. Using as much imagination as you can summon, make this sphere of white light as radiant as you possibly can—even brighter than the Sun on a clear summer's day.

Now imagine, with complete realism, this sphere of radiant white sphere of light moving gradually upward, bathing your feet. Feel the glowing warmth of this energizing radiant white light around your feet, toes and ankles. Feel all remaining tension draining quickly away from your feet. Maintain this visualisation as vividly as possible until all tension completely dissipates from your feet.

Next, imagine the sphere of radiant white light moving slowly up your legs to your calves. Feel this area bathed in this light until both of your calves are completely relaxed.

Now imagine the sphere of radiant white sphere of light moving still further up your legs until it reaches your thighs. The radiant white light can easily expand to fully encompass any area of your body at will. Allow both of your thighs to relax completely bathed in the radiance of the glowing sphere of light.

Repeat this process as the radiant white sphere of light travels further up your body, as it easily expands as necessary, reaching your hips and buttocks, followed by your stomach and lower back, your chest and upper back, arms and shoulders. Your arms should remain totally straight by your sides, allowing the sphere of light to encompass the entire trunk of your body as it progressively makes its way up your body, leaving each area blissfully relaxed.

The sphere radiant white light now reaches your neck. Allow it to bathe your neck for as long as necessary to release all tension.

Finally, sphere of radiant white light reaches your head. Allow it to remain around your head area while all tension completely dissipates from your face and head muscles, leaving them completely relaxed. Finally, imagine the radiant white sphere of light traveling to the top of your head, remaining there while you bask in the wonderful feeling of deep physical relaxation.

Healing Step 3:

Now imagine the sphere of glowing, radiant white light travelling slowly down through your body and out through your feet, leaving you feeling even more relaxed, deeply enjoying a level of relaxation that you have never experiences before, but will wish to, and can achieve again in the future.

Healing Stage 4:

We will now continue with more breathing exercises, but instead of inhaling only through your nose, imagine as realistically as possible that you are also breathing in Energy from the Universe through your entire body.

Imagine that with every single breath, Universal Energy is entering your body through the pores of your skin. This sensation varies from person to person, some feeling the Energy as glowing warmth, others feeling it as a tingling sensation, and others may well feel the pores are actually "breathing" (which they actually are).

Inhale Universal Energy throughout your entire body for a slow count of five, hold your breath for a further slow count of five, and then slowly breathe out for a further slow count of five.

Healing Stage 5:

Know beyond any doubt that this is a Divine, pure, healing Energy directly from The Source of all creation, Energy which constantly flows through and around and sustains you. Should a thought of an ailment enter your Mind, dismiss it immediately and move your full attention back to the healing process.

Now imagine, visualise and know, beyond any possible doubt that your entire body and Being is enjoying only maximum, radiant health throughout, from the tip of your toes to the very top of your head. Feel this absolute, glowing Divine health in every limb, organ and cell of your body, and feeling grateful.

To complete the healing exercise, maintain your state of relaxation, together with your feeling of vibrant health for at least five minutes, after which you can take a few deep breaths, bring yourself back to gradual conscious awareness of your surroundings, and give sincere thanks, to The Universe, The Source, God, knowing, beyond all doubt that you are experiencing only the most perfect glowing, radiant health.

Above all know, beyond any doubt that you are an inseparable, infinite and immortal aspect of God, in Whose image you are truly made, and all you need to do is to realise and express that perfection through you. That perfection, in which you are imaged by God will then express itself in your body as perfect health in every aspect of your Being.

Again, it is extremely important to offer your most grateful thanks for the excellent health you are enjoying before proceeding with your normal routine.

When proceeding with your daily affairs, never dwell on your ailment or on the progress of your healing sessions. Only think in terms of, and know absolute health, feeling the deepest gratitude for it. It is an excellent idea to repeat, as often as possible, "thank you for my perfect health".

If you find yourself thinking about your ailment in any way, even for a moment, immediately repeat an affirmation, such as "I feel so grateful for the complete, radiant health I enjoy throughout my being". Never allow an "ill" thought to enter your Mind under any circumstances whatsoever, and never talk about any ailments with others.

Continue your healing sessions at least twice each day until you are fully healed. Just before sleep at night is an excellent time to do your healing exercises, or at least think in terms of complete health, because at this time we are closest to our Subconscious Mind Which ensures a perfect state of health.

The process for the remote healing of others is very similar to the process of self-healing. By entering into a fully relaxed state you are connecting with the Subconscious Mind of the person to be healed, because, as we know, we are ultimately all One, and "separation" simply does not exist. The objective is to synchronise your Subconscious Mind with the Subconscious Mind of the person being healed, to bring about the same healing as if you were healing yourself, which you really are.

To assist the visualisation process, if you have a photograph of the person you are healing, take as much time as necessary before commencing the healing session to concentrate on the photograph, remembering every detail of the person.

It should be mentioned that it is highly advisable to obtain the permission of the person to be healed. Although your intentions may be entirely honourable, if the person does not wish to be healed for some reason, you will be acting against the freewill of that person, thereby affecting their own path, which could have consequences upon yourself.

Proceed with the remote healing session exactly as above, but this time imagine, visualise and know, beyond any doubt, that this time it is the person being healed that is in perfect health. You can imagine also, inhale Universal Energy as described in the self-healing process, and then, as realistically as possible, imagine that the Energy stored within your body is transmitted to the person from your own heart chakra as a white beam of radiant, healing light This helps to reinforce the connection with the other person and to synchronise the process through your respective Subconscious Minds.

Continue the healing process exactly as you would for healing yourself except that all of your visualisations should be intensively focused with as much concentration as possible on the person being healed rather than yourself. Continue to imagine and visualize with as much feeling and emotion as possible while sending healing Energy from your heart chakra, the perfect health of the person being healed. As always, this must be in the present tense as an absolute reality now – knowing that the other person is in the most perfect health.

Conclude your remote healing session in the same way as a self-healing session. Feel the deepest and most sincere gratitude for the perfect health of the other person, and also be sure to include gratitude for your own perfect health as well.

As you go about your daily affairs, do not think about the other person in as being "ill". If the other person comes to Mind during your normal activities, always think of and imagine them in terms of nothing less than enjoying perfect health, and giving thanks for that perfect health.

In addition to healing yourself and others, you can also heal animals and even the environment using these methods. The process is exactly the same as for remote healing and should be performed in exactly the same way. Visualize the creature being healed, the rainforest or any other aspect of the environment as enjoying complete, vibrant, radiant health. Sending healing Energy to the entire planet and all mankind in this way is similar to the Twin Hearts meditation as previously discussed. Always remember that while this should never be a prime motivation, everything you send out to others or to anything in the Universe will be returned to you in kind.

Finally, always keep in Mind that your absolute objective with any healing exercise and to maintain a perfect body and perfect health is to fully realise the same perfection in which you were imaged by God after the perfection of God, in the image of God, and that a perfect body and perfect health in every way, physically and mentally, is your natural state of Being.

Chapter 99
Living Your Own Reality

We have already discussed many powerful ways of assuming full control over every aspect of our life and destiny—how to achieve deep physical relaxation, concentration, meditation, manifesting, healing and much more.

Living and creating your own reality, as well as remaining in full control of your own destiny, means so much more than simply practicing these abilities when the need arises. It should, as was always intended, be a way of life. The integration of these practices into your life and ongoing Spiritual path should become a completely natural and free-flowing aspect of your very Being.

Remember that you are a true Son or Daughter of The Source, The First Cause, and are therefore immortal and made in the true Spiritual image of God. We are all co-creators in our own Universe, the Microcosm, just as God is the Prime Creator of, and in, the entire Universe, the Macrocosm in all spheres of life. All ongoing actions and thoughts have a profound effect on our reality and the reality of everyone and everything around us.

By being Mindful of, and in full control over your thoughts at all times, and by focusing on your needs, your life will be one of complete peace and harmony with all needs fulfilled from the infinite abundance of the Universe. The pressures and trials of the material world will no longer intrude when you know, beyond doubt, that you have complete control over your own reality and destiny and nothing can ever affect or harm you.

Although others might seek to affect or intrude upon our reality from time to time, either deliberately or unknowingly, only we and we alone can ultimately create and manage our own individual experience, thus ensuring that external influences cannot and will not affect our life, harmony and destiny. Living our own reality includes living consciously in every moment of every day.

As a very basic illustration of how people create their own realities, let us take a look at two people visiting a major city for the very first time. The first person has no real control over his own life and tends to think in a cynical, negative and unfocused way. The second person has full control over his reality and always sees the positive in everything and everyone.

When arriving at the city for the first time, the first person immediately sees only a noisy, grimy, depressing place, with crowded streets, overpriced shops and miserable, unfriendly looking strangers. The second person arriving in the very same city for the first time immediately sees many wonderful places of interest, a vibrant atmosphere, lots of inviting places to shop for bargains and all manner of delightful goods to purchase—a place where everyone is always happy, smiling and friendly.

The first person has a miserable time during their visit to this city, while the second person has a wonderful time. This city is exactly the same place in both cases, but the first person has created a completely negative reality, and the second person has created a positive reality. In this particular example, neither person has tangibly altered the physical reality of the city itself, but each has perceived it very differently. These perceptions, of course, have a profound impact on their respective realities.

When these people interact with the residents and places within this city, their individual realities will affect others in the same way. If many people were to visit exactly the same city, these people would begin to affect the reality of the entire city by propagating either positive or negative vibrations of Energy, which in turn have their effect on the plane of the human Mind of the people in that particular location. This is a simple example of how people can profoundly affect their own immediate reality and that of everyone around them.

As previously discussed, this reality can be extended to encompass the entire planet Earth. If everyone on Earth were to cease focusing on, and observing everything created by humans on the planet, then everything on Earth previously created by the Mind of humans would simply disappear as a physical reality. This is because the collective human Mind would no longer influence the Energy that sustains physical forms, the Energy simply dissipating back into its native form as it was before the influence of humans on Earth.

People who are fully aware of the ways of the Universe can make use of these immense powers of the Mind, including imagination, visualisation and emotions with concentration and intent and gratitude to influence any aspect of their own reality. Of course most people do think positively from time to time in moments of optimism, but any unstructured negative thoughts will always cancel out positive thoughts, resulting in an overall negative bias if negative thoughts are allowed to predominate.

By being totally conscious of, and living in every moment, we an ensure every moment makes a real difference, so that your experience is overwhelmingly positive and creative. You will not only be the master of your own reality but will also become immune to the negative Energy influences of other people. If everyone were to live in conscious, full positive control over their own Mind and individual realities, always living for their own true destiny, while first being of service to others, the world would indeed be the “Kingdom of Heaven on Earth”.

Living your own reality should be a lifelong commitment. The more you can control and master your own inner world, the more you will positively affect and control your outer world. Always see everything around you in the most positive light, with peace, harmony, happiness, and Unconditional Love.

Chapter 100
Our Ultimate Destiny

We are all, without exception, Immortal Spirits made in the true Spiritual image of God, to Whom it is our ultimate destiny to return, in a state of perfection. This is the true, absolute and ultimate meaning of life. When the end of the path is reached, each and every person will have the opportunity to relinquish individuality and reunite with The Source, The All, God, or to retain individuality and continue as a "God person", assisting those aspects of God that are further out, on their own path.

Those who choose to reunite with God will experience an expansion of Consciousness encompassing The All, and finally All in the Universe will become known. It should be mentioned at this stage that as we are already integral aspects of God, when speaking of "Unity with God", we really do mean Unity with The Source, The Prime Creator, The All, the very highest, and most incomprehensible aspect of God, which some refer to as the "Godhead". Unity with God is not however the end of existence, nor is it the end of Consciousness awareness. It is simply the end of the path as an individuated expression of God, while continuing with full conscious awareness of All.

As we ascend ever further along the path, abilities are acquired beyond the wildest dreams of humans at the outer levels of the Universe. During the great ascent on the path to perfection, people are willingly of service to others, before serving themselves, always assisting those further out on the path to perfection, a process that continues at every level of the Universe from the very highest to the very lowest, or more specifically the very inner to the very outer levels, as even now Beings of the inner worlds are assisting humanity on Earth and countless other planets in the outermost reaches of the Universe as a whole, that most know of as the physical Universe.

Everyone living now, who has ever lived, and will ever live, has always existed as an immortal aspect and expression of The Source, The First Cause, of God. When we become an individuated Being for the first time, our Higher Self descends from the Logos, and begins the cycle of incarnations into the physical Universe, on Earth or another planet, to gain sufficient experience, wisdom and qualities to move inwards as a more complete Spiritual Being, with infinitely more experiences ahead.

The physical Universe can be metaphorically likened to first year of kindergarten, while the innermost spheres or life can be metaphorically likened to postgraduate University. No person can ever be born as a child into the physical world and then attend and graduate from University on the same day, and then move on to higher degrees. During the first few years of physical life, a child survives in the physical world by learning the basic requirements for living in a world of physical matter, eventually progressing through all levels of education within the inner levels of the Universe or intelligent, vibrating Energy, until finally graduating from University as a perfected Being.

While many people might believe they enjoy the physical world with all of its materialism and stimulation of the five physical senses, such people at this stage on their path, really have no concept of the true glories, peace, Light, bliss and harmony that await within. Those who are aware of and understand the nature of these inner realities will never knowingly delay their progress simply to gratify the physical senses with ephemeral, material things which are no more than an illusion. Those who choose to turn their back on these realities, thereby delaying their own progress, will trail behind on the sacred path, while their fellow humans are attaining, discovering, and experiencing spheres of glory, splendour and Love beyond the comprehension of those remaining behind.

Chapter 101
Know Thyself

A fundamental requirement for achieving permanent, genuine and valuable progress is to "know yourself". This truth has been taught by the sages of many ancient sources of knowledge throughout the world for thousands of years. Many people simply do not know themselves, even though they may believe they do, merely existing through life without any sense of purpose, reacting to circumstances in an often incoherent and unstructured way, not even realizing why they react as they do. Most people do not even think about these things or the consequences of the way in which they choose to live, simply "existing" from minute to minute, day to day and year to year, in accordance with the "rules" and expectations of family, society, "workplaces" and others, always endeavouring to conform, while never experiencing the freedom of thinking and acting for themselves. Knowing ourselves is an extremely important aspect of personal evolution, not only for true and enduring progress on the Divine path, but also for realising a truly harmonious and peaceful life on Earth.

Knowing yourself can be a very difficult task requiring much discipline, honesty and self-examination. This process can sometimes be upsetting, as you may discover and with the need to face aspects of yourself that you simply do not like. Nevertheless, these are often the very same aspects that can cause the most problems in preventing ultimate happiness.

To know yourself is really only the start. It is extremely important to identify and recognize those aspects of self that are holding you back and to eradicate or transmute those negative aspects of self. This process requires much commitment and perseverance, but the rewards are great, both in life and ongoing evolution. Until our Higher Self has achieved a full spectrum of necessary experience, the cycle of reincarnation into the physical world of matter continues until all lessons have finally been learned, fully integrated and applied, at which point the Higher Self is free of the restrictions and illusions of the physical Universe and Astral planes, and can move on to greater things within the inner Universe of Energy, Spirit and life.

With knowing ourselves comes a further and very important responsibility—never judging others. People who judge others do so by projecting self-judgments toward others based upon their own understanding, ideas and standards, but in so doing judge themselves in accordance with Universal Principles.

The process of ennoblement along the path to perfection on the glorious return to The Source, The First Cause, God, is so crucial for ongoing progression that there have been numerous references made to it over the ages, and indeed forms the basis of many cultures and traditions where it is taught to the people in a number of ways, often including drama, music and dance, as in the cause of the Hindu tradition for example.

The ancient philosophy of "alchemy" for is not merely the transmutation of base metals into gold as is commonly supposed, but is a metaphor for the transmutation of base human imperfections into the gold of perfection, and to that extent everyone, without exception is their own alchemist.

Our ultimate reality is to achieve the opportunity of unity with The Source, The First Cause, God, our Prime Creator from Whence we came in the beginning, and the true meaning of life is to always strive towards the attainment of the ultimate state of perfection necessary to facilitate this most Sacred destiny.

Chapter 102
Subjugating the Ego

One of the biggest challenges facing the evolution of any person is overcoming the relentless demands of the individual Ego. It is simply not possible to achieve enduring and genuine progress and progress to the inner realms of Spirit until the Ego has been brought under complete control.

It is the Ego that constantly demands to be satisfied and satiated, always comparing itself with others. The Ego is responsible for many negative human traits and behaviours, including, but not limited to judgment of others, inflexibility, manipulative behaviour, superior attitudes, arrogance, aloofness, anxiety, fear, hopelessness, mood swings, competitiveness, vanity, addictions, and the need for praise and approval from others. It is the Ego that causes people to take things too seriously or too personally, to feel hurried and driven to do things, feel resentful and guilty, feel the need to have power over others, to cling to the past, and or fail to live in the present moment. All these are seriously negative human traits and ones that can easily make a person's life miserable, as well as causing people to fail to attain their full potential.

The Ego causes an illusory focus on those aspects of the physical world that are not at all important for peace, harmony and happiness and ongoing progression and fulfilment of the reason for being on Earth. The Ego must therefore be considered, from this perspective, to be an unwelcome adversary, focusing on the needs and demands of individual self rather than absolute reality, the sacred path and true meaning of life, as well as the needs of others.

Many people are very quick to blame others or the world generally for their "issues", or blaming their "lot" on such superstitious notions as "luck", "chance" or "fortune". Such people find that it is often much easier to blame everyone and everything else for their situation, rather than take responsibility for their own thoughts and actions. When something adverse happens, the immediate reaction is usually focused on looking for “scapegoats” rather than looking inward for the real cause of the experience. Some people are so much under the control of their own Ego, or even enjoy exerting the influence of their own Ego, that they absolutely convinced that they are always right and accordingly everyone else must always be wrong. The Ego constantly strives to create and perpetuate the belief that the person is not responsible for their own actions.

The Ego constantly strives to be always right in everything, always superior over others, never wrong about anything and never inferior to anyone, always seeking self-importance and power and often control over others, at any cost, regardless of who is hurt.

The Ego is not something that can be destroyed or “transcended” because it is a vital aspect of who we are. The ultimate objective therefore is not to attempt to destroy the Ego, but rather to subjugate the Ego, thereby bringing it under complete control in order to fulfil its real purpose.

The Ego revels in making comparisons, particularly with other people. Comparisons are usually fine for the purposes of making a considered choice, but not when they are allowed to include judgments about other people and everything else. The Ego will for example urge you to take up a sport, hobby or other skill simply as a means of feeling superior to others.

The Ego does, therefore, need to justifiably make comparisons as a function of living in the material world. For example, when walking around a supermarket, comparisons need to be made between the quality and prices of items to be purchased. This sort of comparison serves a purpose and is applied for positive reasons. In this example the reason would not be positive if the shopper was making comparisons simply because they knew it would be better than the equivalent item owned by a family member, friend, or very often a neighbour who the Ego of the person wanted to impress.

The Ego often exerts a particularly strong influence in forming personal relationships. Everyone should be attracted to a partner for genuine qualities and virtues and in particular because they are well-suited to each other. Many people will however be attracted to a partner for much more superficial and Egotistical reasons, in order to satisfy the demands of their own Ego. For example, they may perceive a potential partner to appear "glamorous", "attractive" or "wealthy", and otherwise more "desirable" in the eyes of others. In these cases, the Ego is in full control over something fundamentally important. This is a major reason, of course, why so many marriages fail.

The Ego has delusions of grandeur and likes nothing more than to be noticed, flattered and admired, as well as to experience power and control over others. In reality, nothing ever makes anyone "better" or "superior" to anyone else. Every single person, without exception, irrespective of how they are perceived, is a completely equal aspect of God, made in the true Spiritual image of God. If we judge others, we equally judge ourselves. Acceptance is a most important aspect of life.

The other side of the Ego is when it feels inferior in comparison to others. People might perceive themselves as useless, unworthy, unwanted, unworthy of power and the need to be controlled, and many other such negative perceptions. There really is no difference at all between this side of the Ego and the one suffering from delusions of grandeur. They are all positive and negative extremes of the same thing and equally unbalanced. Ultimately, to subjugate the Ego is to know beyond any doubt whatsoever that everyone is equal in every possible respect, and to live life, and respect others accordingly. God is Perfection, and everyone without exception is an inseparable expression and equal aspect of that same perfection.

The Ego will revel in exerting its influence over the lives of other people. For example, many people like to feel sorry for themselves. Such people will often feel everything is "hopeless", that they feel burdened with demands and responsibilities they believe they cannot handle. They feel unappreciated, misunderstood, badly treated and the victim of "bad luck".

Accepting and taking full responsibility for all such situations is empowering, and those who can achieve this will have considerably more control over every aspect of their lives.

The Ego also revels in always feeling busy. The more a person dwells on this illusion of "busyness", the busier they will believe they really are—a situation that can quickly escalate into a full busyness martyr syndrome. Worse still, if the Ego believes a person is not busy enough, it will create work in order to justify the illusion of busyness, often repeating the same chores and tasks over and over again.

The Ego also often revels in disaster—particularly when it happens to people who are not liked. People often enjoy the misfortunes of others who they feel jealous of for some reason. This is another extremely negative and insidious attribute of the Ego—needing to create an illusion of superiority over others. Of course, this need is often the result of an underlying feeling of inferiority.

Notwithstanding all of its insidious influences, the Ego is a vital aspect of our Being, and one without which we would not exist at all. But until such time as the Ego is subjugated, and its influence fully transcended, true and enduring progress, peace, happiness and harmony cannot be achieved or maintained.

Chapter 103
The Practice of Subjugating the Ego

In order to transcend the negative influences of the Ego, it is necessary to fully recognize the insidious effects it can exert in your life and over the lives of others. As discussed in the previous chapter however, the Ego is an aspect of who we Are, and so we cannot leave the Ego behind or destroy it in any way. Subjugating the Ego therefore involves neutralising all those negative aspects of the Ego that hold us back both in physical life and on our Spiritual path.

Commence the practice of subjugating the Ego by writing down in a suitable notebook a list of all of those things in your life that causes you feel better or superior to others in some way. Do not hurry this exercise, and you must be completely honest with yourself at all times, keeping in mind that the Ego itself will resent your efforts, and wish to retain complete control over every aspect of your life. Think and meditate deeply, ensuring that absolutely nothing is left off your list. There is absolutely nothing at all to be gained by being less than totally honest with yourself during these exercises. It might be better to compose your list over the course of a few days or even weeks in order to ensure nothing is overlooked. It is a very good idea to carry your notebook with you, and whenever you feel superior or better than others in any way whatsoever, immediately write it down before you forget it.

Do not convince or flatter yourself that you do not feel superior in any way, or worse, believe that you that you really are superior—this is the work of the Ego. Continue this process until you are absolutely sure that you have your complete and definitive list, after which you can proceed to the next step.

Sit down quietly and relax in a place where you know you will not be disturbed. Look at the first item on your list and deeply consider, with as much sincerity and emotion as possible, just how absolutely ridiculous it is to feel superior about such a trivial thing. Understand exactly why you believe in your own Mind you feel superior in this particular area and know the reality and the truth that you really are not superior at all, and that it is only your Ego that makes you feel that way.

If, for example, you believe yourself to be a superior cook to someone else, it may well be that this other person may not consider cooking as something important, and therefore does not place the same emphasis upon cooking as you do. You should then be able to see your perceived superiority for the illusion it is. Continue down your list thoroughly and honestly, analyzing and reconciling every single area where you believe yourself to be superior to others. Your Ego will protest most emphatically at this scrutiny. Simply disregard it and continue with this important task. Your Ego will sooner or later have to accept it, because ultimately you have complete control it.

Each area where you feel superior will be different and be caused by different reasons from your past, present, or perceived future. It might have an emotional basis, it might be based on a deeply held desire, or it might be based on jealousy, it might be based upon childhood programming by parents, relatives or others, or for any number of other reasons.

Not until you have completely reconciled an item on your list can you move on to the next item. Until you know beyond any doubt whatsoever that you can proceed without ever feeling superior in that particular area again, do not progress to the next item. You might find some items to be relatively easy to reconcile and others much more difficult, but the more difficult the more of an achievement and worthwhile it is.

It should be noted, however, that this is very much an ongoing process. If you ever find yourself feeling superior about anything at all, immediately write it down and reconcile it at the very first opportunity. The Ego will not be at all happy at being deprived of its perceived superiorities and might constantly strive to replace them with even more. Be constantly vigilant therefore, and over time, the Ego will get the message and reach the realization that creating any more superiorities in your life is futile.

The next stage in subjugating the Ego is to make use of your notebook in order to list all of the situations in the past or present that cause you to "feel sorry for yourself". Note all of the exact circumstances, including whether each feeling is an isolated or ongoing situation.

These feelings might include for example feeling unfairly judged by people, feeling wrongly treated, feeling misunderstood, hopeless, desperate, overcome with burdens, unappreciated, etc. Also make detailed notes of who, if anyone, has made you feel angry and why, and anything and everything else that you can possibly think of associated with causing you to feel like a martyr.

Again, as before, immediately add to your list any new instances where you find yourself feeling sorry for yourself. Also add to your list any such feelings that you might recall from the past. All "sorry feelings" from the past or present should be listed without any exceptions.

For the next stage of this process, as with the previous list of feeling superior, put aside at least ten minutes each day where you can completely relax without being disturbed and reconcile your feeling sorry for yourself list. As before, analyze each situation with complete honesty, asking yourself why you felt sorry for yourself as you did. Ask yourself if you enjoy feeling sorry for yourself. Does it make you feel superior in any way? Do you feel people are more likely to take pity on you? Does it make you feel better or more able to handle the situation? Do you feel you will receive some sort benefit or reward for feeling sorry for yourself? Do you believe feeling sorry for yourself and making yourself suffer is noble in some way? Is feeling sorry for yourself an excuse for avoiding the responsibilities in your life?

For the next stage in this process, write a further list of how you would feel if you did not feel sorry for yourself. Think very deeply about all of the positive effects of shedding these insidiously negative feelings. Consider all of the happiness you can bring into your life by focusing all of your Energy and emotions in a positive way that benefits both yourself and others. Make up your Mind to never feel sorry for yourself again.

If you do catch yourself feeling sorry for yourself, immediately transmute those feelings into positive, happy feelings. Think of someone you love for example, and how wonderful it would be to help someone in some way if you have the opportunity, or actually do help someone or extend some tangible display of kindness.

Think deeply about all those people in the world who really are worse off than yourself, and know that feeling sorry for yourself is fundamentally inappropriate by comparison. However adverse you might feel your own situation to be, you can be sure that there are countless people feeling much worse, and perhaps with good reason. Feel deeply appreciative for your own life as it is right Now. Be constantly on your guard for these feeling sorry feelings that might creep up on you and catch you unawares. Remaining fully aware of your feelings at all times is extremely important.

The next stage in the process of transcending the Ego is to deal with the issue of responsibility. The Ego revels in striving to avoid responsibility or passing responsibility onto others, but must never be allowed to do so. For this exercise, take your journal and think back as far as you possibly can, writing down all of those times when you blamed others for your own actions.

Consider your daily life with complete honesty, and write down all of those areas where you consistently seek to avoid or deny all responsibility. In compiling this list, do not let your Ego convince you it is acceptable not to take responsibility. As you know, we all create and are therefore responsible for our own realities and therefore directly responsible for our own actions.

Next, write a further list of all of those situations where you actually did accept responsibility for your own actions. Write down how positive and empowered you felt at the time. Write down all of the positive benefits directly arising from taking full responsibility for your own actions in each one of those situations. Write down the reasons why you believe that you actually took responsibility in those particular cases. What was your motivation? Why were you prepared to accept responsibility for those particular situations? Were you motivated by the desire to succeed or expected to receive some tangible benefit? Were you motivated by the fear of something negative occurring in your life if you did not accept responsibility? Where you motivated by a superstition? Were you seeking to impress someone else? In all of these cases, ask yourself exactly how you succeeded in accepting responsibility, in particular looking for a common factor.

Finally, over the next few days, resolve to accept the fullest possible responsibility for absolutely everything in your life without exception, including every action, and every thought, a thought still being an action. Do not shy away from any situation where decisions need to be made and positive actions need to be taken. Do not hesitate even for a moment. The very moment a situation arises requiring responsibility, accept that responsibility unhesitatingly, taking all appropriate actions to reconcile it. Make use of your notebook to write down how you felt when you accepted such responsibility.

Enjoy your new freedom, and resolve never to avoid responsibility for your own actions or thoughts again.

The next aspect of the Ego which needs to be addressed is being busy. As before, write down in your journal all of those areas of your life where you have felt that you are always too busy, never have enough time, or feel rushed in some way. When your list is complete, set aside at least ten minutes each day to review and reconcile your "always too busy" list.

Why exactly do you always feel so busy? Is it because you are genuinely busy? Is it perhaps due to a lack of organization in your daily life? Or is it because you feel the need to be busy even though you are not really busy? Perhaps you feel you should be busy in order to impress your boss, spouse, or partner? Perhaps when you are not working, you feel guilty? Why does your life and space feel cluttered? Is it actually cluttered, or do you feel enclosed in some way?

All of these questions need to be considered in depth, with total and complete honesty, taking a very detailed, introspective and sincere look at all relevant aspects of your life, thereby determining the reality and origin of your feelings.

Next, ask yourself how you can simplify your life and become more efficient. If you are seeking to impress someone or are feeling guilty, is it the Ego causing these feelings? Ask yourself honestly exactly why you endeavour to impress people. Is it for some perceived gain or to avoid feeling guilty? Are the people you want to impress actually noticing and responding to you? Are they ever likely to respond to you?

Next, review your daily activities in as much depth and detail as possible. Ask yourself how you can make better use of your time and become more efficient. What could you stop doing altogether that is unnecessary, or perhaps ask someone else to do for you if appropriate? If you are making work for yourself out a sense of guilt, resolve to stop making more work for yourself. This does not imply doing the absolute minimum or not working to the best of your capacity. It means that you should stop overdoing these things for all the wrong reasons.

Finally, and most importantly for this particular aspect of the Ego, review your circumstances and decide exactly where your priorities should really be. Much of the day for many people is taken up in the pursuit of materialism in all of its multiple aspects, and in conforming to the expectations of family, friends and society, all of which, as we now know, is detrimental to true progress, peace and harmony. Being a slave to materialism in order to maintain the illusion of material wealth or to impress others will inevitably lead to misery.

Remind yourself of the true purposes of this life. Everyone is here to learn, to equilibrate karma and evolve as an individual Spiritual being currently in a physical human form, not to conform to the expectations of others.

Of course, everyone needs sufficient money, food and basic possessions in order to provide for their own needs and needs of family, but beyond that, consider just how superfluous material possessions really are and how very little they add in the context of a productive life and genuine progress. Consider how you can manage your life to exclude unnecessary possessions and resolve to manage your life accordingly. The Ego will protest and might well cause you to feel concerned about what others are thinking of you, but you must ignore the protests of the Ego completely, and continue on regardless and relentlessly with your own progress.

The final task in transcending the Ego is to take a very close look at those areas of your life or your past where you have enjoyed disaster in some way, whether it has happened to you or to others. Also, take an honest look at your fantasies for self-destruction or the destruction of others. Put aside at least ten minutes each day to consider and write down in your notebook all potential disasters, melodramas or misfortunes your Mind has flirted with over the years, involving yourself or others.

Having written down all such situations, relax as completely as possible in a place where you will not be disturbed, and visualize yourself in each of these situations one at a time. Do not progress to the next situation until you have fully dealt with the current one. Become completely involved with the scenario, making use of all of your senses and imagination as realistically as possible.

Next, consider your true feelings about the situation. Why do you feel as you do? What real benefits could result from this situation? If it involves others, why would you wish to see them in that same situation? While considering these factors, you must always be totally honest with yourself. If the situation generates fear or suffering, ask yourself why your Ego wishes to subject yourself or someone else to such an experience. What does your Ego really have to gain from this?

Know that negative or destructive thoughts are equally negative or destructive causes, resulting in the correspondingly negative or destructive effects for the originator of those thoughts, either in this life or a future life of the Higher Self. There is quite simply no escape from the immutable Universal principle of Cause and Effect of which karma is an integral aspect. If you wish something negative on others, it will return to you. As you think or do unto others, so it will be done unto you

If the fantasies of misfortune involve yourself, ask why you would wish to suffer this. Is it perhaps because you wish to be noticed? Is it perhaps a shout for help? Is it because you really do have a self-destruction wish?

Finally, you must reach the level of understanding required in order to dismiss these destructive thoughts and fantasies, knowing them for what they really are, and never allow them back into your Mind again. If the Ego attempts to raise them in your Mind, you must bring the Ego back under your complete control immediately. Maintain only the very purest thoughts of peace, harmony and above all Unconditional Love at all times.

By following these simple exercises for just a few minutes each day, you will have taken a very valuable step in transcending the insidious side of your Ego, which will be of immense value both in your daily life and on your evolution and progress along the path.

Always be vigilant. The Ego does not like to be suppressed and controlled and will do everything possible to re-gain full control. It is important to be Mindful of and recognize the often subtle activities of the Ego and react immediately when it attempts to control you in any way. If you cannot deal with the demands of the Ego at the time, write everything down as soon as you possibly can, and put time aside to process these demands, dealing with them permanently and without delay.

In subjugating the influences of the Ego, we make a considerable step forward both in physical life and Spiritual growth. Always keep in Mind however that the Ego is who we Are, is not separate from us, and cannot therefore be left behind in some way. Our task is to recognise the role of the Ego in our lives and Spiritual progression, and to control the Ego instead of allowing it to control us.

Chapter 104
Equilibrium of the Soul

One of the most fundamental aspects of genuine progress, in addition to realising true peace, harmony and happiness in our lives, is not only to know ourselves, but to achieve full equilibrium of our inner selves, of which our Soul is our most immediate focus. Without such equilibrium, true progress cannot be made, the ongoing destiny of all mankind being immediately dependent upon personal perfection and a state of ennoblement.

Ennoblement of the Soul will result in higher vibrations which will in turn enable the transition to higher, or more correctly inner levels of the Astral worlds after the change known as physical "death". Only when the Soul of each Higher Self incarnation has been fully balanced and cleansed can the journey continue and cycle of reincarnation transcended, within the glories, splendours and magnificence of the inner spheres of life and reality—the Mental planes of the Spirit worlds, existing at even higher levels of vibration.

Ennoblement includes subjugating the Ego as practiced in the previous chapter, as well as complete balance of all personal characteristics.

The process of ennoblement fundamentally involves two main stages—full recognition and acceptance of all imperfections and the transmutation of those imperfections into their polar opposite noble characteristics in accordance with the Universal Principle of polarity. Again, as mentioned previously, this is also a solution for the true meaning of "alchemy".

Every negative characteristic, no matter how "bad", small or seemingly insignificant they may seem, must be recognised, faced and transmuted. Of course, an equally important aspect of knowing yourself is recognizing the positive, good and noble aspects of the Soul.

In order to commence this important process, you will, as with the previous chapter, require a notebook. You may use your existing notebook for subjugating the Ego as part of your record of progression, or you may wish to use a separate one. Two lists need to be made in your journal. One of these will be a list of all of your negative or “bad” attributes, and the other will be a list of all of your “good” or positive attributes.

Commence then by setting aside as much time as possible each day for this task in a place where you will not be disturbed. Relax, and consider very deeply and with considerable honesty and deep introspection all of your own shortcomings, your negative characteristics, and write them all down in a list, each on a separate line in your notebook. You should not only list those negative traits appearing in your life today, but also all those negative traits that have appeared in your life in the past.

Continue this process until you have taken yourself as far back in time as you can remember, back to your early childhood ideally. This process should not be hurried and might well take several weeks to complete thoroughly. Should any negative attribute not already on your list appear during your daily activities, note it down immediately before it leaves your Mind. This is very much an ongoing process and one that should never be disregarded. Ideally, you should be able to include at least one hundred such items in your list of negative attributes.

If your list has not yet reached one hundred or more items, it is very worthwhile to continue until your list reaches at least that number. Some people can list many hundreds of negative attributes in their finest details and variations. Again, never shy away from noting any negative attributes however painful they might seem to you. Every single negative attribute must be noted and faced up to without any exceptions. There is nothing whatsoever to be gained by deceiving yourself.

Should you fail to list any particular negative attribute simply because you cannot face it, that particular negative characteristic is probably the very one causing you the most difficulties, and failing to confront it will restrict your progress considerably until you do confront and deal with it.

Your notebook is your own personal private property and should never be shown to anyone else or left in a position where someone else might find and read it. Keep it safely hidden or locked away when not in use. Some people might have difficulty in determining which attributes can be considered to be negative. If in any doubt, note them down anyway.

There are literally thousands of possible negative characteristics, some of which might include for example anger, thoughtlessness, laziness, irresponsibility, shyness, quick temper, hate, apathy, carelessness, defiance, vengefulness, conceit, inconsistency, thoughtlessness, selfishness, jealousy, boastfulness, melancholy, wastefulness, acquiescence, judgementalism, compulsiveness, voracity, addictions, thinking about or craving sex, irritability, quarrelsomeness, immoderation, destructiveness, disinterest, intransigence, shallowness, disdain, indifference, idleness, dishonesty, fickleness, passion for gossip, discrimination, materialism, argumentativeness, disrespect, obsessiveness, gambling, and much more. These are but a very few examples of possible negative attributes. It is for you to probe deeply into your Mind, past and present, to reveal all negative attributes.

Balance is an extremely important aspect of knowing every aspect of yourself, and therefore a more enjoyable task is to make a list of all of your positive attributes. These should be listed in a separate section of your notebook. Positive and negative lists must be maintained separately, and may be considered to be the dark and light sides or polarities of your Soul. Proceed in exactly the same way with listing your positive attributes as you have already done for your negative attributes, noting absolutely every positive attribute you can possibly think of from your past and present.

Again, there are many thousands of possibilities for your positive attributes, but each and every person will be different. Examples of such positive attributes might include the following: respect, modesty, bravery, enthusiasm, responsibility, kindness, generosity, charitableness, humility, eagerness, diligence, optimism, determination, endurance, moderation, lightness, absence of worry, thoroughness, efficiency, circumspection, cheerfulness, daring, courage, optimism, humbleness, joy, soberness, punctuality, prudence, forgiveness, contentment, tenderness, sympathy, empathy, proficiency, willpower, ardency, compassion, mercy, modesty, seriousness, trustfulness, tranquillity, creativity, lucidity, watchfulness, conservationism, conscientiousness, firmness, endurance, and sobriety.

It is important not to be tempted to exaggerate these attributes. Once again, it cannot be stressed enough that complete honesty is required at all times in your introspection, both positive and negative, if true and enduring balance is to result.

The next and most important task is to deal robustly with all of your negative attributes, the objective being to eliminate or transmute every single negative attribute until only your positive attributes remain. There are several ways in which this most important task may be effectively approached, either separately or in combination. Such approaches may include mindfulness and use of the willpower to recognise and deal with negative traits as they arise. Many however do not yet possess the required levels of mindfulness or willpower to achieve this, so in the next chapter we will look at how to make use of one or our most powerful aspects of our Being, the infinite power of the Subconscious Mind.

Chapter 105
Transmutation of Negative Attributes

As we know, the Subconscious Mind is infinitely powerful. Through our Subconscious Mind we can accomplish anything, subject only to our imagination and faith in our own abilities.

Negative attributes originate from the Subconscious Mind. This is not because the Subconscious Mind is "evil" in any way, or "wishes" negative experiences upon us, because as we know from previous discussions, the Subconscious Mind is sublime, and simply acts upon impressions received from the conscious Mind. All negative traits, attributes and desires originating from the Subconscious Mind, are in fact simply a reflection of what has been impressed since birth by the conscious Mind. The task therefore is to undo, or rather transmute these negative impressions that have been impressed over a lifetime.

In the physical world, the Subconscious Mind requires space and time in order to exert its influence. This is the reason why it can take time to impress desires from a normal waking state. If however the influence time and space are limited or withdrawn, as happens for example just before, during and just after sleep, then the influence of space and time can be minimised or removed, and the Subconscious Mind therefore impressed in a much more direct and powerful way.

There are several effective methods of impressing the Subconscious Mind, examples of which include, but are not limited to affirmations, imagination, visualisation and hypnosis, including self-hypnosis when it is performed upon one's self. Self-hypnosis can be a highly effective but complicated process however, with the need to remember the various stages involved as well as the words, and generally managing the entire process. A related, but less complex method is known as "autosuggestion". The use of autosuggestion involves the repetition of a short phrase stating the desired objectives. The construction of this phrase is extremely important for success and should, as with affirmations, always be unambiguous, and stated in the present tense as if already a complete reality. The phrase or "suggestion" is therefore being impressed upon the Subconscious Mind in the present tense as if already a complete reality and not as a request or statement of intent in the future tense. Formulating the correct phrases for autosuggestion is crucial for success.

As with all situations when we wish to impress our desires on the Subconscious Mind, the most effective times to employ autosuggestion are at night just before going to sleep and first thing in the morning, just after awakening but before arising.

Autosuggestion can also be practiced very effectively if waking up temporarily during the night, when the influence of space and time are at a minimum, and accordingly the Subconscious Mind is still highly susceptible to influence. Autosuggestion can also be performed at any time of the day but will be less effective from a normal waking state. If autosuggestion is to be carried out during the day, a state of deep physical relaxation and concentration would be required for significant success.

It is also a very good idea to repeat your autosuggestion as an affirmation whenever possible, thereby helping to reinforce your objectives upon your Subconscious Mind.

The actual practice of autosuggestion is very straightforward. After you have determined an affirmative phrase in the present tense, simply repeat it continuously as you drift off to sleep. The more times the phrase is repeated, the more effective it will be, and the sooner it will manifest into your reality, thus achieving the desired effect. The autosuggestion affirmation you choose should ideally transmute any of your negative attributes into their polar opposites. For example, instead of, *"I am not thoughtless towards others*", it would be much better to affirm, *"I am always very thoughtful towards others"*.

The effectiveness of autosuggestion can also be greatly enhanced if your phrase, or "suggestion" is accompanied by a direct physical action that reinforces the suggestion on the Subconscious Mind. One way to achieve this is to obtain a good length of fine string, cord, or yarn, and tie a knot every five centimetres along its entire length. The string should be long enough to contain at least fifty of these knots, so a total length of two hundred and sixty centimetres would be ideal.

Hold one end of the length of string between two fingers of one hand, and every time you repeat your autosuggestion, pull the string until you feel a knot pass through your fingers. After you have pulled every knot through your fingers, you will have repeated your suggestion fifty times. If you drift off to sleep during this process, don't worry. The purpose is to take your suggestion with you from the waking state into the sleep state where it will have its effect on your Subconscious Mind beyond the influence of space and time.

Proceeding in this way, you can progress through your list of negative attributes, either eradicating them completely in the case of physical tendencies, as for example of smoking, or in the case of mental attributes transmuting them into their polar opposite positive mental attributes. It is very important not to progress to the next suggestion until the previous one has been fully dealt with. If you rush this process, the Subconscious Mind will not have been fully impressed with your suggestion, which can still surface unexpectedly at any time.

As with affirmations, it is extremely important to always state autosuggestion phrases knowing, without doubt, that they are already an absolute reality, feeling the intense gratitude as a result. It is not effective to merely repeat the suggestion mechanically over and over without any meaning or emotion.

It might be worthwhile to sort your list into an order of most negative to least negative attributes, or the other way around. You have a choice as to whether to deal with the most negative attributes or the least negative attributes first. This is a matter of personal preference, but for some people, it might be preferable to commence with the least negative attributes, as these will offer the least resistance and will therefore be the simplest and quickest to eradicate or transmute. This choice also largely depends on the degree of willpower you have at your disposal. If you have strong willpower, it is better to start with the most difficult and pervasive attributes. If you do not yet have strongly developed willpower, it is better to start with the least negative attributes. Each success will provide you with the encouragement to deal with the next and more difficult ones. This is an excellent exercise for strengthening willpower.

The entire process of ennoblement of the Soul might take many months or even years to fully accomplish, but it is advisable not to stop until every single negative characteristic has been completely dealt with, no matter how long it takes. True progression cannot be achieved otherwise, with the cycle of reincarnation of the Higher Self continuing until the necessary level of evolution has been attained, at which point the Higher Self can progress inwards to greater things.

Another method of eradicating negative characteristics is during meditation. While in a state of meditation, thought processes are enhanced dramatically due to a slowing of brainwaves which in turn brings us closer to our Subconscious Mind. A deep meditative state can be used to locate negative characteristics, and transmute them into their polar opposite positive characteristics. You might receive inspiration and guidance from your Higher Self or other inner sources, especially if you request such assistance with deep sincerity.

Meditate deeply that you are enjoying life, and on how much better your life is, not only for yourself, but also those around you. Place yourself with your imagination into the resulting state of peace, harmony and in particular gratitude, knowing beyond all doubt that not only are you enjoying a high quality of life, you are also making progress on the path of perfection back to our Divine Creator. Finally, and most importantly, resolve to actually take positive action in your daily life to realize, enjoy and benefit from these profound experiences.

The final method of eradicating and transmuting negative characteristics requires great presence of mind, and is accomplished by the conscious use of diligence, willpower and circumspection at all times during your daily waking life. This process involves recognizing and unhesitatingly dealing with any negative attributes the instant they arise. If any negative attribute appears in your thoughts, or manifests as an undesirable trait or action, it is crucial to deal with it robustly right away using the sheer power of your Mind and Will, keeping in mind the following three important requirements:

Diligence: instantly recognize the presence of negative traits.

Circumspection: total honesty with yourself, always accepting the existence of a negative trait.

Willpower: immediately dealing with the negative trait, either by eradicating it in the case of a physical trait or by transmuting it into its polar opposite positive mental attribute.

This method calls for considerable focus, self-awareness and willpower, but at the same time will enhance the powers of your Mind at all levels, which in turn will prove to be a great asset as you progress joyfully on your path, with the growing realisation that you truly do control your own destiny.

Chapter 106
Dreams

When we enter a certain state of sleep, normally at night, our Astral body, together with our Mental body, the integral Immortal Spirit, leaves our physical body. During this time, the Energy body is "re-charged" from the activities of the previous day to replenish reserves of Energy for the day ahead. This is one reason why we normally awaken in the morning feeling "refreshed". During this time, our Astral and Mental bodies interact with the inner spheres of the Universe during a process that is similar in many respects to Astral Projection, although there is often no Conscious awareness of the experience.

Although the Astral body retains full awareness and control during these night-time travels within the Astral realms, the physical level of Consciousness is in a state of deep sleep. In the case of light or interrupted sleep, the level of Consciousness is such that the Astral body is content to simply recharge itself with Energy with only a low level interaction with the Astral world. At other times, the Astral body, with a higher level of vibration, will engage in full interaction with the Astral worlds, often resulting in vivid or "lucid" dreams.

There are also several interim states of Consciousness where the Astral body will travel to the level of the Astral planes corresponding to the collective human Consciousness of the sleep state and interact with other people in a sort of collective fantasy dream land. Normal low-level dreaming takes place at the lowest level of the Energy continuum, below that of the human group Consciousness and in the area of the personal Consciousness sometimes known as the individual "psyche". As previously discussed, all projection is a projection into the realms of our own Mind, which, at inner levels, we share with humans and other beings. Here, the Subconscious Mind will create its own scenarios within the Astral Ether, often based upon waking thoughts, and in particular the thoughts that were most prominent in the Mind just prior to drifting off to sleep. This is another reason why it is extremely important to take only the most positive, peaceful, and harmonious thoughts to sleep with you. If you carry negative or chaotic states into your sleep state, these will be reflected and manifest in your dreams and subsequently carried into your normal waking state the following morning, often resulting in awakening with negative feelings including fear, dread and apprehension. During particularly light sleep, dreams will often reflect the activity of the Subconscious Mind. There are many states of dream experience varying from no recollection whatsoever, to a state known as "lucid dreaming". In a lucid dream, everything experienced is extremely vivid and "real" because it is, in fact, very real, and the dreamer becomes fully aware he or she is dreaming, allowing for full control over the dream. In this state, the lucid dreamer can create any scenario using the imagination and become fully involved with their scenario.

Lucid dreaming is an ability that can be learned, and is often used by people for entertainment, living their wildest fantasies, and even for healing. Lucid Dreaming can be valuable for facing and defeating waking fears and phobias. For example, a person who has a fear of spiders can create dreamscapes containing these creatures and face them within the dream.

We have spoken previously of "waking paralysis" or "catalepsy". This is usually experienced immediately upon waking in the morning, when a person finds it difficult or even impossible to move any part of the physical body. This is due to the fact that the Astral and Mental bodies have not yet fully returned to, and re-aligned with, the physical body, and the centre of conscious awareness remains predominantly focussed within the Etheric and Astral bodies. During "waking paralysis" a person might also experience the phenomena of "seeing through closed eyelids". The surroundings of the room are fully, and often vividly "visible" even though the physical eyelids are completely closed. During this time the centre of vision is still based in the Etheric plane, and the impression of viewing the surroundings is actually an Etheric "reflection" of the physical surroundings existing at a higher level of vibration, rather than the actual density of the physical surroundings. During these situations, it is sometimes possible to view "deceased" people or other Etheric Beings. If this happens, do not panic. They mean you no harm, and cannot harm you. The best thing to do is to simply observe without any emotion, and communicate with them, if appropriate.

To interrupt waking paralysis and Astral sight, it is necessary to cause your conjoined Astral and Mental bodies to rejoin your physical body by willing yourself to become fully awake. These cataleptic episodes do not last long and are nothing at all to be alarmed about. It is a completely natural process. Those who practice Out of Body Experiences welcome such a state of catalepsy as an ideal state to project from the physical body.

One extremely useful aspect of Astral travel during deep sleep is the possibility of receiving valuable teachings and other information from inner Beings, sometimes by attending places known as "Astral schools". Although such lessons are not usually remembered at a conscious waking level in the morning after waking, they are nevertheless permanently stored within the Subconscious Mind, and in turn the inner bodies and ultimately Higher Self will also benefit from these experiences.

Sometimes dreams can be "precognitive", which means they include a vision of a probable future. This information received during sleep time can arrive in many different forms including highly graphic dream symbolic imagery that might require interpretation. Whatever the form of information received in dreams, it is a most valuable ability to be able to fully recall dreams in the morning. Maintaining a dream journal is a very convenient and effective way of achieving this.

Chapter 107
The Dream Journal

The process of dream recall is very straightforward, simply involving the maintenance of a dream journal. Dreams can be very long and intricate, involving many different and often unrelated aspects. It is therefore important to recall and note down as much detail as possible immediately upon waking.

A blank notebook is the most flexible for this purpose as you can simply place the date at the top of each entry, and write as much as you need. Write your recollections with the label "Dream recollections" on the left pages and the corresponding interpretations labelled "Dream analysis" on the right pages.

Before going to sleep, it is an excellent idea to get into the habit of repeating an affirmation in order to impress the idea of dream recall on your Subconscious Mind such as: "I always easily totally recall my dreams as soon as I awaken".

Your dream journal and a pen must always be easily available next to your bed. As soon as you awaken in the morning, during the night, or after a nap, immediately recall your dreams. Write down everything you can possibly remember, not leaving out even the slightest detail. Often, it is the smallest details that have the most significance, and crucial to making sense of the dream as a whole. This should become the first thing you do each morning as a daily habit. You will quickly find that recalling your dreams will become progressively easier and more automatic as time goes by as your intent is impressed upon your Subconscious Mind, and the action of recalling and writing down your dreams will become an enjoyable habit and voyage of discovery. As more time progresses, you will very likely find that your intent to recall dreams is impressed upon your Subconscious Mind, which will then accentuate the process, and dreams will become increasingly vivid. You might even start to enjoy Lucid Dreams, as a direct result of maintaining your dream journal.

During the day, set aside some time to analyze your dreams of the night before. It is best to do this while relaxing completely in a place where you will not be disturbed. If possible, enter into meditative state to consider the meaning of dreams, especially when the dreams are symbolic and require deeper levels of interpretation.

First of all, look at each individual dream as a whole, and understand its meaning. Sometimes, the dream will have no apparent meaning. It is important therefore not to attach meanings to your dreams that might not exist at all. This process takes practice, but you will soon be able to differentiate between the meaningful dreams and fantasies. For example, a dream involving a fantasy scenario of being at sea in a luxury liner might simply represent a deeply embedded desire to go on a cruise rather than holding some deeper meaning.

As with all types of introspection and self-analysis, it is extremely important to be totally honest with yourself at all times. Compare each dream with your current waking life, your aspirations, hopes and worries to see if there are any similarities, correlations and connections to be made. If there are similarities, write them down, and determine what the dream is saying about your life. If you are able to determine a definitive message within the dream, you should always follow the guidance of the message immediately.

Dreams are a very important mode of receiving messages from the inner spheres of reality through your Subconscious Mind and from your Higher Self. If you are not immediately able to determine a link between your dream and your waking life, see how the dream might be related to your future aspirations. If your dream seemingly has no relevance to the past, present or future as relates to Earth time, keep the possible message conveyed by your dream in Mind, and remain mindful of circumstances that might arise and be relevant to your dream.

Remember, dreams often originate from within the inner spheres of life and reality, beyond the confines of space and time, where the past, present and probable future, relative to the physical world, all exist concurrently in the "Eternal Now".

Your dreams might, therefore, be telling you something about your future, possibly even your immediate future. The most powerful and important messages are often delivered by recurring dreams, which should therefore receive special attention and should be taken seriously.

An example of a highly symbolic dream might for example be a series of dreams containing blockages, such as blocked pipes, blocked sinks, blocked appliances, and so on. These blockages might well symbolically represent a blockage in your life at either a physical or emotional level.

Sometimes dreams can represent a whole series of messages that will need breaking down into sections in order to analyze the meaning of each section effectively. The aspect you might choose to overlook might be the very aspect of the dream containing a particularly important message, so it is very important to be completely thorough about this entire process.

In summary, dream interpretation is a valuable practice that can have profound benefits in your life and Spiritual growth, and therefore maintaining a dream journal is an excellent way of facilitating this. It is important however to be totally committed to the process of dream recall, in which case you will enjoy the support of your Subconscious Mind which will proceed to make the entire process so much more enjoyable and effective, especially over the longer-term.

Chapter 108
The Inner Voice

The inner voice is an extremely valuable and important source of infinite wisdom and guidance in our lives, but one which often goes unheard in most people. Where it is heard it is often ignored or suppressed as having some sort of "undesirable origin" and in some cases is even associated with mental instability or even insanity. Often people who speak of hearing "voices in their head" are even sent for "psychiatric evaluation" and then "treatment" as a result. For this reason, even those who hear their inner voice endeavour to suppress it, or at least never speak of it to others for fear of being considered to be mentally unstable, "deranged", or even insane.

The truth is, the origin of the inner voice, which is very real and of the utmost importance, is from our "higher" or more "connected" inner sources such as the Higher Self, that more complete aspect of our Being, Who is much more connected with The Source, The First Cause, God, than humans existing in an Earthly state of Consciousness, as individual aspects of the Higher Self can be.

The Higher Self has access to the infinite Universe in all spheres of life and reality beyond the limitations of space and time, as well as every aspect of our infinite and immortal existence, including past, present and probable future physical lives. The Higher Self is most important, both in daily life and for the ongoing journey on the path back to God, constantly advising, guiding, prompting, and inspiring by means of any way that may be heard, always striving for "completeness".

The Higher Self manifests in the individual Consciousness of its individual physical aspects through the Subconscious Mind as the "inner voice" which can be "heard" by anyone who listens and recognizes it for what it is. The Higher Self does not have any agenda beyond our ongoing well-being, and the perfection of the whole, and is incapable of misleading or providing incorrect guidance. The Higher Self is only concerned with our smooth, ongoing journey of each representative on Earth back to the Higher Self with its unique package of information and experience.

The inner voice of the Higher Self is constantly "talking" to us. It is not usually a loud voice, but rather a subtle voice that only becomes apparent when we consciously listen for it. The more we listen for and recognize the inner voice, always respecting and taking heed of its wisdom and guidance, the more apparent it will become within our Consciousness, and the more valuable this channel of communication will become.

Listening to our inner voice and consulting with our Higher Self, which has the benefit of the collective experience of all physical incarnations, is one of the keys for a smooth, harmonious progression of each Higher Self incarnation through physical life and onward through the inner spheres of life, experience and reality on the path back to the Higher Self with its unique package of experience, knowledge and wisdom that goes towards the complete Self. Everyone experiences the guidance of the inner voice from time to time. If you are just about to make a decision, you might suddenly experience a "feeling", or "hear" the voice in your head saying "yes" or "no". If the situation can have a profound effect on your physical life, your Higher Self might act more strongly through sensations such as a "sinking feeling". This feeling in the stomach actually originates from the solar plexus which corresponds to a major Energy centre or "chakra". The solar plexus chakra is a direct connection with our Subconscious Mind, through which all communications from within, including our Higher Self originate. If you ever experience that "sinking feeling" in your solar plexus, always delay what you intended to do until you have had the opportunity to consider the consequences more deeply, rather than taking impulsive actions that may well prove to be adverse to some aspect of your wellbeing.

Most messages from the Higher Self are more subtle, arriving in a variety of ways, often as that little voice in your head or sometimes simply as a feeling, impression, inspiration, intuition or idea. The Higher Self does not only warn about potentially negative situations but is also a most valuable source of encouragement and inspiration for positive experiences and situations.

Many people might regard “voices in the head” as unnatural or even a sign of psychiatric illness, but this is only due to a psychological conditioning in physical life about such things, and a lack of understanding as to the true nature and importance of the inner realms of life and reality. Whenever the Higher Self communicates, it is a telepathic communication through our Subconscious Mind, which in turn manifests into our awareness as inspiration, intuition, voices, feelings or even imagery, especially during dreams.

Those who are vigilant and take heed of, and take actions on the voice of the Higher Self will enjoy a considerably smoother, peaceful and harmonious journey through each physical life as an aspect of the Higher Self. Those who choose to ignore the inner voice do so to their own detriment. Ask yourself how many times you have ignored the whispers, impressions and prompting of your Higher Self (those “gut feelings”) and later deeply regretted it? You instinctively knew that you should take action, but very often, it is the Ego that has the upper hand in these situations, or often the Subconscious conditioning that “hearing voices” is wrong for some reason, often due for example religious teachings, upbringing or pressures of society.

Our Higher Self is our very greatest friend, ally and source of Divine guidance, being after all who we ultimately Are. The Higher Self is a Divine aspect of ourselves, with the benefit of the experience of all physical incarnations, can "see" and know things that on Earth people cannot even begin to comprehend, and can be trusted above all else next to the Source, our Divine Creator, God. Of course, there are other Divine Beings within the inner spheres Who also have our best interests at heart, all of whom should always be respected, providing of course we can be very sure of who they are and what they represent.

There are many ways of establishing and maintaining a strong connection with our Higher Self. First and foremost, learn to recognize the inner voice, intuitions and inspiration of all kinds, arriving in any number of different ways. Whenever you are about to make an important decision, stop for a moment and listen to your inner voice. Be vigilant for any intuition, inspiration, impressions or other feelings you might receive. This should be very straightforward for those who have followed the control of thought exercises earlier in this book. The Mind will then be uncluttered by random thoughts. It is when the Mind is completely silent and focused that the inner voice of the Higher Self can be heard with the highest clarity.

For those who have not yet advanced to the stage of complete Mind control, concentration and focus, a serious attempt should be made at important times to silence the Mind, even for just a few moments at first, and remain vigilant for the inner voice.

There will always, of course, be situations in life that occur suddenly without warning. Never do anything impulsively, however dire, desperate or even threatening the situation might seem. Stop for a moment, quieten your Mind, ask for and listen for the guidance of your Higher Self. Your guidance might arrive as feelings, intuition or the voice from within, but always take heed and proceed accordingly, even though the limited conscious Mind with its often protesting Ego might endeavour to push you in a different direction.

While deeply relaxed or in an established state of meditation, start to communicate with your Higher Self by asking questions in your Mind. It is most important to have complete peace and quiet for this exercise, both around you and within your Mind. At first, you might have difficulty discerning your inner voice or it might seem very quiet. Be patient, and over time, with the help of your Subconscious Mind Who will know what you are wishing to achieve, your inner voice and intuition will become stronger and louder. If you ask your question just before drifting off to sleep, the answer might arrive in the morning as you are awakening, or even in a dream.

Once you have established contact with your Higher Self, you can make requests for guidance, inspiration and for manifesting the things you truly need in life. Over time, communion with your Higher Self will become a daily joy during meditation, and one you will always look forward to. Do not treat your Higher Self as a "fair weather friend", who you only turn to in times of desperation. Instead, endeavour to establish a permanent, strong and intimate relationship with your Higher Self in perfect faith, perfect trust and Unconditional Love, and you will find that your life, reality and personal evolution on the sacred path back to God will be dramatically enhanced.

Chapter 109
The Flow of Life

To be in tune with the flow of life is to live in Spirit. Most people try to force their lives in one direction or another by physical means in response to input of the five physical senses, and often driven by the relentless demands of the Ego, the quest for material things and the pressure to conform to the rules imposed by parents, teachers, "bosses", governments and society. This does not mean that you should blatantly break the rule of "law" or have a disregard for anything imposed by society to maintain peace and stability, but rather that such things contrived by humans should be kept in a proper perspective at all times, and not be allowed to control your life.

To live in the flow of life not only includes listening to, and taking positive action on the promptings of the inner voice of your Higher Self, but also being vigilant for those inner promptings, intuition and inspiration from "higher" sources that seem to be guiding you firmly in a certain direction. Ultimately all inspiration originates from The Source, Our Creator, God, and this Divine guidance should always be heeded.

So how do these impulses manifest in physical life? Perhaps you are looking for something specific on a shopping trip. You decide to go into a particular shop when a sudden impulse causes you to continue walking further down the street. There, you find another shop with exactly what you are looking for, and perhaps in better condition, or at a better price or some other benefit that you might not have even considered.

Many of these impulses are the results of The Law of Attraction, involving the collective Subconscious Minds of many people. All desires, except for personal health or healing, which the Subconscious Mind manages directly, are fulfilled within the Universal Mind, either directly, or very often through other Subconscious Minds which are vibrating in harmony with the Thought Form. These processes always take place in perfect harmony, where all involved benefit, as cooperation between individual conscious and Subconscious Minds, through and within the overall Divine Providence of the Universal Mind, The Source, God.

Of course, there are much more important examples of such guidance involving every possible aspect of life. A more far-reaching example might for example be the purchase of a new home. After many weeks of searching, you finally find a home that you really like and make the decision to place an offer which is subsequently accepted. Suddenly, you feel an impulse to withdraw the offer. Your Higher Self, through your Subconscious Mind, is guiding you away from this situation, and the wise thing to do is take heed. You might well never know why you were compelled not to proceed with the purchase of the home, but had you failed to follow your intuition and proceeded to purchase the home anyway, you would most surely have found out the reasons the hard way.

Going with the flow of life should become a way of life. Always live for the present moment of Now rather than being tempted to plan your life ahead, or by what has "happened" in the "past", keeping in Mind that the "past" and "future" do not actually exist. Your Higher Self is focussed in the Eternal Now and has a complete perspective of our past, present and probable future, but only as these concepts relate to the human idea of "time".

Never let anyone or anything, under any circumstances distract or persuade you from following the flow of your own life, which frees you from having to plan your days and weeks in advance. Being in the flow of life, and living only in the present moment of Now, the Eternal Now, gives you freedom from the pressures of being forced to make decisions by notional external factors and the freedom to fulfil your purpose and ultimate destiny as a channel of creative experience and expression of Source Energy, the First Cause, God.

Everything in the Universe has natural rhythm. There is no place for "chaos" in the perfect order of the Universe. "Chaos" is a human notion that simply cannot be applied to the immutable, Divinely inspired perfection and order of the Universe. When you are enjoying the countryside or anywhere in nature, sit down, completely relax and allow your Mind to become silent of thoughts. Feel the powerful Energy around you, and integrate it into your Being. Become aware and know that everything around you is conscious, intelligent, vibrating Energy originating from the Ultimate Mind of The Source, the flow of Energy and Life that sustains all creation. Everything you see, hear, feel, taste and smell through the mediation of the five physical senses is an integral aspect of the magnificent Universe, all existing within the infinite Mind of God. Tune your own vibrations in harmony with the glories of nature around you, and be completely Mindful of the present moment, feeling the peace and harmony and the most powerful vibration of all—Unconditional Love—sustaining you.

Focus your attention on something that catches your eye such as a flower, an insect, a rock, and send it positive Energy and Unconditional Love, and await the response. The response might arrive in the form of a feeling of warmth, or in numerous other ways in which the object of your Unconditional Love returns that Love to you, a feeling which will be unmistakable for what it truly is, at which point you will understand, know and experience the truth that everything is One in the Universal Mind with which everything in creation is Divinely connected.

Now, find a plant and feel its unique Energy. Hold your hands together, side by side, palms facing downward a few inches above the plant, and relax as much as possible. Soon, you will feel the Energy of the plant as a warm glowing feeling over the palms of your hands. Attune yourself to the Energy of the plant and know it too is every bit as much an aspect of God as you are. Repeat this whenever you have an opportunity, whether in nature or in your own home or garden. You will soon understand that to go with the flow of life is to be in the flow of life and in complete harmony with The Source, and All that Is.

Chapter 110
Respect for All Life and Truth of Nutrition

Nothing in the entire infinite Universe, in any sphere of life and reality, is separate from anything else in the Universe. Everything therefore is an integral aspect of everything else. This applies to everything in creation without exception including all forms of organic life and matter in whatever form it is manifested by God. Everything in the Universe is Life, Energy, Spirit, the unique characteristics of which are defined by Vibration. Nothing exists outside of The Source, The All, The First Cause, The Prime Creator, God, in the Great Mind of Whom we live and move and have our Being, and of Whom all Life, including human Beings are individual channels for the experience and expression of Source Energy, of God.

Everything in the Universe, including all animal, plant and mineral life is accordingly an integral and inseparable aspect of every single one of us who we collectively refer to as "human Beings". Those who would hurt, kill or destroy animals, plants or any living organism, however small, therefore equally hurts or kills a part of themselves. This is an extremely profound truth, the ignorance of which can have serious consequences for your current experience and Spiritual evolution.

Whenever mankind thoughtlessly damages or destroys the environment, very often motivated by selfishness and material greed, through such violent activities as mining, drilling and deforestation, or engage in activities that pollute the environment, or denude Earth of Her natural riches and beauty, those responsible are equally damaging an aspect of themselves. This is one very important reason why Earth, humanity and all life simply cannot withstand the current levels of wanton destruction over the environment we were given by God, and which we all share, for very much longer.

A single physical life is but a temporal moment in the context of infinity on the great path of return to our Divine Creator from whence we came in the beginning as channels of Divine experience and expressions, and therefore to become a slave to material possessions during this temporal moment is to not recognize fundamental Universal realities and the greater meaning of Life, the Universe and Destiny of Mankind.

Hopefully, in the fullness of time, always assuming the coming great transition of the ages facilitates an opportunity, Earth can be restored to the former glory of the days before the influence of so-called “civilized man”. This can only occur when mankind finally understands the complete and utter futility of the constant demand for temporal material possessions, acquired for no other purpose than the gross gratification of the five physical senses, the constant urge to conform to the expectations of others, and the uncontrolled demands of the Ego.

Whether at home, at work, in the garden, in the countryside, on vacation or anywhere else, we should always view and treat everything around us as an integral aspect, and outer expression of ourselves. When out in the garden, walking in nature or anywhere else, we should never knowingly harm any living thing, either accidentally or deliberately, including, but not limited to plucking flowers or treading in places where other wildlife might be peacefully established. We should never, ever harm any living creature, however small, whether it be the largest sea dwelling Whale, or a single celled Amoeba. Each and every creature without exception is an equal aspect of God, The First Cause, our Prime Creator, and therefore of ourselves. All have an equal right to enjoy their rightful places in the Universe, following their own path back to our same Divine Creator. Everything and everyone in the Universe is constantly evolving, and everything and everyone travels a unique but equally important path. All creatures, like everyone and everything else in the entire Universe in all spheres of life and reality, are a conscious creation and channel of experience and expression of The Source, The First Cause, God, and each have an equally important role to fulfil.

People often refer to some small creatures as “vermin”, or unwanted plant life as “weeds”, but these are nothing more than derogatory human concepts arising out of a total lack of understanding and respect for the position in which every creature, every plant, and every other manifestation of life occupies within the infinite Universe. These creatures are only considered to be “vermin” simply because they happen to be perceived as interfering with the material existence of humans.

If you are privileged enough to share your home with smaller creatures such as mice, spiders, or insects, they are not in your home to be vindictive or to cause a “nuisance”—these are human traits. They are simply aspects of ourselves seeking food, shelter and a place to live, just as human Beings do likewise. People might claim that these creatures are harmful in “spreading diseases”, but by comparison with mankind, these creatures are in many ways extremely clean and advanced.

We all create our own reality at all levels. If a person believes that certain creatures “spread diseases”, then that will be the reality experienced. But the disease has not been contracted from the creature in question, but rather by erroneous and wrongful thinking of the person born out of ignorance. If we welcome these wonderful creatures into our home, Love them, feed them and make them feel welcome, then they will return the same, and a mutually harmonious habitat must be the result.

If a person destroys the habitat of a small creature, such as a spider’s web, they have equally destroyed a part of themselves. It is no different at all to someone arriving at your home with heavy machinery and levelling it to the ground simply because they deemed it to be “inconvenient”. How would you feel?

Again, irrational fear or worry about the consequences of allowing these creatures to share your home will attract the same consequences in accordance with The Law of Attraction. If you believe that sharing your home with other creatures will result in disease, damage or other adverse consequences, then you will attract those realities into your experience.

The way to live your life is simple and unambiguous. Feel honoured to share your home with other creatures, and welcome them with complete sincerity as if you were welcoming a member of your own family, which in fact you truly are. Everyone and everything is related as "offspring" of the same Divine Creator. If necessary, provide these creatures with food from your kitchen and anything else they might require. Above all, welcome them with Unconditional Love in the certain knowledge they will return that same Love unconditionally. These same truths apply to plant and mineral life. In a previous chapter, we saw conclusive proof that plants are intelligent and fully capable of thought, even though they do not have a physically observable brain. The physical brain is not the Mind, it is simply an organic interface of non-permanent physical matter between the vibrational level of the human physical body and the much higher vibrations of the inner-self.

Although the Ego of many humans currently leads them to erroneously believe they are the "dominant species", "top of the food chain" or "technologically advanced", humans are only perceiving things from a very temporal perspective. There are Beings, including human Beings who have evolved far beyond the temporal physical Universe. Some of these higher Beings are so evolved in fact that humans might seem to them as a single celled amoeba would seem to human beings. These Beings look upon humanity with compassion, humility and Unconditional Love, as equals before God, whose focus is assisting humanity with its great ascent on the path that one day humans will be like them. Humans should in turn feel the same about "simpler" forms of manifestations of Life on Earth, helping those life-forms on their own Divine path to our Creator just as higher Beings unconditionally help human beings.

Plants also have feelings. They know when they are about to be hurt or destroyed and do not differ from human Beings or animals in that respect. The grand Universal scheme of things does, of course, recognize that the Earth life system requires food for sustenance. The Universe, in immutable perfection, has provided everyone within the Earth-life system with a "food chain". Humans are unique on Earth as being the only species of life to exceed the provisions of that food chain, directly resulting in the multitude of food abuse related diseases that we increasingly witness today.

It has been conclusively proven that the natural human diet is naturally growing harvestable whole foods, often the seed container of the plant, such as with fruits, or the seeds themselves as with grains and pulses, and that people adhering to such a diet are always much healthier, suffer few if any debilitating diseases, and physically live on average 7 years longer. Our true diet is harvestable food from the abundance that The Source has provided, in the form of fruits, nuts, pulses and a multitude of other harvestable food that plants and trees offer unconditionally and with Love as their own contribution to the harmony of Earth and all living Beings. Such food should not include plants that must be uprooted and killed in order to eat it, such as lettuces for example. In addition, cooking any food destroys all of the valuable enzymes contained, and most nutrients, thus rendering it nutritionally almost valueless. The diet therefore that is in complete harmony with both nature and the needs of the physical human body is harvestable plant foods, eaten naturally, not cooked.

The process of eating food and converting it to Energy is in any case a crude one. The only "food" we require to live healthily is Universal Energy. We have the ability to absorb and assimilate Energy directly from the Universe, thus requiring no food or water at all. There are people who happily live this way even now, but in the future this will become a more common occurrence, but only when people remove their perception of food as a form of pleasure—again unique to humans.

The process of eating and assimilation of food through the digestive system is ultimately to convert that food into pure Energy in a form that can be assimilated by the physical body. This is a crude form of sustenance, but one necessary in the course of evolution. During the evolution of humans however just as mankind will progress from speaking through vocal organs to communicating in our native Telepathy, so too will humans progress from consuming organic matter and drinking liquids including water, to consciously absorbing and assimilating all necessary Energy, directly from the Universe

Almost all animals, except for human Beings, who are unique as being the only member of the animal kingdom to exceed the provisions of the food chain, consume only those foods and in those quantities required in order to survive in a healthy and natural state of being. In the case of humans, however, a trip around any supermarket will instantly reveal how the requirement for basic, necessary organic sustenance has degenerated into a gross food-fest designed only to gratify the demands of the physical senses, and made even more attractive to the "consumer" by packaging designed to entice the customer, without regard for the quality, nature or origin of the "food" contained within, while concealing, to the extent possible, additional chemicals, preservatives and other additives designed to enhance flavour and consumer appeal.

In recent decades a particularly damaging category of food, and one that is spreading like an insidious disease around the world where it seems almost no country remains untouched, which is known as "fast food". Fast food is directly responsible for exponentially increasing diseases such as obesity, diabetes in its various forms, heart disease and much more. To make matters much worse, children are a major target of the "fast food industry" with meals served in brightly coloured boxes containing trinkets designed by psychologists to lure children into consuming the dangers that lie deeper in the box in the form of highly processed and chemical impregnated "burgers", "fries", "nuggets" and other so called "junk food". A child eating such fatty, non-nutritional food is instantly exposed to the potential for obesity which will eventually manifest, as well as other diseases, some of which may be debilitating or even fatal. Once fat cells are laid down in the developing body of a child, they remain throughout physical life, and that child will have a pre-disposition to obesity, and a life-long battle with weight gain and the multitude of associated disorders.

Ironically these factors have spawned a whole new "weight-loss" industry, which seeks to convince people who, having abused their bodies with food all those years, can instantly repair the year of abuse and damage simply by taking pills, potions, "diets" with exotic names and many other contrivances, most of which are designed by marketing specialists working for industry as opposed to nutritionists.

This has resulted in a self-perpetuating cycle where "industries" are created that can only result in disease, followed by further industries purporting to "cure" these same diseases they caused in the first place. This has resulted in an incestuous environment, motivated only by greed, the only loser being the "consumer" who often pays, not only in terms of money, but also by way of further serious disease or often "death".

This situation is untenable and cannot and will not be sustained. Everyone needs to wake up to the basic truths about equality of all life in all Divine manifestations, the true meaning of nutrition as it relates to a healthy body, Soul and Spirit, and to wake up to the nefarious agendas of the various factions who put greed before health, children and life itself.

Chapter 111
Selfless Unconditional Service

One of the most important principles of progression in all spheres of life is the offering and provision of unconditional selfless service to others, out of Love, and without any thought of reward. Selfless service to others before service to self is absolutely is a fundamental principle and quality of Spirit, both from an individual perspective and from the perspective of the entire human race, and all life, without which there can be no true progress. Human beings, and indeed all manifestations of life and Spirit in the Universe are One, all aspects of our one Supreme Creator. We are all, whatever our state of evolution, here to help those further out on the path to progress also.

Again—service to others before service to self' is an absolutely fundamental Principle. True, selfless service should be motivated by, extended from of a deep and genuine desire to serve the needs others, before serving the needs of self.

Beings residing within the Astral, Mental, Celestial and Cosmic spheres of life are continually involved in service to humanity, to the extent their circumstances facilitate, the inner always assisting the outer being another fundamental principle within the inner spheres of life as we progress along the path to perfection back to our Divine Creator.

Those within the inner spheres wish to raise those living in the outer Energy spheres of the Universe ever inwards, that they may enjoy the Love, light and bliss they already experience at those levels, with a deep desire to share with fellow Spirits.

This fundamental principle has seriously broken down on Earth, due in no small part to the demands of the Ego, materialism and the pressure to conform at all levels of "society", together with a lack of understanding of the true nature of humanity and of the Universe. Many people today will not consistently help others, especially strangers, without expecting a tangible “reward” in return—very often money. There are, of course, notable exceptions, such as the excellent work carried out by the many charities and volunteer workers.

Of course, people are understandably committed to their own daily needs motivated mostly by a “survival” instinct, only helping each other whenever appropriate. This is as it should be between families and friends. Selfless service, however, extends far beyond the confines of family and friends. The true meaning of selfless service is to unconditionally serve others whenever the need for such assistance is apparent and appropriate, and without any thought of personal gain, providing always that such service is consistent with the well-being of the person to whom the service is being extended, and does not infringe upon their freewill in any way, and thereby their own freedom to learn and evolve through experience.

Such service can be extended in numerous ways, ranging from financial assistance to direct physical help, advice, support, healing and teaching. If all mankind would embrace these extremely important Universal Principles, of service to others before service to self, the greed, selfishness, avarice, materialism, and egocentricity so prevalent in the world today could not and would not be perpetuated, and life on Earth would be harmonious. This is already true of the Astral and Spiritual spheres of life, where every Being, including humans, live on the level of Universal vibration that is in harmony with their individual vibration, and therefore on the same level as other Beings of the same vibration. In these worlds a level harmony always exists relative to that particular level of vibration.

The very outer Astral worlds might well be analogous to a type of “hell” in religious terms, the “dark” nature, the vibration of those realms being in perfect harmony with the nature and therefore vibration of those residing there. However, as previously mentioned, these people will eventually learn their own particular lessons through experience, a fundamental principle of life, and will go on to return to their Higher Self with their own unique package of experience, which in turn contributes to the complete Self in the ongoing quest for perfection and evolution. No experience on Earth, however "dark" or "evil" it is perceived to be, is ever wasted. Without "evil" there would be no reference for "good", and accordingly "good" and "evil" are both relative in accordance with the perceptions of the observer, as well as being points on the same polar axis in accordance with the Universal Principle of Polarity. Before God, there are no "good" people or "bad" people. We are all the Children of God on a unique learning experience in the kindergarten of the Universe called "Earth".

Those who believe "death" will release them from their "issues" in the physical world had better think again because "death" is no escape. Most people, with the exception of those who are ready for the next stage of their journey, or are here for a specific mission from the inner spheres, will transition to the Astral worlds, to a realm that exactly matches their character as determined by their unique vibration, and will be the same person in every respect, with the same memories and "issues", except they will now possess a perceived non-physical as opposed to a physical body.

Selfishness is one of the most serious transgressions against individual Spiritual progression and one which will bring corresponding karmic consequences in accordance with Principles of Cause and Effect and The Law of Attraction. "Do unto others and you would have them do unto you".

Notwithstanding the conditions awaiting a persistently selfish person after physical death, all transgressions will have to be reconciled sooner or later. Relinquishing the habits of a lifetime on Earth or making so called "death bed confessions" is completely meaningless, and does not absolve the "confessor" of a lifetime of selfishness or other negative traits, which have become an integral aspect of the Energy field and therefore vibration of that person. Mere words are not enough. These negative characteristics can only be reconciled by learning the necessary lessons, and transmuting the negative traits into their polar opposite positive traits, which, in the case of selfishness, is by extending selfless service to others.

This equally applies to religious people, many of whom have been led to believe that by going to church, reading the Bible, attending “confession”, having an abstract “faith” and “belief” in God and "accepting Jesus as their saviour" will ensure their place in “Heaven”. Some even go as far as believe that, even after a life of selfishness and other negative traits, if they “embrace Jesus” on their deathbed, they will be “saved” and go to “Heaven”. If only such people knew the truth from the beginning of that life, they would then know how to live their lives joyfully, productively and in service to others, while know, beyond doubt what awaits at the end of their physical days on Earth, and subsequent transition to the Astral worlds.

True progression includes subjugating the Ego, ennoblement of Soul and Spirit on the Divine path to perfection, respect for all life, Unconditional Love and selfless service to others before service to self. No one knows precisely when their current lifetime on Earth will be completed, and no time should be lost in fully embracing these Universal Principles and the true meaning of life. Failing to do so would inevitably mean the Higher Self of the person sending another representative to Earth to learn the lessons that were not learned in that incarnation, thus delaying progression to the inner spheres of life, the glories and splendours of which are beyond the comprehension of Earthly Man. All progression must be out of Unconditional Love and service to others before service to self, and not simply out of a desire for gain, a fundamental Principle that all humans need to embrace sooner or later.

Chapter 112
The Lessons of Life

Each and every physical life on Earth experienced by our Higher Self can be likened to attending the kindergarten of the Universe. The learning process does not end until the path to our Divine Creator is finally reached, which can be likened to graduating with first class honours from University. Even when the Higher Self has transcended the cycle of physical reincarnation on Earth, and the student graduates to the primary school of life, to the great Mental Planes as a more perfect and complete Higher Self, the path ahead back to our Divine Creator is only now truly beginning. This onward path is however much more tranquil and harmonious, with none of the trials and tribulations experienced on Earth life. It should be the primary objective of every single person to graduate from the kindergartens of Earth and the Astral worlds without delay in order to progress to the next phase of Divine education within the Spiritual worlds, beyond the illusion of form. Always keep in Mind that the true meaning of life is to evolve, in a state of perfection, back to God, The Source, The First Cause, from Whom we first came in the beginning, before setting forth on the journey to perfection, as a channel of experience, expression and thereby expansion of God.

We have already discussed in this book many of the factors facilitating true and enduring progress during each physical life of the Higher Self. It is also very important to understand that life is one long learning process from the moment of birth to the moment of transitioning back to the inner spheres of reality where the achievements of the past life can finally be reviewed and reconciled, before finally returning to our Higher Self, our complete Self, with the valuable package of experience that contributes to the Whole Self, experience that not only contributes to our own evolution, but also to the evolution of The Source, The First Cause, God, and therefore the All.

Every single moment, both waking and sleeping, is a valuable opportunity to learn and progress, and none of these lessons should ever be wasted. During life in the physical space-time bound continuum of Earth, the outermost vibration of Source Energy, we all interact with many different people under many different circumstances, and thereby encountering numerous valuable opportunities for learning, gaining experience and for personal evolution, an environment that is unique in the greater continuum of the Universe as a whole. If such opportunities are wasted, the same lessons will present themselves again, either during the current physical Earth life or during a future physical life relative to the human concept of "time, but experienced by another representative of the Higher Self.

It is most important to consider each and every situation in the context its true meaning, and to not "take it personally", to joyfully learn the lessons presented, and take any necessary actions associated with that lesson. We should always listen for and heed the guidance of our Higher Self whenever that voice within "speaks" to us.

Very often such lessons present themselves symbolically. For example, if you suddenly start experiencing blocked sinks, blocked drains, blocked pipes and other blockages appearing in your life on a scale that has never happened before, they might be symbolic representations of a much more fundamental blockage in your life involving some aspect of your Being or personal wellbeing or evolution. Take time meditate or any other means by which this blockage might be identified, and immediately take all necessary steps in order to resolve it. If you do not, do this, you might well be putting off something that could be important or quite likely pivotal in your life such as moving to a different location. Whatever it is, the blockage must be identified and remedied. Every situation has a meaning—nothing "happens" by "chance". Yes we create our own experience with our Mind, in accordance with the Law of Attraction and other Universal Principles, but we always attract things into our lives at many different levels, not all of which we are fully consciously aware of, but all of which nevertheless exist at some level of our continuum of Consciousness.

Frequently, situations will arise that you feel are totally unjust or completely wrong or what you might perceive to be an "injustice". Most people would react strongly to these situations, perhaps by engaging in arguments with others, complaining, or feeling anger, bitterness or even hatred. When faced with such a situation, take a deep breath, count to five, and consider the situation from all perspectives. Suggest to yourself with complete sincerity— "maybe it is I who is wrong in this situation". Consider it from the perspective of the other people involved, and ask yourself what you would do in these very same circumstances. Always keep in mind that the Ego will always endeavour to take control, and will always cause you to feel that you are right in order to maintain its materialistic influence, desires and urge to control at all costs. The Ego does not take kindly to being "wrong", and will do everything it possible can to place the blame on others.

If the uncontrolled Ego is allowed to exert its influence in this way, the lessons of life cannot and will not be learned, karma will not be equilibrated and progress will be adversely affected. There is no avoiding the lessons that need to be learned if true progress is to be made to the next phase of life, so the sooner these lessons are faced up to and surmounted, the better.

Each situation that you are faced, no matter what the origin of that situation might have been, it should be approached with the complete confidence that arises from knowing, beyond doubt, that you are an Immortal, Infinite Spiritual being, a Son or Daughter of The Source, The Prime Creator, God made in the true Spiritual image of God, and absolutely no true harm can ever come to you. Always give thanks for every opportunity you face as a valuable opportunity to learn and experience, and thereby to progress that much nearer to God.

Chapter 113
Pure Unconditional Love

Pure Unconditional Love is the most powerful force, or more specifically vibration in the entire Universe. If the vibration of Unconditional Love were to be withdrawn from the fabric of Universe, the entire Universe would collapse in an instant.

Unconditional Love should never be confused however with sentimental love, sexual love or lust, or even token love of family or friends. In these contexts the word "love" is often used very loosely as a token of friendship, affection or an expression of endearment, or sometimes loosely used without any feelings associated with it at all. Pure Unconditional Love may best be described as a state, or vibratory rate of Energy, emanating from the The Source, The First Cause, God, and the most powerful vibration sustaining all creation in the Universe.

In order to live in complete harmony with the Universe and be a wide open channel of experience and expression of The Source, it is necessary to attune to a personal state of Unconditional Love. In order to maximize our abilities of manifestation, healing, and other inner abilities, Unconditional Love should be experienced as an integral part of our very Being, and not simple as a matter of convenience.

Many people might claim to practice Unconditional Love, but this is often far from the reality. Unconditional Love is not merely "feeling good" toward others, good though that surely is—it is rather a much higher and ongoing state of Being that goes far beyond mere spoken words or displays of affection.

It was out of Purc Unconditional Love that God created and sustains the entire Universe, and all manifestations of life within the Universe. Pure Unconditional Love is the highest and most Divine expression of God, and accordingly, as aspect and expressions of God, what we should all aspire to.

Those wishing to experience total peace and complete harmony with the Universe should strive to become the individual epitome of Pure Unconditional Love. Unconditional Love really does mean "Unconditional" in every possible sense—without any conditions attached. Of course, it is not possible to become Unconditional Love overnight. It is a process commencing with a total and sincere resolve, integrated into daily life, and experienced with genuine and complete dedication until fully realized and assimilated with every aspect of our life and Being at all levels—body, Soul and Spirit. Unconditional Love should be a natural state of Being. However, due to the path upon which humans have chosen to travel over the last few thousand years, becoming more remote from The Source, other, lower emotional states of vibration have come predominant. It is necessary therefore for most people to re-learn the true meaning and experience of Unconditional Love in its truest and purest sense.

Before setting a date in which to commence practicing and becoming at one with Unconditional Love, it is first necessary to contemplate and meditate deeply about what Unconditional Love really means to you, and thereby how you will achieve your objective. It is necessary to fully understand the true nature of Unconditional Love before it can be assimilated.

To practice Unconditional Love is to see and love the Divine essence of absolutely everyone and everything without any exceptions, not only the superficial physical shell, but the Immortal Spirit of everything—the true image of God. You must know, beyond any doubt, in your heart, Soul and Spirit that absolutely everyone, regardless of race, creed, culture, personality, individuality, characteristics, attitude and current Earthly status, is an integral and equal aspect of God.

You cannot be selective about "Unconditional" Love which must always be "Unconditional" by definition. You must radiate and Be Pure Unconditional Love to everyone and everything, including those you might have previously perceived as not worthy of such love, including but not limited to terrorists, murderers, bank robbers, difficult neighbours, annoying co-workers, etc. Every single one of these people, without exception, is an equal aspect of the absolute and immutable perfection of God and therefore of all of us as humans, and to hate such people is to hate God, yourself and the entire Universe. Each of these people has the same ultimate destiny, and all contribute to the complete harmony and balance of the very fabric of the Universal continuum of Energy. Even people considered to be the most "evil" humans on Earth are simply individual aspects of a Higher Self, each of which that must experience a wide range of lives, conditions and experiences, including those considered from a human perception to be "good" or "evil", in order to attain the necessary balance required to eventually ascend back to our Divine Creator in a state of perfection. Everyone and everything is an instrument of learning, and accordingly nothing should be taken personally, or regarded as "evil"—the person you may regard as "evil" is an aspect of yourself. God never discriminates against God's own children anymore than any human being would discriminate against their own children. Therefore as true sons and daughters of God, no human being should ever discriminate against any other human being. Many might say by way of an excuse, "but we are only human after all". In reality, we are God, and God is us.

When you begin to practice being Unconditional Love, you must pour the high Energy vibration of genuine Pure Unconditional Love into everything and everyone you encounter without hesitation, irrespective of your perceptions of that person. You will very quickly discover that Unconditional Love is very expansive and pervasive, and the people around you will begin to receive and assimilate the vibrations of the Energy of Unconditional Love they are receiving from you. People around you will become happier and more peaceful, smile more and become more relaxed.

As the people around you respond in this way, they will radiate more peaceful, harmonious feelings, which will, in turn, be absorbed by people around them. Very soon, your being Unconditional Love will directly or indirectly touch the hearts of many people. In this way, it does not take too many people being Unconditional Love to soon raise the entire world to this most Divine vibration with profoundly positive results for everyone and all life. While practicing Unconditional Love, be vigilant for and reject all negative or unloving thoughts immediately they are recognised. Remember also that with Unconditional Love comes unconditional forgiveness. Always unconditionally forgive those who you believed have or might have wronged you, however bitter or resentful you might feel at the time, and continue to project Unconditional Love in place of any anger or resentment, while learning any valuable lessons you can from the situation to help you on your path.

It is very important to remember and to know that Unconditional Love is much more than a mere token sentiment or something you might say to yourself, such as “I practice Unconditional Love”. It must radiate from your very Being and represent an absolute knowing without thought or effort. Unconditional Love must literally be a state of Being, inseparable from your Soul, Spirit and Higher Self, connected directly with the most Divine vibration of the Energy of God.

Always know that Unconditional Love is projected by God through your Higher Self, through your immortal Spirit, through your Soul and finally to your physical body, through which you send the vibrations to everyone and everything. Very soon your vibration and very Being will be raised to a new level, and you will begin to instinctively understand how to overcome limitations in your life. The door will open for many more possibilities than you would ever have considered or thought possible. Your abilities of creating your own reality, healing and many other powers of the Mind will open wide to you without effort. Not only will you be positively affecting other people, and thereby making a difference in their lives, but you will also be raising vibration and Energy within your own life, thereby experiencing a new level of happiness, peace and harmony with the Universe and those around you.

The first few days of practicing Pure Unconditional Love might prove to be difficult, but as you persevere over the course of weeks and months, it will become a way of life, and you will never want to return to the lower Energy vibration of your previous state. While relaxing or meditating, focus on your heart chakra—the centre of Unconditional Love in your Etheric or Energy body—and see it glowing, sending out its rays to the world. Take every opportunity to perform the Twin Hearts meditation as detailed earlier in this book, sending Pure Unconditional Love to the entire world. The more you become the epitome of Pure Unconditional Love and perform the Twin Hearts meditation, the more your heart chakra will expand and glow brightly. You will clearly feel the warmth and peace as your heart chakra vibrates to the highest Energy vibration of all—the Divine vibration of God. After some time, you will know beyond all doubt that you are connected directly to this ultimate, Divine source of the vibration of Unconditional Love.

In time, you will become a much calmer, happier, peaceful person, which will be reflected in every aspect of your life and Being. You will feel and know, beyond any doubt that you are in tune with the Divine Source of the very highest vibration, which will manifest in your life in many positive ways. You will sleep more peacefully and soundly, and your dreams will be much more vivid, harmonious and intense, opening you to a fuller understanding of your true purpose. Your raised vibrations may also open you to many inner abilities such as Astral Projection, clairvoyance and telepathy.

During the first few days and weeks, the Ego will protest at every turn and demand its own way. Perseverance is the key. Acknowledge the protests and efforts of your Ego to upset your equilibrium of Unconditional Love, but never give in to it. Your Ego will eventually have to accept your desires and cease to place obstacles in your way, because at the final analysis we have the total control over our Ego. The previous chapter in this book, "Subjugating the Ego" is worth re-reading in this context, and to practice the exercises described therein.

Above all, never become disheartened or give up altogether. Always know it is your Divine right as a true Son or Daughter of God, made in the true Spiritual image of God, to be Pure Unconditional Love at all times. Always remember that the Love God has for you is Pure Unconditional Love. God never judges anyone, no matter where a person is on the path—God, The Source, our Creator Unconditionally Loves every aspect of the creation of God without limit or exception.

God always embraces Pure Unconditional Love for all of His/Her Children and creations within the entire multi-dimensional Universe. Unconditional Love has been recognized throughout the millennia as one of the great mysteries of life and of the Universe, and yet, most people in this stage of their evolution do not recognize or attempt to become as one with Unconditional Love. Those who do recognize Unconditional Love, and live their lives accordingly, will realize these profound truths. It can shake you free from the influence of the Ego and allow you to enjoy a new level of freedom which most people would find unimaginable. Only those who become Pure Unconditional Love will know the absolute truth of this reality.

To conclude this section, here is a passage contained within Christian Bible which is most appropriate to the true meaning of Love.

"And now I will show you the most excellent way.

If I speak in the tongues of men and of Angels, but have not Love, I am only a resounding gong or a clanging cymbal.

If I have the gift of prophecy and can fathom all mysteries and all knowledge, and if I have a faith that can move mountains, but have not Love, I am nothing.

If I give all I possess to the poor and surrender my body to the flames, but have not Love, I gain nothing.

Love is patient, Love is kind. It does not envy, it does not boast, it is not proud. It is not rude, it is not self seeking, it is not easily angered, it keeps no record of wrong.

Love does not delight in evil but rejoices with the truth. It always protects, always trusts, always hopes, always perseveres.

Love never fails. But where there are prophesies they will cease, where there are tongues they will be stilled, where there is knowledge, it will pass away.

For we know in part and we prophesy in part. But when perfection comes, the imperfect disappears.

When I was a child I talked like a child. When I became a man, I put childish ways behind me.

Now we see but a poor reflection as in a mirror, then we shall see face to face. Now I know in part, then I shall know fully, even as I am fully known.

And now these three remain; Faith, Hope and Love. And the greatest of these is Love" -- 1 Corinthians 1:13 -13

Chapter 114
The Transition of the Ages

As many readers of this book will no doubt be aware, either by firsthand experience, or by hearing or reading about them from other sources, at the time of writing of this book, major events and changes are occurring at all levels, and increasingly so. These events are not only occurring throughout the world but also beyond, extending deep into our solar system. These events, which are wide-ranging, often profound, and both physical and non-physical in nature, herald the continuance of a great transition of the ages, and one with potentially profound consequences for humanity, life on Earth and Earth Herself.

This great transition, which I have long been aware of, is no doubt a primary factor for the inspiration behind the writing of this book, the principle purpose of which is to reveal to readers your own true Divine nature, purpose and ultimate destiny and above all how to realize it, while there is still time remaining on Earth to do so. I sincerely believe, know and indeed expect that the understanding, assimilation and application of what you learn in this book will prepare you for these approaching events and associated long term consequences as we travel together as One through this great transition of the ages.

I would like to make it absolutely clear from the outset that these events are in no way "random" or "chaotic" in nature, but rather an aspect of the Divine, immutable order and perfection of the Universe, of our Prime Creator, God, and natural cycles of the Universe. I would also like to make it absolutely clear that these events are not part of some "retribution" to "punish" a "wicked" or "sinful" mankind—these are simply superstitions having absolutely no basis in fact whatsoever.

From the outset I would also like to make the following absolutely clear such is its great importance to all humanity:

We must not, under any circumstances, allow ourselves to be influenced in any way whatsoever by external events, "prophecies", sensationalism, purveyors of doomsday scenarios or conspiracies of any type, or by those claiming any special knowledge, powers or connections of any sort in relation to "2012", "the end of the age" or any associated scenarios, or to be influenced in any way by the hidden agendas of governments, those seeking power and control on a global scale or by the popular media and their controllers.

The next few years are absolutely crucial for humanity. We are experiencing a great transition of life representing the culmination of millions of years of evolution of human Beings and all life on Earth as well as Earth, Gaia Herself. The outcome of this transition will not be predetermined in any way, shape or form by "chance" or other superstitious notions.

Only one factor at this stage, at the time of writing can be considered as absolute certainty. **Whatsoever the collective Consciousness of humanity and of all life on Earth expects to happen over the next few years and beyond, will happen.** We are facing the ultimate proof that we really do create our own reality at all levels, both as individual aspects of God, and as the collective Mind and Consciousness of the human race.

We are now experiencing, and will increasingly experience the culmination and transition of a great cycle or "age", an integral aspect of even greater such cycles in the Universe, all of which ultimately originate from The Source, The First Cause, God. These are completely natural cycles of life which exert their presence and influence with immutable precision and perfection, as fundamental aspects of the greater workings of the Universe in all glorious spheres of life and reality.

Cycles are always present in our lives at every level. Some cycles are so tiny they cannot even be measured with scientific instruments, and others so vast that they are far beyond the current perception of humans. However, the truth of the very existence of such cycles is everywhere—we only have to look at nature for example and the cycles of the seasons. Energy, radio waves, sound frequencies can all be measured in terms of distinct "cycles per second". Without such cycles events in the Universe would be chaotic, but this is clearly not the case because the Universe would not be sustainable in such a state of chaos—only Divine order and perfection can exert its immutable influence in maintaining the harmonious equilibrium of the Universe in all spheres of life and reality.

However, herein is the paradox. As with all Energy, this natural cycle is influenced by Mind, aspects of which include thoughts, imagination, expectations, intent and emotions. This cycle of Energy has always existed and will always exist, and, like all Energy, will exert its influence in accordance with the Consciousness of its participants—in this case life on Earth.

We will proceed in this chapter therefore by objectively examining the range of possible scenarios that might exert an influence during the next few years, both in the interests of knowledge, and to form a basis through which we can form a balanced perspective, expectations and state of Consciousness, which may prove to be so crucial in shaping the coming events.

For many people, the first awareness that "something is happening" or will happen, arrived by way of hearing about the now iconic date, December 21, 2012 which, over the last three decades has quite literally assumed a life of its own as a very powerful and pervasive Thought Form. Therein is one of the important issues we face—like any Thought Form it must, in accordance with immutable Universal principles, and the of Energy focused upon it, manifest, and thereby become self-fulfilling in accordance the nature of the thoughts that the majority of people associate with the "2012 Thought Form".

Since this now iconic date of December 21, 2012 first emerged into the Consciousness of humanity there have been countless interpretations spanning the entire spectrum of implications for mankind, ranging from catastrophic to ecstatic and almost all scenarios in between. Let us first then take a closer look at the facts surrounding this date, which has become such a point of focus, trepidation and even fear for so many people, often very worried for the well-being of themselves and families. This is not surprising considering the large and increasing array of "products" appearing on the market about "how to survive 2012", and sensationalism, as well as the widely held but erroneous belief that 2012 means "the end of the world".

As previously mentioned, many people are now focusing thought Energy on "2012", "December 21, 2012", "the end of the world" and other similar thought processes, which in turn, with the thought power of tens of thousands or even millions of people collectively focussing on these concepts, have become very powerful "Thought Forms"—Energy configurations in their own right, which have now literally assumed a life of their own. The more people focusing on these 2012 related thoughts, the more powerful, pervasive and resilient these Thought Forms will become and the less transient they will be in nature.

When in altered states of Consciousness, for example during meditation, in a trance state, or even just before, during and after sleep, we can "connect" with these powerful 2012 related Thought Forms which can present themselves as an "important message from within", with the receiver of the message as the focal point. The Ego of the receiver then takes over and convinces the conscious Mind of the person that they have been the recipient of important "privileged information", or even that they have received a "premonition". Sometimes even the Ego leads the person so far as to believe that they are even a "chosen one" in some way. Such a person then tells family and friends, or even the media, as well as writing about it on the Internet, until soon, in the Minds of many it becomes a fact. Because by now there might well be thousands of people focussing on this single original "message", the original

"Thought Form" that gave rise to it in the Mind of the person gains even more strength, resilience and pervasiveness, and therefore in turn becomes even more "real" to those focussing on it, who in turn then relate it to others as if it were a fact.

This then I believe is a phenomena we are increasingly seeing at the time of writing, specifically, a collection of 2012 related Thought Forms manifesting under the umbrella of a much more pervasive "2012" Thought Form" now reaching a critical mass in the Consciousness of people throughout the world.

Let us continue by putting this Thought Form aside, and investigate some of the fundamental facts surrounding "2012".

It is most notable that before the 1970's, almost no one had ever heard of "the end of the Mayan calendar" or therefore of "2012" and related matters, indeed many had not heard of the Maya themselves. It is only since the Mayan long-count calendar was deciphered in the last 20 years or so that 2012 with its "end of the Mayan calendar" or "end of the world" connotations have entered into the human Consciousness.

Summarizing in a page or so in the context of this chapter the entire 30 or more year history of how the "2012" phenomena came about is most assuredly impractical due to the now vast array of people, factors and theories of all types involved, often supported and motivated by individual agendas and interests. Following however is an overview of the most significant factors for consideration, which will be sufficient to provide the basis for further analysis of these factors in the context of the Transition of the Ages to which this chapter is dedicated.

The Mayan long-count calendar is just one of a larger set of calendars created by the classic Maya people of Mesoamerica around 2000 years ago. The classic Maya were highly advanced in many cosmological, astronomical, astrological, astrophysical and mathematical abilities—considerably more so in fact for the most part, than most of science today.

To the Maya, their calendars were much more than simply measurements of the passage of time for their own convenience in the same way that contemporary calendars, clocks and other measurements of "time" are. They were and still are "books of life", into which are encoded countless levels, collectively charting and predicting cycles of the Universe itself, as well as serving as a reference point for all matters involving the daily lives and Spiritual evolution of the Maya people at all levels of the Mayan culture and society. So important were these calendars that the Mayan people structured their lives and constituted their entire society and infrastructure around them. The Mayan elders and shaman would teach the populous through visual means in the form of ball games and other public performances, conceptually similar to those of the ancient Hindu traditions for example, as well as many cultures that made use of plays, song, dance and other audio-visual methods which serves both as entertainment and education.

The most important calendar of the Maya is known as the "Tzolkin". The Tzolkin measures a year over the course of 260 days as opposed to the 365-day cycle of the Gregorian calendar used today in so called "modern society". The descendants of the classic Maya, of which there are still several million residing in Mesoamerica, still use the Tzolkin today.

The calendar upon which most people are focussing in the context of "2012" is known as the "Long Count". The Mayan long-count calendar is divided into these units:

1 kin = 1 day
20 kins = 1 uinal = 20 days
18 uinals = 1 tun = 360 days
20 tuns = 1 katun = 7,200 days
20 katuns = 1 baktun = 144,000 days

A complete long count great cycle has 13 baktuns in total and so the last great cycle, the end of which we will reach on December 21, 2012, started on August 13, 3114 BCE.

Great cycles measure the “ages” or “suns” of mankind, marking the transformation of mankind to the next level of evolution. These “ages” were not only measured by the Maya, but also by other great civilizations of the past such as the Aztecs in Mesoamerica, the Chinese in the Far East and many other ancient cultures over the preceding three millennia or so.

The end of previous great cycles and the beginning of the next have often been associated with major events that have influenced the destiny of mankind such as the great flood, the destruction of Atlantis, Lemuria and other “lost” civilizations, as well as major ancient cataclysmic events throughout history. In many ancient cultures these cataclysms, as in the great flood, have also regarded as “cleansing” or “purgative”, after which only a small percentage of the original populations survive.

Of course, much of the Mayan long-count calendar, and in particular these historical cataclysmic events precedes modern recorded history, so we know little about most of these ancient events that might have coincided with the end of these cycles or “ages”, “eras” or “suns” going back over millions of years. It is very possible that the huge asteroid or comet that struck the Yucatan Peninsula around 65 million years ago resulting in the end of the age of the dinosaurs, also coincided with the end of one of these “ages”, as did several other known “extinction events”, each one of which heralded a new era and new evolutionary direction for life on Earth, without which humans might not be here today, at least as the “dominant species”.

The Maya are a shamanic culture who made extensive use of Mind-expanding substances known as “entheogens” in order to attain altered states of Consciousness, enabling access to the inner realms of life. Although many entheogens are hallucinatory in nature, there are classes of entheogens that can apparently bring about genuine inner experiences, and which were known to and used by the Maya and many other ancient civilisations. One such class of entheogens belongs to a group of chemical compounds known as the "Dimethyltryptamines", of which there are various derivatives and chemical variations including N,N-dimethyltryptamine (DMT), 5-Methoxy-N,N-Dimethyltryptamine (5-MeO-DMT) and 5-Hydroxy-N,N-Dimethyltryptamine (5-OH-DMT) known as "bufotenine" due, being extracted from the skin of toads of genus "Bufo".

Dimethyltryptamines, usually abbreviated to "DMT", appear to have specific qualities for producing genuine Spiritual experiences. Dr. Rick Strassman conducted extensive research into the effects of DMT on numerous volunteers over a period of years. Subjects frequently reported contacts with all manner of Beings and situations. So conclusive were these findings that Dr. Strassman named DMT "The Spirit Molecule".

Without going too deeply into the way DMT is metabolized and influences Consciousness, the most important effect seems to be related to its interaction with the "pineal gland" of the brain, corresponding to the so-called "3rd eye" or "brow chakra". We already know that the brow chakra is associated with "inner visions" in this way, and especially with clairvoyance. I am of the view that DMT-influenced inner journeys were very likely a major source of the inner knowledge of the Maya.

In addition to the Maya, there have been, and still are, many people using DMT and similar entheogens, returning from inner journeys with information that precisely relates to December 21, 2012 as being a time of transformation for all mankind. Many of these people had previously never heard of the Mayan calendar or of the significance of 2012, but the message is always remarkably similar, an impressive independent confirmation of the significance of a 2012 event.

In addition to advanced, non-terrestrial knowledge acquired by the Mayan shamans in this way, they also engaged in devoted observation of the night sky from their dedicated observatories. The resultant observations, messages and records were recorded in stone structures called "stelae" at their many sacred sites, and on thousands of written records known as "codices", together containing a vast array of information. All but a very few of these valuable codices were later totally destroyed by the Roman Catholic church in their zealous efforts to forcibly convert the Maya and all Mesoamerican races to Christianity, and in particular Roman Catholicism.

The Maya therefore had a great depth of knowledge regarding the cosmos and cosmic cycles, particularly as they relate to the "galactic centre" and above all the pivotal event which is estimated to occur on December 21, 2012, and the basis therefore of the entire 2012 phenomena. This cosmic event is the "galactic alignment" which is alignment of the December solstice sun with the Galactic Equator, an event only occurring every 25,800 years or so, and is a result of the precession of the equinoxes. The galactic alignment coincides with the end of each cycle of the Mayan long count calendar, and is therefore the fundamental basis for the 2012 "end date" phenomena.

The important fact to keep in mind, however, is this - The "end of the Mayan calendar" does not, in and of itself, imply "the end of the world". The "end of the world" is an erroneous interpretation placed upon these events by people, due either to a genuine lack of understanding, or in support of some other motive. The end of one cycle or "age" of the Mayan long count calendar simply marks the beginning of the next calendrical cycle, or "age".

It should be made absolutely clear that the flow of the Universe, The Source, The Prime Creator, The First Cause, God, is, always has been and always will be in the direction of Life and expansion, the only factors to consider being the mode in which these Universal, Divine processes manifest. Contrary to the doctrines of religions, God is not “vengeful”, “jealous” or “angry”, and does not therefore exact “punishments”, “revenge” or “Divine retribution”. God knows only Unconditional Love for all creation, and accordingly all Universal processes extending from the infinite Mind of God are for the ultimate benefit of all creation, including humanity. It is believed in some cultures that these great cycles of Energy, or “ages” alternate between “dark” and “light”, and that we are currently nearing the end of a “dark age” after which will begin an age of light. Hindu teachings define these eras in terms of the “Yuga’s”. We are currently nearing the end of Kali Yuga.

So, the big question is this—what does the end of this current great cycle mean to us experientially both as a race of human Beings, and for each of us as individuals?

In the interests of a balanced approach to these extremely important questions we must consider all possibilities, which, in the very broadest terms consist of the following categories:

1. Catastrophic: A globally destructive cataclysm.
2. Eschatological: A Spiritual transformation
3. Progressive: The continuation of an ongoing process.

1. Catastrophic

The classic Maya, who, as discussed, are at the root of the events life on Earth is facing fundamentally tracked “ages”, or “cycles”, not individual events, and nowhere in the records left by the Maya, to the extent they have been yet discovered, is it suggested that Earth is to experience a cataclysmic event.

As previously noted, it is a fact nevertheless that there is growing evidence in support of such events in the distant past, which may very well have coincided with the end of previous ages. It is entirely possible that a global cataclysm is necessary as a purgative prelude to, and catalyst for a major transformation or change in direction for humans, in order to clear away the millennia of dross that now subsumes the Consciousness of humanity, buried under which humanity has become substantially blind to its own true Spiritual nature. Humanity could on the other hand move towards the high path of enlightenment and evolution by conscious freewill.

From an observational perspective, there are currently few known factors that the Maya could have tracked with the potential to result in a catastrophic outcome in the near future, although numerous theories and unsubstantiated claims have emerged in recent years. There are however most certainly known factors that the ancient Maya would have known about, and which could well form the basis of any predictive aspect of their long count calendar which ends on 21 December 2012.

One compelling and very real factor with the potential to precipitate profound changes on Earth and solar system generally is increasing solar activity, i.e. from the Sun, the cycles of which the Maya could certainly have tracked. Solar activity has at the time of writing, been at an unusually high level, and at a time when such activity is historically indicated to be at a minimum. Also at the time of writing, Earth has been subjected to an unusually high level of activity from the Sun including but not limited to powerful X class solar flares and the much more powerful "coronal mass ejection" or "CME", in the form of super-heated radioactive plasma. These events were most certainly not in isolation, and are very highly likely to increase as we move towards the next solar maxima, expected most significantly to occur around the year 2012. Current indications are that this coming solar maxima could be unprecedented in recorded history in its sheer magnitude. We cannot determine at this stage just how high this level of solar activity will attain, but, if it is as seems possible, the effects upon Earth due to solar storms in the form of CME's and other powerful solar emissions could be profound in many ways. Such a possibility most certainly includes Earth receiving a "broadside" from a single massive coronal mass ejection, the effects of which could well be catastrophic for most life on Earth. It is entirely possible therefore that around 2012 life could face the cataclysmic consequences of one or more powerful solar events with highly unpredictable consequences for humans, all life, and all life-sustaining infrastructure.

It should be mentioned that current climatic extremes are being blamed on so called "climate change", erroneously associated with so called "greenhouse gasses", the use of "fossil fuels" and other environmentally polluting by-products of human activity. While no form of environment polluting activity should ever be condoned, to solely blame such agents for "climate change" is to be dangerously and naively oblivious to the real causes, notably solar activity and other wider ranging Energy influences originating from beyond Earth, which, for the most part are at frequencies of Energy beyond those measurable by current scientific instruments. This can be demonstrated by virtue of similar changes occurring on other planets in our solar system, thus conclusively eliminating human so called "greenhouse gases" or "fossil fuels" as a cause. While scientists, governments, industry and others would seek to commercialise "climate change" or "global warming", the true and most important origin of the changes Earth is increasingly being subjected to are being largely and dangerously overlooked with potentially catastrophic results.

Another major "wild card" associated with these and other possible events seems to be the precipitation of a "pole shift" which can either be geomagnetic in nature where the north and south poles exchange places, an event that is known to happen over long periods of time, or geophysical whereby the current position of the physical poles, in relation to the Sun, suddenly move by several degrees, or even by twenty degrees or more. Such an event could imply profound consequences for Earth and all life on Earth, in ways which we cannot fully predict.

There is increasing evidence being discovered by sea divers of the extensive remains of major ancient civilisations, now lying 2000 feet or more under the sea. How did they get there? Many have heard of the fabled lost civilisations of Atlantis and Lemuria as well as others. Most people have heard of the biblical "Great Flood". Further evidence suggests that the north and south poles have not always been cold, and indeed in the quite recent past Antarctica may have been abundant with life. We can only speculate in the context of 2012, but clearly strong evidence most certainly exists for profound and very sudden geophysical events occurring in the past, which seem to happen with immutable frequency, often coinciding with the catastrophic submerging and subsequent destruction and consequential loss of once great and advanced civilisations.

The classic Maya based much or their long count calendar and in particular the 2012 end date around observations of our Galaxy, and in particular the Galactic Centre where the super-massive black hole almost certainly exists. It is very possible in my view that as we transition through the galactic alignment that was being tracked by the Maya, which is likely occurring now, the effects of this alignment, the mechanism for which has been previously described, and in particular the massive Energy influence of the super-massive black hole could well pull the solar system, including the Sun, all planets and Earth into alignment with it, resulting in a geophysical pole shift of perhaps 20 degrees or more. As previously mentioned, this could well be catastrophic, resulting in massive geophysical effects including earthquakes, massive volcanic eruptions, huge tsunamis and much more. Most life on Earth would be very seriously compromised as has likely happened many times in Earth history. Again, the Maya would most definitely know about these galactic cycles and would also be aware of their consequential transformative potential in many possible ways, including the potential for evolution or destruction, being dependent on the Mind state and consciousness of human beings and all life on Earth before and during these events.

2. Eschatological

In this scenario, the outcome of the transition of the ages may manifest as a potential Spiritual transformation or enlightenment of mankind, being, as previously emphasised, ultimately depend on the thoughts, expectations and Spiritual status, i.e. Consciousness of both the collective Mind of the human race and of each individual. It should also be made absolutely clear that in no way will religious devotion be a factor. The only factor relevant to each individual will be true Spiritual evolution—an immutable Universal Principle.

Mankind is currently in the grips of an escalating downward social spiral precipitated by many factors, including but not limited to rampant materialism and often greed fuelled by the demands of the Ego. This cannot and will not be sustained. The root causes of this situation is that most humans perceive everyone and everything as being separate from themselves, and view the gaining of money as the basis for happiness. Existence therefore becomes competitive, adversarial and aggressive, with people fighting for material supremacy while protecting themselves against perceived threats from "others". In reality there is no such separation. The illusion of separation is perpetuated only by the five physical senses. Everything in the entire Universe is an equal, integral and Divine aspect of everything else in the Universe and of The Source, The First Cause, God. We all exist as individuated Energy fields within the Great Universal Mind of conscious, intelligent, vibrating Energy in which we live and move and have our Being.

Should we experience an eschatological event associated with the transition of the ages, in my view one of the most likely outcomes of such an event would be the veil of the illusion of separation that has blinded humans of their true Spiritual nature for so long would dissipate, along with the related illusions of "time" and "space", thereby leaving people "Spiritually naked" in a true multi-dimensional state of awareness, with the twin illusions of "space" and "time" no longer exerting an influence over Consciousness, and where our thoughts manifest instantly as opposed to the currently perceived time delays. This will enable those who are Spiritually prepared to view life, reality and people in a different way, with an emphasis on Oneness, service and Unconditional Love, with materialism, lack and competitiveness no longer being meaningful. The effects of The Law of Attraction would be experienced instantly. So by what mechanism could these events possibly manifest?

As previously discussed, the classic Maya almost certainly fixed the end of their long count calendar to coincide with the galactic alignment and were also certainly aware of the super massive "black hole" that exists at the very centre of our galaxy, and which could well exert its influence at the time of the galactic alignment. In addition to the physical implications of this galactic event, there are also Energetic and therefore Spiritual implications. Again, and this is most important: **How humanity and all life on Earth experiences this event will be entirely determined by one primary factor – Consciousness.**

Einstein's Law of Relativity describes, among other things, the rate of time, and scale of space. For example a clock may be observed to run slower at lower altitudes, where the gravitational potential exerted on the clock is higher. The gravitational potential of a black hole, in this case the galactic centre is so massive that "time" itself is suspended and the dimensions of "space" reduced to zero. In other words "space" and "time" as experienced on Earth cease to exist altogether.

We, along with all life on Earth, are currently bound together in the same shared quantum reality by virtue of the fact that we are all at the extremity of, and thereby subjected to, the same extreme gravitational potential, and have been since before recorded history. As we approach 2012 and beyond we may well be travelling through the spiral arms of the black hole at the galactic centre, associated with greatly modified gravitational potential to which we will all become progressively subjected as this process progresses, as will every planet in our solar system and beyond. Without going into the extensive and complex quantum mechanics behind this process, the ultimate outcome of this scenario will be that the twin illusions of "space" and "time" would cease to exert their influence. When this finally takes place, and this process is accelerating even now, as mentioned previously, humans will be left "Spiritually naked" in an environment where everything is perceived for what it really is, and where our thoughts, feelings emotions and other powers of the Mind will manifest into our experience instantly. This will be a pivotal juncture for all humanity. Each of us and all life will be freed to realise our true Spiritual potential based upon our individual state of Spiritual evolution knowledge, wisdom and other factors. Those who are thus ready will transition to a quantum reality, a plane of vibration that most closely matches their individual vibration. Although this would happen in due course anyway, this could be a "mass evolution" event. Those not Spiritually prepared will gravitate to another "time-space" bound reality. It should also be mentioned that the galactic alignment could also result in other unknown consciousness influencing effects including magnetic, radiation and other Energy influences.

Although this is largely conjecture, my dedicated involvement in these important matters has enabled me to observe an ongoing awakening of Consciousness of humanity on many levels that leads me to believe that this process could already be taking place and exponentially accelerating. This also leads me to feel that humanity is experiencing the potential for a glorious opportunity in its Spiritual evolution, towards realising our ultimate reality. It is however still for each individual to realise and accept this, and to prepare themselves accordingly. Humanity is facing events that could result in almost total catastrophe, or enlightenment and evolution, and again the eventual outcome will be decided by humanity and life itself.

3. Progressive

This final scenario is based upon my observation that natural Spiritual transformation and transition processes are already very much in progress and appear to be exponentially increasing at this time. This leads me to consider the possibility that December 21, 2012 simply represents a symbolic date in recognition of this ongoing event, as opposed to representing the final date of any causation in absolute terms. In other words, this iconic date simply represents a convenient marker in time as measured by the Gregorian calendar, in recognition of a series of ongoing cosmic events that will continue to progress through 21 December, 2012 and on into the "future". As discussed previously, it is thought that the Maya derived the basis of their "long count calendar" upon cosmic observation conducted over a long period of time, extrapolating these observations to form the basis of a calendrical system representing galactic cycles of around 25,800 years, the end of which is marked or symbolised by the so called "galactic alignment"—an event resulting from the "precession of the equinoxes". In brief, this "precession" arises from the fact that Earth wobbles very slowly about its axis, which in turn causes the relative position of the equinox to move backwards, i.e. to "precess" at the rate of around 1 degree every 71.5 years. The entire precessional cycle takes around 25,800 years to complete, culminating in the end of a Maya "long count" calendrical cycle, and the beginning of the next cycle. Thus it may be seen that the end of the calendar, or cycle is not the "end of the world" as has been erroneously widely supposed, but rather the end of the current single Mayan long count cycle. The question therefore is this - is the "galactic alignment" a symbolic or a causal event in and of itself as previously discussed in the previous scenarios.

It might be that the actual date of December 21, 2012 could simply be a convenient symbolic representation, based upon the galactic alignment, of a much greater cosmic event the Maya were tracking, and which they expected to exert its influence during this period, but with a different origin of causation that humanity may well not be yet aware of. There is very strong evidence at many levels, both physical and non-physical to suggest that we are indeed in the throes of such an ongoing process. At a physical level we are seeing and experiencing increasing extremes of weather and associated anomalies, increased volcanic and seismic activity, and of course an exponentially increasing climatic warming trend. These types of changes appear to be occurring throughout the entire solar system, not only on Earth, and cannot therefore be the result of any localised pollution and other such influences.

From my own perspective, as a person who receives messages from, and communicates with numerous people around the world, I am observing a very real "Spiritual awakening" taking place, with increasing numbers of people becoming progressively aware of their true infinite, unlimited, immortal, Spiritual, Divine, nature, needing to know what it all means, and how they should make changes in their lives accordingly.

In addition, we are seeing various factions, many negative or dark in nature, often with very selfish motives, which, realising there is not much time left before the Minds and lives of people can no longer be controlled as they are currently, are doing everything they can to bring forward and execute their agendas of domination and control, regardless of the wider consequences for humanity and life on Earth. We will not discuss these factions lest we give them more power, but suffice it to say, by comparison with the Universal forces of change currently exerting themselves, the efforts of these dark agencies are completely futile, and can be likened to someone standing on a beach with view to holding back the tides. Giving serious attention to these factions is therefore neither useful, productive or appropriate—they are best completely ignored.

Planet Earth Herself, a great planetary Spirit, often known as "Gaia", with Whom we are inexorably connected, is currently in the process of making Her own joyous evolutionary transition to the next vibrational level of the Universe on the path of Her own glorious return to our Divine Creator, in exactly the same way that humans, all life, and everything in creation will inevitably do sooner or later. There is compelling evidence that this process is underway right now. The Schumann Cavity Resonance, often referred to as the "heartbeat" of Earth, has always in the past maintained a steady frequency or resonance of 7.8Hz. In the last few of years, however, the resonance has recently increased to around 12Hz with 13Hz being pivotal. Gaia is increasing the frequency of Her own Spiritual body as She prepares to make Her own evolutionary transition, something we should all celebrate.

In conclusion, we can see that regardless of the theories and agendas of the various groups interested in this process for whatever reason, there is indeed very real and important changes occurring that must ultimately affect all mankind, life on Earth and the solar system, and planet Earth, Gaia herself.

Due to the multitude of such theories, factions and agendas exerting themselves during this natural process, many people are understandably becoming very confused, bewildered and concerned for the future of themselves and families, particularly in view of the increasing number of "survive 2012" type agendas appearing, implying a pending global catastrophe. We must recognise the many unsubstantiated ideas, theories and agendas for what they are, choosing instead to focus within, and on what we know to be incontrovertible true, based upon what we personally experience, know and intuitively feel.

My own message is clear and unequivocal. We are all, both as individuals and equal aspects of the human race and of all life on Earth and of the Universe, experiencing a completely natural cycle of transition, orchestrated by Divine intelligence, Who Unconditionally Loves us all. How we experience and emerge from this transition, both individually and collectively as the human race will, as always, be determined by one factor and one factor only – individual and collective Consciousness, and our own unique state of Spiritual attainment and evolution. What we have discussed in this chapter and are witnessing and experiencing at all levels is the confluence of an infinite number of quantum probabilities, quantum potential, any or all of which can exert themselves in precise alignment with the influence of Mind and therefore individual and collective Consciousness over the next few years. What we ultimately experience as the transition progresses therefore is already taking shape in our own Mind and therefore Universal Mind in Which we all experience our collective Consciousness. We each create our own reality, and never has there been a greater opportunity to realise this great truth than the age in which we are living now. Nothing is to be gained by focussing on material, outer events, however dramatic they may seem – they are an illusion and a distraction. Nothing is to be gained and everything is to be lost by listening to the voices of doom, or those who claim to represent your "best interests" as events unfold. They are pursuing their own agendas that are very often biased towards power, fear and control, rather than evolution.

If you really wish to know the outcome of the transition of the ages, or of December 21, 2012, or of any related event, then rejoice, because you have the power to determine and experience that outcome, both individually and as a member of the human race. Humanity can have and achieve anything it desires during the coming age, so choose Peace, Harmony, Love, Service and true Spiritual Evolution, and they shall be yours with everyone else sharing the same glorious new reality.

We must therefore focus within in order to realise our own true reality, in the absolute knowledge that once the transition of the ages is complete, only those who have turned to focus within, and rediscovered their own true, infinite, immortal, Self, and are ready and prepared to progress beyond the material illusion of the physical world, will emerge to become the first members of the next Divine evolution of human beings – Homo Spiritus.

Chapter 115
Our Ultimate Reality

On your journey of discovery through this book, we have discussed the true nature of the glorious Universe and all of the magnificent realms in which we live we live and move and have our Being, a Universe known simply as God, The All, Spirit, and by numerous other names, and the truth of the one primary Principle behind all life, creation and Being—Mind.

We have revealed the mysteries of the inner realms of life and reality through which sooner or later we will all journey on the way to the realization of our most true, ultimate and sacred destiny as infinite, immortal Spiritual Beings of the Universal Mind with Whom we are all equal aspects and joyful creators.

We have observed how each and every person creates their own individual reality, as well as participating in, and helping to shape the consensus reality of the human race, and ultimately of the entire Universe, by virtue of the freewill granted by our Divine creator to Whom we are all ultimately destined to return once our quest for perfection is complete.

It is the most sacred objective of every single individual to travel the sacred path back to Our Source, while always selflessly assisting others further behind on the path, in the Spirit of service to others before service to self, and out of Pure Unconditional Love, the most powerful vibration in the entire Universe, and the Divine force behind all creation.

As increasingly more people on Earth begin to awaken to these inner realities and sense of true purpose, an expansion of collective Consciousness of the human race is occurring and will continue to occur and accelerate, in turn a catalyst for increasingly more people awakening to their own true nature.

During the great transition of the ages which we are all blessed to be experiencing, this transformational process is already well underway, as a great Spiritual awakening increasingly pervades the Consciousness of all humanity and ultimately of all life on Earth and of Earth Herself.

Every reader of this book will now know, beyond any doubt that the true meaning of life for every single person and indeed all life, without exception, is both simple and profound—to evolve back to The First Cause, Our Prime Creator, God, on a journey of learning, experience and growth, to finally realise the ultimate vibration and pinnacle of perfection—God.

This Divine journey within Universal Mind should be joyfully embraced and never delayed, even for a single moment. We should always be Mindful that we are sharing this journey with fellow travellers to Whom we should always be of Service before serving ourselves, in the Spirit of the most powerful vibration and force in the Universe—Unconditional Love.

Epilogue

It is my sincerest hope that this book has succeeded in revealing to you your own glorious, infinite and Divine nature and true destiny, and that your life will be thus enriched.

I must also however add the following important caveat.

The truth I have detailed within the pages of this book is my own truth—the truth of over 40 years of sincere seeking, finding, and Divine inspiration. It is a truth of which I myself have not even the very slightest doubt. I know my own truth to be the absolute truth. If I did not believe that to be so, I would never have received the inspiration to share my truth with you.

However, you must also discover your own truth, because at the final analysis, your own truth is the only truth that is right truth for you during your own, unique individual journey back to our Creator from Whence you came in the beginning.

Within the pages of this book, I have provided you with the seeds of truth. Sow those seeds of truth within the fertile ground of your own Mind and Being, and water and nourish them frequently by sincerely seeking with an open heart and open Mind. Love and care for those seeds of truth that you have sown in your Mind with all your heart, as if they are your own child, never doubting, even for a single moment that they will germinate, grow, flourish and in due course bloom into a vibrant flower of Life, Light and Truth.

No amount of reading or theoretical knowledge can ever, in and of itself, enable you to fulfil your own glorious destiny. Only with a totally conscious decision to understand, realise and embrace your own true Spiritual nature, potential and ultimate reality, and to live your life accordingly, with the absolute knowledge, joy and Unconditional Love that comes with knowing precisely who you Are, what you can achieve, and where you are ultimately going, will you prevail.

Always know, beyond any doubt, that you are not simply a random person, experiencing a single physical life on the physical world we call Earth, housed within a physical body of matter. You are, always have been and always will be, a glorious Immortal Spiritual Being, a Child of the Universe—an infinite, immortal and inseparable aspect of the Divine, The First Cause, The All, The Source, Universal Mind, our Prime Creator, also known by many other names, but mostly often known simply as the Mind of "God", in Whose Perfect Image we are all made, and Who Loves us all—Unconditionally.

There has potentially never been a better time to be a human on Earth as we journey together through the transition from one great age of evolution to the next. The ultimate outcome of this transition of the ages will however ultimately be determined by one factor only—individual and collective Consciousness. In view of the close proximity of the changes we are all facing, and the potential consequences of those changes, it would be wise for each and every person to turn away from the current distractions of the human race without, in order to focus on the realising God and therefore of our true Spiritual nature within.

I would finally like to personally thank you for your time in reading this book, and wish you every possible success in the greatest Peace, Light, Truth, Harmony and Unconditional Love, as you progress towards the realisation and fulfilment of your own true reality and ultimate destiny—your glorious return to our Divine Creator of Whom we are all immortal, infinite, eternal, inseparable, Unconditionally Loved aspects, and in Whose Perfect Image we are each truly made.

Printed in the United States
126073LV00005BA/1-18/A

9 780979 91060